Springer Series in Transitional Justice

Series Editor:
Olivera Simic

More information about this series at http://www.springer.com/series/11233

Lionel Nichols

The International Criminal Court and the End of Impunity in Kenya

Lionel Nichols
Honorable Society of the Inner Temple
London, England

Faculty of Law
University of Tasmania
Tasmania, Australia

ISBN 978-3-319-10728-8   ISBN 978-3-319-10729-5 (eBook)
DOI 10.1007/978-3-319-10729-5
Springer Cham Heidelberg New York Dordrecht London

Library of Congress Control Number: 2014951718

© Springer International Publishing Switzerland 2015
This work is subject to copyright. All rights are reserved by the Publisher, whether the whole or part of the material is concerned, specifically the rights of translation, reprinting, reuse of illustrations, recitation, broadcasting, reproduction on microfilms or in any other physical way, and transmission or information storage and retrieval, electronic adaptation, computer software, or by similar or dissimilar methodology now known or hereafter developed. Exempted from this legal reservation are brief excerpts in connection with reviews or scholarly analysis or material supplied specifically for the purpose of being entered and executed on a computer system, for exclusive use by the purchaser of the work. Duplication of this publication or parts thereof is permitted only under the provisions of the Copyright Law of the Publisher's location, in its current version, and permission for use must always be obtained from Springer. Permissions for use may be obtained through RightsLink at the Copyright Clearance Center. Violations are liable to prosecution under the respective Copyright Law.
The use of general descriptive names, registered names, trademarks, service marks, etc. in this publication does not imply, even in the absence of a specific statement, that such names are exempt from the relevant protective laws and regulations and therefore free for general use.
While the advice and information in this book are believed to be true and accurate at the date of publication, neither the authors nor the editors nor the publisher can accept any legal responsibility for any errors or omissions that may be made. The publisher makes no warranty, express or implied, with respect to the material contained herein.

Printed on acid-free paper

Springer is part of Springer Science+Business Media (www.springer.com)

For Zhanna

Acknowledgements

As might be expected for a piece of work which was five years in the making, its completion would not have been possible but for the generosity of a great many persons, the most significant of which I would like to take this opportunity to acknowledge.

First, I would like to thank all of those who so generously provided the funding for this research, without which this project would not have been possible. In particular, I would like to thank the Rhodes Trust for funding tuition at the University of Oxford and providing such an enriching community during my studies. In particular, I am extremely grateful to Warden Don Markwell for the outstanding support he provided throughout this project. Special thanks also to Don Ferencz and the Planethood Foundation for their generous funding of the Global Justice Research Fellowship at St. Anne's College. I also wish to acknowledge Lincoln College and the Faculty of Law for their assistance in funding my fieldwork. I am especially thankful to all of those involved in establishing the Tim Hawkins Memorial Scholarship and thereby affording me the opportunity to enter the world of international criminal law.

I also owe a great deal of thanks to the many people who provided such helpful guidance, advice, supervision and feedback. In particular, I wish to acknowledge the contribution of Dr. Phil Clark, who was involved in this project from the very beginning and was heavily influential in transforming a thread of an idea into this completed manuscript. I am tremendously grateful to Phil for his outstanding academic input, practical advice and good humour throughout this project. I also owe a great deal of thanks to Dr. Fernanda Pirie for so adeptly guiding me through to the completion of this work. Special thanks also to those who provided such insightful and helpful feedback on my work at various stages, including Professor David Anderson, Professor Dapo Akande, Professor Daniel Branch and Dr. Gabrielle Lynch. I also wish to acknowledge the contributions of the Oxford Transitional

Justice Research network, the Centre for Criminology, the Centre for Socio-Legal Studies and the British Institute in East Africa.

Thank you also to all of those in Kenya, The Hague and elsewhere who so generously gave up their time in answering my questions and assisting with my research. Special thanks to Francis Okomo-Okello for the active role he played in this regard. Most of all, however, I am most grateful to the many Kenyans who helped this *dogo mzungu* feel so welcome in their country.

Finally, I owe the greatest thank you of all to Ekaterina Aristova, whom I met during the early stages of this project and by its completion had become my wife. I am most grateful for her love and support throughout this project.

Contents

1	**Introduction**	1
	1 The Prosecutor's Promise	2
	2 The Effectiveness of International Criminal Justice	4
	3 Methodology	8
	3.1 Scope	8
	3.2 Research Method	9
	3.3 Assessing the ICC's Impact	11
	4 Ending Impunity	12
	4.1 The OTP and the End of Impunity	13
	4.2 The Ending of Impunity for Kenyans	14
	4.3 Assessing the End of Impunity	16
	5 Precursors for Positive Complementarity	17
	6 Structure of Project	20
	Bibliography	24
2	**The Strategy of Positive Complementarity**	29
	1 Origins of Positive Complementarity	30
	1.1 Complementarity and the Rome Statute	30
	1.2 The Birth of Positive Complementarity	31
	2 OTP's Understanding of Positive Complementarity	32
	2.1 The Two Dimensions of Complementarity	33
	2.2 Strategy for Encouraging Prosecutions	34
	3 Positive Complementarity in Practice	38
	3.1 Early Years and Negative Complementarity	38
	3.2 Success Stories?	40
	3.3 The Shadow Side of Complementarity	42
	4 Conclusion	43
	Bibliography	44

3	**Kenya's Post-Election Violence and History of Impunity**		47
	1 Kenya's Post-Election Violence		48
		1.1 Disputed Presidential Elections and the Road to Violence	48
		1.2 Causes of the Violence	51
	2 History of Institutionalised Impunity		53
		2.1 Colonial Era	53
		2.2 Post-Independence	55
		2.3 The Institutionalisation of Impunity	59
		2.4 Culture of Impunity	61
	3 Conclusion		64
	Bibliography		65
4	**From Nairobi to The Hague**		69
	1 Phase One: Commencement of Preliminary Examinations (February 2008–July 2009)		70
		1.1 Monitoring the Situation	70
		1.2 The Waki Report and the Sealed Envelope	71
		1.3 Strike One	72
	2 Phase Two: Encouragement of Domestic Prosecutions (June 2009–November 2009)		74
		2.1 The Complementarity Contract and the Delivery of the Sealed Envelope	74
		2.2 Strike Two and the Division of Labour	75
	3 Phase Three: ICC Investigations (December 2009–December 2010)		78
		3.1 Strike Three and Investigations Proprio Motu	78
		3.2 Continued Encouragement of Domestic Proceedings	80
	4 Phase Four: ICC Pre-Trial Stage (December 2010–March 2013)		82
		4.1 The 'Ocampo Six'	82
		4.2 The 'Ocampo Four'	84
		4.3 The 'Ocampo Three'	85
	5 Conclusion		86
	Bibliography		87
5	**Prosecuting Perpetrators**		91
	1 A Yardstick for Success		91
	2 The Small Fish		93
		2.1 Prosecutions by Numbers	95
		2.2 Prosecutions by Crimes	99
		2.3 The OTP's Influence	101
	3 The Big Fish		102
	4 The Foreign Affairs Façade		103
		4.1 The Special Tribunal and Motion Without Movement	104
		4.2 Justice Delayed but Justice Assured	106
		4.3 Investigating the Ocampo Six	108

	5	Kenyans in The Hague	110
		5.1 Local Support for ICC Intervention	110
		5.2 A Blow to Impunity	114
	6	Impunity Gaps	115
	7	The Shadow Side of Complementarity	119
		7.1 Increased Threats to Witnesses	119
		7.2 Politicisation of the ICC	121
	8	Conclusion	125
	Bibliography		127
6	**Don't Be Vague, Go to The Hague!**		**133**
	1	An Unsuitable Strategy	134
		1.1 Political Suicide	135
		1.2 Domestic Inability	136
	2	The OTP's Influence	139
		2.1 Not the Initial Impetus	139
		2.2 Influencing Leaders	142
		2.3 Imminent but not Inevitable	147
		2.4 Vested Interests	151
	3	Foreign Affairs Façade	156
		3.1 Reneging on Referral	156
		3.2 Rescuing the Ocampo Six	157
		3.3 Withdrawal from the Rome Statute	158
		3.4 Security Council Deferral and Shuttle Diplomacy	159
		3.5 Article 19 Application	160
		3.6 East African Court of Justice	162
		3.7 African Court of Justice and Human Rights	163
		3.8 Motions Without Movement	164
		3.9 Obstructing Investigations	165
	4	The Shadow Side of Complementarity	169
		4.1 Discouragement of Local Prosecutions	170
		4.2 A Mechanism We Can Control	171
	5	Conclusion	174
	Bibliography		176
7	**Rule of Law Reforms: Post Hoc Ergo Propter Hoc?**		**183**
	1	The OTP and Rule of Law Reform	184
	2	The Tenth Parliament's Rule of Law Reforms	186
		2.1 Constitution	188
		2.2 Criminal Justice System	189
		2.3 Electoral Process	191
		2.4 National Reconciliation	192
	3	Catalysts for Reform	194
		3.1 The Ongoing Reform Process	194
		3.2 The Post-Election Violence	198
		3.3 Legacies and Campaigns	200

		3.4	International Pressures	202
		3.5	Domestic Pressures	204
	4	The OTP's Impact		206
		4.1	The International Crimes Act 2008	206
		4.2	Witness Protection	208
		4.3	Judicial and Security Sector Reforms	212
		4.4	Simultaneous but Separate	213
	5	The Shadow Side of Complementarity		216
		5.1	The Government of National Disunity	216
		5.2	Delays and Distractions	220
		5.3	Illusory Reforms	221
	6	Conclusion		223
	Bibliography			225
8	**Culture of Impunity**			233
	1	Ending the 'Culture of Impunity'		234
	2	Judging the Judges		236
	3	Policing the Police		239
	4	The Shadow Side of Complementarity		243
	5	Conclusion		246
	Bibliography			246
9	**Conclusion**			249
	Bibliography			254
Appendix: Timeline				257
Index				265

Abbreviations

ACJHR	African Court of Justice and Human Rights
AG	Attorney General
ASP	Assembly of States Parties
CAR	Central African Republic
CID	Criminal Investigations Division
CREAW	Centre for Rights Education and Awareness Women
DPP	Director of Public Prosecutions
DRC	Democratic Republic of the Congo
EACJ	East African Court of Justice
ECK	Electoral Commission of Kenya
FIDA-K	Federation of Women Lawyers-Kenya
GLJOS	Governance, Justice, Law and Order Sector reform programme
GNU	Government of National Unity
HRW	Human Rights Watch
IBA	International Bar Association
ICC	International Criminal Court
ICG	International Crisis Group
ICJ-K	International Commission of Jurists-Kenya
ICPC	International Centre for Policy and Conflict
ICTR	International Criminal Tribunal for Rwanda
ICTY	International Criminal Tribunal for the former Yugoslavia
IEBC	Independent Electoral and Boundaries Commission
IIEC	Interim Independent Electoral Commission
JMVB	Judges and Magistrates Vetting Board
JSC	Judicial Services Commission

KHRC	Kenya Human Rights Commission
KNCHR	Kenya National Commission on Human Rights
KNDR	Kenya National Dialogue and Reconciliation process
LRA	Lord's Resistance Army
LSK	Law Society of Kenya
NCIC	National Cohesion and Integration Commission
ODM	Orange Democratic Movement
OHCHR	Officer of the High Commissioner for Human Rights
OSI	Open Society Institute
OTP	Office of the Prosecutor
PTC	Pre-Trial Chamber
SCCED	Special Court on the Events in Darfur
TJRC	Truth, Justice and Reconciliation Commission
VPRS	Victims Participation and Reparations Section
WPA	Witness Protection Agency

About the Author

Lionel Nichols is a barrister of the Honourable Society of the Inner Temple and an Adjunct Lecturer in Law at the University of Tasmania. He has previously worked on the trials of Radovan Karadzic at the ICTY and Charles Taylor at the SCSL. He is the former convenor of the Oxford Transitional Justice Research group and was the University of Oxford's Global Justice Research Fellow. He lives in London with his wife and daughter.

Chapter 1
Introduction

The Prosecutor of the International Criminal Court ('ICC'), Luis Moreno-Ocampo, promised that there would be no impunity for crimes against humanity committed during Kenya's post-election violence of 2007/2008.[1] The two months following the 2007 presidential election were the most violent and traumatic in the country's history. At least 1,113 were killed, 350,000 forcibly displaced and countless more subjected to crimes of sexual violence and other inhumane acts.[2] As the Office of the Prosecutor ('OTP') has finite resources that permits it to prosecute only a handful of persons, it sought to enhance its impact by encouraging domestic investigations and prosecutions as part of its strategy of positive complementarity. The Prosecutor insisted that impunity would not be an option and held meetings with senior government ministers in The Hague and Nairobi in an attempt to pressure the government into supporting local prosecutions. He was assisted by a sealed envelope containing the names of those believed to be the most responsible for the violence, which Kofi Annan threatened to deliver to the Prosecutor should a special tribunal not be established to try the suspects. The government, however, failed to ensure that those most responsible for the 2007/2008 post-election violence were held accountable for their actions and the Prosecutor responded by commencing his own investigations and prosecutions. Six persons, colloquially known as the Ocampo Six, were named as suspects and for the first time in history Kenyans witnessed their leaders being held to account. Before these trials could commence, however, two of these suspects, Uhuru Kenyatta and William Ruto, were elected President and Vice President, respectively. The OTP was faced with an unprecedented situation—trying a sitting head of state for crimes against humanity.

---

[1] Anthony Kariuki, 'Ocampo: ICC has strong case in Kenya chaos', *Daily Nation,* 7 November 2009.
[2] *Final Report from Kenya's Commission of Inquiry into Post-Election Violence*, 15 October 2008 ('Waki Report'), 305, 346.

So what was the ICC's impact in Kenya? Did the Prosecutor realise his stated objective of ending impunity? To what extent did the OTP succeed in encouraging domestic investigations and prosecutions? What impact did the commencement of criminal proceedings against Kenyatta and Ruto have on the country? Did the ICC's involvement serve as a catalyst for the country's subsequent constitutional, judicial, security sector and witness protection reforms? Did its intervention have any negative impacts? And what lessons may be learned for the implementation of the strategy of positive complementarity in future situations? This five-year empirical case study seeks to answer these questions.

1 The Prosecutor's Promise

The Prosecutor's promise to end impunity in Kenya should not be seen as an isolated undertaking but rather as part of an ongoing commitment to this objective. The OTP's self-defined mandate and its strategy for realising its stated objectives may be ascertained by reference to official policy papers and public statements made by the Prosecutor. From these it is apparent that the OTP seeks to do more than merely prosecuting suspected perpetrators of serious crimes. Rather, it attempts to 'maximise its impact' on the situation countries in which it becomes involved.[3] According to Moreno-Ocampo, '[y]ou can't measure [the ICC's] success only by trials. We must be judged by our impact on the conflict'.[4] This is why in the Kenyan situation the Prosecutor promised that the OTP's intervention would serve as a 'world example of managing violence'.[5]

An impact that the OTP has sought to have in many situation countries, including Kenya, has been to 'end impunity', an objective that is mentioned in the fifth preambular paragraph of the Rome Statute.[6] The Prosecutor publicly affirmed this to be the OTP's goal in Kenya on at least seven occasions between July 2009 and December 2010. He made this undertaking during meetings with a government delegation in

---

[3] International Criminal Court, Office of the Prosecutor, *Paper on some policy issues before the Office of the Prosecutor*, September 2003' ('2003 OTP Policy Paper'), 3; International Criminal Court, Office of the Prosecutor, *Prosecutorial Strategy 2009–2012*, 1 February 2010 ('Prosecutorial Strategy 2009–2012') [23].

[4] Phil Clark, 'Grappling in the Great Lakes: the Challenges of International Justice in Rwanda, the Democratic Republic of Congo and Uganda' in Brett Bowden, Hilary Charlesworth and Jeremy Farrall (eds) *Great Expectations: the Role of International Law in Restructuring Societies after Conflict* (Cambridge University Press, 2009).

[5] International Criminal Court Office of the Prosecutor, 'ICC Prosecutor: Kenya Can Be an Example to the World', 18 September 2009; Oliver Mathenge, 'Reforms: Annan heads to Kenya', *Daily Nation*, 1 October 2009; Mutinda Mwanzia, 'Ocampo's actions plans', *Standard*, 9 April 2010; Emma Thomasson, 'Interview—Darfur, Kenya courts to complement ICC-prosecutor', *Reuters*, 30 October 2009.

[6] Rome Statute of the International Criminal Court, opened for signature 17 July 1998, 2187 UNTS 90 (entered into force 1 July 2002) ('Rome Statute'), Preamble.

The Hague, when he received the sealed envelope less than two weeks later, during a September 2009 conference on international criminal justice, during a meeting with civil society in The Hague, during a meeting with President Kibaki and Prime Minister Odinga in Nairobi, after conducting official investigations in Kenya and upon announcing names of the Ocampo Six.[7] Moreno-Ocampo's successor as Prosecutor, Fatou Bensouda, also declared that the OTP's objective in Kenya was to 'end impunity[8] and has committed the OTP to this goal in future situations.[9]

The OTP seeks to end impunity by ensuring that those responsible for serious crimes face criminal prosecutions. As the OTP is forced to operate with limited resources, it does not seek to prosecute all perpetrators but instead focuses its attention on prosecuting 'those who bear the greatest responsibility for the crimes'.[10] According to the OTP, this commitment of its scarce resources to a limited number of targeted prosecutions will ultimately have the effect of ending of impunity not only in the situation country, but also throughout the world.[11]

Since the OTP may only prosecute a limited number of persons in any given conflict, it attempts to avoid an 'impunity gap' by encouraging local prosecutions for the lower-ranking perpetrators wherever possible.[12] As part of this strategy of positive complementarity, the OTP uses various techniques to persuade the national government to conduct its own investigations and prosecutions. As such the OTP will commence its own proceedings 'only where there is a clear case of failure to act by the state or states concerned'.[13] Indeed, as a consequence of this strategy of positive

---

[7] International Criminal Court Office of the Prosecutor, "Agreed minutes of the meeting between Prosecutor Moreno-Ocampo and the delegation of the Kenyan Government", 3 July 2009; International Criminal Court Office of the Prosecutor, 'ICC Prosecutor Receives Materials on Post-Election Violence in Kenya', 16 July 2009; International Criminal Court Office of the Prosecutor, 'Waki Commission List of Names in the Hands of ICC Prosecutor', 16 July 2009 ('OTP Second Statement on the Sealed Envelope'); Luis Moreno-Ocampo, 'Session 1: Office of the Prosecutor of the ICC', Consultative Conference on International Criminal Justice, 9 September 2009; OTP, 'Kenya can be an example to the world' (see Footnote 5); International Criminal Court Office of the Prosecutor, 'Kenya Authorities Committed to Cooperate as ICC Prosecutor Informs them that in December he will Request ICC Judges to Open an Investigation into Post-Election Violence', 6 November 2009 ('OTP Proprio Motu Statement'); Kariuki (2009) (see Footnote 1); 'Kenya: Ocampo Show Over', *Radio Netherlands Worldwide,* 13 May 2010; International Criminal Court, Office of the Prosecutor, 'Kenya's post election violence: ICC Prosecutor presents case against six individuals for crimes against humanity', 15 December 2010 ('OTP Ocampo Six Statement').

[8] International Criminal Court Office of the Prosecutor, 'Statement by the Prosecutor of the International Criminal Court Mrs. Fatou Bensouda at the press conference at the conclusion of Nairobi segment of ICC Prosecutor's visit to Kenya, Nairobi', 25 October 2012 ('OTP Second Statement on Bensouda's Visit to Kenya').

[9] International Criminal Court Office of the Prosecutor, *Strategic Plan June 2012–2015*, 11 October 2013 ('OTP Strategic Plan 2012–2015-2015').

[10] 2003 OTP Policy Paper (see Footnote 3).

[11] Ibid.

[12] Ibid.

[13] Ibid, 2–3; International Criminal Court Office of the Prosecutor, 'Address by the Prosecutor to the Third Session of the Assembly of States Parties', 6 September 2004; Luis Moreno-Ocampo, 'Statement of the Prosecutor to the Diplomatic Corps', 12 February 2004 ('February 2004 Speech').

complementarity, the OTP has stated that a 'major success' for the Court would not be the successful prosecution of cases in The Hague, but rather 'the absence of trials before [the ICC] as a consequence of the regular functioning of national institutions'.[14]

In summary, through its strategy of positive complementarity, the OTP seeks to encourage prosecutions at the domestic level so as to ensure that there is no impunity gap and in this way maximise its impact on the situation country. The Prosecutor's promise to end impunity in Kenya may therefore be seen to be consistent with these broader policy objectives and strategies and by evaluating the ICC's impact in Kenya important lessons may be learned for future situations.

2 The Effectiveness of International Criminal Justice

Research into the effectiveness of the ICC as an institution fits within the broader category of scholarship on transitional justice, which may be defined as 'that set of practices, mechanisms and concerns that arise following a period of conflict, civil strife or repression, and that are aimed directly at confronting and dealing with past violations of human rights and humanitarian law'.[15] A common feature of transitional justice strategies has been to ensure that perpetrators are held accountable for their acts through prosecutions before international criminal tribunals. Such tribunals have been set up to respond to crimes committed in Germany, Japan, the former Yugoslavia, Rwanda, Sierra Leone, Cambodia, East Timor and Lebanon. In 2002, the ICC was established as a permanent, international court to try those most responsible for genocide, crimes against humanity, war crimes and the crime of aggression.

Despite the existence of a significant body of literature in the fields of transitional justice and international criminal justice, to date little academic attention has been paid to the *effectiveness* of transitional justice mechanisms generally or international criminal tribunals specifically. Kritz, for example, has suggested that 'there is a clear need for serious empirical research on the impacts of transitional justice mechanisms'.[16] This is especially the case for international criminal tribunals. Ryngaert, editor of a 2009 volume entitled *The Effectiveness of International Criminal Justice*, has observed that researchers 'have not conducted empirical research into the effectiveness of the international criminal tribunals *on the ground* in the (post-) conflict area'.[17] Empirical research is especially lacking with respect to the effectiveness of the

---

[14] Luis Moreno-Ocampo, 'Statement Made at the Ceremony for the Solemn Undertaking of the Chief Prosecutor of the ICC', The Hague, 16 June 2003 ('Moreno-Ocampo June 2003 Statement').

[15] Naomi Roht-Arriaza and Javier Mariezcurrena (eds), *Transitional Justice in the Twenty-First Century* (Cambridge, 2006), 2.

[16] Neil Kritz, 'Policy Implications of Empirical Research on Transitional Justice' in Hugo van der Merwe, Victoria Baxter and Audrey R Chapman (eds), *Assessing the Impact of Transitional Justice: Challenges for Empirical Research* (United States Institute of Peace Press, 2009).

[17] Cedric Ryngaert, 'Introduction' in Cedric Ryngaert (ed), *The Effectiveness of International Criminal Justice* (Intersentia, 2009), xvi (emphasis in original).

OTP's strategy of positive complementarity. For example, Stahn, co-editor of a two-volume collection on the subject has stated that '[t]he broader implications of complementarity in international relations and domestic societies are not yet well understood and researched'.[18]

Contemporary studies on the dynamic relationship between international courts and national governments were first conducted in relation to the International Criminal Tribunal for the former Yugoslavia ('ICTY') and the International Criminal Tribunal for Rwanda ('ICTR'). Peskin, Lamont, El Zeidy and Melman have considered issues such as the political impact of these tribunals, state compliance with international obligations and the division of labour between the international court and the domestic courts.[19]

The establishment of the ICC added a new layer of complexity to studies on the relationship between international courts and national governments. Whereas the ICTY and ICTR were granted primacy over local courts, the ICC was established to be *complementary* to domestic criminal justice systems. The drafters of the Rome Statute agreed that where a state is investigating or prosecuting a case, that case shall be inadmissible before the ICC unless that state is unwilling or unable to carry out genuine investigations and prosecutions.[20] Over the past decade, a substantial body of literature has emerged that considers this unprecedented arrangement of 'complementarity'. In his comprehensive 2008 study, El Zeidy provides a history of the ICC's complementarity regime.[21] Others consider the ambiguous and contentious legal issues that arise from the complementarity relationship.[22] Foudladvand and Hussanein approach the issue of complementarity from a different perspective,

---

[18] Carsten Stahn, 'Introduction: bridge over troubled waters?' in Carsten Stahn and Mohamed M. El Zeidy (eds), *The International Criminal Court and Complementarity From Theory to Practice* (Cambridge University Press, 2011), 3.

[19] Victor Peskin, *International Justice in Rwanda and the Balkans: Virtual Trials and the Struggle for State Cooperation* (Cambridge University Press, 2008); Christopher Lamont, *International Criminal Justice and the Politics of Compliance* (Ashgate, 2010); Mohamed El Zeidy, 'From Primacy to Complementarity and Backwards: (Re)-Visiting Rule 11bis of the Ad Hoc Tribunals' (2008) 57(2) *International & Comparative Law Quarterly* 403; Jesse Melman, 'The Possibility of Transfer(?): A Comprehensive Approach to the International Criminal Tribunal for Rwanda's Rule 11bis to Permit Transfer to Rwandan Domestic Courts' (2010–2011) 79 *Fordham Law Review* 1271.

[20] Rome Statute, Article 17(1).

[21] Mohamed El Zeidy, *The Principle of Complementarity in International Criminal Law: Origin, Development and Practice* (Brill, 2008).

[22] Jo Stigen, *The Relationship between the International Criminal Court and National Jurisdictions: The Principle of Complementarity* (Martinus Nijhoff, 2008); Florian Razesberger, *The International Criminal Court: The Principle of Complementarity* (Peter Lang, 2006); Jan Kleffner, 'The Impact of Complementarity on National Implementation of Substantive International Criminal Justice' (2003) 86(1) *Journal of International Criminal Justice* 86; Claire Brighton, 'Avoiding Unwillingness: Addressing the Political Pitfalls Inherent in the Complementarity Regime of the International Criminal Court' (2012) 12(4) *International Criminal Law Review* 629; Jakob Pichon, 'The Principle of Complementarity in the Cases of the Sudanese Nationals Ahmad Harun and Ali Kushayb before the International Criminal Court' (2008) 8 *International Criminal Law Review* 185; Darryl Robinson, 'The Mysterious Mysteriousness of Complementarity' (2010) 21(1) *Criminal Law Forum* 67.

focusing on the implications that the regime has for OTP policy.[23] Meanwhile, authors such as Schabas, Stahn, Politi and Gioia, analyse the impact of complementarity by reference to the division of labour between the ICC and national courts.[24]

In more recent times, the OTP has focused on a strategy of *positive* complementarity. That is, rather than passively waiting to see if domestic prosecutions take place (as the drafters of the Rome Statute envisaged), the OTP now seeks to encourage domestic prosecutions in the hope that international prosecutions become unnecessary. Consequently, another group of authors discuss the potential for the threat of ICC prosecutions to serve as a catalyst for domestic prosecutions. Some commentators have expressed a great deal of enthusiasm for the strategy, perhaps none more so than Burke-White, who suggests that it 'offers the best and perhaps the only way for the ICC to meet its mandate and help end impunity'.[25] According to Burke-White, 'the threat of international prosecution by the ICC may generate a positive set of incentives for national governments to pursue prosecutions themselves'.[26]

Commentators offer varying explanations as to why positive complementarity has the potential to serve as a catalyst for domestic prosecutions. Robinson, Schabas and Mégret all suggest that the very existence of the ICC creates an incentive for national governments to strengthen their own legislative capacities to prosecute international crimes, long before those crimes are committed and the OTP begins imposing pressure.[27] Cryer and Burke-White argue that when the OTP threatens to commence prosecutions, states are more likely to support proceedings at the local level.[28] Another group, comprising Stahn, Ellis, Burke-White, Kleffner, Akhavan, Finnemore and Sikkink claim that the shame, embarrassment, stigmatisation and

---

[23] Shahrzad Foudladvand, 'Complementarity and Cultural Sensitivity: Decision-Making by the ICC Prosecutor in Relation to the Situations in the Darfur Region and the Democratic Republic of the Congo (DRC)', Doctor of Philosophy Thesis, University of Sussex, January 2012; Ahmed Samir Hassanein, 'The Principle of Complementarity between International and National Criminal Courts', Doctor of Philosophy Thesis, University of Aberdeen, 2010.

[24] William Schabas, 'Complementarity in Practice: Some Uncomplimentary Thoughts' (2008) 19 *Criminal Law Forum* 7; Carsten Stahn, 'Libya, the International Criminal Court and Complementarity' (2012) 10 *Journal of International Criminal Justice* 325; Mauro Politi and Federica Gioia, *The International Criminal Court and National Jurisdictions* (Ashgate, 2008).

[25] William Burke-White, 'Proactive Complementarity: the International Criminal Court and National Courts in the Rome System of International Justice' (2008) 49(1) *Harvard International Law Journal* 53; William Burke-White, 'Implementing a Policy of Positive Complementarity in the Rome System of Justice' (2008) 19(1) *Criminal Law Forum* 59.

[26] William Burke-White, 'Reframing positive complementarity: reflections on the first decade and insights from the US federal criminal justice system' in Stahn and El Zeidy (2011) (see Footnote 18), 344.

[27] Darryl Robinson, 'The Rome Statute and its Impact on National Law' in Antonio Cassese, Paola Gaeta and John Jones (eds), *The Rome Statute of the International Criminal Court: a commentary* (Oxford University Press, 2002), 1849; William Schabas, *An Introduction to the International Criminal Court* (Cambridge University Press, 2001), 19; Frédéric Mégret, 'Too much of a good thing? Implementation and the uses of complementarity' in Stahn and El Zeidy (2011) (see Footnote 18), 362.

[28] Robert Cryer, *Prosecuting International Crimes: Selectivity and the International Criminal Law Regime* (Cambridge University Press, 2005).

cathartic feedback that accompany international prosecutions may induce national governments to carry out domestic proceedings.[29]

To date, however, there has been very little empirical research that considers whether the strategy of positive complementarity is effective in serving as a catalyst for domestic prosecutions. The small amount of research that has been published in this area suggests that the strategy of positive complementarity has had only limited success in encouraging local proceedings. Jurdi, who has analysed the ICC's impact in the Ugandan situation, concluded that the hope of positive complementarity 'has not yet been realised' and compared the ICC to a 'giant without arms and legs'.[30] While Burke-White and Schiff claim that the ICC's intervention in the Democratic Republic of the Congo ('DRC') caused some government officials to launch reforms of the national judiciary and attempt the creation of a truth commission, Burke-White has nevertheless observed that the 'ICC's record for encouraging national prosecutions is decidedly mixed'.[31] More recently, Nouwen has published the findings of her empirical research into whether the ICC has served as a catalyst in Uganda and Sudan, concluding that 'an increase in domestic proceedings for crimes within the ICC's jurisdiction is barely observable in either state'.[32]

Writing in relation to the Kenyan situation, Sriram and Brown are a little more positive, suggesting that 'the ICC's strategy of positive complementarity may have influenced the political calculus by influencing national debates on accountability mechanisms in response to the violence and provided extra momentum for broader rule of law reforms'.[33] In a separate article, the same authors conclude that '[o]nly after ICC prosecutions became imminent did the government invoke plans for prosecutions through regular national courts in a bid to forestall international action'.[34]

---

[29] Carsten Stahn, 'Taking complementarity seriously: on the sense and sensibility of 'classical', 'positive' and 'negative' complementarity' in Stahn and El Zeidy (2011) (see Footnote 18), 250; Mark Ellis, 'The International Criminal Court and its Implications for Domestic Law and National Capacity Building' (2002–2003) 15 *Florida Journal of International Law* 215; Burke-White (2008b) (see Footnote 25); Jan Kleffner, *Complementarity in the Rome Statute and National Criminal Jurisdictions* (Oxford University Press, 2008); Payam Akhavan, 'Beyond Impunity: Can International Criminal Justice Prevent Future Atrocities?' (2001) 95 *American Journal of International Law* 7; Martha Finnemore and Kathryn Sikkink, 'International Norma Dynamics and Political Change' (1998) 52(4) *International Organisation* 887, 892.

[30] Nidai Nabil Jurdi, *The International Criminal Court and National Courts: A Contentious Relationship* (Ashgate, 2011), 258–263.

[31] William Burke-White, 'Complementarity in Practice: The International Criminal Court as Part of a System of Multi-level Global Governance in the Democratic Republic of Congo' (2005) 18 *Leiden Journal of International Law* 557; Benjamin Schiff, *Building the International Criminal Court* (Cambridge University Press, 2008), 213; Burke-White in Stahn and El Zeidy (2011) (see Footnote 18), 342.

[32] Sarah Nouwen, *Complementarity in the Line of Fire: The Catalysing Effect of the International Criminal Court in Uganda and Sudan* (Cambridge University Press, 2013).

[33] Chandra Sriram and Stephen Brown, 'Kenya in the Shadow of the ICC: Complementarity, Gravity and Impact' (2012) 12(2) *International Criminal Law Review* 219.

[34] Stephen Brown and Chandra Sriram, 'The Big Fish Won't Fry Themselves: Criminal Accountability for Post-Election Violence in Kenya' (2012) 111(443) *African Affairs* 244.

In addition to these writings on the potential of positive complementarity and studies of its impact, some attention has also been paid to the unintended consequences that may follow from the strategy. In an important 2006 article, Heller suggests that there is a 'shadow side' of complementarity, namely 'its effect on the likelihood that the defendants will receive due process in national proceedings'.[35] Heller cites as an example the Specialised Court in Sudan, established in response to the ICC's intervention, which admitted confessions obtained through torture, held trials in secret, regularly denied defendants the right to legal counsel and often ignored the presumption of innocence. Burke-White, Schiff and Clark highlight what might be considered to be another shadow side of positive complementarity—the manipulation of the ICC process by savvy politicians for their own political benefit.[36] For this reason, this study also considers any 'shadow sides' of positive complementarity that may have emerged as a result of the OTP's intervention in Kenya.

This study provides empirical evidence to address gaps in the literature on the effectiveness of transitional justice mechanisms, international criminal tribunals and the OTP's strategy of positive complementarity. By conducting an in-depth case study on the ICC's involvement in Kenya, it is possibly to assess not only the effectiveness of the strategy of positive complementarity, but also any other impacts that the Court may have had. Kenya has been chosen as a case study because, despite being the fifth situation in which the ICC became involved, it may be regarded as the OTP's first genuine attempt to implement its strategy of positive complementarity. As demonstrated in Chap. 2, in relation to Uganda, the DRC and the Central African Republic ('CAR'), the OTP did not seek to encourage domestic investigations and prosecutions, but rather solicited self-referrals of the situation so that early cases could be tried in The Hague. The ICC's fourth situation, that concerning Darfur, was initiated as the result of a United Nations Security Council resolution and the OTP does not appear to have gone to any great effort to encourage national proceedings. As such, the Kenyan situation may be regarded as the first situation in which the OTP actively encouraged domestic prosecutions and therefore the first opportunity to conduct empirical research into the effectiveness of the strategy of positive complementarity.

3 Methodology

3.1 Scope

The scope of this project is limited by subject, place and time. First, with respect to the subject matter, the focus is on the work of the OTP and, in particular, its strategy of positive complementarity. References are at times made to other organs of

---

[35] Kevin Jon Heller, 'The Shadow Side of Complementarity: The Effect of Article 17 of the Rome Statute on National Due Process' (2006) 17 *Criminal Law Forum* 255.

[36] Burke-White (2008b) (see Footnote 25); Schiff (2008) (see Footnote 31), 194–213; Clark (2009) (see Footnote 4).

the Court but the project primarily considers the OTP's actions and their impact. Second, discussion is of course limited to the case study of the Kenyan situation. Where relevant, comparisons are made with other situations in which the ICC has become involved, but the focus of the thesis is on the OTP's impact in Kenya. Finally, the thesis is limited in temporal scope to the OTP's actions and impact between February 2008 and March 2013. This 5-year period corresponds with the full term of Kenya's Tenth Parliament. The earlier date also coincides with the month in which the OTP commenced its strategy of positive complementarity in Kenya, which occurred just weeks before the first session of Kenya's Tenth Parliament.[37] The March 2013 latter date is also of significance because it was the month in which Kenya held its first general elections since the 2007 violence and this appears to have served as a self-imposed deadline for the Prosecutor.[38] This project therefore evaluates the ICC's impact during on five-year parliamentary term.

3.2 Research Method

The general methodology employed for this project is that of a qualitative case study, which is most appropriate where there is little quantitative data available and the focus of the research is on the process by which events and actions take place and the causal relationships among observed phenomena.[39] Reliance has been placed upon multiple sources and methods so as to enhance the credibility of the conclusions reached.[40]

To begin with, I conducted an extensive documentary analysis of a variety of sources. To identify the OTP's objectives and strategies, I examined all OTP policy documents and public statements made by the Prosecutor. These documents are a key resource for an institution's representations of itself and for enabling the external and public consumption of its practices and processes.[41]

To assess the influence of the OTP's actions over the Kenyan government, I compiled, reviewed, coded and analysed a total of 256 relevant Parliamentary sessions, as reported in Hansard. The same process was also followed for more than 1,700 public statements made by senior politicians to Kenya's print, television and radio media.

---

[37] International Criminal Court Office of the Prosecutor, 'OTP Statement in Relation to Events in Kenya', 5 February 2008 ('OTP February 2008 Statement').
[38] 'ICC seeking speedy trials', *BBC News*, 7 November 2009; Manthenge (2009) (see Footnote 5); Bernard Namunane, 'The Hague beckons for suspects', *Daily Nation*, 26 November 2009; Bernard Namunane and Oliver Mathenge, 'I'll nail suspects in 6 months', *Daily Nation*, 8 May 2010; 'Cases will ensure peaceful 2012 election, says Ocampo', *Daily Nation*, 15 December 2010; OTP Second Statement on the Sealed Envelope (see Footnote 7).
[39] Joseph Maxwell, *Qualitative Research Design: An Interactive Approach*, 3rd ed (Sage, 2012).
[40] Ibid, 93–94.
[41] Paul Atkinson and Amanda Coffey, 'Analysing Documentary Realities' in David Silverman (ed), *Qualitative Research: Theory, Method and Practice*, 2nd ed (Sage, 2004), 45–46.

To account for any potential media biases, these sources were generally relied upon only for quotations and where possible the accuracy of these quotes was verified by a second independent source. Observations on the government's reactions to the ICC were also informed by 21 official government reports on issues relating to the post-election violence and the implementation of rule of law reforms. Reliance was also placed upon the data and observations of 78 non-governmental and inter-governmental reports on Kenya during the relevant period.

This documentary analysis was complemented by 68 semi-structured interviews and focus groups conducted with OTP staff in The Hague and during two three-month research expeditions to Kenya. These were arranged to coincide with significant moments in the OTP's involvement in Kenya. The first (March 2010–May 2010) was conducted at the same time that the OTP commenced official investigations in Kenya, which included a 5-day visit from the Prosecutor to the country. The second (July 2011–September 2011) coincided with the two ICC pre-trial hearings, the first time that the six accused were confronted with the details of the charges against them. The semi-structured interview technique was selected because it allowed an insight into what an interviewee sees as important and relevant.[42] As a consequence, part of the interview was structured with a set of questions asked sequentially while other parts were unstructured and were designed to explore the views of the interviewee in detail.[43]

Interviews were conducted with OTP staff members, politicians, judges, lawyers, civil servants, civil society organisations, victims and other Kenyan citizens. Many of the interviews were arranged upon the recommendation of other interviewees, following the 'snowball' technique.[44] Interviewees were contacted in advance and asked to participate in a conversation with a researcher from the University of Oxford. They were not provided with questions prior to the interview and their answers were spontaneous. Interviewees were given no incentives, financial or otherwise, for their participation. Anonymity was granted when requested and records of interview were made through hand notation. The majority of these interviews were conducted in Nairobi, but focus group sessions were also arranged in Naivasha, Nakuru and Eldoret. Male and female persons self-identifying as belonging to the Kikuyu, Luhya, Kalenjin and Luo communities were interviewed.

In seeking to discover the ICC's influence in Kenya, I asked open-ended questions about the post-election violence, Kenya's legal system and its history of impunity. Only where the interviewee failed to mention the ICC did I raise the subject. When the ICC was being discussed, I asked participants for their views on what the ICC had done and what they believed the ICC ought to do in the future.

---

[42] Alan Bryman, *Social Research Methods* (Oxford University Press, 2000), 265.
[43] Alice Bloch, 'Doing Social Surveys' in Clive Seale (ed), *Researching Society and Culture*, 2nd ed (Sage, 2004), 165.
[44] Sara Arber, 'Designing Samples' in Nigel Fielding (ed), *Researching Social Life* (Sage, 1993), 73–74.

3.3 Assessing the ICC's Impact

Perhaps the greatest challenge for a project of this kind is developing a means by which the ICC's impact may be assessed and measured. Akhavan is correct when he states that no 'mechanical cause and effect operates between international criminal tribunals and domestic politics'.[45] Rather, the impact, if any, of international criminal tribunals on political behaviours is likely to be subtle and long term.[46] Hall has specifically referred to this as being a challenge for researchers who attempt to assess the effectiveness of the strategy of positive complementarity:

> Determining causality in human activity is often difficult or impossible. People have a wide range of motivations, not always known to themselves, for their actions. Therefore, absent any statements by legislators or government officials that one of the various types of positive complementarity led to law reform or investigations and prosecutions (and assuming that such statements are accurate), it is difficult to demonstrate that positive complementarity has worked effectively so far as to persuade states to investigate and prosecute genuinely such crimes. However, it is quite possible to conclude in those instances where positive complementarity was known to be involved and failed to lead to new or amended legislation or genuine criminal investigations and prosecutions that it was not effective.[47]

The only way in which the effectiveness of the strategy of positive complementarity may be assessed is through an in-depth case study, which is thus far lacking in the literature. Conducting such a case study employing the research methodology described above is the only means by which any link may be identified between the OTP's strategy of positive complementarity on the one hand, and action on the part of the target state, on the other. While the decisions of individual members of government are likely to be influenced by a range of considerations, the comprehensive documentary analysis and in-depth interviews reveal whether it is possible to isolate the OTP's intervention as an influencing factor. Observing this process over a period of 5 years provides the opportunity to assess whether the extent of this influence changed over time. The breadth of sources considered permits conclusions to be made not just on the direct and positive impact of the OTP, but also any indirect and negative impacts.

A number of factors were taken into account when considering any influence that the OTP may have had over the government. First, whether the particular action taken by the government was within close temporal proximity to a development at the ICC. Second, the extent to which the government's actions, or promised actions, coincided with the OTP's stated desires. Third, whether or not the government made reference to the ICC in general or specific terms, to either admit or deny the Court's influence. Fourth, evidence of members of the Kenyan government altering their position over time, particularly where such changes took place following the imposition of pressure from the OTP. At all times, due regard was had to any other factors that may have influenced the government with respect to a particular course of action and where relevant these are noted in the study.

---

[45] Akhavan (2001) (see Footnote 29), 10–11.
[46] Ibid.
[47] Christopher Hall, 'Positive complementarity in action' in Stahn and El Zeidy (2011) (see Footnote 18), 1034.

4 Ending Impunity

The first step in evaluating whether the OTP's strategy of positive complementarity contributed to the ending of impunity in Kenya is to identify what is meant by 'ending impunity' in this project. The Rome Statute explicitly lists 'ending impunity' as being one of the mandates of the Court, but does not provide a definition. Similarly, despite the OTP's regular reference to this objective, some uncertainty exists as to what it means by this self-defined mandate. Surprisingly, despite the existence of a rich body of literature in the field of transitional justice that concerns the subject of impunity, there has been little academic attention devoted to the meaning of this concept, particularly in the context of international criminal justice. Indeed, even texts that contain the word 'impunity' within their title do not provide much clarification as to what is meant by this concept.[48] As Penrose noted in a 1999 literature review on the subject, while the objective itself was not contested, there was no agreement on precisely what it meant to 'end impunity'.[49] Some progress had been made by 2005 when the United Nations published a report which included what now become the authoritative definition of 'impunity':

> the impossibility, de jure or de facto of bringing the perpetrators of violence to account—whether in criminal, civil, administrative or disciplinary proceedings—since they are not subject to any inquiry that might lead to their being accused, arrested, tried and, if found guilty, sentenced to appropriate penalties, and to making reparations to their victims.[50]

While this definition is a useful starting point, the more crucial issue for this study is whether this is what the OTP intended when it promised to end impunity in Kenya. Primary reliance for this exercise is placed upon OTP policy documents. These sources are complemented by public statements made by the Prosecutor or senior OTP staff and opinions expressed by OTP staff during the course of interviews conducted in The Hague.

This study goes further, however, to also consider what Kenyans understood the Prosecutor to have meant when he promised to end impunity. This investigation has been undertaken for two reasons. First, since ending impunity is ultimately pursued for the benefit of victims, their families and the citizenry-at-large, such persons should have some input into what is meant by this objective. In short, whatever understanding of 'ending impunity' that the OTP adopts, an intervention can hardly

---

[48] See, for example, Mauro Politi and Giuseppe Nesi, *The Rome Statute of the International Criminal Court: a Challenge to Impunity* (Ashgate, 2001); Naomi Roht-Arriaza, *Impunity and Human Rights in International Law and Practice* (Oxford University Press, 1995); Ramesh Thakur and Petrus Malcontent, *From Sovereign Impunity to International Accountability: the Search for Justice in a World of States* (United Nations University, 2004); Yves Beigbeder, *International Justice against Impunity: Progress and New Challenges* (Martinus Nijhoff, 2005).

[49] Mary Margaret Penrose, 'Impunity—Inertia, Inaction and Invalidity: A Literature Review' (1999) 17(2) *Boston University International Law Journal* 269, 271.

[50] United Nations Economic and Social Council Commission on Human Rights, *Report of the Independent Expert to Update the Set of Principles to Combat Impunity*, E/CN.4/2005/102/Add.1, 8 February 2005.

be regarded as a success where a significant proportion of the local population, including the victims of the conflict, consider impunity to endure. Second, it is entirely possible that the OTP's strategy of positive complementarity could fail to end impunity according to its own definition, but nevertheless make a significant contribution to ending impunity according to some other understanding. Fairness to the OTP therefore requires consideration of all possible contributions to ending impunity that the Office may have had.

4.1 The OTP and the End of Impunity

For the OTP, its promise to end impunity in Kenya was limited to the prosecution of the perpetrators of the post-election violence. According to the Prosecutor, '[his] job [was] to prosecute, period'.[51] Throughout the period of the OTP's involvement in Kenya, the Prosecutor therefore distanced the OTP from other objectives, such as the encouragement of rule of law reforms.[52] These statements were consistent with general OTP policy, which dictated that the OTP would not become engaged in 'reforming domestic judiciaries' since 'such activities belong[ed] to other rule of law organisations'.[53]

The OTP's strategy at the first instance was to encourage these prosecutions to take place at the local level, with the Prosecutor regularly emphasising that the Kenyan government retained the primary responsibility for investigations and prosecutions.[54] When such prosecutions did not eventuate, the OTP assumed responsibility for prosecuting those individuals whom it believed to be most responsible for the violence, while at the same time continuing to encourage local prosecutions of all remaining suspects in order to ensure that there would be no 'impunity gap'.[55] The Prosecutor continuously stressed the limitations of the Court, such as in May 2010 when he said 'don't expect everything from me. I will only prosecute two to six cases and the rest is up to you'.[56]

---

[51] Joe Mbuthia, 'ICC has 'no witness in Kenya'', *Daily Nation*, 24 March 2010.

[52] Luis Moreno-Ocampo, 'Kenya National Dialogue and Reconciliation, Two Years On, Where are We?', Statement, Nairobi, 2 December 2010; 'Cases will ensure peaceful 2012 election, says Ocampo', *Daily Nation*, 15 December 2010; Thomasson (2009) (see Footnote 5).

[53] Luis Moreno-Ocampo, 'A positive approach to complementarity: the impact of the Office of the Prosecutor' Stahn and El Zeidy (2011) (see Footnote 18).

[54] 'Justices beckons as Ocampo visits Kenya', *Daily Nation*, 6 May 2010; Emeka-Mayaka Gekara, 'Ocampo to step in if Kenya does shoddy job', *Daily Nation*, 19 June 2009; Lucianne Limo, Beauttah Omanga and Vincent Bartoo, 'Ocampo asks Kenyans not to expect too much', *Standard*, 11 May 2010; Thomasson (2009) (see Footnote 5); Beauttah Omanga, 'Nowhere to hide as The Hague alerts states on chaos suspects', *Standard*, 27 April 2010; Peter Leftie, "Small fish' now put on notice', *Daily Nation*, 3 December 2010;'Cases will ensure peaceful 2012 election, says Ocampo', *Daily Nation*, 15 December 2010; Beauttah Omanga, 'Why Ocampo needs two years on Kenya', *Standard*, 13 May 2010.

[55] Luis Moreno-Ocampo (2010) (see Footnote 52); Omanga (2010) (see Footnote 54); Kariuki (2009) (see Footnote 1).

[56] Limo et al. (2010) (see Footnote 54).

Some OTP staff members suggested a broader interpretation of 'ending impunity' that may include the ICC acting as a catalyst for domestic rule of law reforms and serving as a deterrent for the commission of future crimes. They spoke confidently about the potential for ICC intervention to produce these outcomes within Kenya. Nevertheless, these staff members stressed that the OTP would not actively pursue such objectives but would instead limit itself to ensuring that there was no 'impunity gap' in Kenya. In this way, they suggested, the OTP could end impunity not just in Kenya, but throughout the world. In short, as far as the OTP was concerned, ending impunity meant holding accountable through domestic or international prosecutions, those responsible for the post-election violence.

4.2 The Ending of Impunity for Kenyans

The focus groups I conducted with victims, as well as interviews I conducted with members of government and civil society, confirmed that Kenyans also strongly supported criminal prosecutions as a necessary precondition for ending impunity. Kenyans agreed with the OTP that ending impunity meant not only prosecuting the *leaders* of the violence, but also the *direct perpetrators*. A Kenya National Dialogue and Reconciliation ('KNDR') survey of more than 9,000 Kenyans in 47 counties revealed that that 90 % of respondents wanted the perpetrators of the post-election violence suspects prosecuted, with 81 % believing that prosecuting 'low-level perpetrators' was also necessary to end impunity.[57] Moreover, Kenyans consistently told me that they expected the ICC to assume responsibility for the prosecution of low-level perpetrators since the Kenyan criminal justice system could not be relied upon to carry out this task with impartiality, competence and efficiency.

Kenyans insisted, however, that even if all perpetrators of the post-election violence were investigated, prosecuted, convicted and sentenced, this would not necessarily mean the end of impunity in the country. They stressed that impunity had existed in Kenya long before the occurrence of the 2007 post-election violence and could be traced back to the colonial era.

According to interviewees, the ending of impunity required widespread reforms to state institutions. It was on this basis that politicians made impassioned speeches in Parliament calling for reforms as part of an 'anti-impunity agenda'.[58] In its submissions to the ICC's Pre-Trial Chamber in March 2011, the government admitted that ending impunity required not only investigations and prosecutions, but also reforms to the country's constitution, judiciary, police and witness protection

---

[57] South Consulting, Kenya National Dialogue and Reconciliation Monitoring Project, *Draft Review Report*, April 2011 ('KNDR April 2011 Report'), vi; South Consulting, Kenya National Dialogue and Reconciliation Monitoring Project, *Review Report*, June 2011 ('KNDR June 2011 Report'), 9.

[58] Hansard, National Assembly, Official Report, 27 January 2009; Hansard, National Assembly, Official Report, 22 December 2010.

programme.[59] Lawyer Godfrey Musila said that, in the Kenyan situation, it was necessary to 'broaden [one's] understanding of impunity to consider the broad legal and institutional context within which the rule of law has been eroded thereby creating favourable conditions for impunity'.[60] Not only did Kenyans believe that ending impunity required institutional reform and a restoration of confidence in the rule of law, they believed that it was the ICC's place to effect such change. Kenyans had lost faith in their leaders' desire to implement the necessary reforms because they believed that their politicians had attained their positions through entrenched impunity. They therefore regarded the ICC as their last hope and expressed a strong desire for the ICC to assist with much-needed rule of law reforms.

Victim's also under the Prosecutor's promise to include the provision of reparations to victims of the post-election violence. According to Robins' 2011 study of 276 victims, they considered reparations to be equally as important as prosecutions.[61] During focus group sessions, victims told me that ending impunity meant having their property returned, being provided with sufficient finances to re-open their businesses, having their medical bills paid and receiving compensation for the loss of loved ones. Similar statements were also made by victims' groups to the press.[62] Significantly, victims who had little faith in the government to meet such demands insisted that this should be the role of the ICC. Victims of Kenya's post-election violence displayed an advanced knowledge of the ICC's reparations procedure and asked questions concerning the burden of proof and the rate at which interest would be calculated.

Finally, Kenyans expressed hope that the ICC could end impunity by deterring politicians and businesspersons from organising future violence. They emphasised that violence had accompanied every general election since the reintroduction of multi-party politics in 1992 and would continue to do so unless the ICC prosecuted those responsible for the post-election violence. According to a KNDR survey conducted in April 2011, 81 % of Kenyans believed that prosecuting those responsible for the violence was the best way to prevent future violence and would be more effective at realising this objective than promoting peace and reconciliation, fighting tribalism or ensuring free and fair elections.[63] In summary, Kenyans considered

---

[59] *Prosecutor v William Samoei Ruto, Henry Kiprono Kosgey and Joshua Arap Sang*, ICC-01/11, Application on Behalf of the Government of the Republic of Kenya Pursuant to Article 19 of the ICC Statute, ICC-01/09–01/11–19, 31 March 2011 ('Article 19 Application').

[60] Godfrey Musila, 'The Accountability Process in Kenya: Context, Themes and Mechanisms' in Waruguru Kaguongo and Godfrey Musila (eds), *Judiciary Watch Report: Addressing Impunity and Options for Justice in Kenya—Mechanisms, Issues and Debates* (International Commission of Jurists, 2009) ('ICJ-K, Judiciary Watch Report'), 34.

[61] Simon Robins, *To Live as Other Kenyans Do: A Study of the Reparative Demands of Kenyan Victims of Human Rights Violations* (International Centre for Transitional Justice, 2011).

[62] Vitalis Kimutai, 'Poll chaos victims upbeat on trials as Ocampo prepares to nail six at Hague', *Standard*, 13 December 2010; Dennis Odunga, 'Ocampo's list splits victims of violence', *Daily Nation*, 21 December 2010; Gakuu Mathenge, 'Why Ocampo list has angered PNU members', *Standard*, 18 December 2010.

[63] KNDR April 2011 Report (see Footnote 57).

ending impunity to involve four facets: prosecutions, rule of law reforms, reparations and deterrence.

4.3 Assessing the End of Impunity

The foregoing discussion demonstrates the differences in understanding between the OTP and Kenya as to what the Prosecutor was undertaking to do when he promised to end impunity. Since this project initially sets out to evaluate the OTP against its own stated objectives, it is essential that this includes a discussion of the extent to which the strategy of positive complementarity ensured that those responsible for the post-election violence were held accountable for their actions.

This project goes further, however, by also considering the extent to which the OTP's strategy of positive complementarity strengthened the rule of law in Kenya. This has been included for four reasons. First, notwithstanding the OTP's official position, the Prosecutor did attempt to encourage progress in certain rule of law reforms, particularly the truth commission and the country's witness protection programme. Second, even if the OTP did not seek to influence rule of law reforms, it is entirely possible that its strategy of positive complementarity had such an impact and fairness to the OTP requires this to be considered. Third, there has been very little academic attention on the link between the strategy of positive complementarity and rule of law reform and in the one study on Kenya suggests that the OTP *did* have a positive impact on Kenya's reform agenda.[64] Finally, Kenyans and local NGOs hoped and expected that the ICC would make a significant contribution to ending impunity by removing the 'lords of impunity' and thereby paving the way for necessary reforms.

The third facet of ending impunity identified by Kenyans—reparations for victims—has been excluded from consideration in this study because it clearly falls outside of the OTP's mandate. The ICC is unique as an international criminal tribunal in the sense that it makes provision for victims to receive reparations and has established a Trust Fund for Victims.[65] In addition, upon obtaining a conviction, a trial chamber may order the perpetrators to pay reparations. The OTP, however, has no capacity to award reparations to victims and for this reason it would not be appropriate to include such considerations in a study focussed upon the OTP.

Kenyans' fourth facet of ending impunity, deterrence, has also been excluded from consideration in this study. An assessment of the ICC's deterrent effect in a situation country would be ambitious and worthy of its own dedicated research project. Indeed, such a study has never before been attempted within the field of international criminal justice, possibly because of the methodological difficulties that would confront such a project. Proving a connection between international

---

[64] Sriram and Brown (2012) (see Footnote 33); Christine Bjork and Juanita Goebertus, 'Complementarity in Action: The Role of Civil Society and the ICC in Rule of Law Strengthening in Kenya' (2011) 14 *Yale Human Rights & Development Law Journal* 205.
[65] Rome Statue, Article 75.

prosecutions and the deterrence of future crimes would require many in-depth interviews with elites known to be contemplating the commission of such crimes. It would further require these elites being candid about their motivations and thought processes. Indeed, even those who argue that the ICC has the potential to serve as a deterrent concede that 'it may never be possible to show a causal relationship between the Court and decreased violence'.[66] For these reasons, considerations of the ICC's deterrent effect have been excluded from this project.

Finally, in evaluating the OTP's impact upon ending impunity, it must of course be conceded that 'ending impunity' is an aspirational objective that can never be completely realised. It should be recognised that the Prosecutor's promise to end impunity is largely rhetorical and, consequently, it would be both unrealistic and unfair to hold the OTP to this impossible ideal. Nobody would suggest that the OTP would have failed to realise its objective simple because a small number of perpetrators escaped accountability or some rule of law reforms remained outstanding. This project therefore adopts a more modest and reasonable assessment of the OTP's impact—whether the strategy of positive complementarity made a *significant contribution* to the ending of impunity in Kenya.

In summary, this project considers the extent to which the OTP's strategy of positive complementarity made a significant contribution to ending impunity in Kenya, confining this analysis to the OTP's impact upon domestic prosecutions and rule of law reforms. Any negative impacts (or 'shadow sides') are also considered. This study is limited to consideration of the *OTP's immediate* impact over the first five years of its involvement in a situation country.

5 Precursors for Positive Complementarity

This project provides empirical evidence to challenge many assumptions on the practical operation and impact of the strategy of positive complementarity. I suggest that the strategy does not operate in the same way in all situation countries and that its effectiveness depends on the existence of certain factors, which I call the 'precursors for positive complementarity'. Where these are present, the strategy is more likely to succeed in realising its objective of ending impunity.

First, the target state should have the present ability to investigate and prosecute suspects. This includes having passed the necessary criminal legislation (including for Rome Statute crimes); sufficient numbers of professionally trained and well-funded police, prosecutors and judges; and an effective witness protection programme. Where any of these features are absent or lacking, reforms will be necessary before perpetrators may be held accountable for their actions. Such reforms will often take a considerable period of time to complete and during this period witnesses may disappear and evidence may be destroyed, thereby reducing the likelihood of successful future prosecutions at the local or international level.

---

[66] Burke-White (2005) (see Footnote 31).

Second, suspected perpetrators should not occupy positions of power in the government, judiciary or security forces. Although Schabas may be correct when he suggests that the Rome Statute will challenge prosecutors and judges to repress serious human rights violations with 'greater zeal', this is unlikely to be the case where the prosecutors, judges or politicians are themselves implicated in the crimes or allied to others who are so implicated.[67] The evidence from the Kenyan situation suggests that in such circumstances the threat of international prosecutions is unlikely to encourage elites to commit 'professional suicide' by overseeing their own prosecutions.

Third, the domestic criminal justice system should command public confidence. Victims and witnesses will be reluctant to report crimes or to testify in court where they believe prosecutors, judges or politicians to be supportive of a culture of impunity. Criminal justice systems are reliant upon public cooperation for their effectiveness and no amount of pressure exerted by the OTP will encourage domestic prosecutions where there is an absence of public confidence.

Finally, the strategy of positive complementarity is more likely to be successful where the target state considers international prosecutions to be imminent but not yet inevitable. Where international prosecutions are seen to be far-fetched or remote, the OTP is likely to have little influence as its threat is lacking in immediacy. Likewise, where the OTP commences its own investigations and this induces the target state into believing international prosecutions to be inevitable, a major incentive for conducting domestic prosecutions is removed, thereby significantly diminishing the OTP's influence.

Where some or all of these precursors are lacking but the strategy of positive complementarity is nevertheless pursued, the target state is likely to seek to avoid accountability at both the domestic and international level by engaging in a foreign affairs facade. This involves the target state making little or no progress in domestic prosecutions while simultaneously providing continued assurances of a commitment to ending impunity in order to save itself from international embarrassment and deter the ICC from intervening. Although Burke-White correctly predicts that the threat of international prosecutions may generate negative publicity, the target state's response may not be to pursue domestic prosecutions but to instead to merely give the appearance of so doing.[68] Additionally, or in the alternative, should proceedings commence in The Hague the target state is likely to give assurances of cooperation while at the same time engaging in practices designed to frustrate and delay the progress of the prosecutions. By doing so, the target state reduces the likelihood of convictions at either the domestic or local level while simultaneously minimising stigmatisation and cathartic feedback.

Where the OTP pursues a strategy of positive complementarity where some of these precursors are absent, some shadow sides of complementarity may result. First, and somewhat paradoxically, the threat of international prosecutions may *discourage* domestic prosecutions. Those in government with a genuine desire to

---

[67] Schabas (2008) (see Footnote 24), 19.
[68] Burke-White in Stahn and El Zeidy (2011) (see Footnote 18), 344.

end impunity may throw their support behind international intervention believing the ICC to be better placed to provide impartial and effective justice than a politicised and compromised local mechanism. Likewise, those with blood on their hands may demonstrate their commitment to accountability by professing to favour ICC prosecutions for the same reasons, while at the same time taking steps to undermine that process. The strategy of positive complementarity therefore provides each group with an incentive for favouring international prosecutions over domestic prosecutions.

Second, to the extent that the strategy of positive complementarity serves as a catalyst for local prosecutions, it may be that it encourages the establishment of a defective local mechanism. Contrary to Ellis' prediction, it may be that the target state does not 'aggressively and fairly pursue domestic prosecutions'.[69] Likewise, Cryer may be mistaken in his prediction that positive complementarity creates a strong interest for states 'not to cheat'.[70] Rather, the Kenyan situation suggests that political elites who are reluctant to commit professional suicide by prosecuting themselves or their allies are likely to support a local justice mechanism designed to either be completely ineffective or to effective in merely prosecuting political adversaries.

Third, the pressure exerted by the OTP has the potential to cause or exacerbate disunity within the government of the target state. This shadow side is of particular concern where the government in question is a fragile power-sharing coalition. Factions within the government may disagree on how to respond to the OTP's threat and as a consequence may withhold their cooperation on other important items on the political agenda. Likewise, precious parliamentary time and scarce government resources may be devoted to the target state's resistance to the ICC and this may have the consequence of delaying or jeopardising a crucial reform agenda. In this way, the ICC may not force legislators to strengthen their own legislative capacity to confront the persistent problem of impunity, as Robinson suggests, but may instead present a major obstacle to such reforms.[71]

A fourth shadow side is that the target government may manipulate the ICC issue for its own political advantage. Political elites may seek to discredit opponents by calling for such persons to be tried in The Hague. Where leaders are named as suspect themselves, they may attempt to portray themselves as martyrs of a politicised ICC process that threatens state sovereignty. Savvy politicians may go further and employ this victimisation narrative as a means of mobilising their supporter base. As such, although Akhavan suggests that individuals named as suspects by international tribunals may experience stigmatisation, it is also possible that such persons may see an *increase* in domestic support following the issuance of indictments.[72]

Fifth, where the target state does not have an effective witness protection programme, the OTP's threat of international prosecutions may lead to a significant increase in the intimidation of victims, witnesses and their families. The Prosecutor has previously identified the protection of victims to be the objective of his mission,

---

[69] Ellis (2002–2003) (see Footnote 29), 239.
[70] Cryer (2005) (see Footnote 28), 164.
[71] Robinson (2002) (see Footnote 27), 1849.
[72] Akhavan (2001) (see Footnote 29).

the avoidance of new killings to be his 'basic duty' and the interests of victims to be one of the four 'fundamental principles' guiding OTP policy.[73] As such, this potential shadow side of complementarity ought to be of particular concern to the OTP.

Finally, should the OTP commence its own investigations and prosecutions, this may have the effect of undermining public confidence in the domestic criminal justice system, thereby making future local prosecutions more difficult. As Burke-White has recognised, the commencement of international prosecutions demonstrates that national governments 'have failed to meet their legal obligation to prosecute crimes domestically'.[74] The local criminal justice system may then be subject to international criticism (including from the Court itself), as well as from domestic civil society. This is likely to have the consequence of making victims and witnesses less willing to report crimes to local authorities and in this way the cycle of impunity may be perpetuated. In time, local actors may place increased reliance upon the ICC as a substitute for domestic proceedings.

6 Structure of Project

This project is divided into nine chapters. Following this introduction, Chap. 2 provides greater detail on the OTP's strategy of positive complementarity, which is now routinely pursued whenever the OTP receives reports of Rome Statute crimes being committed on the territory of an ICC Member State. While conducting its preliminary assessment on whether a situation is admissible (a process that often takes months or years), the OTP seeks to encourage the national government in question to uphold its obligations under the Rome Statute to investigate and prosecute crimes within the ICC's jurisdiction. It does this by applying increasing amounts of pressure upon the Member State, initially by announcing that it is monitoring the situation. Should cooperation not be forthcoming, the OTP may elect to hold meetings with senior government officials, enter into a 'complementarity contract', agree upon a 'division of labour', seek to mobilise civil society, threaten international prosecutions and, ultimately, request the Court's permission to conduct official investigations. The OTP's hope is that by prosecuting the leaders, this then opens up the possibility of prosecutions proceeding at the local level. Even after international proceedings have commenced at the ICC, the Prosecutor continues to encourage domestic proceedings by emphasising the Court's limited capacity to conduct prosecutions. The chapter then briefly summarises the OTP's implementation of its strategy of complementarity in other situation countries, arguing that in its early years it did not pursue such a policy and instead actively sought self-referrals in the Ugandan and DRC situations. As such, the Kenyan situation represents perhaps one

---

[73] Moreno-Ocampo June 2003 Statement (see Footnote 14); Prosecutorial Strategy 2009–2012 (see Footnote 3).

[74] Burke-White in Stahn and El Zeidy (2011) (see Footnote 18), 344.

of the first instances in which the OTP has committed to the strategy and, therefore, provides the first opportunity to empirically evaluate its effectiveness.

Chapter 3 introduces the Kenyan case study. It first provides a summary of the 2007 post-election violence that led to OTP involvement and briefly discusses some of the major causes of this violence, one of which was the prevalence of impunity. It then traces Kenya's history of impunity from the colonial period, through its period of one-party rule, the return to multi-party politics and, ultimately, to the commencement of the 2007 violence. It demonstrates how impunity had become institutionalised through constitutional amendments that augmented the powers of the executive at the expense of the other branches of government. With the president of the day exercising a great deal of control over the legislature, the judiciary and the police, Kenyans lost faith in their political and legal institutions, resulting in a 'culture of impunity'. This lack of confidence in the State's security apparatus led to the formation of vigilante groups, which became increasingly responsible for providing protection for citizens and the subsequent commoditisation of security. As such, by the time of the post-election violence the State had lost its monopoly over the legitimate use of force, providing a fertile environment for widespread and systematic violence.

Chapter 4 provides an overview of the ICC's involvement in Kenya and, in particular, the implementation of the OTP's strategy of positive complementarity. It shows the means by which the OTP announced that it was monitoring the situation, met with government delegations, entered into a complementarity contract, agreed to a division of labour, threatened international prosecutions and initiated official investigations. As the OTP conducted these investigations, it continued to stress the importance of domestic prosecutions in order to end impunity. Following the OTP's announcement of its six suspects, however, the OTP's exertion of pressure largely diminished and the ICC prosecutions took centre stage. Ultimately, three persons were called to face trial for crimes against humanity, including Kenyatta and Ruto.

The evaluation of the OTP's involvement in Kenya commences in Chap. 5, which considers the extent to which the perpetrators of the post-election violence were held accountable for their actions through criminal prosecutions, either at the domestic or the international level. Relying upon official government reports on the status of domestic investigations and prosecutions, it is argued that the OTP's strategy of positive complementary had very little impact in ensuring that low- or high-level perpetrators were held accountable for their role in the violence. The data available suggests that no politician, public servant, businessman, tribal elder or police officer was convicted by a Kenyan court during the period under consideration. Indeed, despite the existence of at least 9,000 reported case files in relation to crimes committed during the post-election violence, only approximately 350 resulted in successful convictions, mostly for less serious crimes. Consequently, the citizenry's hopes for prosecutions rested upon the trial of the accused before the ICC. Although these trials did not commence during the period under consideration, the naming of the accused and their appearance in court during the pre-trial stages was welcomed by Kenyans as being significant steps in the fight against impunity. Notwithstanding the commencement of proceedings in The Hague, however, significant impunity gaps remained. It is suggested that the major influence of the OTP's strategy of positive complementarity was to encourage the government to engage in a foreign affairs façade, whereby the government felt compelled to commit to illusory reforms designed to give assurances that progress was being made in domestic investigations and prosecutions. Finally, this chapter argues that the OTP's commencement of international prosecutions as part of its strategy of positive complementarity had two shadow sides—an increased threat to witnesses and domestic politicisation of the ICC process. This latter shadow side may have assisted two suspects, Kenyatta and Ruto, to be elected as President and Vice President, respectively.

Although the OTP's strategy of positive complementarity did not succeed in realising its desired objective of serving as a catalyst for domestic prosecutions, it does not necessarily follow that it had *no* influence upon the government. Chapter 6 seeks to identify this influence by examining the government's attempts to establish a special tribunal and its reaction to the commencement of Hague prosecutions. It suggests that the threat of international prosecutions did not so much convince politicians to support domestic investigations and prosecutions as merely to give the appearance of doing so in the hope that this would curtail international proceedings. When this tactic proved unsuccessful, sections of the government then sought to subvert the ICC process through legal challenges and the withholding of evidence. The OTP's strategy of positive complementarity therefore encouraged the government to engage in another foreign affairs façade, this time by providing continued assurances of cooperation with the Court while simultaneously seeking to obstruct the Court's progress. It also suggests that the OTP's encouragement of domestic prosecutions may have had further shadow sides. First, there is evidence that the strategy of positive complementarity may have discouraged the establishment of a local mechanism to try post-election violence suspects. Second, to the extent that the OTP served as a catalyst for domestic prosecutions, it was to encourage the establishment of a defective local mechanism that was capable of being manipulated by political elites.

Discussion of the OTP's impact in strengthening the rule of law in Kenya commences in Chap. 7. Although the time frame under consideration in this project coincided with perhaps the greatest sustained period of legal reforms in Kenya's history, this chapter argues that there is little evidence linking the OTP's involvement to the passing of a new Constitution, the establishment of a truth commission or fundamental changes to the country's judiciary, criminal justice system, security sector or witness protection programme. It is instead suggested that the scale and intensity of the post-election violence was the major catalyst for these reforms, with many politicians supporting the reform agenda because of national shame and anxiety over the future. Other politicians saw the rule of law agenda as an opportunity to preserve their legacy as they prepared for retirement or as a means by which they could boost their credentials as they prepared for the next elections. While it is possible that the OTP's strategy of positive complementarity in Kenya may have made *some* contribution to this reform process, the data would suggest that the majority of the credit should go to the Annan-led KNDR initiative and to Kenya's Tenth Parliament. Again, there is evidence of a potential shadow side of ICC involvement, with some reforms appearing to have been delayed as some members of government focused their attention on delaying and subverting the ICC process. Further, the ICC process appears to have contributed to divisions within the power-sharing government, with these divisions threatening to derail the reform process altogether.

This discussion of the ICC's impact on the rule of law continues in Chap. 8, which considers Kenyans' perceptions of their political and legal institutions following the ICC's involvement. In other words, to what extent did the OTP's strategy of positive complementarity contribute to the restoration of public confidence in domestic legal institutions? It argues that, while public confidence in the judiciary and the police force improved after the ICC's intervention, the evidence suggests that this was more due to the KNDR process than the ICC's involvement. Indeed, in another example of a shadow side, the OTP's commencement of investigations and prosecutions appears to have undermined confidence in local institutions since it confirmed to the public that the Kenyan judiciary and police were unwilling or unable to carry out these responsibilities.

Some concluding remarks are made in Chap. 9, not only in relation to the OTP's impact in Kenya, but also what lessons may be learned for future situations. The OTP remains committed to its strategy of positive complementarity and continues to routinely implement this strategy in other situations. This chapter suggests that the OTP should carefully consider whether a strategy of positive complementarity is appropriate in *all* situations. In particular, the strategy is less likely to be successful where one or more of the precursors of positive complementarity is absent or lacking. In such circumstances, the target state may be expected to engage in a foreign affairs façade. Further, prior to committing to positive complementarity, the OTP may wish to consider any 'shadow sides' that its involvement may have.

Practitioners and commentators alike continue to embrace and promote positive complementarity because of its theoretical potential to serve as a catalyst for domestic prosecutions and rule of law reform. To date, however, there is little empirical evidence to support these assumptions other than circumstantial evidence of domestic prosecutions having commenced in some countries soon after the OTP has commenced preliminary examinations. No serious attempt has been made to demonstrate a causal link or correlation between the OTP's strategy of positive complementarity on the one hand, and domestic prosecutions and rule of law reform, on the other. In addition, minimal attention has been paid to the 'shadow side of complementarity' or to situations in which positive complementarity has failed to serve as a catalyst for domestic proceedings. This study seeks to make a modest contribution to this gap in the literature by providing a detailed consideration of the impact that positive complementarity has had on ending impunity in Kenya, commencing with a brief overview of Kenya's post-election violence that prompted ICC involvement.

Bibliography

'Cases will ensure peaceful 2012 election, says Ocampo', Daily Nation, 15 December 2010
'ICC seeking speedy trials', *BBC News*
'Justice beckons as Ocampo visits Kenya', *Daily Nation*, 6 May 2010
'Kenya: Ocampo Show Over', *Radio Netherlands Worldwide,* 13 May 2010
Akhavan, Payam, 'Beyond Impunity: Can International Criminal Justice Prevent Future Atrocities?' (2001) 95 *American Journal of International Law* 7
Arber, Sara, 'Designing Samples' in Nigel Fielding (ed), *Researching Social Life* (Sage, 1993)
Atkinson, Atkinson and Coffey, Amanda, 'Analysing Documentary Realities' in David Silverman (ed), *Qualitative Research: Theory, Method and Practice*, 2nd ed (Sage, 2004)
Beigbeder, Yves, International Justice against Impunity: Progress and New Challenges (Martinus Nijhoff, 2005)
Bjork, Christine and Goebertus, Juanita, 'Complementarity in Action: The Role of Civil Society and the ICC in Rule of Law Strengthening in Kenya' (2011) 14 *Yale Human Rights & Development Law Journal* 205
Bloch, Alice, 'Doing Social Surveys' in Clive Seale (ed), *Researching Society and Culture*, 2nd ed (Sage, 2004)
Brighton, Claire, 'Avoiding Unwillingness: Addressing the Political Pitfalls Inherent in the Complementarity Regime of the International Criminal Court' (2012) 12(4) *International Criminal Law Review* 629
Brown, Stephen and Sriram, Chandra, 'The Big Fish Won't Fry Themselves: Criminal Accountability for Post-Election Violence in Kenya' (2012) 111(443) *African Affairs* 244
Bryman, Alan, *Social Research Methods* (Oxford University Press, 2000)
Burke-White, William, 'Complementarity in Practice: The International Criminal Court as Part of a System of Multi-level Global Governance in the Democratic Republic of Congo' (2005) 18 *Leiden Journal of International Law* 557
Burke-White, William, 'Implementing a Policy of Positive Complementarity in the Rome System of Justice' (2008) 19(1) *Criminal Law Forum* 59
Burke-White, William, 'Proactive Complementarity: the International Criminal Court and National Courts in the Rome System of International Justice' (2008) 49(1) *Harvard International Law Journal* 53
Burke-White, William, 'Reframing positive complementarity: reflections on the first decade and insights from the US federal criminal justice system' in Carsten Stahn and Mohamed M. El Zeidy (eds), *The International Criminal Court and Complementarity From Theory to Practice* (Cambridge University Press, 2011)
Clark, Phil, 'Grappling in the Great Lakes: the Challenges of International Justice in Rwanda, the Democratic Republic of Congo and Uganda' in Brett Bowden, Hilary Charlesworth and Jeremy Farrall (eds) *Great Expectations: the Role of International Law in Restructuring Societies after Conflict* (Cambridge University Press, 2009)
Cryer, Robert, Prosecuting International Crimes: Selectivity and the International Criminal Law Regime (Cambridge University Press, 2005)
Ellis, Mark, 'The International Criminal Court and its Implications for Domestic Law and National Capacity Building' (2002-2003) 15 *Florida Journal of International Law* 215
El Zeidy, Mohamed, 'From Primacy to Complementarity and Backwards: (Re)-Visiting Rule 11bis of the Ad Hoc Tribunals' (2008) 57(2) *International & Comparative Law Quarterly* 403
El Zeidy, Mohamed, The Principle of Complementarity in International Criminal Law: Origin, Development and Practice (Brill, 2008)
Final Report from Kenya's Commission of Inquiry into Post-Election Violence, 15 October 2008
Finnemore, Martha and Sikkink, Kathryn, 'International Norma Dynamics and Political Change' (1998) 52(4) *International Organisation* 887
Foudladvand, Shahrzad, 'Complementarity and Cultural Sensitivity: Decision-Making by the ICC Prosecutor in Relation to the Situations in the Darfur Region and the Democratic Republic of the Congo (DRC)', Doctor of Philosophy Thesis, University of Sussex, January 2012

Gekara, Emeka-Mayaka, 'Ocampo to step in if Kenya does shoddy job', *Daily Nation*, 19 June 2009

Hall, Christopher, 'Positive complementarity in action' in Carsten Stahn and Mohamed M. El Zeidy (eds), *The International Criminal Court and Complementarity From Theory to Practice* (Cambridge University Press, 2011)

Hansard, National Assembly, Official Report, 27 January 2009

Hansard, National Assembly, Official Report, 22 December 2010

Hassanein, Ahmed Samir, 'The Principle of Complementarity between International and National Criminal Courts', Doctor of Philosophy Thesis, University of Aberdeen, 2010

Heller, Kevin John, 'The Shadow Side of Complementarity: The Effect of Article 17 of the Rome Statute on National Due Process' (2006) 17 *Criminal Law Forum* 255

International Criminal Court, Office of the Prosecutor, 'Address by the Prosecutor to the Third Session of the Assembly of States Parties', 6 September 2004

International Criminal Court, Office of the Prosecutor, 'Agreed minutes of the meeting between Prosecutor Moreno-Ocampo and the delegation of the Kenyan Government', 3 July 2009

International Criminal Court, Office of the Prosecutor, 'ICC Prosecutor: Kenya Can Be an Example to the World', 18 September 2009

International Criminal Court, Office of the Prosecutor, 'ICC Prosecutor Receives Materials on Post-Election Violence in Kenya', 16 July 2009

International Criminal Court, Office of the Prosecutor, 'Kenya Authorities Committed to Cooperate as ICC Prosecutor Informs them that in December he will Request ICC Judges to Open an Investigation into Post-Election Violence', 6 November 2009

International Criminal Court, Office of the Prosecutor, 'Kenya's post election violence: ICC Prosecutor presents case against six individuals for crimes against humanity', 15 December 2010

International Criminal Court, Office of the Prosecutor, 'OTP Statement in Relation to Events in Kenya', 5 February 2008

International Criminal Court, Office of the Prosecutor, *Paper on some policy issues before the Office of the Prosecutor*, September 2003

International Criminal Court, Office of the Prosecutor, *Prosecutorial Strategy 2009–2012*, 1 February 2010

International Criminal Court, Office of the Prosecutor, 'Statement by the Prosecutor of the International Criminal Court Mrs. Fatou Bensouda at the press conference at the conclusion of Nairobi segment of ICC Prosecutor's visit to Kenya, Nairobi', 25 October 2012

International Criminal Court, Office of the Prosecutor, *Strategic Plan June 2012-2015*, 11 October 2013

International Criminal Court, Office of the Prosecutor, 'Waki Commission List of Names in the Hands of ICC Prosecutor', 16 July 2009

Jurdi, Nidai Nabil, The International Criminal Court and National Courts: A Contentious Relationship (Ashgate, 2011)

Kariuki, Anthony 'Ocampo: ICC has strong case in Kenya chaos', *Daily Nation,* 7 November 2009

Kimutai, Vitalis, 'Poll chaos victims upbeat on trials as Ocampo prepares to nail six at Hague'

Kleffner, Jan, Complementarity in the Rome Statute and National Criminal Jurisdictions (Oxford University Press, 2008)

Kleffner, Jan, 'The Impact of Complementarity on National Implementation of Substantive International Criminal Justice' (2003) 86(1) *Journal of International Criminal Justice* 86

Kritz, Neil, 'Policy Implications of Empirical Research on Transitional Justice' in Hugo van der Merwe, Victoria Baxter and Audrey R Chapman (eds), *Assessing the Impact of Transitional Justice: Challenges for Empirical Research* (United States Institute of Peace Press, 2009)

Lamont, Christopher, International Criminal Justice and the Politics of Compliance (Ashgate, 2010)

Leftie, Peter, '"Small fish" now put on notice', *Daily Nation*, 3 December 2010

Limo, Lucianne, Omanga, Beauttah and Bartoo, Vincent, 'Ocampo asks Kenyans not to expect too much', *Standard*, 11 May 2010

Mathenge, Gakuu, 'Why Ocampo list has angered PNU members', *Standard*, 18 December 2010

Mathenge, Oliver, 'Reforms: Annan heads to Kenya', *Daily Nation*, 1 October 2009

Maxwell, Joseph, Qualitative Research Design: An Interactive Approach, 3rd ed (Sage, 2012)

Mbuthia, Joe, 'ICC has "no witness in Kenya"', *Daily Nation*, 24 March 2010

Mégret, Frédéric, 'Too much of a good thing? Implementation and the uses of complementarity' in Carsten Stahn and Mohamed M. El Zeidy (eds), *The International Criminal Court and Complementarity From Theory to Practice* (Cambridge University Press, 2011)

Melman, Jesse, 'The Possibility of Transfer(?): A Comprehensive Approach to the International Criminal Tribunal for Rwanda's Rule 11bis to Permit Transfer to Rwandan Domestic Courts' (2010-2011) 79 *Fordham Law Review* 1271

Moreno-Ocampo, Luis, 'A positive approach to complementarity: the impact of the Office of the Prosecutor' Carsten Stahn and Mohamed M. El Zeidy (eds), *The International Criminal Court and Complementarity From Theory to Practice* (Cambridge University Press, 2011)

Moreno-Ocampo, Luis, 'Kenya National Dialogue and Reconciliation, Two Years On, Where are We?', Statement, Nairobi, 2 December 2010

Moreno-Ocampo, Luis, 'Session 1: Office of the Prosecutor of the ICC', Consultative Conference on International Criminal Justice, 9 September 2009

Moreno-Ocampo, Luis, 'Statement Made at the Ceremony for the Solemn Undertaking of the Chief Prosecutor of the ICC', The Hague, 16 June 2003

Moreno-Ocampo, Luis, 'Statement of the Prosecutor to the Diplomatic Corps', 12 February 2004

Musila, Godfrey, 'The Accountability Process in Kenya: Context, Themes and Mechanisms' in Waruguru Kaguongo and Godfrey Musila (eds), *Judiciary Watch Report: Addressing Impunity and Options for Justice in Kenya—Mechanisms, Issues and Debates*

Mwanzia, Mutinda, 'Ocampo's actions plans', *Standard*, 9 April 2010

Namunane, Bernard, 'The Hague beckons for suspects', *Daily Nation*, 26 November 2009

Namunane, Bernard and Mathenge, Oliver, 'I'll nail suspects in 6 months', *Daily Nation*, 8 May 2010

Nouwen, Sarah, Complementarity in the Line of Fire: The Catalysing Effect of the International Criminal Court in Uganda and Sudan (Cambridge University Press, 2013)

Odunga, Dennis, 'Ocampo's list splits victims of violence', *Daily Nation*, 21 December 2010

Omanga, Beauttah, 'Nowhere to hide as The Hague alerts states on chaos suspects', *Standard*, 27 April 2010

Omanga, Beauttah, 'Why Ocampo needs two years on Kenya', *Standard*, 13 May 2010

Penrose, Mary Margaret, 'Impunity—Inertia, Inaction and Invalidity: A Literature Review' (1999) 17(2) *Boston University International Law Journal* 269

Peskin, Victor, International Justice in Rwanda and the Balkans: Virtual Trials and the Struggle for State Cooperation (Cambridge University Press, 2008)

Pichon, Jakob, 'The Principle of Complementarity in the Cases of the Sudanese Nationals Ahmad Harun and Ali Kushayb before the International Criminal Court' (2008) 8 *International Criminal Law Review* 185

Politi, Mauro and Gioia, Federica, The International Criminal Court and National Jurisdictions (Ashgate, 2008)

Politi, Mauro and Nesi, Giuseppe, The Rome Statute of the International Criminal Court: a Challenge to Impunity (Ashgate, 2001)

Prosecutor v William Samoei Ruto, Henry Kiprono Kosgey and Joshua Arap Sang, ICC-01/11, Application on Behalf of the Government of the Republic of Kenya Pursuant to Article 19 of the ICC Statute, ICC-01/09-01/11-19, 31 March 2011

Roht-Arriaza, Naomi, Impunity and Human Rights in International Law and Practice (Oxford University Press, 1995)

Roht-Arriaza, Naomi and Mariezcurrena, Javier (eds), *Transitional Justice in the Twenty-First Century* (Cambridge, 2006)

Razesberger, Florian, The International Criminal Court: The Principle of Complementarity (Peter Lang, 2006)

Robins, Simon, To Live as Other Kenyans Do: A Study of the Reparative Demands of Kenyan Victims of Human Rights Violations (International Centre for Transitional Justice, 2011)

Robinson, Darryl, 'The Mysterious Mysteriousness of Complementarity' (2010) 21(1) *Criminal Law Forum* 67

Robinson, Darryl, 'The Rome Statute and its Impact on National Law' in Antonio Cassese, Paola Gaeta and John Jones (eds), *The Rome Statute of the International Criminal Court: a commentary* (Oxford University Press, 2002)

Rome Statute of the International Criminal Court, opened for signature 17 July 1998, 2187 UNTS 90 (entered into force 1 July 2002)

Ryngaert, Cedric, 'Introduction' in Cedric Ryngaert (ed), *The Effectiveness of International Criminal Justice* (Intersentia, 2009)

Schabas, William, *An Introduction to the International Criminal Court* (Cambridge University Press, 2001)

Schabas, William, 'Complementarity in Practice: Some Uncomplimentary Thoughts' (2008) 19 *Criminal Law Forum* 7

Schiff, Benjamin, *Building the International Criminal Court* (Cambridge University Press, 2008)

South Consulting, Kenya National Dialogue and Reconciliation Monitoring Project, *Draft Review Report*, April 2011

South Consulting, Kenya National Dialogue and Reconciliation Monitoring Project, *Review Report*, June 2011

Sriram, Chandra and Brown, Stephen, 'Kenya in the Shadow of the ICC: Complementarity, Gravity and Impact' (2012) 12(2) *International Criminal Law Review* 219

Stahn, Carsten, 'Introduction: bridge over troubled waters?' in Carsten Stahn and Mohamed M. El Zeidy (eds), *The International Criminal Court and Complementarity From Theory to Practice* (Cambridge University Press, 2011)

Stahn, Carsten, 'Libya, the International Criminal Court and Complementarity' (2012) 10 *Journal of International Criminal Justice* 325

Stahn, Carsten, 'Taking complementarity seriously: on the sense and sensibility of 'classical', 'positive' and 'negative' complementarity' in Carsten Stahn and Mohamed M. El Zeidy (eds), *The International Criminal Court and Complementarity From Theory to Practice* (Cambridge University Press, 2011)

Stigen, Jo, The Relationship between the International Criminal Court and National Jurisdictions: The Principle of Complementarity (Martinus Nijhoff, 2008)

Thakur, Ramesh and Malcontent, Petrus, From Sovereign Impunity to International Accountability: the Search for Justice in a World of States (United Nations University, 2004)

Thomasson, Emma, 'Interview—Darfur, Kenya courts to complement ICC-prosecutor', *Reuters*, 30 October 2009

United Nations Economic and Social Council Commission on Human Rights, *Report of the Independent Expert to Update the Set of Principles to Combat Impunity*, E/CN.4/2005/102/Add.1, 8 February 2005

Chapter 2
The Strategy of Positive Complementarity

Although the Rome Statute's fifth preambular paragraph declares the ICC to have been established to 'end impunity', it does not define this phrase and provides little guidance on how this objective is to be realised. Instead, this is left for the various organs of the Court to develop their own interpretations and strategies. The OTP has sought to provide some guidance in this regard by publishing a series of policy papers. As these papers identify, the dilemma that the OTP faces is how it can make a significant contribution towards ending impunity with finite resources that permit just a handful of trials per year. The OTP's proposed solution, as stated in its first policy paper, is to encourage states to conduct their own domestic proceedings:

> The Court is an institution with limited resources. The Office will function with a two-tiered approach to combat impunity (sic). On the one hand, it will initiate prosecutions of the leaders who bear the most responsibility for the crimes. On the other hand, it will encourage national proceedings, where possible, for the lower-ranking perpetrators, or work with the international community to ensure that the offenders are brought to justice by some other means.[1]

Under this strategy of positive complementarity, the OTP actively encourages domestic investigations and prosecutions with the objective of rendering international trials unnecessary. Indeed, according to the Prosecutor, a success for the OTP would be the absence of trials before the ICC as a consequence of functioning domestic criminal justice systems.[2] The OTP has now identified the strategy of positive complementarity to be one of the four 'fundamental principles' that guide prosecutorial policy, alongside 'focussed investigations and prosecutions', 'addressing the interests of the victims' and 'maximising the impact of the Office's work'.[3]

---

[1] International Criminal Court, Office of the Prosecutor, *Paper on some policy issues before the Office of the Prosecutor,* September 2003' ('2003 OTP Policy Paper'), 3.
[2] Luis Moreno-Ocampo, 'Statement Made at the Ceremony for the Solemn Undertaking of the Chief Prosecutor of the ICC', The Hague, 16 June 2003 ('Moreno-Ocampo June 2003 Statement').
[3] International Criminal Court, Office of the Prosecutor, *Prosecutorial Strategy 2009–2012,* 1 February 2010 ('Prosecutorial Strategy 2009–2012') [23].

This chapter provides an overview of the strategy of positive complementarity and discusses its potential to make a significant contribution to ending impunity. Relying upon official policy papers, OTP practice, public statements from the Prosecutor and interviews, this chapter provides a background on the origins of the strategy, a description of its components and an explanation of how it has been applied in the past. This chapter also discusses the concept of the 'shadow side of complementarity', a term used to describe any unintended and detrimental effects that the strategy may have had on the target state.

1 Origins of Positive Complementarity

1.1 Complementarity and the Rome Statute

Perhaps the most remarkable aspect of the OTP's strategy of positive complementarity is that it was never contemplated by those responsible for establishing the ICC, despite the fact that one of the principal considerations for the drafters of the Rome Statute was the relationship between the Court and domestic criminal justice systems.[4,5] According to one of the principal negotiators, John Holmes, throughout the negotiation process a majority of states made clear that the most effective and viable system was one based on national procedures complemented by an international court.[6] Negotiators therefore displayed an eagerness to move away from the primacy models adopted by both the ICTY and ICTR under which the domestic courts served as a residual mechanism for suspects not tried by the international courts.

The Preamble to the Rome Statute provides that 'the International Criminal Court established under this Statute shall be complementary to national criminal jurisdictions'. This is reinforced by Article 1, which states that the ICC 'shall be complementary to national jurisdictions'. The heart of the complementarity regime, however, is Article 17, which provides in relevant part as follows.

1. Having regard to paragraph 10 of the Preamble and article 1, the Court shall determine that a case is inadmissible where:

    (a) The case is being investigated or prosecuted by a State which has jurisdiction over it, unless the State is unwilling or unable genuinely to carry out the investigation or prosecution;
    (b) The case has been investigated by a State which has decided not to prosecute the person concerned, unless the decision resulted from the unwillingness or inability of the State genuinely to prosecute;
    (c) The person concerned has already been tried for conduct which is the subject of the complaint, and a trial by the Court […]

---

[4] Mauro Politi, 'Reflections on complementarity at the Rome Conference and beyond' in Stahn and Zeidy (2011).

[5] Carsten Stahn and Mohamed M. El Zeidy (eds), *The International Criminal Court and Complementarity From Theory to Practice* (Cambridge University Press, 2011), 3.

[6] John Holmes, 'The Principle of Complementarity' in Rory Lee (ed) *The International Criminal Court: The Making of the Rome Statute, Issues, Negotiations, Results* (Kluwer Law International, 1999); Schabas, 'The rise and fall of complementarity', in Stahn and El Zeidy (2011) (see Footnote 5), 154.

1 Origins of Positive Complementarity

When states ratify the Rome Statute they are entrusted with the primary responsibility for conducting investigations and prosecutions. Where a state has conducted investigations or prosecutions, or is in the process of conducting investigations or prosecutions, the case will be inadmissible before the ICC. This regime is strengthened by Articles 18 and 19, which permit states and the Court, respectively, to initiate motions to challenge the admissibility of cases on the basis of the requirements in Article 17. It is therefore clear that the drafters of the Rome Statute intended that the principle of complementarity should uphold state sovereignty and serve as a barrier to admissibility to the ICC. No serious consideration was given during the negotiation process to the possibility that the ICC might wish to actively *encourage* domestic prosecutions so that international prosecutions become unnecessary.[7]

1.2 The Birth of Positive Complementarity

The ICC and its complementarity regime came into force in 2002, but by this time a rather different conception of complementarity was emerging through the practice of the two *ad hoc* international criminal tribunals. The Security Council had exerted pressure upon the ICTY to complete its work as quickly as possible and to facilitate this process passed resolutions that authorised the ICTY to refer cases involving lower-level perpetrators to competent domestic courts in the region.[8] The ICTY then became instrumental in the formation of the War Crimes Chambers in Serbia and Bosnia and Herzegovina. The ICTY shared its expertise during the drafting process and allowed each of these local justice mechanisms to access its legal database.[9] Meanwhile, ICTR legal experts began training investigators, lawyers and judges in order to build the capacity of Rwandan courts to try suspects locally.[10] These developments demonstrated that cooperation between international courts and their domestic counterparts was not only possible, but also *necessary* in order to reduce the impunity gap.

As a result of the developments at the ICTY and the ICTR, policy makers within the OTP entertained the idea of re-interpreting the Rome Statute's complementarity regime. In 2003, the OTP established an expert consultation process on 'complementarity in practice'. The experts agreed that a court with global reach but limited resources could not realise its mandate of ending impunity for the world's most serious crimes merely by acting as a safety net for domestic courts. The experts therefore concluded that the OTP could make its greatest contribution to ending impunity by actively encouraging domestic proceedings:

---

[7] Holmes (1999) (see Footnote 6).
[8] UNSC Res 1503 (28 August 2003) UN Doc S/Res/1503/2003; UNSC Res 1534 (26 March 2004) UN Doc S/Res/1534/2004.
[9] Human Rights Watch, *Selling Justice Short: Why Accountability Matters for Peace* (Human Rights Watch, 2009) ('HRW, Selling Justice Short').
[10] Hassan Jallow, 'International criminal justice: reflections on the past and the future' (2010) 36(2) *Commonwealth Law Bulletin* 269, 273.

Consistent with its mandate to help ensure that serious international crimes do not go unpunished, it should be a high priority for the Office of the Prosecutor to actively remind States of their responsibility to adopt and implement effective legislation and to encourage them to carry out effective investigations and prosecutions.[11]

Less than 3 weeks after the first meeting of the experts, Moreno-Ocampo was sworn in as the first Prosecutor of the ICC, promising to 'establish links with prosecutors and judges from all over the world' because 'they continue to bear the primary responsibility for investigating and prosecuting crimes within the jurisdiction of the Court'.[12] During the same speech, the Prosecutor made the following statement:

As a consequence of complementarity, the number of cases that reach the Court should not be a measure of its efficiency. On the contrary, the absence of trials before this Court, as a consequence of the regular functioning of national institutions, would be a major success.

The idea of actively encouraging domestic prosecutions was novel and not one which was contemplated as the ICC was being established.[13] It took until 2006 for the OTP to adopt a name for this new strategy: '*positive* complementarity'.[14] Commentators now distinguish 'positive complementarity' from 'passive complementarity', the approach contemplated by the drafters of the Rome Statute under which the ICC is seen as a backstop or safety net for national jurisdictions.[15] In short, rather than waiting for domestic prosecutions to commence and initiating international prosecutions where they do not (*passive* complementarity), the OTP now seeks to actively promote domestic prosecutions in the hope that international prosecutions will not be necessary (*positive* complementarity).

2 OTP's Understanding of Positive Complementarity

Five major policy papers have now been released that make reference to the strategy of positive complementarity and some further detail has been provided through the Prosecutor's speeches and writings.[16, 17] By analysing these sources, it

---

[11] International Criminal Court Office of the Prosecutor, *Informal Expert Paper: The principle of complementarity in practice*, 2003 ('Informal Expert Paper').

[12] Moreno-Ocampo June 2003 Statement (see Footnote 2).

[13] Schabas, 'The rise and fall of complementarity', in Stahn and El Zeidy (2011) (see Footnote 5), 154.

[14] International Criminal Court Office of the Prosecutor, *Report on Prosecutorial Strategy*, 14 September 2006 ('2006 Policy Paper').

[15] John Holmes, 'Complementarity: National Courts versus the ICC' in Antonio Cassese, Paola Gaeta and John Jones (eds), *The Rome Statute of the International Criminal Court: a commentary* (Oxford University Press, 2002), 1849, 667; William Burke-White, 'Implementing a Policy of Positive Complementarity in the Rome System of Justice' (2008b) 19(1) *Criminal Law Forum* 59, 56.

[16] 2006 Policy Paper (see Footnote 14); Prosecutorial Strategy 2009–2012 (see Footnote 3); International Criminal Court Office of the Prosecutor, *Draft Policy Paper on Preliminary Examinations*, 4 October 2010 ('Preliminary Examinations Policy Paper'); International Criminal Court, Office of the Prosecutor, *Policy Paper on the Interests of Justice*, September 2007 ('Interests of Justice Policy Paper'); International Criminal Court Office of the Prosecutor, *Strategic Plan June 2012–2015* 11 October 2013 ('OTP Strategic Plan 2012–2015') (2011) (n 53).

[17] Luis Moreno-Ocampo, 'A positive approach to complementarity: the impact of the Office of the Prosecutor' in Stahn and El Zeidy (2011) (see Footnote 5).

is possible to gain a rudimentary understanding of what the OTP means by 'positive complementarity', what it aims to accomplish through this strategy and how it works in practice.

2.1 The Two Dimensions of Complementarity

According to the Prosecutor, complementarity has two dimensions: an admissibility dimension and a second, related dimension known as 'positive complementarity'.[18] Under this first dimension, the OTP conducts a preliminary examination of the referred situation in order to determine whether the Rome Statute permits the Court to intervene. As a first step, the OTP decides whether there is a reasonable basis for believing that a crime within the jurisdiction of the Court has been committed.[19] Once this task has been completed, the OTP then inquires into whether the crimes have been investigated and prosecuted at the domestic level and whether the state is unwilling or unable to take such action.[20] Next, the OTP considers whether the case is of sufficient gravity to warrant ICC prosecutions, taking into account such factors as the number of victims, the nature of the crimes, the manner of the commission of the crimes and the impact of the crimes.[21] Finally, the OTP determines whether it would be in the 'interests of justice' to commence investigations and prosecutions.[22]

Throughout this (potentially lengthy) preliminary examinations phase, the OTP implements its strategy of positive complementarity by encouraging investigations and prosecutions at the local level. According to the Prosecutor, the preliminary examinations phase 'offers the most promising, or at a minimum, the first opportunity, for the OTP to serve as a catalyst for the initiation of national proceedings'.[23] The OTP provides encouragement for the trial of suspected perpetrators before national courts. Should these trials not commence, the OTP then commences its own investigations and prosecutions, focusing its efforts on those bearing the greatest responsibility for the most serious crimes.[24] One objective of these trials is that they themselves serve as a catalyst for domestic proceedings and the OTP therefore continues to encourage national prosecutions for other alleged perpetrators in order to avoid an 'impunity gap'.[25] In other words, the ICC prosecutions themselves may form part of the OTP's strategy of positive complementarity in furtherance of its objective to end impunity.

According to the OTP, as a consequence of this strategy, impunity can be ended not only in the targeted state, but also throughout the world. The Prosecutor has said

---

[18] Moreno-Ocampo (2011) (see Footnote 17).
[19] Article 53(1)(b).
[20] Article 17.
[21] Article 17(1)(d). See also Preliminary Examinations Policy Paper (see Footnote 16) [70].
[22] Article 53(1)(c). See also Interests of Justice Policy Paper (see Footnote 16).
[23] Moreno-Ocampo (2011) (see Footnote 17), 25.
[24] Ibid.
[25] Moreno-Ocampo (2011) (see Footnote 17).

that the impact of international prosecutions will be felt not only by the concerned state, but also by all other States Parties, as well as non-states parties.[26] According to the Prosecutor, 'one court ruling in an individual case can affect a multiplicity of other cases' and 'such behavioural change may well be considered as the main impact of the Court'.[27] In support of this contention, the Prosecutor suggests a causal link between the trial of Congolese warlord Thomas Lubanga in The Hague and 'debates in far-flung countries such as Colombia, a State Party, or Sri Lanka and Nepal, two non-states parties'.[28]

2.2 Strategy for Encouraging Prosecutions

The OTP commences its strategy of positive complementarity immediately upon receipt of information that crimes within the Court's jurisdiction may have been committed. According to the Prosecutor, this referral presents the OTP with its '*first opportunity*' to 'serve as a catalyst for the initiation of national proceedings'.[29] It may be deduced from this statement that the OTP commences its strategy of positive complementarity only *after* crimes have been committed and a situation has been referred. This is significant, as it suggests that the OTP does not see itself as being responsible for such activities as encouraging non-parties to ratify the Rome Statute, or encouraging States Parties to pass domestic legislation that facilitates future investigations and prosecutions should they become necessary. Rather, these initiatives are left for other organs of the Court, particularly the Presidency and the Registry.[30]

The OTP therefore waits until crimes within the Court's jurisdiction have been committed before commencing its strategy. In accordance with the Rome Statute, the OTP may receive referrals from either a State Party[31] or the Security Council[32] or communications from individuals or organisations.[33] As an initial response, the OTP may publicise that it has commenced preliminary examinations into the situation. According to the Prosecutor, such an action may serve 'as a potential incentive to national proceedings'.[34] In its first two years of operation, the OTP indicated that it would not disclose which situations were under preliminary examination, but this policy was reversed in 2007.[35] Such information is now made public, subject to confidentiality requirements,

---

[26] Ibid, 21.

[27] Ibid, 30.

[28] Ibid.

[29] Ibid, 25 (emphasis added).

[30] International Criminal Court Assembly of States Parties, *Report of the Court on complementarity*, 11 November 2011 ('ASP 2011 Report').

[31] Article 14.

[32] Article 13(b).

[33] Article 15(1); See also Preliminary Examinations Policy Paper (see Footnote 16) [30].

[34] Moreno-Ocampo (2011) (see Footnote 17), 25.

[35] Paul Seils, 'Making complementarity work: maximising the limited role of the Prosecutor' in Stahn and El Zeidy (2011) (see Footnote 5), 998.

because 'this information can then be factored in by all states and relevant organisations in order to promote timely accountability efforts at the national level'.[36] Typically, this first step will involve the OTP releasing a statement during the course of the conflict, or soon after hostilities have ceased, declaring that the OTP has opened a preliminary examination and is 'closely monitoring' the situation.[37]

Should the target government fail to make any progress with domestic investigations or prosecutions, the Prosecutor may make official visits to situation countries to meet delegations,[38] or receive delegations from these countries in The Hague.[39] The Prosecutor will remind the state of its international obligations to investigate and prosecute, and inquire into what progress has been made in furtherance of these obligations. The Prosecutor may also use these meetings as an opportunity to enter into a 'complementarity contract' with the government, whereby benchmarks and deadlines are agreed as being necessary for the government to satisfy in order to avoid international prosecutions.[40] Alternatively, the Prosecutor may enter into negotiations with the state regarding an appropriate division of labour between local courts and the ICC.[41]

The OTP may also seek to mobilise other groups into exerting further pressure upon the government to initiate domestic investigations and prosecutions. At the local level, the Prosecutor may make an official visit to the situation country in order to meet with victims, community leaders, civil society and the local population.[42] Such meetings may inspire grassroots lobbying for domestic prosecutions, thereby placing further pressure upon state institutions. At the international level, the Prosecutor may network with international organisations in order to persuade the

---

[36] Moreno-Ocampo (2011) (see Footnote 17), 26.

[37] International Criminal Court Office of the Prosecutor, 'ICC Prosecutor confirms situation in Georgia under analysis', 20 August 2008; International Criminal Court, Office of the Prosecutor, 'ICC Prosecutor: alleged war crimes in the territory of the Republic of Korea under preliminary examination', 6 December 2010; International Criminal Court, Office of the Prosecutor, 'ICC Prosecutor confirms situation in Guinea under examination', 14 October 2010.

[38] International Criminal Court Office of the Prosecutor, 'Georgia preliminary examination: OTP concludes second visit to the Russian Federation', 4 February 2011; International Criminal Court Office of the Prosecutor, 'OTP delegation to visit Guinea', 18 May 2010 ('OTP Guinea Statement'); ICC Prosecutor is working with the Russian Federation to promote justice for all victims of Georgian conflict—OTP and Russian Federation pledge co-operation at conclusion of Moscow visit', 10 March 2010; International Criminal Court Office of the Prosecutor, 'ICC Prosecutor visits Colombia', 21 August 2008 ('Colombia 2008 Press Release').

[39] International Criminal Court Office of the Prosecutor, 'OTP preliminary examination in Georgia: ICC Prosecutor receives Georgian Justice Minister', 19 March 2010; International Criminal Court Office of the Prosecutor, 'ICC Prosecutor receives Palestinian Justice Minister, Arab League and Independent Fact-Finding Committee', 16 October 2009.

[40] Carsten Stahn, 'Taking complementarity seriously: on the sense and sensibility of 'classical', 'positive' and 'negative' complementarity' in Stahn and El Zeidy (2011) (see Footnote 5).

[41] Luis Moreno-Ocampo, 'Statement of the Prosecutor to the Diplomatic Corps', 12 February 2004 ('February 2004 Speech').

[42] International Criminal Court Office of the Prosecutor, 'ICC Prosecutor meeting local communities in DRC', 9 July 2009; International Criminal Court Office of the Prosecutor, 'ICC Prosecutor visits Central African Republic to meet with victims and local population', 21 January 2008.

international community, including donors, to support rule of law reforms that would complement the work of the Court.[43] The objective of this networking is to ensure that such international organisations give due consideration to Rome Statute issues when designing policies on conflict management, legal reform and development, thereby providing another source of encouragement for domestic institutions.[44]

The OTP may further increase pressure upon the state by privately or publicly threatening to initiate a formal investigation should domestic proceedings fail to eventuate.[45] In making such a threat, the OTP hopes that local authorities will be prompted to act so as to avoid being shamed on the international stage. Where cooperation is still not forthcoming, the Prosecutor may use his or her *proprio motu* powers to request the Pre-Trial Chamber for permission to conduct investigations.[46] Even after the OTP has commenced its own investigations and prosecutions, its strategy of positive complementarity continues. The OTP will stress that the limitations of the Court restrict it to prosecuting only 'those situated at the highest echelons of responsibility, in particular those who ordered, financed or organised the alleged crimes'.[47] The Prosecutor has indicated that the OTP will continue to encourage local prosecutions even when international proceedings are underway.[48] In other words, it would appear that the OTP's policy is to continue to pursue its strategy of positive complementarity even with trials in The Hague ongoing.

Some have suggested that the OTP should go further than merely seeking to encourage domestic prosecutions by providing material support for the conduct of these proceedings.[49] This latter strategy has been described as '*proactive* complementarity'. The OTP has been inconsistent as whether it supports such a strategy although it seems that initially the OTP was open to the idea of contributing its own resources for the purposes of domestic law reform. In 2003, the Prosecutor told the Assembly of States Parties that the OTP's 'first task' was to help national jurisdictions fulfil their mission and that the OTP would 'help them improve their efficiency'.[50] The Prosecutor even went so far as to suggest the possibility of the OTP providing training and technical support to States Parties.[51] In more recent times, however, the Prosecutor has sought to distance the OTP from being involved in domestic law reform initiatives. In 2009, the Prosecutor was quoted as saying that the ICC had to

---

[43] Moreno-Ocampo (2011) (see Footnote 17), 28.

[44] ASP 2011 Report (see Footnote 30).

[45] International Criminal Court Office of the Prosecutor, 'Côte d'Ivoire: ICC Prosecutor ready to request judges for authorisation to open an investigation', 22 June 2011; International Criminal Court Office of the Prosecutor, 'ICC Prosecutor visits Colombia', 21 August 2008 ('Colombia 2008 Press Release').

[46] Article 15(1).

[47] Moreno-Ocampo (2011) (see Footnote 17), 26.

[48] Ibid.

[49] Mark Ellis, 'International Justice and the Rule of Law: Strengthening the ICC through Domestic Prosecutions' (2009) 1(1) *Hague Journal on the Rule of Law* 79.

[50] Luis Moreno-Ocampo, 'Address to the Assembly of States Parties', New York, 22 April 2003 ('Moreno-Ocampo Inaugural Address').

[51] Ibid.

be 'modest' and recognise that it 'can't train lawyers and prosecutors'.[52] In a chapter published in 2011, the Prosecutor wrote that the OTP would not become engaged in 'reforming domestic judiciaries' because 'such activities belong to other rule of law organisations'.[53] The Prosecutor has, however, affirmed that the OTP will provide assistance by sharing its legal resources and case information with domestic authorities.[54] For example, the OTP has developed a comprehensive online 'legal knowledge system' which it has made publicly available free of charge, thereby providing judges, lawyers and civil society with a valuable resource in the prosecution of international crimes.[55] In addition, as outlined in Article 93(10) of the Rome Statute, the OTP may share evidentiary materials with domestic investigators, prosecutors and courts, if a request to do so has been received.[56]

In other words, the OTP's strategy of positive complementarity involves assisting domestic investigations and prosecutions through the sharing of legal resources and information, but does not go so far as to involve the ICC in the process of reforming domestic institutions. The OTP's understanding of positive complementarity would therefore appear to accord with that of an ICC working group which was formed to consider the matter:

> Positive complementarity refers to all activities/actions whereby national jurisdictions are strengthened and enabled to conduct genuine national investigations and trials of crimes included in the Rome Statute, without involving the Court in capacity building, financial support and technical assistance, but instead leaving these actions and activities for States, to assist each other on a voluntary basis.[57]

In summary, the OTP commences its strategy of positive complementarity upon receipt of information that crimes within the Court's jurisdiction may have been committed and continues until domestic proceedings are finalised, even if trials in The Hague have commenced by this stage. Through meetings with senior members of government, the making of public statements and the issuance of press releases, the OTP seeks to encourage the commencement of national proceedings. The OTP may threaten international prosecutions, enter into a complementarity contract or agree to a division of labour. Where appropriate, the OTP may provide assistance for domestic prosecutions by sharing legal resources and information, but it will not go further in providing training for lawyers and judges or actively assisting with rule of law reforms. Should domestic prosecutions fail to proceed, the Prosecutor will use his or her *pro-*

---

[52] Phil Clark, 'Grappling in the Great Lakes: the Challenges of International Justice in Rwanda, the Democratic Republic of Congo and Uganda' in Brett Bowden, Hilary Charlesworth and Jeremy Farrall (eds) *Great Expectations: the Role of International Law in Restructuring Societies after Conflict* (Cambridge University Press, 2009).

[53] Moreno-Ocampo (2011) (see Footnote 17), 25.

[54] Ibid.

[55] Morten Bergsmo, Olympia Bekou and Annika Jones, 'Complementarity and the construction of national ability' in Stahn and El Zeidy (2011) (see Footnote 5).

[56] Moreno-Ocampo (2011) (see Footnote 17), 26.

[57] International Criminal Court Assembly of States Parties, *Report of the Bureau on Stocktaking: complementarity*, 18 March 2010 ('ASP March 2010 Report') [16].

prio motu powers to commence an ICC investigation. When this occurs, the OTP focuses its efforts on those bearing the greatest responsibility for the crimes in the hope these trials might themselves serve as a catalyst for domestic prosecutions.

3 Positive Complementarity in Practice

In November 2012, the OTP published its *Report on Preliminary Examination Activities*.[58] This revealed that, from the ICC's formation in July 2002, the OTP had received 9,717 communications.[59] By October 2013, a further 597 communications had been received.[60] To date, communications have led to the opening of 21 publicly confirmed preliminary examinations, eight of which have resulted in the OTP launching its own official investigations.[61] Although there have been very few empirical studies that evaluate the OTP's impact in these situations, it would appear that the success of strategy of positive complementarity has been mixed, at best.

3.1 Early Years and Negative Complementarity

Despite the OTP promising from as early as 2003 that it would seek to encourage and assist domestic prosecutions, its practice in its early years suggests that it was in fact doing precisely the opposite—encouraging states to abdicate their responsibilities so that the Court could solicit its first cases.[62] Supporters of the strategy of positive complementarity were surprised and disappointed with the OTP's approach to its first two situations, which involved States Parties with functioning domestic criminal justice systems voluntarily self-referring cases to the ICC.

---

[58] International Criminal Court Office of the Prosecutor, *Report on Preliminary Examination Activities 2012*, November 2012 ('2012 Preliminary Examinations Report').

[59] Ibid [17].

[60] International Criminal Court Office of the Prosecutor, *Report on Preliminary Examination Activities 2013*, November 2013 ('2013 Preliminary Examinations Report') [16].

[61] The eight situations currently being investigated by the OTP are Central African Republic, Côte d'Ivoire, Darfur (Sudan), Democratic Republic of the Congo, Kenya, Libya, Mali and Uganda.

The OTP has completed preliminary examinations in two situations but decided not to proceed—Palestine and Venezuela.

The OTP continues to conduct preliminary examinations in a further eleven situations—Afghanistan, CAR (a second investigation), Colombia, Comoros, Georgia, Guinea, Honduras, Iraq, Nigeria, Republic of Korea and Ukraine

[62] Antoine Buyse, 'The Other Path to Peace: Restitution as a Method to Undo Past Injustice' in Cedric Ryngaert (ed), *The Effectiveness of International Criminal Justice* (Intersentia, 2009), xvi (emphasis in original).

In its first official policy paper, the OTP promised to 'encourage national proceedings, where possible',[63] but less than 3 months later it had accepted a voluntary referral from Uganda. On 16 December 2003, President Museveni sent a confidential letter to the Prosecutor referring the situation concerning the Lord's Resistance Army ('LRA') in northern Uganda to the ICC, a referral that was made public on 29 January 2004.[64] Significantly, there appears to be no evidence of the OTP actively encouraging or assisting domestic prosecutions at this time. Clark's research suggests that the opposite was in fact true—that Uganda's self-referral was made only after the Prosecutor approached an initially reluctant Museveni and persuaded the President to hand over the LRA cases to the ICC for prosecution.[65] This referral was made despite the fact that the Ugandan criminal justice system was, according to Clark, 'one of the most proficient and robust in Africa' and 'unquestionably willing to prosecute serious cases such as those involving the LRA'.[66] The Prosecutor's sole justification for accepting the referral was that Uganda had been unable to arrest those persons bearing the greatest responsibility for the crimes in northern Uganda. The ICC has, however, equally been unable to arrest such persons and 10 years after the referral of the situation, four indicted persons remain fugitives.

At the same time that the OTP was encouraging a self-referral from Uganda, it was also soliciting work in relation to the situation in the neighbouring DRC. President Kabila followed his Ugandan counterpart by signing a letter referring the situation to the ICC, a referral that was made public in July 2004.[67] Again, there appears to have been no serious attempt by the OTP to proactively encourage and assist domestic prosecutions.[68] Rather, the Prosecutor told the Assembly of States Parties on 8 September 2003 that the OTP's role 'could be facilitated by a referral or active support from the DRC'.[69] The OTP's primary objective was not to serve as a catalyst for domestic prosecutions, but rather to present the strongest possible case that domestic prosecutions were not feasible. Evidence that one of the suspects, Thomas Lubanga, was already in the custody of local authorities and preparing to face prosecution was

---

[63] 2003 OTP Policy Paper (see Footnote 1).

[64] International Criminal Court Office of the Prosecutor, 'President of Uganda refers situation concerning the Lord's Resistance Army (LRA) to the ICC', 29 January 2004; International Criminal Court Presidency, 'Letter from Chief Prosecutor Moreno Ocampo to President Kirsch', 17 June 2004, appendix to 'Decision Assigning the Situation in Uganda to Pre-Trial Chamber II', 5 July 2004.

[65] Phil Clark, 'Chasing Cases: The ICC and the politics of state referral in the Democratic Republic of Congo and Uganda' in Stahn and El Zeidy (2011) (see Footnote 5); Payam Akhavan, 'The Lord's Resistance Army Case: Uganda's Submission of the First State referral to the International Criminal Court' (2005) 99(2) *American Journal of International Law* 403, 415.

[66] Clark (2011) (see Footnote 65), 1202.

[67] International Criminal Court Office of the Prosecutor, 'Prosecutor receives referral of the situation in the Democratic Republic of Congo', 19 April 2004.

[68] International Criminal Court Office of the Prosecutor, 'Communications received by the Office of the Prosecutor of the ICC', 16 July 2003.

[69] International Criminal Court Assembly of States Parties, Second Assembly of the States Parties to the Rome Statute of the International Criminal Court, *Report of the Prosecutor of the ICC, Mr Luis Moreno-Ocampo*, 8 September 2003.

rebutted by unsubstantiated rumours that Lubanga might be released prior to trial.[70] Likewise, evidence of the Congolese justice system having recently conducted successful prosecutions for crimes against humanity,[71] and expressions of willingness from the local authorities to try Lubanga and his fellow suspects[72] were ignored in favour of the letter from President Kabila declaring that the DRC's justice system was not capable of conducting investigations or prosecutions.[73] Ultimately, Lubanga avoided prosecution in Bunia for crimes against humanity and genocide by instead answering charges in The Hague for the less grave charges of recruiting and using child soldiers.

The OTP's actions in Uganda and DRC suggest that it was somewhat disingenuous in its commitment to positive complementarity during this time. It would appear that in these early years the OTP was in fact *discouraging* local investigations and prosecutions so that some cases could be heard by the ICC.[74] In other words, it is perhaps best to describe this strategy as one of '*negative* complementarity'. Having found cases to fill the ICC's judicial docket, the OTP appears to have moved away from this strategy of discouraging local prosecutions and encouraging self-referrals. In more recent years, the OTP has actively encouraged domestic prosecutions in a manner that more closely resembles its promised strategy of positive complementarity. The Kenyan situation, which arose at the end of 2007, therefore presents one of the first opportunities to evaluate the OTP's strategy.

3.2 Success Stories?

Perhaps the best example of the OTP genuinely acting in accordance with its strategy of positive complementarity is the situation in Colombia, which has been engaged in a civil war since 1964. In a letter dated 3 March 2005, the Prosecutor informed the Colombian government that there was a reasonable basis for believing that war crimes and crimes against humanity had been committed by paramilitary groups and members of the armed forces.[75] The OTP's preliminary examination of the situation became public in 2006 and, in October 2007 and August 2008, the Prosecutor

---

[70] Situation in the Democratic Republic of the Congo, Decision on the Prosecutor's Application for Warrants of Arrest, Article 58, International Criminal Court Pre-Trial Chamber I, ICC-01/04–01/07, 10 February 2006 ('DRC Arrest Warrants Decision') [33].

[71] HRW, Selling Justice Short (see Footnote 9).

[72] Clark (2011) (see Footnote 65), 1192–1193.

[73] DRC Arrest Warrants Decision (see Footnote 70) [35].

[74] William Burke-White, 'Proactive Complementarity: the International Criminal Court and National Courts in the Rome System of International Justice' (2008) 49(1) *Harvard International Law Journal* 53; William Burke-White, 'Implementing a Policy of Positive Complementarity in the Rome System of Justice' (2008) 19(1) *Criminal Law Forum* 59.

Nidal Nabil Jurdi, 'The Prosecutorial Interpretation of the Complementarity Principle: Does it Really Contribute to Ending Impunity on the National Level?' (2010) 10 *International Criminal Law Review* 73

[75] ASP 2011 Report (see Footnote 30) [33].

led missions to Colombia in which he met with members of the government, judges, prosecutors, police and civil society.[76] Following the OTP's first involvement in the Colombian situation in 2005, there were significant developments in holding perpetrators accountable and ending impunity. On 22 July 2005, President Uribe signed the Justice and Peace Law which provided a framework for truth telling, reparations and prosecutions. In 2009, the Prosecutor announced that the commencement of domestic cases against paramilitaries, guerrillas and the military was evidence that the Colombian justice system 'was working' and that it was therefore not necessary for the OTP to intervene.[77] The Prosecutor claimed this development as a success for the OTP's strategy of positive complementarity:

> In Colombia, the prospect of the ICC attaining jurisdiction was mentioned by prosecutors, courts, legislators and members of the Executive Branch as a reason to make policy choices in implementing the Justice and Peace Law, thus ensuring that the main perpetrators of the crimes would be prosecuted.[78]

Others, however, are reticent to label Colombia as a triumph for positive complementarity. Seils, for example, challenges the assertion that the ICC served as a catalyst for the Justice and Peace Law.[79] Burke-White, meanwhile, refutes the claim that the Justice and Peace Law has made a significant contribution to ending impunity in Colombia, suggesting that 'the scope of accountability that the law provides is questionable'.[80]

Nevertheless, the OTP remains buoyed by the results of its involvement in Colombia and in recent years has sought to replicate this impact elsewhere. The OTP announced the commencement of preliminary examinations in Georgia on 14 August 2008 and made two official visits to monitor the progress of national investigations.[81] The OTP then received confirmation from both Georgian and Russian prosecutors that they had commenced investigations and both governments continue to update the OTP on the progress of these investigations.[82] Similarly, the OTP announced the opening of preliminary examinations in Guinea on 14 October 2009, after which it received a Guinean delegation and conducted three missions to the country.[83] The Guinean government responded by appointing three judges to investigate crimes committed during the 28 September 2009 massacre in Conakry.[84] According to the OTP, 'the situation in Guinea is a clear example of the impact of the Office's

---

[76] Ibid.

[77] Bryon Wells, 'Colombian Judicial System Works: ICC Official', *Colombia Reports*, 9 December 2009.

[78] Moreno-Ocampo (2011) (see Footnote 17), 30.

[79] Seils (2011) (see Footnote 35), 998.

[80] William Burke-White, 'Reframing positive complementarity: reflections on the first decade and insights from the US federal criminal justice system' in Stahn and El Zeidy (2011) (see Footnote 5), 344, 347.

[81] International Criminal Court Office of the Prosecutor, *Report on Preliminary Examination Activities*, 13 December 2011 [100].

[82] Ibid [102].

[83] Ibid [114]–[115].

[84] Ibid.

preliminary examinations activities in triggering national proceedings in accordance with the Rome Statute'.[85]

Some commentators, however, remain sceptical over the OTP's claim to be succeeding in its stated ambition of encouraging domestic prosecutions. According to Hall, 'there is little evidence that these threats have encouraged States Parties to investigate or prosecute genuinely'.[86] Similarly, Seils has observed that 'there is little reason to believe that the Rome Statute has provided the catalyst for genuine national proceedings that was hoped for'.[87] For these commentators, it is premature to conclude that the OTP's strategy of positive complementarity has encouraged genuine domestic prosecutions on the basis of the circumstantial evidence that has thus far been provided by the OTP. Rather, what is required in order to evaluate the success of the strategy of positive complementarity is a more thorough and robust evaluation of the OTP's involvement in post-conflict situations and the impact it has had.

3.3 The Shadow Side of Complementarity

Conspicuously absent from the OTP's observations on the impact of positive complementarity are any unintended or detrimental effects. The potential for positive complementarity to produce undesired results was first raised by Heller in his article on the 'shadow side of complementarity'.[88] Heller provides the example of the Special Criminal Court on the Events in Darfur ('SCCED'), which was established the day after the Prosecutor's 2005 announcements that the OTP was commencing formal investigations. According to the Sudanese Justice Minister, this local justice mechanism was intended to serve as a 'substitute to the International Criminal Court'.[89] The SCCED, however, held proceedings in secret, regularly denied defendants the right to legal representation, admitted evidence obtained through torture and often ignored the presumption of innocence.[90] Heller therefore concludes that 'a downside of complementarity is that it exposes perpetrators to national judicial systems that are far less likely than the ICC to provide due process'.[91] In other words, in encouraging domestic prosecutions, the OTP may inadvertently be promoting proceedings that do not meet international fair trial standards.

---

[85] ASP 2011 Report (see Footnote 30) [33].

[86] Christopher Hall, 'Positive complementarity in action' in Stahn and El Zeidy (2011) (see Footnote 5), 1034, 1029.

[87] Seils (2011) (see Footnote 35), 991.

[88] Kevin Jon Heller, 'The Shadow Side of Complementarity: The Effect of Article 17 of the Rome Statute on National Due Process' (2006) 17 *Criminal Law Forum* 255.

[89] 'National court to try suspects of Darfur crimes', *IRIN News*, 15 July 2005.

[90] Heller (2006) (see Footnote 89).

[91] Ibid.

A second example of this shadow side of complementarity is the potential for savvy and opportunistic politicians to exploit the ICC for their own political benefit. Clark has alluded to the possibility that President Museveni's decision to self-refer the situation in northern Uganda was made only after the Prosecutor had given assurances that the ICC would prosecute rebel forces but not government forces for alleged crimes.[92] According to Clark, this has led to a common perception in the region that 'the ICC has become Museveni's political tool'.[93] Similarly, Peskin has demonstrated the effectiveness of the Balkan and Rwandan governments in manipulating the ICTY and ICTR respectively, in order to further their own political agendas.[94]

Finally, it has been alleged that governments increasingly respond to the threat of ICC prosecutions by creating defective and biased local tribunals that convict political adversaries or a handful of lower-level perpetrators, but shield government elites and their allies from prosecution. For example, Human Rights Watch has criticised the SCCED for prosecuting ordinary crimes, such as theft and possession of stolen goods rather than crimes against humanity, and for targeting foot soldiers rather than senior officials.[95] In other words, the strategy of positive complementarity may provide an incentive for domestic governments to merely give the appearance of ending impunity as part of a foreign affairs façade so as to avoid ICC prosecutions, rather than genuinely taking steps to hold accountable those persons responsible for the atrocities.

4 Conclusion

The OTP seeks to realise its objective of ending impunity through its strategy of positive complementarity under which it actively encourages domestic investigations and prosecutions. The OTP may also provide assistance in the form of sharing of legal resources and information, but it has indicated that it will not contribute to developing domestic legal institutions, which it considers to be a role best reserved for development organisations.

The strategy of positive complementarity commences after crimes have been committed and the situation has been communicated to the OTP. The OTP then conducts preliminary examinations to determine whether Rome Statute crimes have been committed, whether these are being investigated and prosecuted, whether these crimes are of sufficient gravity to justify ICC involvement and whether it would be in the interests of justice to commence investigations and prosecutions. Throughout this preliminary examination phase, the OTP encourages domestic prosecutions by announcing that it is monitoring the situation, making official visits to the situation country to monitor progress, mobilising others at the international

---

[92] Phil Clark (2009) (see Footnote 52).
[93] Ibid.
[94] Victor Peskin, *International Justice in Rwanda and the Balkans: Virtual Trials and the Struggle for State Cooperation* (Cambridge University Press, 2008).
[95] Human Rights Watch, *Lack of Conviction: The Special Criminal Court on the Events in Darfur* (Human Rights Watch, 2006).

and grassroots level to also demand the government to take action, threatening ICC intervention should local proceedings fail to commence and continuing to encourage domestic prosecutions even after international proceedings have commenced by stressing the limitations of the Court.

Practitioners and commentators alike continue to embrace and promote positive complementarity because of its theoretical potential to serve as a catalyst for domestic prosecutions and rule of law reform. To date, however, there is little empirical evidence to support these assumptions other than circumstantial evidence of domestic prosecutions having commenced in some countries soon after the OTP has commenced preliminary examinations. No serious attempt has been made to demonstrate a causal even a correlation between the OTP's strategy of positive complementarity on the one hand, and domestic prosecutions and rule of law reform, on the other. In addition, minimal attention has been paid to the 'shadow side of complementarity' or to situations in which positive complementarity has failed to serve as a catalyst for domestic proceedings. This study seeks to make a modest contribution to this gap in the literature by providing a detailed consideration of the impact that positive complementarity has had on ending impunity in Kenya, commencing with a brief overview of Kenya's post-election violence that prompted ICC involvement.

Bibliography

'National court to try suspects of Darfur crimes', *IRIN News*, 15 July 2005

Akhavan, Payam, 'The Lord's Resistance Army Case: Uganda's Submission of the First State referral to the International Criminal Court' (2005) 99(2) *American Journal of International Law* 403

Bergsmo, Morten, Bekou, Olympia and Jones, Annika, 'Complementarity and the construction of national ability' in Carsten Stahn and Mohamed M. El Zeidy (eds), *The International Criminal Court and Complementarity From Theory to Practice* (Cambridge University Press, 2011)

Burke-White, William, 'Implementing a Policy of Positive Complementarity in the Rome System of Justice' (2008) 19(1) *Criminal Law Forum* 59

Burke-White, William, 'Proactive Complementarity: the International Criminal Court and National Courts in the Rome System of International Justice' (2008) 49(1) *Harvard International Law Journal* 53

Burke-White, William, 'Reframing positive complementarity: reflections on the first decade and insights from the US federal criminal justice system' in Carsten Stahn and Mohamed M. El Zeidy (eds), *The International Criminal Court and Complementarity From Theory to Practice* (Cambridge University Press, 2011)

Buyse, Antoine, 'The Other Path to Peace: Restitution as a Method to Undo Past Injustice' in Cedric Ryngaert (ed), *The Effectiveness of International Criminal Justice* (Intersentia, 2009)

Clark, Phil, 'Chasing Cases: The ICC and the politics of state referral in the Democratic Republic of Congo and Uganda' in Carsten Stahn and Mohamed M. El Zeidy (eds), *The International Criminal Court and Complementarity From Theory to Practice* (Cambridge University Press, 2011)

Clark, Phil, 'Grappling in the Great Lakes: the Challenges of International Justice in Rwanda, the Democratic Republic of Congo and Uganda' in Brett Bowden, Hilary Charlesworth and Jeremy Farrall (eds) *Great Expectations: the Role of International Law in Restructuring Societies after Conflict* (Cambridge University Press, 2009)

Ellis, Mark, 'International Justice and the Rule of Law: Strengthening the ICC through Domestic Prosecutions' (2009) 1(1) *Hague Journal on the Rule of Law* 79

Hall, Christopher, 'Positive complementarity in action' in Carsten Stahn and Mohamed M. El Zeidy (eds), *The International Criminal Court and Complementarity From Theory to Practice* (Cambridge University Press, 2011)

Heller, Kevin John, 'The Shadow Side of Complementarity: The Effect of Article 17 of the Rome Statute on National Due Process' (2006) 17 *Criminal Law Forum* 255

Holmes, John, 'Complementarity: National Courts versus the ICC' in Antonio Cassese, Paola Gaeta and John Jones (eds), *The Rome Statute of the International Criminal Court: a commentary* (Oxford University Press, 2002)

Holmes, John, 'The Principle of Complementarity' in Rory Lee (ed) *The International Criminal Court: The Making of the Rome Statute, Issues, Negotiations, Results* (Kluwer Law International, 1999)

Human Rights Watch, Lack of Conviction: The Special Criminal Court on the Events in Darfur (Human Rights Watch, 2006)

Human Rights Watch, Selling Justice Short: Why Accountability Matters for Peace (Human Rights Watch, 2009)

International Criminal Court Assembly of States Parties, *Report of the Bureau on Stocktaking: complementarity*, 18 March 2010

International Criminal Court, Assembly of States Parties, *Report of the Court on complementarity*, 11 November 2011

International Criminal Court, Assembly of States Parties, Second Assembly of the States Parties to the Rome Statute of the International Criminal Court, *Report of the Prosecutor of the ICC, Mr Luis Moreno-Ocampo*, 8 September 2003

International Criminal Court, Office of the Prosecutor, 'Communications received by the Office of the Prosecutor of the ICC', 16 July 2003

International Criminal Court, Office of the Prosecutor, 'Côte d'Ivoire: ICC Prosecutor ready to request judges for authorisation to open an investigation', 22 June 2011

International Criminal Court, Office of the Prosecutor, *Draft Policy Paper on Preliminary Examinations*, 4 October 2010

International Criminal Court, Office of the Prosecutor, 'Georgia preliminary examination: OTP concludes second visit to the Russian Federation', 4 February 2011

International Criminal Court, Office of the Prosecutor, 'ICC Prosecutor: alleged war crimes in the territory of the Republic of Korea under preliminary examination', 6 December 2010

International Criminal Court, Office of the Prosecutor, 'ICC Prosecutor confirms situation in Georgia under analysis', 20 August 2008

International Criminal Court, Office of the Prosecutor, 'ICC Prosecutor confirms situation in Guinea under examination', 14 October 2010

International Criminal Court, Office of the Prosecutor, 'ICC Prosecutor meeting local communities in DRC', 9 July 2009

International Criminal Court, Office of the Prosecutor, 'ICC Prosecutor is working with the Russian Federation to promote justice for all victims of Georgian conflict – OTP and Russian Federation pledge co-operation at conclusion of Moscow visit', 10 March 2010

International Criminal Court, Office of the Prosecutor, 'ICC Prosecutor receives Palestinian Justice Minister, Arab League and Independent Fact-Finding Committee', 16 October 2009

International Criminal Court, Office of the Prosecutor, 'ICC Prosecutor visits Central African Republic to meet with victims and local population', 21 January 2008

International Criminal Court, Office of the Prosecutor, 'ICC Prosecutor visits Colombia', 21 August 2008

International Criminal Court, Office of the Prosecutor, Informal Expert Paper: The principle of complementarity in practice, 2003

International Criminal Court, Office of the Prosecutor, 'OTP delegation to visit Guinea', 18 May 2010

International Criminal Court, Office of the Prosecutor, 'OTP preliminary examination in Georgia: ICC Prosecutor receives Georgian Justice Minister', 19 March 2010

International Criminal Court, Office of the Prosecutor, *Paper on some policy issues before the Office of the Prosecutor*, September 2003

International Criminal Court, Office of the Prosecutor, *Policy Paper on the Interests of Justice*, September 2007

International Criminal Court, Office of the Prosecutor, 'President of Uganda refers situation concerning the Lord's Resistance Army (LRA) to the ICC', 29 January 2004

International Criminal Court, Office of the Prosecutor, *Prosecutorial Strategy 2009–2012*, 1 February 2010

International Criminal Court, Office of the Prosecutor, 'Prosecutor receives referral of the situation in the Democratic Republic of Congo', 19 April 2004

International Criminal Court, Office of the Prosecutor, *Report on Preliminary Examination Activities*, 13 December 2011

International Criminal Court, Office of the Prosecutor, *Report on Preliminary Examination Activities 2012*, November 2012

International Criminal Court, Office of the Prosecutor, *Report on Preliminary Examination Activities 2013*, November 2013

International Criminal Court, Office of the Prosecutor, *Report on Prosecutorial Strategy*, 14 September 2006

International Criminal Court, Presidency, 'Letter from Chief Prosecutor Moreno Ocampo to President Kirsch', 17 June 2004, appendix to 'Decision Assigning the Situation in Uganda to Pre-Trial Chamber II', 5 July 2004

Jallow, Hassan, 'International criminal justice: reflections on the past and the future' (2010) 36(2) *Commonwealth Law Bulletin* 269

Jurdi, Nidal Nabil, 'The Prosecutorial Interpretation of the Complementarity Principle: Does it Really Contribute to Ending Impunity on the National Level?' (2010) 10 *International Criminal Law Review* 73

Moreno-Ocampo, Luis, 'Address to the Assembly of States Parties', New York, 22 April 2003

Moreno-Ocampo, Luis, 'A positive approach to complementarity: the impact of the Office of the Prosecutor' Carsten Stahn and Mohamed M. El Zeidy (eds), *The International Criminal Court and Complementarity From Theory to Practice* (Cambridge University Press, 2011)

Moreno-Ocampo, Luis, 'Statement Made at the Ceremony for the Solemn Undertaking of the Chief Prosecutor of the ICC', The Hague, 16 June 2003

Moreno-Ocampo, Luis, 'Statement of the Prosecutor to the Diplomatic Corps', 12 February 2004

Peskin, Victor, International Justice in Rwanda and the Balkans: Virtual Trials and the Struggle for State Cooperation (Cambridge University Press, 2008)

Politi, Mauro, 'Reflections on complementarity at the Rome Conference and beyond' in Carsten Stahn and Mohamed M. El Zeidy (eds), *The International Criminal Court and Complementarity From Theory to Practice* (Cambridge University Press, 2011)

Schabas, William, 'The rise and fall of complementarity', in Carsten Stahn and Mohamed M. El Zeidy (eds), *The International Criminal Court and Complementarity From Theory to Practice* (Cambridge University Press, 2011)

Seils, Paul, 'Making complementarity work: maximising the limited role of the Prosecutor' in Carsten Stahn and Mohamed M. El Zeidy (eds), *The International Criminal Court and Complementarity From Theory to Practice* (Cambridge University Press, 2011)

Situation in the Democratic Republic of the Congo, Decision on the Prosecutor's Application for Warrants of Arrest, Article 58, International Criminal Court Pre-Trial Chamber I, ICC-01/04-01/07, 10 February 2006

Stahn, Carsten, 'Taking complementarity seriously: on the sense and sensibility of 'classical', 'positive' and 'negative' complementarity' in Carsten Stahn and Mohamed M. El Zeidy (eds), *The International Criminal Court and Complementarity From Theory to Practice* (Cambridge University Press, 2011)

United Nations Security Council Resolution 1503 (28 August 2003) UN Doc S/Res/1503/2003

United Nations Security Council Resolution 1534 (26 March 2004) UN Doc S/Res/1534/2004

Wells, Byron, 'Colombian Judicial System Works: ICC Official', *Colombia Reports*, 9 December 2009

Chapter 3
Kenya's Post-Election Violence and History of Impunity

On 27 December 2007, Kenyans went to the polls for just the fourth time since the reinstatement of multi-party politics in 1992. Incumbent Mwai Kibaki, representing the Party of National Unity ('PNU') was controversially declared the winner and hurriedly sworn in as President. Within hours of this announcement, supporters of Raila Odinga's Orange Democratic Movement ('ODM') protested this result through violent attacks upon suspected PNU supporters. Hostilities escalated when ethnic leaders from both sides of politics organised, funded and incited youths to commit acts of brutality against opponents. By the time that this two months of bloodshed had ceased, at least 1,113 persons had been killed, more than 350,000 forcibly displaced and countless more subjected to sexual violence and other inhumane acts.[1] A peace settlement was negotiated by an international mediation team, led by Kofi Annan, which culminated in the formation of a power-sharing government with Kibaki as President and Odinga as Prime Minister. The Government of National Unity ('GNU') was entrusted with the responsibility of ensuring that the violence did not recommence and that the next elections were held peacefully. This included, *inter alia*, addressing the country's history of impunity and ensuring that those responsible for the post-election violence faced criminal prosecutions.

This chapter introduces the Kenyan case study by providing an overview of the post-election violence and its causes, including that of the country's institutionalised impunity. Reliance has been placed upon interviews with victims and civil society as well as NGO reports on human rights violations in Kenya, including eight

---

[1] *Final Report from Kenya's Commission of Inquiry into Post-Election Violence*, 15 October 2008 ('Waki Report'), 305, 346.

© Springer International Publishing Switzerland 2015
L. Nichols, *The International Criminal Court and the End of Impunity in Kenya*, Springer Series in Transitional Justice,
DOI 10.1007/978-3-319-10729-5_3

that were published specifically on the post-election violence.² Particular regard has been had to the findings contained of the Commission of Inquiry into the Post-Election Violence ('Waki Commission' or 'Waki Report'). This 529-page report was produced by an independent three-member commission chaired by Justice Philip Waki of the Court of Appeal. Between June 2008 and September 2008, the Waki Commission conducted public hearings and private interviews with victims, civil society and members of government, publishing its findings and recommendations on 15 October 2009. In providing a history of impunity in Kenya, particular reference is made to a 481-page Human Rights Watch report, published in 1991, entitled *Taking Liberties*.³ This report relies upon interviews, newspaper reports and government reports to provide a comprehensive history of state-sanctioned violence in Kenya up until the reinstatement of multi-party politics.

1 Kenya's Post-Election Violence

1.1 *Disputed Presidential Elections and the Road to Violence*

The scale and intensity of the violence was largely unexpected for a country that had prided itself as a bastion of peace in an otherwise volatile and unstable region.⁴ Prior to the violence, Nairobi was leading humanitarian assistance efforts in East Africa, had a prosperous economy that was growing at a healthy 7 % per annum and had held presidential elections five years earlier that the European Union declared to be free and fair.⁵

---

²Ibid; Kenya National Commission on Human Rights, *On the brink of the precipice: a human rights account of Kenya's post-2007 election violence*, 15 August 2008 ('KNCHR Post-Election Violence Report'); Office of the High Commissioner for Human Rights, *Report from OHCHR fact-finding mission to Kenya*, 6–28 February 2008 ('OHCHR Post-Election Violence Report'); UNICEF, UNFPA, UNIFEM and Christian Children's Fun, *A rapid assessment of gender-based violence (GBV) during the post-election violence in Kenya*, Jan-Feb 2008 ('Gender-Based Violence Post-Election Violence Report'); Federation of Women Lawyers, *Submission to the CIPEV on behalf of the inter agency gender-based violence (GBV)*, 11 September 2008 ('FIDA-K Post-Election Violence Report'); Centre for Rights Education and Awareness, *Women paid the price*, 2008 ('CREAW Post-Election Violence Report'); Human Rights Watch, *From Ballots to Bullets*, March 2008 ('HRW Post-Election Violence Report'); International Crisis Group, *Kenya in Crisis*, 21 February 2008 ('ICG Post-Election Violence Report').
³Human Rights Watch, Kenya: *Taking Liberties, an African Watch Report*, 1991 ('HRW, Taking Liberties').
⁴JW Nasongo, JSK Achoka and LLM Wamocha, 'Is Forgiveness and Amnesty a Panacea to Kenya's Post-Conflict Crisis?' (2009) 3(4) *African Journal of Political Science and International Relations* 122.
⁵Axel Harneit-Sievers and Ralph-Michael Peters, 'Kenya's 2007 General Election and its Aftershocks' (2008) 43 *Africa Spectrum* 133; Maina Kiai, 'The Crisis in Kenya' (2008) 19 *Journal of Democracy* 162; Jacqueline Klopp, 'Kenya's Unfinished Agendas' (2009) 62(2) *Journal of International Affairs* 143, 145; Edwin Odhiambo Abuya, 'Consequences of a Flawed Presidential Election' (2009) 29(1) *Legal Studies* 127, 130; Clark Gibson and James Long, 'The Presidential and Parliamentary Elections in Kenya, December 2007' (2009) 28 *Electoral Studies* 492, 497; Mwangi wa Gĩthĩnji and Frank Holmquist, 'Kenya's Hopes and Impediments: The Anatomy of a Crisis of Exclusion' (2008) 2(2) *Journal of Eastern African Studies* 344, 345.

The catalyst for the violence was the presidential election, held on 27 December 2007. Initial results over the first three days of counting suggested an Odinga victory but on 30 December 2007, the Electoral Commission of Kenya ('ECK') declared that Kibaki had prevailed by just over 200,000 votes.[6] Independent observers from the European Union, the Commonwealth, the East African Community and the International Republican Institute all questioned the integrity of the elections.[7] Some members of the ECK admitted that there were serious problems with the vote tallying and its chairman later claimed to have been subjected to intense pressure from ruling political elites.[8] Kibaki was sworn in at a hastily arranged ceremony and Kenyan Internal Security Minister John Michuki ordered a media blackout 'in the interests of public safety'.[9] This in fact led to an escalation in tensions as citizens spread gossip and innuendo via mobile phones and social media.[10] Odinga accused the ECK of having 'doctored the results' but refused to challenge the results in the courts, largely because it had taken the judiciary over a year to hear and reject an electoral challenge from 1997.[11] Those who claimed the 2007 election to have been stolen pointed to the fact that less than two months before the election, Kibaki replaced all of the ECK commissioners and appointed his former lawyer as the ECK vice-chairman.[12]

Many ODM supporters launched violent protests in the streets within minutes of the elections results being announced. Mobs in Nairobi, Kisumu, Eldoret and Mombasa targeted the Kikuyu ethnic group because they were perceived to be loyal to Kibaki. In less than 24 hours, hundreds of persons from these areas had been killed.[13] Property belonging to Kikuyu persons was burned, looted and vandalised and thousands of persons were forced to flee their homes.[14] This phase of violence appears to have been spontaneous and unplanned.[15]

This may be distinguished from *organised* ethnic attacks that took place throughout January 2008. In an apparent attempt to redress long-standing grievances over land and access to resources, opportunistic elites used the election controversy to mobilise their own ethnic groups into violence against rival ethnic groups. Politicians, businessmen, religious leaders and tribal elders held meetings in town halls to organise the attacks, promising cash payments to those who participated

---

[6] Ted Dagne, *Kenya: The December 2007 Elections and the Challenges Ahead* (Congressional Research Service, 2008).

[7] David Throup, 'The Count' (2008) 2(2) *Journal of East African Studies* 290; KNCHR Post-Election Violence Report (see Footnote 2); Abuya (2009) (see Footnote 5).

[8] Dagne (2008) (see Footnote 6), 3.

[9] Maarit Mäkinen and Mary Wangu Kuira, 'Social Media and Postelection Crisis in Kenya' (2008) 13(3) *International Journal of Press/Politics* 328.

[10] Jennifer Coffman, Vigdis Broch-Due, Peter Little, Mwenda Ntarangwi, Miroslava Prazak and Parker Shipton, 'Understanding Kenya's Postelection Violence' (2009) 1(1) *Beliefs and Values* 53.

[11] Mäkinen and Kuira (2008) (see Footnote 9).

[12] Susanne Mueller, 'The Political Economy of Kenya's Crisis' (2008) 2(2) *Journal of Eastern African Studies* 185.

[13] ICG Post-Election Violence Report (see Footnote 2).

[14] Waki Report (see Footnote 1), 164–174.

[15] Ibid, 159.

in the violence.[16] Throughout the Rift Valley, Kalenjin persons loyal to Odinga's ODM targeted the non-Kalenjin communities.[17] Thousands of Kalenjin youths brandishing machetes, bows and poisonous arrows attacked non-Kalenjin and their properties.[18] In the most infamous incident of the entire period of violence, an estimated 35 people were burned alive in a Kiamba church in which they had sought refuge.[19] A Kalenjin youth's chilling explanation for the group's motivation in setting the church alight demonstrates that these political attacks were ethnically motivated: 'We want to send a very very strong message to Kibaki. Because we cannot get him, we are going to work on his ethnic group, the Kikuyu'.[20]

Members of the Kikuyu community responded by organising revenge attacks, signalling a third phase of the violence. From 24 to 28 January 2008, members of the Kikuyu ethnic group attacked the Rift Valley towns of Nakuru and Naivasha, targeting persons of Kalenjin and Luo ethnicity.[21] In one arson attack in Naivasha, 19 members of the Luo community were killed when they were trapped inside their burning homes.[22] Like the other ethnic attacks in the Rift Valley, there is evidence that this violence was organised, with Kikuyu politicians and businessmen organising, sponsoring and inciting the Mungiki criminal sect to carry out the attacks.[23]

Kenya's police force was ill-equipped and unprepared for the violence and many officers responded in a heavy-handed fashion, which resulted in the fourth and final phase of the violence. An estimated 405 people were killed by the police, accounting for more than 35 % of all deaths during this period.[24] While the police later claimed that their decision to use force was necessary in the circumstances, this claim is discredited by evidence that more than half of those persons who were shot had gunshot wounds to the back.[25] There are many tragic stories of police brutality, such as the shooting of a 13-year-old girl who had bent down to pick up a doll.[26] There is also evidence that security forces were responsible for looting, gang rapes and inciting violence during the conflict period.[27]

Sexual violence was a feature of all four phases of violence. The 900 women who were recorded as having been treated in hospital for sexual violence are

---

[16] Waki Report (see Footnote 1), vii.

[17] International Criminal Court Pre-Trial Chamber II, Decision Pursuant to Article 15 of the Rome Statute on the Authorisation of an Investigation into the Situation in the Republic of Kenya, 31 March 2010 ('PTC Authorisation to Conduct Investigations').

[18] Waki Report (see Footnote 1), 42–43.

[19] KNCHR Post-Election Violence Report (see Footnote 2), 67.

[20] Ibid.

[21] David Anderson and Emma Lochery, 'Violence and Exodus in Kenya's Rift Valley, 2008: Predictable and Preventable?' (2008) 2(2) *Journal of Eastern African Studies* 328.

[22] KNCHR Post-Election Violence Report (see Footnote 2), 4.

[23] Waki Report (see Footnote 1), 102–104.

[24] Waki Report (see Footnote 1), 331.

[25] Ibid, 192.

[26] ICG Post-Election Violence Report (see Footnote 2).

[27] Waki Report (see Footnote 1), 99, 396.

believed to have been just the 'tip of the iceberg'.[28] Women were sexually assaulted, gang raped and sodomised, resulting in some becoming pregnant and other contracting HIV or Hepatitis.[29] A smaller number of men were also the victims of sexual violence, with some sodomised and others forcibly circumcised.[30]

On 24 January 2008, Kofi Annan and the Panel of Eminent African Personalities commenced a mediation process that involved representatives from both PNU and ODM. In less than two weeks, the leaders of the respective parties had agreed to four agenda items that later formed the basis of the peace agreement. The two parties agreed to: (1) take immediate steps to stop the violence; (2) take immediate measures to address the humanitarian crisis; (3) negotiate a power-sharing agreement; and (4) address the long-term causes of the violence. On 28 February 2008, Kibaki and Odinga signed a power-sharing agreement, signalling the end of the conflict.

With the country at peace and the power-sharing agreement concluded, the GNU was quickly sworn in and immediately turned its attention to identifying and addressing the long-term causes of the violence. 'Agenda Item IV', as it became known, served as the blueprint for the GNU's massive reform agenda. It identified a wide range of issues that had to be addressed in order to ensure there would be no repeat of the violence, including 'constitutional, legal and institutional reforms, land reforms, tackling youth unemployment, tackling poverty, inequity and regional development imbalances, consolidating national unity and cohesion, and addressing impunity, transparency and accountability'.[31]

1.2 Causes of the Violence

The organised phases of the violence were the result of several historical factors. First, Kenyans regarded presidential elections to be high stakes because 32 amendments to the Constitution over four decades had significantly augmented the powers of the president.[32] By 2007, the presidency had become all powerful, as described by Kenyan human rights advocate Maina Kiai:

> It is a country where the president doles out public lands and forests to anyone he fancies. He alone decides who becomes a judge. He alone appoints members to the Electoral Commission. He can create any public office and staff it with anyone he wants at whatever salary he wishes. He can fire almost anyone at will. He decides if Parliament will sit for 30 years a year or 180. He decides which regions will be given resources for development and which ones will remain marginalised.[33]

---

[28] Ibid, 248.

[29] FIDA-K Post-Election Violence Report (see Footnote 2).

[30] Waki Report (see Footnote 1), 248.

[31] South Consulting, *The Kenya National Dialogue and Reconciliation (KNDR) Monitoring Project*, January 2009 ('KNDR January 2009 Report').

[32] Mueller (2008) (see Footnote 12).

[33] Maina Kiai, Keynote Address to the Fifth Assembly of the World Movement for Democracy, Kyiv, 6 April 2008.

Historically, Kenya's presidents tended to use their excessive powers to favour their own ethnic tribes. This commenced under the country's first president, Jomo Kenyatta, a Kikuyu who encouraged and supported those from his own ethnicity to settle on fertile land in the Rift Valley that had previously belonged to the Kalenjin.[34] Government nepotism continued under his successor, Daniel Arap Moi, who awarded land allocations to members of his own Kalenjin tribe as part of a process that became known within Kenya as 'land grabbing'.[35] This feature of Kenyan politics led some ethnic groups to argue that when a president of their own ethnicity was elected, it was 'our turn to eat'.[36] The widespread belief that the presidency brought advantages to the president's ethnic group caused communities to 'exert violence to attain and keep power'.[37] In addition, the allocation of land to persons of particular ethnic groups resulted in a 'quasi residential apartheid'.[38] Traditional land owners were regarded as 'insiders', those who migrated to the land labelled as 'outsiders'.[39] Elections provided the impetus for marginalised groups to express their grievances. Following the 1992 and 1997 elections, ethnic clashes led to the death of more the 3,000 people and the forcible displacement of over 300,000 others.[40] The 2007 post-election violence was in many ways a continuation of this pattern.

Some politicians chose to exploit these ethnic cleavages during their 2007 election campaigns and this politicisation of ethnicity provided a second cause of the violence. ODM's campaign strategy portrayed the contest as 'Kenya against the Kikuyu' and 'forty-one tribes against one', causing fear and resentment amongst the Kikuyu community.[41] In response, prominent PNU politicians publicly stated that Odinga could not lead the country because he was a Luo and therefore uncircumcised.[42] This inflammatory language was picked up by ethnic radio stations which incited violence throughout the post-election period.[43]

A third cause of the violence is what Mueller describes as the state's loss of monopoly on the legitimate use of force.[44] While Kenyatta had relied upon state institutions to forcefully and systematically eliminate political opponents, Moi did

---

[34] Gabrielle Lynch, 'Courting the Kalenjin: The Failure of Dynasticism and the Strength of the ODM Wave in Kenya's Rift Valley Province' (2008) 107 *African Affairs* 541; Dennis Otieno Oricho, 'Advocacy Campaign Design for Interethnic Violence Reforms in Kenya' (2009) 1(2) *Journal of Law and Conflict Resolution* 47, 50.

[35] Daniel Branch and Nic Cheeseman, 'Democratisation, Sequencing, and State Failure in Africa: Lessons from Kenya' (2008) 108(430) *African Affairs* 1.

[36] Mueller (2008) (see Footnote 12).

[37] Waki Report (see Footnote 1), vii.

[38] Ibid, 31–32.

[39] Ibid.

[40] Nic Cheeseman, 'The Kenyan Elections of 2007: an Introduction' (2008) 2(2) *Journal of East African Studies* 166.

[41] Peter Kagwanja and Roger Southall, 'Introduction: Kenya—a democracy in retreat?' (2009) 27(3) *Journal of Contemporary African Studies* 259.

[42] Klopp (2009) (see Footnote 5).

[43] Waki Report (see Footnote 1), 217.

[44] Mueller (2008) (see Footnote 12).

not have the same level of trust in the public security forces and so protected his regime through a system of privatised violence. As a result, Mueller suggests that violence became 'commodified' as politicians employed their own bodyguards and recruited youth groups to commits acts of political violence on their behalf.[45] Several armed militia groups emerged, the most prominent being the ethnically exclusive and pro-Kikuyu Mungiki sect that was employed to commit acts of violence in the Rift Valley during the third phase of the post-election violence. In some cases, these vigilante groups were considered by the local population to be a form of community policing, with the groups often consulting with police officers in relation to operations.[46] With the state having lost its monopoly on the legitimate use of force, wealthy businessmen and politicians felt justified in encouraging youth groups, and even some members of the police force, to violently target persons of rival ethnicity.[47]

A fourth cause of the violence was Kenya's history of impunity, which enabled the country's security forces and youths to commit crimes confident in the knowledge that they would not be held accountable for their actions. Perpetrators felt assured that they would be shielded from criminal prosecution by the political elites on whose behalf they were acting. Indeed, the Waki Commission considered Kenya's history of institutionalised impunity to be 'at the heart of the post-election violence'.[48] During my interviews with victims, citizens and human rights activists, they explained that the 2007/08 post-election violence could not be considered in isolation and must instead be placed within the contact of Kenya's history of institutionalised impunity.

2 History of Institutionalised Impunity

2.1 Colonial Era

The British government colonised Kenya in 1885 and, considering much of the country's land to be unoccupied, passed a succession of regulations that expropriated much of Kenya's most fertile land for government use.[49] In the process several tribes, particularly the Kikuyu and Maasai, lost large tracts of their traditional homelands.[50] Those who protested against British rule were often silenced. This included Koitalel Arap Samoei, who was assassinated in 1905, and his son Koitalel Arap Samoei,

---

[45] Ibid.
[46] Patricia Kameri Mbote and Migai Akech, Kenya: Justice Sector and the Rule of Law (Open Society Foundation, March 2011) ('OSI Rule of Law Report'), 14.
[47] Waki Report (see Footnote 1), 27.
[48] Ibid, 444.
[49] HRW, Taking Liberties (see Footnote 3), 1–2.
[50] Ibid.

who was imprisoned for 42 years.[51] Native Kenyans who had been forced off their lands relocated to the slums of Nairobi, where they were often harassed by police and charged with a criminal offence if they failed to pay a bribe.[52] In response, many young Kikuyu persons organised themselves into an armed resistance group with the objective of forcing all Europeans to leave Kenya.[53] This group was the genesis of the nationalist, anti-colonial insurgency group known as the Mau Mau. Group members participated in oathing ceremonies before commencing a guerrilla war against their colonial oppressors.[54]

The British response to this insurgency was brutal. Governor Sir Evelyn Baring declared a state of emergency on 22 October 1952 and in the eight years that followed British troops engaged in systematic acts of violence with impunity.[55] According to official statistics, 11,500 Africans were killed during the uprising (as well as 32 white settlers) but these figures do not include the many Africans buried in mass graves or who died in detention centres.[56] The Kenya Human Rights Commission ('KHRC') estimates that 90,000 Kenyans were executed, tortured or maimed during the counter-insurgency, and 160,000 were detained in appalling conditions.[57] Detainees were intimidated, beaten and tortured until they confessed.[58] Despite the prevalence of violence, no British official was ever prosecuted for their actions during the suppression.

After obtaining confessions through torture, the British would then hold show trials in colonial courts. A total of 1,090 Africans were sentenced to death and many more to lengthy periods of incarceration.[59] The trial of the man who was later to become the country's first president illustrates how these proceedings were conducted without due process. Kenyatta was convicted of conspiracy to murder all white settlers in Kenya on the basis of evidence from a prosecution witness who testified only after being offered free tuition at an English university and a government job upon his return to Kenya.[60] The judge, who had been provided with an ex gratia payment of £20,000 for hearing the case, sentenced Kenyatta to an indefinite period of detention and seven years of hard labour.[61]

---

[51] HRW, Taking Liberties (see Footnote 3), 9–10.

[52] Robert Edgerton, *Mau Mau: an African Crucible* (Tauris, 1990), 35.

[53] Ibid.

[54] Wunyabari Maloba, *Mau Mau and Kenya* (Indiana University Press, 1993), 3.

[55] David Anderson, *Histories of the Hanged: Britain's Dirty War and the End of the Empire* (Pheonix, 2006); Caroline Elkins, *Britain's Gulag: The Brutal End of Empire in Kenya* (Jonathan Cape, 2005).

[56] FD Cordfield, *The Origins and Growth of Mau Mau: An Historical Survey* (Colony and Protectorate of Kenya, 1960), 316.

[57] 'Mau Mau case: UK government cannot be held liable', *BBC News*, 7 April 2011.

[58] Josiah Mwangi Kariuki, *'Mau Mau' Detainee* (Oxford University Press, 1976).

[59] Anderson (2006) (see Footnote 55).

[60] Martin Meredith, *The State of Africa: A History of Fifty Years of Independence* (Free Press, 2005), 86–87.

[61] Ibid, 86–87.

2.2 Post-Independence

In 1963, soon after the Mau Mau uprising had been suppressed, Kenya attained its independence. Kenyatta was released from prison and as president inherited the institutions of his oppressors, including 'a demoralised judiciary, a violent, oppressive, and corrupt police force, and a contemptuous and venal bureaucracy'.[62] The Kenyatta regime used this legal framework to violently and systematically suppress dissidents. Kenyatta augmented his inherited powers by making Kenya a de facto one-party state, and by creating the power to appoint judges and declare states of emergency without parliamentary approval.[63] A plethora of other powers were also infused in the presidency, including the power to appoint and dismiss public servants at will.

Less than one year after independence, Kenyatta faced his own insurrectionist movement as ethnic Somalis in the North Eastern Province sought to join with the newly formed Somali Republic. One of the government's permanent secretaries suggested that they should 'take a leaf from the operations carried out during the emergency against the Mau Mau movement'.[64] The government's response bore similarities to that of the colonialists, legislating for detention without trial, imposing a mandatory death penalty for possession of firearms and engaging in widespread extrajudicial killings.[65] In 1970, the government passed the *Indemnity Act* which shielded government agents and security forces from legal action resulting from any acts they committed during this four-year Shifta War.

Kenyatta was just as harsh in the suppression of political opponents. As Mbote and Akech note, 'the Kenyatta era was characterised by political assassinations, the criminalisation of the freedoms of expression and assembly and police brutality'.[66] There is evidence that individuals who challenged the establishment were harassed, detained without trial and tortured.[67] Tom Mboya, a one-time ally of Kenyatta's who publicly challenged his policies and was seen as a potential threat to the presidency, was assassinated in 1969.[68] Mboya's murderer was hanged, but prior to his execution asked 'Why don't you go after the big man?'[69] Despite much conjecture that elites within the Kenyatta regime may have been responsible for the assassination, no judicial inquiry was held. Other political assassinations were to follow and,

---

[62] Nasongo et al. (2009) (see Footnote 4), 2.

[63] Ibid; Kim Matthews and William Coogan, 'Kenya and the Rule of Law: The Perspective of Two Volunteers' (2008) 60 *Maine Law Review* 561.

[64] John Kamau, 'How Kenya Averted War with Somalia', *East African Standard*, 18 January 2004.

[65] HRW, Taking Liberties (see Footnote 3), 6.

[66] OSI Rule of Law Report (see Footnote 46), 33.

[67] Kenya Human Rights Commission, *Surviving After Torture: A Case Digest on the Struggle for Justice by Torture Survivors in Kenya* (Kenya Human Rights Commission, 2009) ('KHRC, Surviving After Torture').

[68] HRW, Taking Liberties (see Footnote 3), 30.

[69] 'Kenya: Unanswered Questions', *Time*, 5 December 1969.

although in at least one case a parliamentary inquiry was conducted and government official implicated, no person was ever prosecuted.[70]

When Moi assumed the presidency in 1978, the prevalence and severity of state-sanctioned violence rose sharply.[71] Once again, it was the Somalis in North Eastern Province who experienced the harshest treatment. In November 1980, Kenyan security forces burned down an entire village in Garissa as retaliation for the killing of six government officials. Hundreds of people were killed as they attempted to flee, with bodies thrown into a mass grave. Thousands of Somalis were then rounded up, interrogated, beaten and raped by the security forces.[72] The government eventually succumbed to pressure and commissioned a public inquiry but this was never made public and no person was held responsible for the massacre. One minister reportedly told newspapers that 'the only good Somali is a dead one'.[73]

Worse was to follow, as on 10 February 1994 approximately 6,000 men were stripped naked and forced to lie face down on the Wagalla Airstrip for five days without food or water.[74] Security forces then doused the men in petrol and set them alight, resulting in the death of an estimated 2,000 persons.[75] According to Africa Watch, the plan was sanctioned by the president's office and the leaders of the operation were awarded gifts and large tracts of land for their actions.[76] The government conceded that 57 persons had died but argued that this was part of a 'necessary action' against 'inter-tribal fighting'.[77] No investigation was conducted, no apology made, no compensation provided and no conviction secured.

Four years later, the government unilaterally annexed the Elemi Triangle from Sudan and in the process killed at least 500 civilians. Later that same year, Kenyan helicopter gunships and paramilitary forces returned to the area to massacre many hundreds more civilians in Kibish. These killings were never officially acknowledged and no persons were ever held accountable.[78]

Throughout his 24-year rule Moi suppressed political opponents, often violently. In 1982, Moi prevented a new political party from being registered by arranging for an amendment to the Constitution that made Kenya a de jure one-party state.[79] Later that year, the Moi administration suppressed an attempted coup, allegedly through a shoot-to-kill policy that resulted in the death of as many as 1,800 persons.[80]

---

[70] Orich (2009) (see Footnote 34); HRW, Taking Liberties (see Footnote 3), 7.

[71] Human Rights Watch, *Divide and Rule: State-Sponsored Ethnic Violence in Kenya* (Human Rights Watch, 1993).

[72] HRW, Taking Liberties (see Footnote 3), 272–273.

[73] Ibid.

[74] Mutuma Ruteere, *Where Terror Rules: Torture by Kenyan Police in North Eastern Kenya* (Kenya Human Rights Commission, 1998), 6.

[75] HRW, Taking Liberties (see Footnote 3), 274.

[76] Ibid, 277.

[77] Ibid, 275.

[78] Ibid, 336.

[79] Ibid, 19.

[80] Ibid, 10–11.

Following the attempted coup, Moi's regime became even more oppressive. Thousands of political activists, students, businessmen and academics were arbitrarily arrested and imprisoned, including Odinga who was detained without trial for six years.[81] While in detention, many pro-democracy advocates were tortured and subjected to humiliating treatment until they confessed to sedition charges.[82] Prisoners were then convicted on the basis of these confessions in trials that lasted less than five minutes.[83] A major report written by Amnesty International in 1991 concluded that torture was continuing to be committed in Kenya 'because of a lack of effective action taken by the government to stamp it out'.[84]

The political assassinations that were a feature of Kenyatta's regime continued under Moi. The most well known was the 1990 murder of Robert Ouko, the Foreign Affairs Minister who was preparing a report on high-level political corruption. Ouko's body was found charred almost beyond recognition, prompting massive student demonstrations and riots.[85] In response, the government commissioned Scotland Yard to investigate the murder, but this report was never fully released to the public.[86] A judicial commission and a parliamentary committee were established, but neither produced a conclusive report.[87]

Multi-party politics was restored to Kenya in 1992 but this only encouraged Moi to use further violence in order to retain power. Forces loyal to Moi employed gangs in the Rift Valley and elsewhere to intimidate, forcibly displace and kill opposition supporters in the lead up to the 1992 elections.[88] In total, 779 persons were killed and a further 654 injured during the pre-election violence.[89] Moi won this election comfortably, as he did in 1997 by employing similar tactics. Despite two government inquiries and two human rights reports naming those believed to have been responsible for the electoral violence, none of these persons were ever prosecuted.[90] When the government received the report from the Akiwumi Commission that recommended prosecutions of certain individuals, it kept the report confidential for three years, before eventually rejecting the report and producing a response that recommended naming and admonishing rather than prosecuting.[91]

In the final years of Moi's presidency a new form of impunity emerged—unpunished political corruption. While there were several instances of corruption during the Moi era, the most notable was the Goldenberg Scandal, in which as much as $1 billion

---

[81] Ibid, 58–60; KHRC, Surviving After Torture (see Footnote 67).

[82] HRW, Taking Liberties (see Footnote 3), 83–108.

[83] Ibid, 134–143.

[84] Amnesty International Kenya, *Ending the Cycle of Impunity* (Amnesty International, 2001).

[85] HRW, Taking Liberties (see Footnote 3), 28–29.

[86] Ibid, 35.

[87] Kenya Human Rights Commission, *Lest We Forget: The Faces of Impunity in Kenya* (Kenya Human Rights Commission, 2011) ('KHRC, Lest We Forget'), 9.

[88] Waki Report (see Footnote 1), 26.

[89] Ibid.

[90] Ibid.

[91] Ibid, 446–447.

was siphoned through the Goldenberg International company and its networks for gold and diamonds that were never imported, with the money then used to finance the incumbent government's 1992 election campaign.[92] The report of the judicial inquiry established to investigate the matter concluded that criminal charges should be laid against Vice President George Saitoti and that further investigations should be conducted into Moi's involvement.[93] In 2006, however, the Constitutional Court ruled that Saitoti could not be charged. Saitoti went on to serve as the Minister for Internal Security in the GNU and, prior to his death in 2012 had announced his intention to run for the presidency. Another person implicated in the affair, Mutula Kilonzo, was also never charged and went on to serve as the GNU's Justice Minister.

In 2002, Kibaki swept to a landslide victory on an anti-corruption platform. At his inauguration speech Kibaki promised that 'corruption will now cease to be a way of life in Kenya'.[94] In his first year in office, Kibaki's government passed the *Anti-Corruption and Economic Crimes Act* and appointed John Githongo to serve as the country's first anti-corruption commissioner. In 2005, however, Githongo resigned without explanation, later becoming a whistle-blower who accused four senior government ministers, including Vice President Moody Awori, of siphoning hundreds of millions of dollars into a non-existent company called Anglo Leasing and Finance in order to fund Kibaki's 2007 re-election campaign.[95] Githongo also claimed that he had shown Kibaki 'incontrovertible' evidence of the scam but that the President had elected not to act.[96] To date, no prosecutions have commenced against any of the alleged perpetrators.

The Kibaki regime also sought to eliminate the Mungiki criminal sect and, in furtherance of this objective, allegedly ordered a shoot-to-kill policy for any person found to be in possession of illegal firearms.[97] On 3 June 2007, one MP gave a speech about the Mungiki and promised to 'pulverise and finish them off'.[98] According to a report written by the Kenya National Commission on Human Rights ('KNCHR'), in the three months that followed this speech approximately 500 persons were killed or had disappeared as a result of this policy.[99] A UN special rapporteur concluded that there was 'zero accountability' for killings conducted by these 'police death squads'.[100]

---

[92] Oscar Gakuo Mwangi, 'Political Corruption, Party Financing and Democracy in Kenya' (2008) 46(2) *Journal of Modern African Studies* 267.

[93] *Report of the Judicial Commission of Inquiry into the Goldenberg Affair*, October 2005.

[94] 'New Kenya leader promises reform', *BBC News*, 30 December 2002.

[95] Michela Wrong, *It's Our Turn to Eat: The Story of a Kenyan Whistleblower* (Fourth Estate, 2009).

[96] 'Githongo: Kibaki knew about Anglo Leasing', The *Standard*, 23 January 2006.

[97] 'Fury at Kenya shoot-to-kill order', *BBC News*, 23 March 2005.

[98] Kenya National Commission on Human Rights, *Follow-up Report on: Extrajudicial Killings and Disappearances*, August 2008.

[99] Ibid.

[100] Philip Alston, *Mission to Kenya 16–25 February 2009* (United Nations Special Rapporteur on Extrajudicial Killings, Arbitrary or Summary Executions, 2009) ('Alston Report').

Further, as was the case under the Moi regime, there was also a vast amount of violence in the lead-up to the 2007 election. In the three months before polling day, some 600 persons were killed.[101] There was a sharp increase in violence in the Rift Valley and by mid-December 2007, approximately 10,000 persons had been forced to flee Kuresoi to neighbouring Molo.[102] A spike in violence in Mount Elgon caused thousands of persons to be displaced.[103] Very few suspects were arrested in relation to this pre-election violence and many of those who were arrested were released without charge.[104]

This brief history reveals a pattern of killing, torture, involuntary detention and corruption, either sanctioned or condoned by governments, both colonial and post-colonial, without perpetrators ever being held accountable. Often no investigations were conducted into the atrocities (as in the case of the Mau Mau counter-insurgency, the Wagalla Massacre, Moi's torture chambers and the Anglo-Leasing Scandal). On other occasions, investigations were conducted but the reports were not made public for a substantial period of time (such as the Akiwumi report into electoral violence), or the report was never released (the inquiry into the Garissa Massacre). Where the reports were released, they sometimes failed to name suspects (as occurred for the three inquiries into the assassination of Robert Ouko). Even when perpetrators were named (as was the case with the reports into electoral violence and the Goldenberg Scandal), the respective governments took no steps to hold such persons accountable. In total, successive presidents established at least 25 commissions of inquiry in relation to these excesses of state power. Although valuable reports were produced and recommendations made, they were regularly ignored or, in the words of human rights advocates, 'left to collect dust'.[105] It is this history of impunity that allowed the organisers and perpetrators of the 2007 post-election violence to commit atrocities with the confidence that they would never be investigated or prosecuted for their crimes. The occurrence of so many egregious acts over more than half a century with little or no accountability would suggest that impunity had to some extent become institutionalised.

2.3 The Institutionalisation of Impunity

At the time of the 2007 post-election violence, impunity had become institutionalised in the state security sector. Although Kenya had a criminal code and constitutional protection for the most fundamental human rights, its security forces by and large failed to enforce these laws largely because of a lack of independence from government elites. Section 108 of the Constitution provided the President with an unfettered

---

[101] Kagwanja and Southall (2009) (see Footnote 41), 262.
[102] Anderson and Lochery (2008) (see Footnote 21), 331.
[103] Cheeseman (2008) (see Footnote 40), 262.
[104] Waki Report (see Footnote 1), 41.
[105] OSI Rule of Law Report (see Footnote 46), 10.

power to appoint the Commissioner of Police.[106] Recruitment into the police service was for some time 'characterised by irregularities ranging from nepotism, tribalism and political patronage to favouritism and corruption, with wide-ranging negative effects on service delivery'.[107] The led to bias within the police force, with some officers refusing to enforce the law because of a 'reluctance to tread on the toes of powerful political personalities'.[108] The entire security sector was routinely underfunded, which made it difficult for the police to enforce the law and investigate crimes.[109] Police officers were often poorly paid, thereby increasing temptation for officers to 'engage in corruption and other opportunistic behaviour as a survival strategy'.[110]

Police officers rarely investigated serious crimes and, if they did, tended to focus on lower-level perpetrators.[111] When witnesses made reports to the police, they were often treated with 'callous indifference' or 'outright hostility'.[112] For example, when victims in Eldoret reported crimes to the police, they were told 'Now is not the time to call us. Now is the time to call your God'.[113] When the police took suspects into custody, these persons were often released without charge, even when there was overwhelming evidence of their guilt.[114] Should a case proceeded to the stage where it was on the verge of being tried, it was susceptible to being sabotaged by a corrupt police prosecutor who had been bribed to lose the file. In Kiambu, for example, a pit latrine was used as a dumping ground for files for over two years.[115] Even if the police prosecutor decided to proceed with the case, the Attorney General, another presidential appointee, had constitutional powers to terminate the criminal case at his discretion.

By the time of the post-election violence, impunity had also become institutionalised within the judiciary. In 1993 and 1994, two High Court judges who decided against Moi in an electoral matter had their contracts terminated.[116] In 2006, two judges who ruled against the interests of the Kibaki administration were transferred to a new post 200 kilometres away.[117] According to a major report produced by the International Commission of Jurists ('ICJ-Kenya') in 2005, judges' insecurity over

---

[106] Antony Laibuta, 'Constitutional and Institutional Reform: What role in Addressing Impunity' in ICJ-K Judiciary Watch Report.

[107] OSI Rule of Law Report (see Footnote 46), 131.

[108] Waki Report (see Footnote 1), 63, 108.

[109] International Bar Association and International Legal Assistance Consortium, *Restoring Integrity: An assessment of the needs of the justice system in the Republic of Kenya* (International Bar Association and International Legal Assistance Consortium, February 2010) ('IBA Report'), 74.

[110] OSI Rule of Law Report (see Footnote 46), 132.

[111] Ibid, 420.

[112] Ibid, 257.

[113] Ibid, 94.

[114] Ibid, 99, 133–134.

[115] 'HRW, Taking Liberties (see Footnote 3), 87–89.

[116] KNCHR Post-Election Violence Report (see Footnote 2), 22.

[117] Nasongo et al. (2009) (see Footnote 4), 4.

lack of tenure affected the way they carried out their judicial functions.[118] Judges and their clerks were also sometimes bribed to lose files, slow the progress of cases or decide a case in a particular manner.[119] In 2002, a panel of Commonwealth judges investigating judicial independence in Kenya said that they were 'shocked and dismayed' by the widespread allegations of judicial bribery.[120] Those who suffered prejudice to their case as a result of these bribes were provided with no recourse, because no appropriate legal mechanism existed to investigate alleged judicial misconduct.[121] Any cases that did proceed through the courts made slow progress, as the court houses struggled in the absence of stenographers, recording devices and computers.[122] As Kenyans went to the polls in 2007, the judiciary was struggling to cope with a backlog of some 800,000 cases.[123]

2.4 Culture of Impunity

As a consequence of this institutionalisation of impunity, Kenyans had developed a 'culture of impunity'. That is, regardless of whether or not impunity *in fact* existed in Kenya, there was a commonly held *belief* amongst Kenyans that crimes could be committed without their perpetrators being held accountable. According to a survey conducted in 2005 by the Economic Commission for Africa, fewer than 2 % of experts in Kenya believed that civil and political rights as enshrined in the Constitution were always or usually respected, placing Kenya last on the list of all African countries surveyed (Fig. 3.1).[124]

Much of this lack of confidence in the justice system derived from Kenyans' negative experiences in dealing with the police. Many Kenyans perceived public security forces as an 'inefficient, brutal, anti-people institution that lacked transparency and accountability'.[125] Nearly half of all Kenyan households rated police performance as 'bad or very bad', again placing it as one of the worst in Africa (Fig. 3.2).[126] The other major reason for Kenyans' belief in impunity was their lack of faith in their judges. Experts in Kenya were more sceptical about citizens

---

[118] International Commission of Jurists, *Kenya: Judicial Independence, Corruption and Reform* (International Commission of Jurists, 2005) ('ICJ-K Judicial Independence Report').
[119] Alston Report (see Footnote 100).
[120] ICJ-K Judicial Independence Report (see Footnote 119).
[121] Ibid.
[122] Nasongo et al. (2009) (see Footnote 4), 5.
[123] Antonina Okuta, 'National Legislation for Prosecution of International Crimes in Kenya' (2009) 7(5) *Journal of International Criminal Justice* 1063.
[124] Economic Commission for Africa, *African Governance Report 2005* (Economic Commission for Africa, 2005) ('African Governance Report 2005'), 177.
[125] Christine Alai and Njonjo Mue, *Kenya: Impact of the Rome Statute and the International Criminal Court* (International Centre for Transitional Justice, 2010).
[126] African Governance Report (see Footnote 125).

Share of experts surveyed, by country (%)

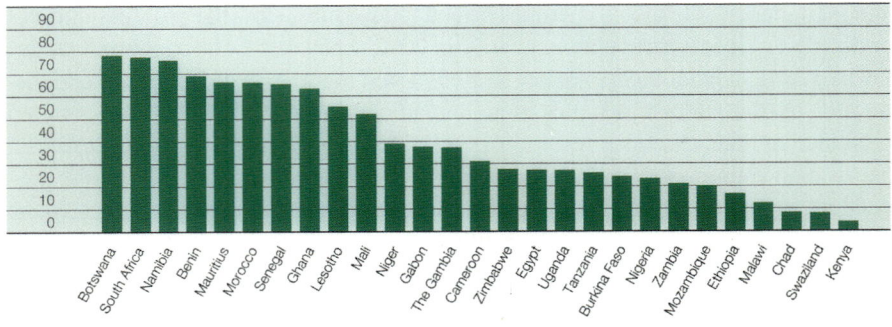

Source: ECA governance survey of experts

Fig. 3.1 Expert opinion that civil and political rights provided for in the constitution are always or usually being respected

Share of households surveyed, by country (%)

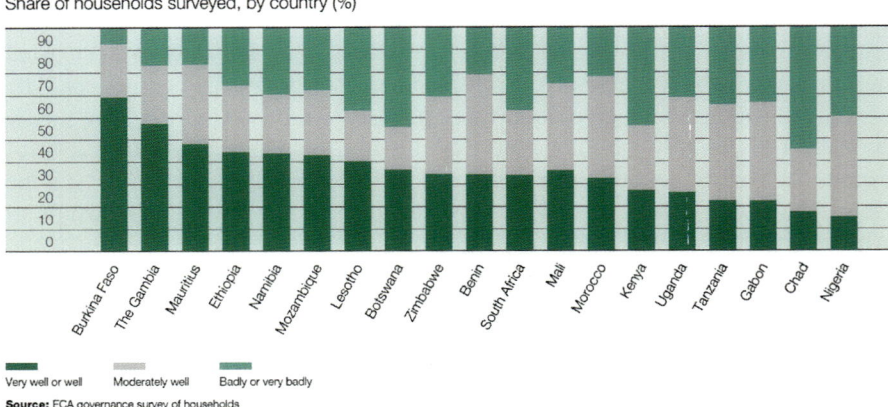

Very well or well   Moderately well   Badly or very badly
Source: ECA governance survey of households

Fig. 3.2 Household opinion on police performance

obtaining full access to justice than their counterparts in all other African countries surveyed (Fig. 3.3).[127] Such was the perceived level of corruption in Kenya that during my interviews, citizens commonly asked rhetorically: 'Why hire a lawyer when you can buy a judge?' More than half of Kenyans expected both judges and public prosecutors to demand bribes, which meant that Kenya's judges had a worse reputation than almost all African countries (Fig. 3.4).[128]

This culture of impunity had two major consequences, each of which further contributed to the institutionalisation of impunity. First, victims and witnesses were reluctant to report crimes. 45 % of sexual violence victims did not report the crime

---

[127] Ibid.
[128] Ibid.

Share of experts surveyed, by country (%)

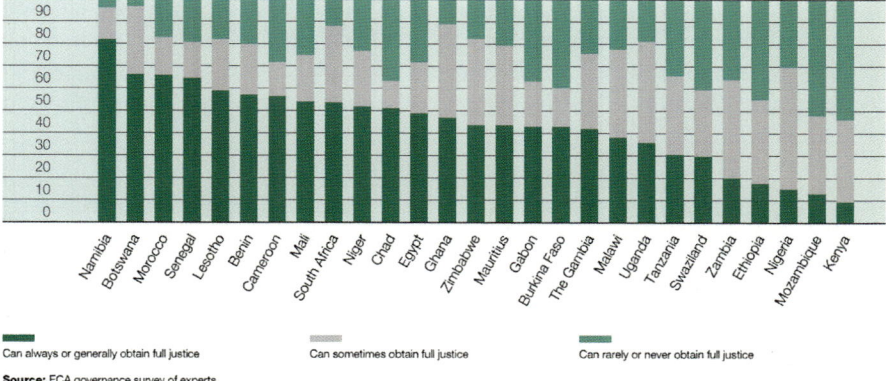

Fig. 3.3 Expert opinion on citizen access to justice in court irrespective of economic or social status

Share of households surveyed, by country (%)

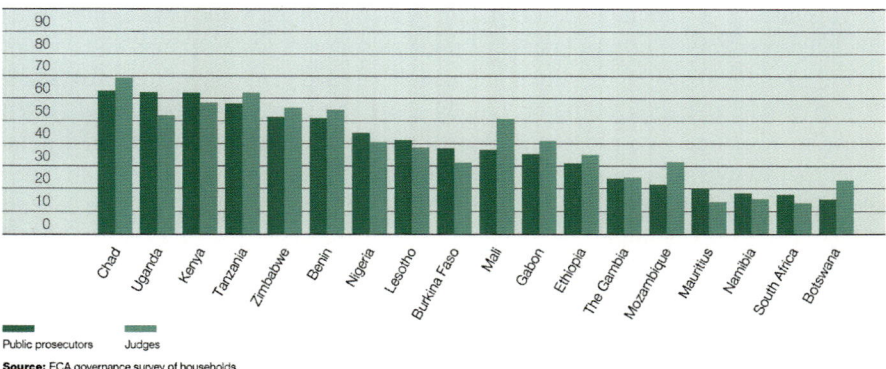

Fig. 3.4 Household opinion that public prosecutors and judges are expected to demand bribes

because they believed that nothing would be done.[129] The Attorney General himself admitted that witnesses were 'reluctant to record statements, reluctant to participate in identification parades, unwilling to appear in court and give evidence for fear of reprisals'.[130] As a consequence, criminal prosecutions either did not commence or were discontinued because of a lack of evidence. Second, this lack of faith in the criminal justice system prompted aggrieved persons to turn to extrajudicial methods of dispute resolution. Kenya's culture of impunity meant that ODM supporters elected to express their frustration at Kibaki's 2007 electoral victory through political violence rather than by challenging the results in the courts. Further, those who

---

[129] Waki Report (see Footnote 1), 246.
[130] Ibid, 395–396.

felt aggrieved by historical land injustices did not feel that they could seek redress through formal legal mechanisms and so instead took advantage of the post-election pandemonium to extract crude vigilante justice. In short, a lack of public confidence in state institutions provided further impetus for violence and an unwillingness to cooperate with the criminal justice system to the extent necessary for perpetrators to be held accountable.

3 Conclusion

Systematic acts of violence committed with impunity due to weak or corrupt political and legal institutions were a feature of Kenya's history for more than half a century. Governments, both colonial and post-colonial, were responsible for massacres, political assassinations, extrajudicial killings, arbitrary detention and torture.[131] No person in power was ever held accountable for these actions and violations went almost entirely unpunished.

This history of impunity was one factor that contributed to the post-election violence. Perpetrators of crimes knew that under-resourced, under-trained and corrupt security forces would be unwilling and unable to enforce the law. They also knew that, even when victims did report crimes, these same security forces would often refuse to investigate or prosecute. Perpetrators were further emboldened by the belief that Kenya's overworked justice system would struggle to process all crimes and that criminal liability could be averted by elites pressuring and bribing corrupt judges. This lack of faith in the Kenyan justice system may have also provided further impetus for some to seek revenge for perceived historical injustices through violence rather than resolving grievances through legal mechanisms. Other reasons for the violence included centralisation within the power of the presidency, historical injustices, the politicisation of ethnicity and the state's loss of monopoly on the legitimate use of force. These factors together provided the means and motivation for organised political violence. The opportunity, however, was provided by Kenya's history of impunity which, by the time of the post-election violence had become institutionalised.

It can therefore be concluded that ending impunity was a necessary but not sufficient precondition for long-lasting peace in Kenya. Citizens were overwhelmingly supportive of ending impunity but had little confidence in the government or its institutions to deliver on this objective. A great deal of faith was placed in the ICC Prosecutor, who had promised to end impunity in Kenya and to make the country an example for the rest of the world.

---

[131] Kenya Human Rights Commission, *Justice Delayed: A Status Report on Historical Injustices in Kenya* (Kenya Human Rights Commission, 2011).

Bibliography

'Fury at Kenya shoot-to-kill order', *BBC News*, 23 March 2005
'Githongo: Kibaki knew about Anglo Leasing', The *Standard*, 23 January 2006
'Kenya: Unanswered Questions', *Time*, 5 December 1969
'Mau Mau case: UK government cannot be held liable', *BBC News*, 7 April 2011
'New Kenya leader promises reform', *BBC News*, 30 December 2002
Abuya, Edwin Odhiambo, 'Consequences of a Flawed Presidential Election' (2009) 29(1) *Legal Studies* 127 at 130
Alai, Christine, and Mue, Njonjo, *Kenya: Impact of the Rome Statute and the International Criminal Court* (International Centre for Transitional Justice, 2010)
Alston, Philip, *Mission to Kenya 16-25 February 2009* (United Nations Special Rapporteur on Extrajudicial Killings, Arbitrary or Summary Executions, 2009)
Amnesty International Kenya, *Ending the Cycle of Impunity* (Amnesty International, 2001)
Anderson, David, Histories of the Hanged: Britain's Dirty War and the End of the Empire (Phoenix, 2006)
Anderson, David and Lochery, Emma, 'Violence and Exodus in Kenya's Rift Valley, 2008: Predictable and Preventable?' (2008) 2(2) *Journal of Eastern African Studies* 328
Branch, Daniel and Cheeseman, Nic, 'Democratisation, Sequencing, and State Failure in Africa: Lessons from Kenya' (2008) 108(430) *African Affairs* 1
Centre for Rights Education and Awareness, *Women paid the price*, 2008
Cheeseman, Nic, 'The Kenyan Elections of 2007: an Introduction' (2008) 2(2) *Journal of East African Studies* 166
Coffman, Jennifer, Broch-Due, Vigdis, Little, Peter, Ntarangwi, Mwenda, Prazak Miroslava and Shipton, Parker, 'Understanding Kenya's Postelection Violence' (2009) 1(1) *Beliefs and Values* 53
Cordfield, FD, *The Origins and Growth of Mau Mau: An Historical Survey*, (Colony and Protectorate of Kenya, 1960)
Dagne, Ted, Kenya: The December 2007 Elections and the Challenges Ahead (Congressional Research Service, 2008)
Economic Commission for Africa, *African Governance Report 2005* (Economic Commission for Africa, 2005)
Edgerton, Robert, *Mau Mau: an African Crucible* (Tauris, 1990)
Elkins, Caroline, Britain's Gulag: The Brutal End of Empire in Kenya (Jonathan Cape, 2005)
Federation of Women Lawyers, Submission to the CIPEV on behalf of the inter agency gender-based violence (GBV), 11 September 2008
Final Report from Kenya's Commission of Inquiry into Post-Election Violence, 15 October 2008
Gibson, Clark and Long, James, 'The Presidential and Parliamentary Elections in Kenya, December 2007' (2009) 28 *Electoral Studies* 492
Gĩthĩnji, Mwangi wa and Holmquist, Frank, 'Kenya's Hopes and Impediments: The Anatomy of a Crisis of Exclusion' (2008) 2(2) *Journal of Eastern African Studies* 344
Harneit-Sievers, Axel and Peters, Ralph-Michael, 'Kenya's 2007 General Election and its Aftershocks' (2008) 43 *Africa Spectrum* 133
Human Rights Watch, Divide and Rule: State-Sponsored Ethnic Violence in Kenya (Human Rights Watch, 1993)
Human Rights Watch, *From Ballots to Bullets*, March 2008
Human Rights Watch, Kenya: Taking Liberties, an African Watch Report, 1991
International Bar Association and International Legal Assistance Consortium, *Restoring Integrity: An assessment of the needs of the justice system in the Republic of Kenya* (International Bar Association and International Legal Assistance Consortium, February 2010)
International Commission of Jurists, *Kenya: Judicial Independence, Corruption and Reform* (International Commission of Jurists, 2005)
International Criminal Court, Pre-Trial Chamber II, Decision Pursuant to Article 15 of the Rome Statute on the Authorisation of an Investigation into the Situation in the Republic of Kenya, 31 March 2010

International Crisis Group, *Kenya in Crisis*, 21 February 2008

Kagwanja, Peter and Southall, Roger, 'Introduction: Kenya—a democracy in retreat?' (2009) 27(3) *Journal of Contemporary African Studies* 259

Kamau, John, 'How Kenya Averted War with Somalia', *East African Standard*, 18 January 2004

Kariuki, Josiah Mwangi, *'Mau Mau' Detainee* (Oxford University Press, 1976)

Kenya Human Rights Commission, *Justice Delayed: A Status Report on Historical Injustices in Kenya* (Kenya Human Rights Commission, 2011)

Kenya Human Rights Commission, *Lest We Forget: The Faces of Impunity in Kenya* (Kenya Human Rights Commission, 2011)

Kenya Human Rights Commission, Surviving After Torture: A Case Digest on the Struggle for Justice by Torture Survivors in Kenya (Kenya Human Rights Commission, 2009)

Kenya National Commission on Human Rights, Follow-up Report on: Extrajudicial Killings and Disappearances, August 2008

Kenya National Commission on Human Rights, On the brink of the precipice: a human rights account of Kenya's post-2007 election violence, 15 August 2008

Kiai, Maina, Keynote Address to the Fifth Assembly of the World Movement for Democracy, Kyiv, 6 April 2008

Kiai, Maina, 'The Crisis in Kenya' (2008) 19 *Journal of Democracy* 162

Klopp, Jacqueline, 'Kenya's Unfinished Agendas' (2009) 62(2) *Journal of International Affairs* 143

Laibuta, Antony, 'Constitutional and Institutional Reform: What role in Addressing Impunity' in Waruguru Kaguongo and Godfrey Musila (eds), *Judiciary Watch Report: Addressing Impunity and Options for Justice in Kenya—Mechanisms, Issues and Debates*

Lynch, Gabrielle, 'Courting the Kalenjin: The Failure of Dynasticism and the Strength of the ODM Wave in Kenya's Rift Valley Province' (2008) 107 *African Affairs* 541

Mäkinen, Maarit, and Kuira, Mary Wangu, 'Social Media and Postelection Crisis in Kenya' (2008) 13(3) *International Journal of Press/Politics* 328

Maloba, Wunyabari, *Mau Mau and Kenya* (Indiana University Press, 1993)

Matthews, Kim and Coogan, William, 'Kenya and the Rule of Law: The Perspective of Two Volunteers' (2008) 60 *Maine Law Review* 561

Mbote, Patricia Kameria and Akech, Migai, *Kenya: Justice Sector and the Rule of Law* (Open Society Foundation, March 2011)

Meredith, Martin, The State of Africa: A History of Fifty Years of Independence (Free Press, 2005)

Mueller, Susanne, 'The Political Economy of Kenya's Crisis' (2008) 2(2) *Journal of Eastern African Studies* 185

Mwangi, Oscar Gakuo, 'Political Corruption, Party Financing and Democracy in Kenya' (2008) 46(2) *Journal of Modern African Studies* 267

Odhiambo Abuya, Edwin, 'Consequences of a Flawed Presidential Election' (2009) 29(1) *Legal Studies* 127

Office of the High Commissioner for Human Rights, *Report from OHCHR fact-finding mission to Kenya*, 6-28 February 2008

Okuta, Antonina, 'National Legislation for Prosecution of International Crimes in Kenya' (2009) 7(5) *Journal of International Criminal Justice* 1063

Otieno Oricho, Dennis, 'Advocacy Campaign Design for Interethnic Violence Reforms in Kenya' (2009) 1(2) *Journal of Law and Conflict Resolution* 47

Nasongo, JW, Achoka, JSK and Wamocha, LLM, 'Is Forgiveness and Amnesty a Panacea to Kenya's Post-Conflict Crisis?' (2009) 3(4) *African Journal of Political Science and International Relations* 122

Report of the Judicial Commission of Inquiry into the Goldenberg Affair, October 2005

Ruteere, Mutuma, Where Terror Rules: Torture by Kenyan Police in North Eastern Kenya (Kenya Human Rights Commission, 1998)

South Consulting, The Kenya National Dialogue and Reconciliation (KNDR) Monitoring Project, January 2009

Throup, David, 'The Count' (2008) 2(2) *Journal of East African Studies* 290
UNICEF, UNFPA, UNIFEM and Christian Children's Fun, A rapid assessment of gender-based violence (GBV) during the post-election violence in Kenya, Jan-Feb 2008
Wrong, Michela, It's Our Turn to Eat: The Story of a Kenyan Whistleblower (Fourth Estate, 2009)

Chapter 4
From Nairobi to The Hague

After more than half a century of impunity, Kenyans were desperate for the perpetrators of the post-election violence to be held accountable for their actions. Impunity had become so institutionalised and entrenched, however, that they had very little confidence that the GNU would deliver on this demand. Kenyans therefore provided overwhelming support for the OTP and its promise to end impunity.

This chapter explains how the OTP sought to end impunity in Kenya through its strategy of positive complementarity by providing a chronology of the OTP's involvement. In doing so, it summarises the tactics employed by the OTP to encourage the government to conduct its own investigations and prosecutions and the government's response to these tactics. This includes meetings held between the Prosecutor and senior members of government in Nairobi and The Hague at which the parties agreed that impunity would not be an option, entered into a complementarity contract and agreed to a division of labour.

A prominent feature for much of this period was the Waki Commission's sealed envelope containing the names of suspected perpetrators, which Annan was under instructions to deliver to the Prosecutor should a special tribunal not be established. Notwithstanding this threat, Parliament voted against establishing the proposed special tribunal in February 2009, Cabinet rejected a revised proposal in July 2009 and politicians boycotted debates of a third proposed tribunal in November 2009. The Prosecutor responded by using his *proprio motu* powers for the first time in the Court's history. This culminated in the naming of the Ocampo Six, which then became the Ocampo Four and the Ocampo Three. By this time, two of the suspects, Uhuru Kenyatta and William Ruto, had been elected President and Vice President, respectively, which presented the OTP with the difficult prospect of requesting state cooperation while at the same time prosecuting its two most powerful politicians.

It must be recognised, however, that the OTP was not alone in seeking to persuade the government to end impunity. At various stages during this period the Panel of Eminent African Personalities, the United Nations Human Rights Council, the United Nations Human Rights Committee, the United States government and the European Union all exerted pressure upon the government to end impunity. Similar demands were also regularly made by Kenya's civil society.[1] This chapter therefore also makes reference at appropriate times to these other institutions that sought to influence the government between February 2008 and March 2013.

The OTP's involvement in Kenya between 2008 and 2013 may be divided into four phases. During phase one (from February 2008 until July 2009), the OTP commenced preliminary examinations in which it monitored the government's response to the post-election violence without imposing any overt pressure. The most sustained period of pressure was during phase two (July 2009 - November 2009) in which the OTP actively encouraged the government to conduct its own investigations and prosecutions. When such cooperation was not forthcoming, the OTP entered phase three (December 2009 - December 2010) in which it conducted its own investigations into the crimes committed during the violence. When no significant progress had been made with respect to local prosecutions, the OTP entered phase four (December 2010 - March 2013) in which it proceeded to prepare for trials in The Hague.

1 Phase One: Commencement of Preliminary Examinations (February 2008–July 2009)

1.1 Monitoring the Situation

As demonstrated in Chap. 2, the OTP's strategy of positive complementarity commences after crimes have been committed and the situation has been communicated. The OTP will undertake preliminary examinations and while doing so encourage the target state to conduct its own investigations and prosecutions. As an initial step, the OTP will commonly announce that it is monitoring the situation so as to put the government on notice that crimes within the Court's jurisdiction may have been committed.

In mid-January 2008, with the post-election violence still in its most intense phase, Kenya's ODM party sent a communication to the OTP, advising that serious crimes had been committed within the territory of Kenya.[2] The OTP responded on 5 February 2008 by issuing a statement declaring it was 'carefully considering all information' on crimes that may have been committed in Kenya.[3]

The OTP sent letters requesting additional information to the government, PNU, ODM, KNHRC and KNCHR.[4] On 26 August 2008, the OTP received a copy of the KNCHR report entitled, *On the Brink of the Precipice: a Human Rights Account of Kenya's Post-2007 Election Violence*. This 221-page report publicly named 219 alleged perpetrators of the violence, including high-profile and powerful ministers

---

[1] Including the Law Society of Kenya ('LSK'), the International Centre for Policy and Conflict ('ICPC'), the KNCHR, the KHRC and ICJ-K.

[2] Kenya Human Rights Institute, *Clarifying Human Rights Violations in the Kenyan Post-Election Crisis* (Kenya Human Rights Institute 2008).

[3] International Criminal Court Office of the Prosecutor, 'OTP Statement in Relation to Events in Kenya', 5 February 2008 ('OTP February 2008 Statement').

[4] International Criminal Court, Situation in the Republic of Kenya, Request for authorisation of an investigation pursuant to Article 15, ICC-01/09, 26 November 2009 ('OTP Request for Authorisation').

Uhuru Kenyatta and William Ruto.[5] In total, the OTP received communications and reports from 30 individuals and groups concerning the crimes committed during the post-election violence. Pressure from the OTP remained limited at this time, however, as it afforded the government the opportunity to take ownership of its problems by 'addressing both the need for accountability and the need for structural reforms'.[6]

With the OTP remaining passive, it was the Annan-led KNDR which assumed the leading role in encouraging the coalition government to end impunity. In February 2008, Annan secured agreement from the two sides to what became known as Agenda Item IV, which among other objectives stressed the need for the GNU to take measures to end impunity. Following the conclusion of the peace negotiations, Annan announced that he would be leaving Nairobi but would 'never be far way' and 'would be looking in on the talks from time to time'.[7] Annan and the KNDR group monitored the coalition government's progress in its commitment to conduct an independent review of the post-election violence. In May 2008, approximately one month after Cabinet was sworn in, it announced that it was fast-tracking the establishment of the Waki Commission. As the Waki Commission was undertaking its investigations, Annan returned to Kenya and received assurances from Kibaki and Odinga of their commitment to implementing the Agenda Item IV reforms.[8]

1.2 The Waki Report and the Sealed Envelope

The Waki Commission delivered its report to Kibaki and Odinga on 15 October 2008. The Report provided a detailed narrative of the violence and recommended comprehensive reform of the police force, witness protection programme and freedom of information regime, as well as the passing of legislation that would domestically implement Kenya's obligations under the Rome Statute. The Report's major recommendation was that the coalition government establish a special tribunal which would 'seek accountability against persons bearing the greatest responsibility for crimes, particularly crimes against humanity, relating to the 2007 general elections in Kenya'.[9] The Waki Report recommended that the special tribunal be based in Kenya, but for its staff to be predominantly international so as to avoid perceptions of judicial corruption.

A major concern for the Waki Commission was that its report might be 'shelved and left to gather dust like other official reports in Kenya's history'.[10] In an attempt to counter this possibility, the Waki Commission included an ingenious

---

[5] Kenya National Commission on Human Rights, *On the brink of the precipice: a human rights account of Kenya's post-2007 election violence*, 15 August 2008 ('KNCHR Post-Election Violence Report').

[6] Luis Moreno-Ocampo, 'A positive approach to complementarity: the impact of the Office of the Prosecutor' Stahn and El Zeidy (2011).

[7] African Union Panel of Eminent African Personalities, Press Statement by Kofi Annan, 1 March 2008 ('Annan March 2008 Statement').

[8] African Union, Panel of Eminent African Personalities, Press Statement by Kofi Annan, 23 September 2008 ('Annan September 2008 Statement').

[9] Final Report from Kenya's Commission of Inquiry into Post-Election Violence, 15 October 2008 ('Waki Report'), 305, 346, 472.

[10] Interview with Justice Philip Waki (Nairobi, 16 April 2010).

self-implementation mechanism designed to ensure that justice for the post-election violence would not once again be denied through a political cover-up. This began with the Waki Commission's decision not to publicly name persons suspected of having been responsible for the violence. Instead, the names of the alleged perpetrators, together with the supporting evidence, were placed in a sealed envelope and handed to Annan. The Waki Commission recommended that an agreement to establish the special tribunal be concluded within 60 days of the publication of the report and that enabling legislation be enacted within a further 45 days. The Waki Commission advised the government that should it fail to meet either of these deadlines, Annan would forward the envelope to the ICC Prosecutor who would 'be requested to analyse the seriousness of the information received with a view to proceeding with an investigation and prosecuting such suspected persons'.[11]

As the government began to implement the Waki Commission's recommendations, the OTP took no action to encourage domestic proceedings. Instead, it was left for Annan and the KNDR to oversee the implementation of the Waki Report and the establishment of the special tribunal. Two days after the Waki Report's release, Annan visited Nairobi and called on the government 'to move expeditiously to deal with the recommendations'.[12] On 16 December 2008, one day before the expiration of the Report's first deadline, Kibaki and Odinga signed a document agreeing to implement each of its recommendations, including the establishment of the special tribunal.[13] Annan issued a statement in support of this development, but also took the opportunity to urge Kenya's leaders to redouble their efforts to implementing the recommendations because such proposals would 'go a long way towards ending the culture of impunity and spearheading much needed institutional reforms in the country'.[14] Similar sentiments were expressed by several non-governmental organisations in Kenya, which were broadly supportive of establishing the special tribunal, provided that it was free from political manipulation.[15] These groups considered the Special Tribunal for Kenya ('STriKe' for short) to have the potential to hold perpetrators accountable for the post-election violence.

1.3 Strike One

According to the Waki Commission's second deadline, the government was required to enact legislation establishing the special tribunal by no later than 29 January 2009. This in fact required the passing of two pieces of legislation: the *Special Tribunal for Kenya Bill 2009* that set out the structure and jurisdiction of the special

---

[11] Waki Report (see Final Report from Kenya's Commission of Inquiry into Post-Election Violence, 15 October 2008, 305, 346), 473.

[12] African Union Panel of Eminent African Personalities, Address by Kofi Annan delivered during the 29th graduation of the University of Nairobi, 17 October 2008.

[13] Republic of Kenya Office of the President, 'Special Tribunal to be set up', 17 December 2008.

[14] African Union, Panel of Eminent African Personalities, Statement of Kofi Annan on the Implementation of the Report of the Commission of Inquiry on Post-Election Violence (CIPEV) & Independent Review Commission (IREC), 19 December 2008.

[15] Oliver Mathenge and Sadiki Sudhir, 'Lawyers fault proposed tribunal on Waki', *Daily Nation*, 3 December 2008.

tribunal and the *Constitutional Amendment Bill 2009* to ensure that the tribunal was constitutional. As the latter required a two-thirds majority to be passed, it was debated first. This legislation, however, was not introduced into Parliament until after the expiration of the 29 January deadline. Annan did not at this time, however, hand over the sealed envelope to the Prosecutor. On 11 February 2009, with Parliament still yet to debate the legislation, the OTP issued another statement, similar to the statement that had released 12 months earlier, affirming that it was continuing to 'follow-up whether national proceedings into the post-election violence in Kenya in early 2008 [were] being conducted'.[16] On the following day, the proposed special tribunal was rejected when 101 MPs voted in favour and 93 against, well short of the 145 votes affirmative votes required to amend the Constitution.

The failure to establish the special tribunal prompted Annan to travel to Nairobi to meet with Odinga to encourage the government to reconsider its position.[17] Annan followed this up with a letter dated 23 February 2009, addressed to Kibaki and Odinga, indicating that he considered it appropriate to grant an extension to the Waki Commission's deadlines. In a subsequent letter, Annan informed the two principals that they had until 31 August 2009 to establish the special tribunal.[18] During the period of this extension, Annan continued to monitor the government's progress, but the OTP for the first time began to assume an active role in exerting pressure. In March 2009, OTP representatives attended a 2-day meeting in Geneva to discuss the reform process in Kenya. The Prosecutor's special advisor, Beatrice le Fraper Du Hellen, met Cabinet ministers Amos Wako, Martha Karua and Moses Wetangula to discuss the government's progress in establishing special tribunal. The special advisor warned that the OTP would act 'relentlessly and immediately' should the special tribunal not be created.[19]

A UN special rapporteur also joined the OTP and Annan in calling for an end to impunity, though not specifically in the context of the post-election violence. In February 2009, Philip Alston conducted a 10-day fact-finding mission and published a report claiming that Kenyan security forces regularly committed extrajudicial killings 'at will and with utter impunity'.[20] Alston recommended comprehensive and urgent reforms, commencing with the immediate dismissal of the Commissioner of Police and the Attorney General. In its official response, the government denied Alston's allegations, reaffirmed its commitment to human rights and insisted that

---

[16] International Criminal Court Office of the Prosecutor, 'ICC Prosecutor Reaffirms that the Situation in Kenya is Monitored by his Office', 11 February 2009 ('OTP February 2009 Statement').

[17] Lucas Barasa, 'Annan roots for local tribunal', *Daily Nation*, 17 February 2009.

[18] African Union, Panel of Eminent African Personalities, Note on handover of CIPEV materials to the Prosecutor of the ICC, 29 July 2009 ('Annan Sealed Envelope Statement').

[19] OTP Request for Authorisation (see Footnote 4); Bernard Namunane, 'The Hague vows to act swiftly', *Daily Nation*, 31 March 2009.

[20] Philip Alston, *Mission to Kenya 16–25 February 2009* (United Nations Special Rapporteur on Extrajudicial Killings, Arbitrary or Summary Executions, 2009) ('Alston Report').

most of Alston's recommendations were already in the process of being implemented well before he embarked on his fact-finding mission.[21]

2 Phase Two: Encouragement of Domestic Prosecutions (June 2009–November 2009)

2.1 The Complementarity Contract and the Delivery of the Sealed Envelope

From June 2009 the Prosecutor began to actively encourage domestic prosecutions in Kenya and Annan assumed a less prominent role. The Prosecutor gave an interview to local newspaper the *Daily Nation* which was published on 19 June 2009.[22] He emphasised that the Kenyan authorities bore the primary responsibility for investigating and prosecuting all crimes committed on Kenyan territory but that if these did not commence then the OTP would intervene. Less than three weeks later, a Kenyan delegation led by Justice Minister Mutula Kilonzo and Attorney General Amos Wako travelled to The Hague to meet with the Prosecutor. The Prosecutor and the Kenyan delegation agreed that 'impunity was not an option' and that if the Kenyan authorities carried out genuine judicial proceedings against those most responsible for the post-election violence, the ICC would have no grounds to intervene. At this meeting, the two parties entered into a 'complementarity contract'. They agreed that if the government did not establish a specific judicial mechanism for handling the post-election violence cases, it would voluntarily refer the situation to the ICC by June 2010.[23] As part of this commitment, the Kenyan delegation promised that by 30 September 2009 it would provide the OTP with reports on: (1) the status of the special tribunal; (2) the extent of investigations and prosecutions conducted; and (3) the witness protection measures put in place.[24]

With this complementarity contract concluded, Annan considered his earlier extension to no longer be necessary and that it would be 'wholly inappropriate' to continue holding the envelope under such circumstances.[25] Consequently, on 9 July 2009, Annan delivered the sealed envelope and six boxes of supporting materials to

---

[21] Government of the Republic of Kenya, Response to the Report of the Special Rapporteur on Extrajudicial. Arbitrary or Summary Executions, Professor Philip Alston, on his Mission to Kenya from 16 to 25 February, 2009 ('Government Response to Alston Report').

[22] Emeka-Mayaka Gekara, 'Ocampo to step in if Kenya does shoddy job', *Daily Nation*, 19 June 2009.

[23] International Criminal Court Office of the Prosecutor, 'ICC Prosecutor Receives Materials on Post-Election Violence in Kenya', 16 July 2009 ('OTP First Statement on the Sealed Envelope').

[24] International Criminal Court Office of the Prosecutor, 'Agreed minutes of the meeting between Prosecutor Moreno-Ocampo and the delegation of the Kenyan Government', 3 July 2009 ('OTP Complementarity Contract Statement').

[25] Annan Sealed Envelope Statement (see Footnote 19).

the OTP. According to Annan, the contents of these materials would assist the OTP in assessing the extent to which the government was in a position to initiate local investigations and prosecutions.[26] On 16 July 2009 the Prosecutor opened the envelope, examined its contents and resealed it, before reaffirming the complementarity contract that had been agreed two weeks earlier:

> There is a consensus that there will be no impunity for the crimes that have been committed. This is the only way to prevent the commission of new crimes during the next elections. The main responsibility now lies with the Kenyan Government.[27]

2.2 Strike Two and the Division of Labour

With the support of a two-thirds majority of Parliament proving difficult to secure, the government adopted a different strategy in its second attempt to establish the special tribunal by seeking the support of Cabinet. On 14 July 2009, Kilonzo presented revised versions of the two pieces of legislation to Cabinet. The four-hour meeting that followed, however, failed to produce a consensus.[28] Cabinet met again on 30 July 2009 but agreed that Kenya would not establish the special tribunal. Instead, it undertook to accelerate far-reaching reforms of the police and judiciary to enable them to investigate and prosecute perpetrators of the post-election violence in the future.[29] In the interim, the post-election violence cases would be handled by the recently established Truth Justice and Reconciliation Commission ('TJRC').[30] Cabinet also took the opportunity to reaffirm its commitment to the ICC and pledged to cooperate with the Court.[31] On 5 August 2009, a coalition of nearly 60 organisations condemned Cabinet's decision in an open letter to Kibaki and Odinga.[32] The letter accused Cabinet of a 'collective conspiracy to protect suspects responsible for the horrendous atrocities of the 2007/2008 post-election violence from criminal responsibility'.[33]

Although Cabinet's lack of support for the establishment of the special tribunal appeared on its face to have been contrary to the OTP's objective under its strategy of positive complementarity, the Prosecutor was initially supportive of this development. On 1 August 2009, he welcomed Cabinet's commitment to the ICC, stating that he

---

[26] Ibid.

[27] International Criminal Court Office of the Prosecutor, 'Waki Commission List of Names in the Hands of ICC Prosecutor', 16 July 2009 ('OTP Second Statement on the Sealed Envelope').

[28] Bernard Namunane and Lucas Barasa, 'Cabinet rejects draft laws on local tribunal', *Daily Nation*, 14 July 2009.

[29] Republic of Kenya Office of the President, 'Cabinet Decides on TJRC', 30 July 2009.

[30] Ibid.

[31] Ibid.

[32] International Centre for Policy and Conflict and others, 'Open Letter to President Mwai Kibaki and Prime Minister Raila Odinga', 5 August 2009 ('Civil Society TJRC Open Letter').

[33] Civil Society TJRC Open Letter (see Footnote 33).

respected the Kenyan authorities' efforts to end impunity and confirmed that he had not yet decided whether to open an investigation.[34] The following week, the Prosecutor continued to apply pressure upon the government to deal with the suspects domestically, saying that he would be 'closely monitoring the judicial mechanisms that [would] be utilised to conduct national investigations and prosecutions of those most responsible for the post-election violence'.[35] The Prosecutor also delivered this message when he met with the Minister for Lands, James Orengo, on 17 September 2009 and the Foreign Affairs Minister, Moses Wetangula, on 29 September 2009.[36]

Other sections of the international community continued to impose pressure upon the government to hold post-election violence suspects accountable and to undertake legal reforms. The European Union threatened to withhold approximately $500 million in donor funding should the special tribunal not be established.[37] Likewise, Washington stated that it would not conduct 'business as usual' with Nairobi should it fail to implement the reform agenda.[38] Washington sent letters to 15 prominent Kenyans threatening to impose travel bans prohibiting them from visiting the US should they continue to obstruct the reform agenda.[39] Similarly, in August 2009 the British High Commissioner to Kenya, Robert Macaire, announced that 20 Kenyans would be denied visas to visit the UK.[40] Meanwhile, the secretariat of the Panel of Eminent African Personalities continued to brief Annan on the progress of reforms through quarterly progress reports and Annan made periodic visits to Kenya to meet with politicians and civil society.

Despite the government's assurances that post-election violence suspects would be held accountable, as the first deadline under the complementarity contract approached, it was not certain whether the suspects would be tried by the ICC, a special tribunal, the TJRC, the ordinary Kenyan courts or some combination of these mechanisms. The Prosecutor therefore took the opportunity to outline a 'division of labour'. On 30 September 2009, the Prosecutor announced that he favoured a three-pronged approach to addressing the crimes committed during the post-election violence.[41] Under this proposal, the OTP would prosecute individuals bearing the greatest responsibility; the special tribunal or other local mechanism

---

[34] 'Kenyan Cabinet in the eye of a storm', *Daily Nation*, 1 August 2009.

[35] 'Truth commission "unlikely to try suspects"', *Daily Nation*, 10 August 2009.

[36] Peter Leftie, 'Ocampo wants trials split in three', *Daily Nation*, 17 September 2009; John Ngirachu, 'Wetangula allays ICC prosecution fears', *Daily Nation*, 29 September 2009.

[37] 'EU wants Waki, Kriegler reports implemented', *Standard*, 19 November 2008; Bernard Namunane, 'EU piles pressure on Kenya over poll trials', *Daily Nation*, 27 July 2009; Oliver Mathenge, 'Kenya, EU mulls withholding TJRC funds', *Daily Nation*, 7 August 2009; Oliver Mathenge, 'Resign, NCCK tells Cabinet over post-poll chaos trials', *Daily Nation*, 31 July 2009.

[38] Dave Opiyo, 'US warns Kenya on reforms', *Daily Nation*, 15 August 2009.

[39] David Ohito, 'Travel ban: Obama jolts Cabinet ministers', *Standard*, 25 September 2009.

[40] Peter Leftie, 'Violence suspects may face UK travel ban', *Daily Nation*, 4 August 2009.

[41] International Criminal Court Office of the Prosecutor, 'ICC Prosecutor supports three-pronged approach to justice in Kenya', 30 September 2009 ('OTP Division of Labour Statement').

would prosecute low-level perpetrators; while other reforms and mechanisms such as the TJRC would address historical injustices and the underlying causes of the violence. The Prosecutor boldly proclaimed that Kenya would be 'a world example on managing violence'.[42]

The government failed to meet the deadline imposed under the complementarity contract, just as it had missed the second Waki deadline earlier in the year. Although the Attorney General had delivered reports on the status of witness protection and domestic investigations, a report on the status of the establishment of the special tribunal remained outstanding. As far as the Prosecutor was concerned, the government had run out of chances. It had been three months since the delivery of the sealed envelope, eight months since the expiry of the second Waki deadline, nine months since Kibaki's and Odinga's undertaking to establish a special tribunal and 18 months since the cessation of hostilities, but still no significant progress had been made in the establishment of a local mechanism. The Prosecutor therefore decided that the ICC would intervene in Kenya.

On 9 October 2009, the Prosecutor requested a meeting with Kenyan authorities and told the media that 'decisive consultations between the Prosecutor and the Kenyan principals will take place in the coming weeks'.[43] On 27 October 2009, the Prosecutor wrote a letter to the principals, informing them of his decision and requesting that they keep their promise from July 2009 to self-refer the situation to the ICC.[44] When this was not immediately forthcoming, the Prosecutor then made this request in person during a meeting in Nairobi with Kibaki, Odinga and other Cabinet ministers on 5 November 2009. The Prosecutor told the delegation that prosecutions were necessary to 'put an end to impunity' and again requested a voluntary self-referral.[45] The principals, however, reneged on their earlier promise to voluntarily refer the situation to the ICC. In a statement to Parliament, Odinga said the Kenyan authorities refused to self-refer because this was an option reserved for failed states, which Kenya was not since it had a functioning government.[46] The Prosecutor informed the Kenyan authorities that he would commence an investigation *proprio motu* and, on the same day, he wrote to the President of the ICC informing him of the situation.[47] In response, Kibaki and Odinga issued a joint statement in which they promised to cooperate with the OTP in its investigations and to establish a local judicial mechanism to prosecute the perpetrators of the post-election violence.[48]

---

[42] Ibid.
[43] OTP Request for Authorisation (see Footnote 4).
[44] Ibid.
[45] International Criminal Court Office of the Prosecutor, 'Kenya Authorities Committed to Cooperate as ICC Prosecutor Informs them that in December he will Request ICC Judges to Open an Investigation into Post-Election Violence', 6 November 2009 ('OTP Proprio Motu Statement').
[46] Hansard, National Assembly, Official Report, 18 November 2009.
[47] OTP Request for Authorisation (see Footnote 4).
[48] Ibid.

3 Phase Three: ICC Investigations (December 2009–December 2010)

3.1 Strike Three and Investigations *Proprio Motu*

As the Prosecutor was seeking a self-referral, MP Gitobu Imanyara commenced a third attempt to establish the special tribunal, this time through a private member's bill. Imanyara, in consultation with other backbenchers and representatives from civil society, amended the legislation that Kilonzo had proposed to Cabinet and gazetted this new version on 26 August 2009. Despite continued assurances from Kibaki and Odinga that they were committed to holding perpetrators accountable at the local level, it took more than two months for the legislation to be introduced into Parliament. When the legislation was finally tabled, its passing was prevented by a parliamentary boycott. Just 18 of Kenya's 222 MPs were present as the legislation was read for the first time, well short of the 30 needed to make a quorum.[49] On 19 November 2009, Imanyara again attempted to pass the legislation, but another boycott ensued with just eight MPs attending the session on this occasion.[50]

One week later, on 26 November 2009, the Prosecutor requested the Pre-Trial Chamber for authorisation to conduct investigations in Kenya, the first time in the Court's history that the Prosecutor had used such powers.[51] In the 42-page application, the OTP submitted that there was a reasonable basis for believing that crimes against humanity had been committed in Kenya and that the situation was admissible because the Kenyan authorities had conducted only a 'limited number of proceedings for less serious offences'.[52] On 18 February 2010, the Pre-Trial Chamber requested the OTP to provide it with further information on the individuals to be investigated and their alleged links to the crimes committed.[53] This occurred on 3 March 2010 when the OTP provided a confidential list of 20 persons believed to have been involved in the organisation, incitement or financing of widespread or systematic attacks against civilians.[54] On 31 March 2010, a majority of the Pre-Trial Chamber found that there was a reasonable basis for believing that crimes against

---

[49] Beauttah Omanga and Alex Ndegwa, 'Debate on Imanyara Bill stalls as MPs stay away', *Daily Nation*, 12 November 2009.

[50] 'MPs snub Imanyara Bill debate, yet again', *Standard*, 19 November 2009.

[51] OTP Request for Authorisation (see Footnote 4).

[52] Ibid.

[53] International Criminal Court, Situation in the Republic of Kenya, Decision Requesting Clarification and Additional Information, ICC-01/09, 18 February 2010.

[54] International Criminal Court, Situation in the Republic of Kenya, Prosecutor's Response to Decision Requesting Clarification and Additional Information, ICC-01/09, 3 March 2010.

humanity had been committed in Kenya during the post-election violence and therefore authorised the OTP to commence investigations.[55]

The Prosecutor embarked upon a five-day visit to Kenya, from 8 May 2010 to 12 May 2010. While in the country, the Prosecutor reiterated that his 'only job [was] to end impunity for past crimes and prevent future crimes'.[56] The Prosecutor met with victims, civil society and Cabinet ministers, promising to 'follow the evidence' and 'prosecute those most responsible'.[57] Thereafter, OTP investigators remained in the country to gather evidence. The Prosecutor promised that investigations would be completed and the evidence presented to the Pre-Trial Chamber by the end of 2010.[58]

As the OTP conducted its investigations, other organs of the ICC also became involved in the Kenya situation. Three staff members from the Victims Participation and Reparations Section ('VPRS') visited Kenya in December 2009 to meet with victims and receive their representations.[59] On 4 September 2010 the Outreach Unit distributed 200,000 copies of the publication *Understanding the ICC*. The booklet, with an estimated readership of 20 million, explained the Court's mandate, structure and operations, and answered frequently asked questions.[60] The Outreach Unit was also responsible for the launch of a programme entitled *Understanding the International Criminal Court*, which was broadcast through 13 vernacular and community radio stations,[61] and a series entitled *Ask the Court* which was broadcast on all major Kenyan television and radio stations.[62]

Meanwhile, the government remained under pressure from other international actors to maintain momentum for its reform agenda. In May 2010, the UN Human

---

[55] International Criminal Court Pre-Trial Chamber II, Decision Pursuant to Article 15 of the Rome Statute on the Authorisation of an Investigation into the Situation in the Republic of Kenya, 31 March 2010 ('PTC Authorisation to Conduct Investigations'). Judge Kaul dissented, finding that there was no evidence of a State or organisational policy to commit an attack on a civilian population. While Judge Kaul accepted that the post-election violence may have been organised and planned in advance, the absence of an 'organisation' implementing a policy to attack a civilian population prevented His Excellency from being satisfied that there was a reasonable basis for concluding that crimes against humanity had been committed.

[56] David Clarke and Matthew Tostevin, 'Interview—ICC prosecutor targets up to six Kenyans', *Reuters*, 12 May 2010.

[57] International Criminal Court Office of the Prosecutor, 'ICC Prosecutor to visit Kenya to meet victims and listen to all Kenyans', 4 May 2010.

[58] Bernard Namunane and Oliver Mathenge, 'I'll nail suspects in 6 months', *Daily Nation*, 8 May 2010.

[59] International Criminal Court Pre Trial Chamber II, Situation in the Republic of Kenya, Public Redacted Version of Report Concerning Victims' Representations (ICC-01/09-6-Conf-Exp) and annexes 2 to 10, ICC-01/09, 29 March 2010 ('PTC Victims Report').

[60] International Criminal Court, 'ICC distributes 200,000 copies of the booklet Understanding the ICC', 4 September 2010.

[61] International Criminal Court, 'The ICC launches Outreach Programme radio campaign in Kenya', 3 December 2010.

[62] International Criminal Court, 'ICC releases episode two of the Kenyan-wide TV series Ask the Court', 15 April 2011.

Rights Council conducted its universal periodic review of Kenya's human rights record, during which the US delegation expressed concern over the allegations raised in the Alston Report and the UK urged the government to establish a special tribunal to complement the ICC. In response, the Kenyan delegation reaffirmed the government's commitment to human rights and assured the Council of its commitment to cooperating with the ICC.[63]

3.2 Continued Encouragement of Domestic Proceedings

The OTP was concerned to avoid an impunity cap and so continued to encourage domestic proceedings throughout the investigatory period. The OTP did not want to give the impression, however, that domestic proceedings would halt the progress of the ICC cases. Consistent with the three-pronged strategy first outlined in September 2009, the OTP explained that domestic proceedings were to be complementarity to the ICC trials, rather than an alternative to them. The OTP attempted to achieve this through two distinct and simultaneous narratives.

On the one hand, the Prosecutor regularly made statements that suggested ICC prosecutions were inevitable. The Prosecutor emphasised the strength of the OTP's evidence against those bearing the greatest responsibility for the post-election violence, affirmed that no person would be immune from prosecution and promised that the cases would proceed expeditiously.[64] On the other hand, the Prosecutor

---

[63] United Nations General Assembly Human Rights Council, Working Group of the Universal Periodic Review, *Report of the Working Group on the Universal Periodic Review, Kenya*, A/HRC/15/8, 17 June 2010 ('Human Rights Council Universal Periodic Review').

[64] 'I think I have a strong case because the Waki Commission is a very good report, it's full of information and there are other reports; the UN report; different other human rights groups reports. I believe I have a very strong case' (Kariuki 2009).

'There is no doubt that I will be able to present a very strong case against at least six key suspects before the ICC judges' (Omanga 2010). 'We have great evidence. This includes details of meetings that planned the attacks'. Murithi Mutiga, 'Ocampo: I have solid evidence against six Kenyan suspects', *Daily Nation*, 21 September 2011.

'The important point is that no-one is immune from Prosecution before the ICC; politicians, businessmen or security officers may all potentially be brought to account in accordance with their criminal responsibility … It happened with Slobodan Milosevic; it happened with Charles Taylor' (Gekara 2009) (see Footnote 22).

'I saw in my country President Videla who had a lot of power when he took office and one day we prosecuted him in court … I saw General Pinochet who was arrested when he was in London. I saw President Milosevic who was arrested in his own country. I saw Charles Taylor arrested and in The Hague. We are living in a new world in which power is not allowing you to commit massive crimes'. Michael Onyiego, 'ICC Prosecutor promises justice for Kenyas', *Voice of America*, 13 May 2010.

'We are investigating massive crimes against humanity faster than ever thought possible' (Gekara 2009) (see Footnote 22).

'Everyone is worried about the next election in Kenya in 2012. That is why I understand the importance of speed'. 'ICC seeking speedy trials', *BBC News*, 7 November 2009.

'We are trying to be as fast as possible. Individuals should face justice in 2010' (Namunane 2009).

'It will be very fast. At the end of the year, we will present the cases that I want tried to the judges' (Namunane and Mathenge 2010) (see Footnote 58).

continued to highlight the importance of the government establishing a local mechanism to conduct prosecutions. The Prosecutor regularly stressed that the ICC could not be expected to prosecute all alleged perpetrators and would limit itself to the prosecution of up to six persons bearing the greatest responsibility.[65] As a consequence of this limitation, the Prosecutor emphasised that for there to be an end to impunity in Kenya, the government would have to assume responsibility for prosecuting the remaining perpetrators.[66]

For the most part, the Prosecutor elected to deliver these messages through press statements and media interviews, rather than through face-to-face meetings with senior members of government. Indeed, between May 2010 and December 2010, the Prosecutor did not visit Kenya or host any Kenyan delegations, instead using this time to implement the strategy of positive complementarity strategy in Guinea and Georgia.[67] The OTP's only interaction with members of government during this seven-month period was when it met with Ruto in November 2010. The purpose of this meeting, however, was not for the OTP to once again encourage domestic investigations and prosecutions, but rather to afford Ruto, a potential suspect, the opportunity to explain his role in the post-election violence.[68]

On 1 December 2010, the Prosecutor returned to Nairobi to meet with Kibaki, Odinga and Annan. The Prosecutor briefed the principals on the OTP's progress in its investigations and the principals reaffirmed their commitment to the ICC.[69] The Prosecutor also took the opportunity to encourage Kenya to 'move ahead and implement the Constitution'.[70] On the following day, the Prosecutor said that he had completed his investigations and within the next two weeks would reveal the names of the six persons whom the OTP would seek to prosecute at the ICC.[71]

---

[65] 'The Prosecutor will present in court a limited number of cases, two or three, against those persons considered the most responsible. Only some of the gravest incidents will be presented at trial' (Kariuki 2009).

'We cannot prosecute thousands of people at The Hague. Young men raped and killed, but who gave the order? Who paid the money?' Anthony Kariuki, 'Ocampo says no suspects in Kenya chaos', *Daily Nation*, 8 May 2010.

[66] 'We still emphasise the need for a special tribunal and other national proceedings to ensure a holistic approach to criminal responsibility for these crimes'. 'Justice beckons as Ocampo visits Kenya', *Daily Nation*, 6 May 2010.

'Don't expect everything from me. I will only prosecute two to six cases and the rest is up to you'.

[67] International Criminal Court Office of the Prosecutor, 'OTP delegation to visit Guinea', 18 May 2010 ('OTP Guinea Statement').

[68] Murithi Mutiga, 'Now Ruto wants Kenya's principals charged by ICC', *Daily Nation*, 6 November 2010.

[69] Lucas Barasa, 'We'll arrest suspects, Big Two tell Ocampo', *Daily Nation*, 1 December 2010.

[70] Lucas Barasa, 'Annan, Ocampo meet Kenya principals', *Daily Nation*, 1 December 2010.

[71] Bernard Namunane, 'Your time is up, Ocampo tells chaos suspects', *Daily Nation*, 2 December 2010.

4 Phase Four: ICC Pre-Trial Stage (December 2010– March 2013)

4.1 The 'Ocampo Six'

On 15 December 2010, the Prosecutor publicly named six suspects and requested the Pre-Trial Chamber to issue summonses in relation to each. According to the Prosecutor, these persons, colloquially known as the 'Ocampo Six', bore the greatest responsibility for the crimes against humanity committed during Kenya's postelection violence. The Prosecutor presented the names to the Pre-Trial Chamber in two separate cases, each containing three suspects. The first case (labelled 'Kenya One' by OTP staff) focussed on the crimes committed by ODM supporters against PNU supporters in the immediate aftermath of the 2007 election. The suspects consisted of the Minister for Agriculture, William Ruto; ODM chairman, Henry Kosgey; and radio broadcaster Joshua Sang.[72] The second ('Kenya Two') centred on PNU's response to the violence, including crimes committed by the police and the Mungiki criminal sect. The Prosecutor named Deputy Prime Minister Uhuru Kenyatta; the head of the public service, Francis Muthaura; and the former Commissioner of Police, Mohammed Ali.[73] According to the Prosecutor:

> These senior leaders, from both PNU and ODM parties were guided by political objectives to retain or gain power. They utilised their personal, government, business and tribal networks to commit the crimes. They implemented their policy with the involvement of a number of State officers and public or private institutions, such as members of the Parliament, senior government officers, the police force and youth gangs.[74]

The Prosecutor promised that these prosecutions would 'break the cycle of impunity for massive crimes' and provide victims and their families with justice.[75]

Two days prior to the Prosecutor's announcement, Cabinet met to discuss possible responses. Its first preference was to 'establish a credible local process for the investigation and prosecution of the six persons' so that the government could challenge the admissibility of the cases before the ICC. The second option considered by Cabinet was to seek a Security Council deferral of the cases for twelve months on the basis that progressing with the prosecutions would threaten international

---

[72] Situation in the Republic of Kenya, Prosecutor's Application Pursuant to Article 58 as to William Samoei Ruto, Henry Kiprono Kosgey and Joshua Arap Sang, Public Redacted Version of Document ICC-01/09-30-Conf-Exp, 15 December 2010 ('OTP Kenya One Application').

[73] Situation in the Republic of Kenya, Prosecutor's Application Pursuant to Article 58 as to Francis Kirimi Muthaura, Uhuru Muigai Kenyatta and Mohammed Hussein Ali, Public Redacted Version of Document ICC-01/09-31-Conf-Exp, 15 December 2010 ('OTP Kenya Two Application').

[74] International Criminal Court Office of the Prosecutor, 'ICC Prosecutor to Judges: Kenya crimes resulted from a policy by identifiable leaders', 3 March 2010.

[75] International Criminal Court, Office of the Prosecutor, 'Kenya's post election violence: ICC Prosecutor presents case against six individuals for crimes against humanity', 15 December 2010 ('OTP Ocampo Six Statement').

peace and security. Should each of these responses prove unsuccessful, Cabinet's third preference was to withdraw from the Rome Statute. Finally, Cabinet's fourth and least-preferred response was to allow the ICC process to 'take its own course'.[76]

Following the announcement of the Ocampo Six, sections of the government pursued a number of initiatives that had the potential to frustrate the progress of the ICC trials. In the same month that the Ocampo Six was announced, Parliament passed a motion calling upon the government to withdraw from the Rome Statute. This was followed by a request to the Security Council in March 2011 for a deferral of the cases and an unsuccessful application to challenge the admissibility of the cases before the ICC later that same month. In January 2012 the government sought to suspend the ICC cases by arranging for suspects to be tried by the East African Court of Justice ('EACJ') and, in May 2012 pursued a similar strategy in relation to the African Court of Justice and Human Rights ('ACJHR').

Despite these distractions, the two ICC cases continued to proceed through the pre-trial stage. On 8 March 2011, the Pre-Trial Chamber issued summonses for the Ocampo Six to appear before the ICC and the suspects made their initial appearances on 7 and 8 April 2011. The Pre-Trial Chamber held confirmation of charges hearings in September and October 2011, then retired to consider whether there was a reasonable basis for believing that the Ocampo Six were responsible for crimes against humanity. On 23 January 2012, a majority of the Pre-Trial Chamber confirmed the charges against four of the six suspects.[77] The Pre-Trial Chamber dismissed the charges against Kosgey, determining the uncorroborated testimony of a single anonymous witness to be an insufficient basis upon which to confirm the charges. It also dismissed the charges against Ali on the basis that it was not satisfied that police officers had committed crimes against humanity during the post-election violence. The Pre-Trial Chamber did, however, confirm the charges against Ruto, Sang, Kenyatta and Muthaura and those decisions were ultimately upheld on appeal.[78] The Ocampo Six had become the Ocampo Four.

---

[76] Hansard, National Assembly, Official Report, 16 December 2010.

[77] *Prosecutor v William Samoei Ruto, Henry Kiprono Kosgey and Joseph Arap Sang*, Decision on the Confirmation of Charges Pursuant to Article 61(7)(a) and (b) of the Rome Statute, ICC-01/09-01/11, 23 January 2012 ('PTC Confirmation of Charges, Kenya One'); *Prosecutor v Francis Kirimi Muthaura, Uhuru Muigai Kenyatta and Mohammed Hussein Ali*, Judgment on the appeal of the Republic of Kenya against the decision of Pre-Trial Chamber II of 30 May 2011 entitled 'Decision on the Confirmation of Charges Pursuant to Article 61(7)(a) and (b) of the Rome Statute', ICC-01/09-02/11-274, 31 January 2012 ('PTC Confirmation of Charges, Kenya Two').

[78] *Prosecutor v William Samoei Ruto and Joseph Arap Sang*, Decision on the appeals of Mr William Samoei Ruto and Mr Joshua Arap Sang against the decision n of Pre-Trial Chamber II of 23 January 2012 entitled 'Decision on the Confirmation of Charges Pursuant to Article 61(7)(a) and (b) of the Rome Statute', ICC-01/09-01/11, 24 May 2012; *Prosecutor v Francis Kirimi Muthaura and Uhuru Muigai Kenyatta*, Decision on the appeals of Mr Francis Kirimi Muthaura and Uhuru Muigai Kenyatta against the decision n of Pre-Trial Chamber II of 23 January 2012 entitled 'Decision on the Confirmation of Charges Pursuant to Article 61(7)(a) and (b) of the Rome Statute', ICC-01/09-02/11, 24 May 2012.

On the same day that the Pre-Trial Chamber confirmed the charges against four of the suspects, Kibaki issued a statement in which he emphasised that the government was continuing to work towards ending impunity through reforms to the judiciary, police, investigatory institutions and the witness protection regime.[79] The Prosecutor responded the following day, calling upon the government to address the concerns of the country's displaced persons.[80] The statement, however, contained no language that suggested that the OTP was continuing to encourage domestic investigations and prosecutions as part of its strategy of positive complementarity. Rather, all that was included was the rather vague assertion that it was 'in the hands of Kenyans themselves to solve the problems in Kenya'.[81] This suggests that from January 2012, the OTP had abandoned its attempts to encourage domestic prosecutions and instead focussed its attention on the trial of the Ocampo Four.

4.2 The 'Ocampo Four'

The four remaining ICC suspects voluntarily appeared in The Hague on 11 and 12 June 2012 to attend status conferences in order to make all necessary arrangements for the remainder of the pre-trial stage. With Moreno-Ocampo in the final week of his nine-year term, his successor, Fatou Bensouda, represented the OTP as Prosecutor. Each of the parties agreed to a March 2013 commencement date for the two trials, despite the fact that Ruto and Kenyatta were two of the leading candidates for the 4 March 2013 presidential election. On 9 July 2012, the Pre-Trial Chamber ordered that the Kenya One case would commence on 10 April 2013 and that the Kenya Two case would begin on the following day. Later that month, the head of the OTP's JCCD division, Phakiso Mochochoko, travelled to Nairobi to reassure Kenyans that the trials would continue, irrespective of the outcome of the presidential election.[82]

As the ICC cases progressed, the OTP did little to encourage domestic investigations and prosecutions. The OTP received no Kenyan delegations in The Hague, nor did it arrange any meetings with the principals throughout this period. In May 2012, Ocampo and Bensouda conducted a joint tour of African countries as part of the latter's appointment as Prosecutor, but the two elected not to include Kenya on their itineraries. The OTP also ceased releasing press statements that called upon the government to adhere to its Rome Statute obligations to investigate and prosecute and neither Moreno-Ocampo nor Bensouda made any public statements on this issue.

The international community, however, continued to apply pressure upon Nairobi. For three days in July 2012, the UN Human Rights Committee conducted

---

[79] Office of the President, 'Statement by His Excellency Hon Mwai Kibaki CGH MP, President and Commander-in-Chief of the Defence Forces of the Republic of Kenya following the decision by the International Criminal Court Pre-Trial Chamber', 23 January 2012.

[80] 'Victims do not have to wait for a conviction before they receive help. The Government of Kenya has a responsibility to help its citizens. And to protect them. The Office is concerned about allegations of attacks against victims of the crimes'. International Criminal Court Office of the Prosecutor, 'Statement by the Prosecutor of the International Criminal Court on Kenya ruling', 24 January 2012.

[81] Ibid.

[82] Nzau Musau, 'Kenya: Uhuru, Ruto must go to ICC even if elected', *The Star*, 27 July 2012.

its periodic review of Kenya's compliance with the International Covenant on Civil and Political Rights, with the sessions broadcast live on Kenyan television. At the conclusion of the review, the Committee issued a number of recommendations, including that Kenya should 'as a matter of urgency, pursue all cases of the post-2007 election violence to ensure that the perpetrators are brought to justice and that victims are adequately compensated'.[83]

4.3 The 'Ocampo Three'

In late October 2012, Bensouda undertook a five-day trip to Kenya, her first official visit to the country as Prosecutor and the first from the OTP since Moreno-Ocampo's meeting with the principals in Nairobi on December 2010. The Prosecutor met with Kibaki and Odinga, newly appointed Chief Justice Willy Mutunga, members of civil society and victims to discuss a variety of matters. Once again, however, absent from these were attempts to encourage the government to conduct its own investigations and prosecutions to complement the ICC trials. Instead, the Prosecutor focused on securing pledges of cooperation from the government in relation to the two cases.[84] For the first time, the Prosecutor admitted that the OTP was having some difficulty in compiling strong cases against the suspects. The Prosecutor revealed that the OTP was 'facing challenges', such as interference with witnesses and the government's withholding of evidence.[85] The Prosecutor claimed that there had been 'serious efforts, and timeless efforts, to find out where witnesses [were and] threaten them and their families'.[86] On 18 March 2013, a key insider witness in the Muthaura case recanted his testimony, forcing the OTP to drop charges against that suspect.[87] In essence, the Ocampo Six had become the Ocampo Three.

On 4 March 2013, Kenya held its first presidential election since the 2007/2008 post-election violence. Kenyatta was declared the victor with 50.07 % of the popular vote, narrowly avoiding the need for a run-off election. Odinga was once again the runner-up but in contrast to 2007/2008 elected to challenge the results in the courts. The election results were ultimately upheld on 25 March 2013. Fifteen days later, Kenyatta was sworn in as the country's fourth President, with Ruto becoming his Vice President.

---

[83] United Nations Human Rights Committee, *Concluding observations adopted by the Human Rights Committee at its 105th session*, 9–27 July 2012, CCPR/C/KEN/CO/3, 26 July 2012 ('UN Human Rights Committee Concluding Observations').

[84] International Criminal Court Office of the Prosecutor, 'Statement by the Prosecutor of the International Criminal Court Mrs. Fatou Bensouda at the press conference at the conclusion of Nairobi segment of ICC Prosecutor's visit to Kenya, Nairobi', 25 October 2012 ('OTP Second Statement on Bensouda's Visit to Kenya').

[85] International Criminal Court Office of the Prosecutor, 'Statement by the Prosecutor of the International Criminal Court Mrs. Fatou Bensouda', press release, 22 October 2012 ('OTP First Statement on Bensouda's Visit to Kenya').

[86] Koome Kimonye and Alex Chamwada, 'Kenyan Gov't not cooperative, says ICC', *Citizen News*, 17 February 2013.

[87] *Prosecutor v Francis Kirimi Muthaura and Uhuru Muigai Kenyatta*, Decision on the withdrawal of charges against Mr Muthaura, ICC-01/09-02/11, 18 March 2013 ('Decision to Withdraw Charges Against Muthaura').

For the first time in history, therefore, an international court was faced with the prospect of arranging a trial for a sitting head of state. Over the months that followed, the various organs of the ICC contemplated how it would confront this unprecedented challenge. Initially, the Kenya One case, involving Ruto and Sang, was scheduled to commence on 10 April 2013, with the Kenyatta trial to begin on the following day. The start date for each of the two trials, however, was delayed on multiple occasions. Kenyatta's trial, which was originally scheduled to commence on 11 April 2013[88] was postponed until 9 July 2013,[89] then to 12 November 2013,[90] then to 5 February 2014[91] then to 7 October 2014[92]. Three weeks before the latest revised start date, the Trial Chamber again vacated the date and instead ordered status conferences for 7 and 8 October 2014 to discuss the progress of the trial.[93] The OTP again sought an adjournment of the the trial but on 3 December 2014 the Trial Chamber rejected this request, stating that the OTP had to either indicate a readiness to proceed to trial or withdraw the charges.[94] Two days later, the Prosecutor withdrew all charges against Kenyatta.[95] The Ocampo Six had become the Ocampo Two. Although the case against Ruto and Sang did commence, it was ultimately postponed until 10 September 2013, with the Vice-President being granted permission to be absent for large parts of the trial.[96]

5 Conclusion

The OTP first received a communication alerting it to the commission of crimes against humanity in Kenya in mid-January 2008 and commenced its strategy of positive complementarity the following month when it announced that it was 'carefully considering all information' on crimes that may have been committed. The OTP placed little overt pressure upon the government, however, between February 2008 and June 2009, with

---

[88] *Prosecutor v Francis Kirimi Muthaura and Uhuru Muigai Kenyatta*, Decision on the schedule leading up to trial, ICC-01/09-02/11, 9 July 2012.

[89] *Prosecutor v Francis Kirimi Muthaura and Uhuru Muigai Kenyatta*, Order concerning the state date of trial, ICC-01/09-02/11, 7 March 2013.

[90] *Prosecutor v Uhuru Muigai Kenyatta*, Public redacted version of 'decision on commencement date of trial', ICC-01/09-02/11, 20 June 2013.

[91] *Prosecutor v Uhuru Muigai Kenyatta*, Decision adjourning the commencement of trial, ICC-01/09-02/11, 31 October 2013.

[92] *Prosecutor v Uhuru Muigai Kenyatta*, Decision on Prosecution's application for a finding of non-compliance pursuant to Article 87(7) and for an adjournment of the provisional trial date, ICC-01/09-02/11, 31 March 2014.

[93] Prosecutor v Uhuru Muigai Kenyatta, Order vacating trial date of 7 October 2014, convening two status conferences, and addressing other procedural matters, ICC-01/09-02/11, 19 September 2014

[94] Prosecutor v Uhuru Muigai Kenyatta, Decision on Prosecution's application for a further adjournment, ICC-01/09-02/11, 3 December 2014

[95] International Criminal Court Office of the Prosecutor, Statement of the Prosecutor of the International Criminal Court, Fatou Bensouda, on the withdrawal of charges against Mr. Uhuru Muigai Kenyatta, 5 December 2014

[96] *Prosecutor v William Samoei Ruto and Joshua Arap Sang*, Decision on Mr Ruto's request for excusal from continuous presence at trial, ICC-01/09-01/11, 18 June 2013

Annan and the KNDR group assuming the leading role during this period. The OTP most actively pursued its strategy of positive complementarity between June 2009 and November 2009. During this five-month period, the Prosecutor met with Kenyan officials on four occasions, took delivery of the sealed envelope, entered into a 'complementarity contract', outlined a 'division of labour' and threatened international prosecutions. Ultimately, however, these measures failed to convince the government to try suspects domestically, resulting in the Prosecutor taking the unprecedented step of using his *proprio motu* powers to launch an investigation. While the OTP was conducting investigations it persevered with its strategy of positive complementarity by emphasising the limitations of the Court and stressing the importance of local proceedings to complement the Court's work so as to avoid an impunity gap. From mid-2010, however, the Prosecutor's calls for domestic trials gradually diminished as the OTP focused its resources on preparing the cases for trial and on implementing the strategy of positive complementarity in other situations. Indeed, from January 2011 when the charges against the Ocampo Four were confirmed and the Prosecutor declared that it was 'in the hands of Kenyans themselves to solve the problems in Kenya', it appears that the OTP made no overt attempt to persuade the government to conduct domestic prosecutions. By the time that Bensouda assumed office in June 2012, the OTP had moved away from encouraging domestic proceedings and instead focused on securing cooperation from the government for the ICC trials.

Throughout this period, the government continued to be subjected to a great deal of pressure from both international and domestic sources to end impunity. UN agencies, foreign embassies, the Panel of Eminent African Personalities and Kenyan NGOs all regularly called upon the government to not only try suspected perpetrators, but also to expedite rule of law reforms outlined in Agenda Item IV.

Having provided this chronology, it is now possible to consider the extent to which the OTP's strategy of positive complementarity contributed to the ending of impunity in Kenya. This commences with a consideration of the extent to which those responsible for the post-election violence were held accountable at either the local or international level and, if so, the contribution that the OTP's strategy of positive complementarity may have had on these prosecutions.

Bibliography

'EU wants Waki, Kriegler reports implemented', *Standard*, 19 November 2008
'ICC seeking speedy trials', *BBC News*, 7 November 2009
'Justice beckons as Ocampo visits Kenya', *Daily Nation*, 6 May 2010
'MPs snub Imanyara Bill debate, yet again', *Standard*, 19 November 2009
'Truth commission 'unlikely to try suspects'', *Daily Nation*, 10 August 2009
African Union, Panel of Eminent African Personalities, Address by Kofi Annan delivered during the 29th graduation of the University of Nairobi, 17 October 2008
African Union, Panel of Eminent African Personalities, Note on handover of CIPEV materials to the Prosecutor of the ICC, 29 July 2009

African Union, Panel of Eminent African Personalities, Press Statement by Kofi Annan, 1 March 2008
African Union, Panel of Eminent African Personalities, Press Statement by Kofi Annan, 23 September 2008
African Union, Panel of Eminent African Personalities, Statement of Kofi Annan on the Implementation of the Report of the Commission of Inquiry on Post-Election Violence (CIPEV) & Independent Review Commission (IREC), 19 December 2008
Alston, Philip, *Mission to Kenya 16–25 February 2009* (United Nations Special Rapporteur on Extrajudicial Killings, Arbitrary or Summary Executions, 2009)
Barasa, Lucas, 'Annan, Ocampo meet Kenya principals', *Daily Nation*, 1 December 2010
Barasa, Lucas, 'Annan roots for local tribunal', *Daily Nation*, 17 February 2009
Barasa, Lucas, 'We'll arrest suspects, Big Two tell Ocampo', *Daily Nation*, 1 December 2010
Clarke, David and Tostevin, Matthew, 'Interview—ICC prosecutor targets up to six Kenyans', *Reuters*, 12 May 2010
Final Report from Kenya's Commission of Inquiry into Post-Election Violence, 15 October 2008
Gekara, Emeka-Mayaka, 'Ocampo to step in if Kenya does shoddy job', *Daily Nation*, 19 June 2009
Hansard, National Assembly, Official Report, 18 November 2009
Hansard, National Assembly, Official Report, 16 December 2010
International Centre for Policy and Conflict and others, 'Open Letter to President Mwai Kibaki and Prime Minister Raila Odinga', 5 August 2009
International Criminal Court, 'ICC distributes 200,000 copies of the booklet Understanding the ICC', 4 September 2010
International Criminal Court, 'ICC releases episode two of the Kenyan-wide TV series Ask the Court', 15 April 2011
International Criminal Court, 'The ICC launches Outreach Programme radio campaign in Kenya', 3 December 2010
International Criminal Court, Office of the Prosecutor, 'Agreed minutes of the meeting between Prosecutor Moreno-Ocampo and the delegation of the Kenyan Government', 3 July 2009
International Criminal Court, Office of the Prosecutor, 'ICC Prosecutor confirms situation in Guinea under examination', 14 October 2010
International Criminal Court, Office of the Prosecutor, 'ICC Prosecutor Reaffirms that the Situation in Kenya is Monitored by his Office', 11 February 2009
International Criminal Court, Office of the Prosecutor, 'ICC Prosecutor Receives Materials on Post-Election Violence in Kenya', 16 July 2009
International Criminal Court, Office of the Prosecutor, 'ICC Prosecutor supports three-pronged approach to justice in Kenya', 30 September 2009
International Criminal Court, Office of the Prosecutor, 'ICC Prosecutor to Judges: Kenya crimes resulted from a policy by identifiable leaders', 3 March 2010
International Criminal Court, Office of the Prosecutor, 'ICC Prosecutor to visit Kenya to meet victims and listen to all Kenyans', 4 May 2010
International Criminal Court, Office of the Prosecutor, 'Kenya Authorities Committed to Cooperate as ICC Prosecutor Informs them that in December he will Request ICC Judges to Open an Investigation into Post-Election Violence', 6 November 2009
International Criminal Court, Office of the Prosecutor, 'No impunity for crimes committed in Georgia: OTP concludes second visit to Georgia in context of preliminary examinations', 26 June 2010
International Criminal Court, Office of the Prosecutor, 'OTP Statement in Relation to Events in Kenya', 5 February 2008
International Criminal Court Office of the Prosecutor, 'Statement by the Prosecutor of the International Criminal Court Mrs. Fatou Bensouda', press release, 22 October 2012
International Criminal Court, Office of the Prosecutor, 'Statement by the Prosecutor of the International Criminal Court Mrs. Fatou Bensouda at the press conference at the conclusion of Nairobi segment of ICC Prosecutor's visit to Kenya, Nairobi', 25 October 2012
International Criminal Court Office of the Prosecutor, Statement of the Prosecutor of the International Criminal Court, Fatou Bensouda, on the withdrawal of charges against Mr. Uhuru Muigai Kenyatta, 5 December 2014
International Criminal Court, Office of the Prosecutor, 'Statement by the Prosecutor of the International Criminal Court on Kenya ruling', 24 January 2012

Bibliography

International Criminal Court Office of the Prosecutor, 'Waki Commission List of Names in the Hands of ICC Prosecutor', 16 July 2009
International Criminal Court, Situation in the Republic of Kenya, Decision Requesting Clarification and Additional Information, ICC-01/09, 18 February 2010
International Criminal Court, Situation in the Republic of Kenya, Prosecutor's Application Pursuant to Article 58 as to Francis Kirimi Muthaura, Uhuru Muigai Kenyatta and Mohammed Hussein Ali, Public Redacted Version of Document ICC-01/09-31-Conf-Exp, 15 December 2010
International Criminal Court, Situation in the Republic of Kenya, Prosecutor's Application Pursuant to Article 58 as to William Samoei Ruto, Henry Kiprono Kosgey and Joshua Arap Sang, Public Redacted Version of Document ICC-01/09-30-Conf-Exp, 15 December 2010
International Criminal Court, Situation in the Republic of Kenya, Prosecutor's Response to Decision Requesting Clarification and Additional Information, ICC-01/09, 3 March 2010
International Criminal Court, Situation in the Republic of Kenya, Public Redacted Version of Report Concerning Victims' Representations (ICC-01/09-6-Conf-Exp) and annexes 2 to 10, ICC-01/09, 29 March 2010
International Criminal Court, Situation in the Republic of Kenya, Request for authorisation of an investigation pursuant to Article 15, ICC-01/09, 26 November 2009
Interview with Justice Philip Waki (Nairobi, 16 April 2010)
Kariuki, Anthony 'Ocampo: ICC has strong case in Kenya chaos', *Daily Nation*, 7 November 2009
Kariuki, Anthony, 'Ocampo says no suspects in Kenya chaos', *Daily Nation*, 8 May 2010
Kenya Human Rights Institute, Clarifying Human Rights Violations in the Kenyan Post-Election Crisis (Kenya Human Rights Institute, 2008)
Kenya National Commission on Human Rights, On the brink of the precipice: a human rights account of Kenya's post-2007 election violence, 15 August 2008
Kimonye, Koomer and Chamwada, Alex, 'Kenyan Gov't not cooperative, says ICC', Citizen News, 17 February 2013
Leftie, Peter, 'Ocampo wants trials split in three', *Daily Nation*, 17 September 2009
Leftie, Peter, 'Violence suspects may face UK travel ban', *Daily Nation*, 4 August 2009
Leftie, Peter, Wanyoro, Charles, Majefa, Mwakera and Mathenge, Oliver, 'Kenya Cabinet in the eye of a storm', *Daily Nation*, 2 August 2009
Limo, Lucianne, Omanga, Beauttah and Bartoo, Vincent, 'Ocampo asks Kenyans not to expect too much', *Standard*, 11 May 2010
Mathenge, Oliver, 'Kenya, EU mulls withholding TJRC funds', *Daily Nation*, 7 August 2009
Mathenge, Oliver, 'Resign, NCCK tells Cabinet over post-poll chaos trials', *Daily Nation*, 31 July 2009
Mathenge, Oliver and Sudhir, Sadiki, 'Lawyers fault proposed tribunal on Waki', *Daily Nation*, 3 December 2008
Moreno-Ocampo, Luis, 'A positive approach to complementarity: the impact of the Office of the Prosecutor' Carsten Stahn and Mohamed M. El Zeidy (eds), *The International Criminal Court and Complementarity From Theory to Practice* (Cambridge University Press, 2011)
Musau, Nzau, 'Kenya: Uhuru, Ruto must go to ICC even if elected', The Star, 27 July 2012
Mutiga, Murithi, 'Now Ruto wants Kenya's principals charged by ICC', *Daily Nation*, 6 November 2010
Mutiga, Murithi, 'Ocampo: I have solid evidence against six Kenyan suspects', *Daily Nation*, 21 September 2011
Namunane, Bernard, 'EU piles pressure on Kenya over poll trials', *Daily Nation*, 27 July 2009
Namunane, Bernard, 'The Hague beckons for suspects', *Daily Nation*, 26 November 2009
Namunane, Bernard, 'The Hague vows to act swiftly', *Daily Nation*, 31 March 2009
Namunane, Bernard, 'Your time is up, Ocampo tells chaos suspects', *Daily Nation*, 2 December 2010
Namunane, Bernard and Barasa, Lucas, 'Cabinet rejects draft laws on local tribunal', *Daily Nation*, 14 July 2009
Namunane, Bernard and Mathenge, Oliver, 'I'll nail suspects in 6 months', *Daily Nation*, 8 May 2010
Ngirachu, John, 'Wetangula allays ICC prosecution fears', *Daily Nation*, 29 September 2009
Ohito, David, 'Travel ban: Obama jolts Cabinet ministers', *Standard*, 25 September 2009
Omanga, Beauttah, 'Why Ocampo needs two years on Kenya', *Standard*, 13 May 2010

Omanga, Beauttah and Ndegwa, Alex, 'Debate on Imanyara Bill stalls as MPs stay away', *Daily Nation*, 12 November 2009

Onyiego, Michael, 'ICC Prosecutor promises justice for Kenyans', *Voice of America*, 13 May 2010

Opiyo, David, 'US warns Kenya on reforms', *Daily Nation*, 15 August 2009

Prosecutor v Francis Kirimi Muthaura and Uhuru Muigai Kenyatta, Decision on the appeals of Mr Francis Kirimi Muthaura and Uhuru Muigai Kenyatta against the decision n of Pre-Trial Chamber II of 23 January 2012 entitled 'Decision on the Confirmation of Charges Pursuant to Article 61(7)(a) and (b) of the Rome Statute', ICC-01/09-02/11, 24 May 2012

Prosecutor v Francis Kirimi Muthaura and Uhuru Muigai Kenyatta, Decision on the schedule leading up to trial, ICC-01/09-02/11, 9 July 2012

Prosecutor v Francis Kirimi Muthaura and Uhuru Muigai Kenyatta, Decision on the withdrawal of charges against Mr Muthaura, ICC-01/09-02/11, 18 March 2013

Prosecutor v Francis Kirimi Muthaura and Uhuru Muigai Kenyatta, Order concerning the state date of trial, ICC-01/09-02/11, 7 March 2013

Prosecutor v Francis Kirimi Muthaura, Uhuru Muigai Kenyatta and Mohammed Hussein Ali, Judgment on the appeal of the Republic of Kenya against the decision of Pre-Trial Chamber II of 30 May 2011 entitled 'Decision on the Confirmation of Charges Pursuant to Article 61(7)(a) and (b) of the Rome Statute ', ICC-01/09-02/11-274, 31 January 2012

Prosecutor v Uhuru Muigai Kenyatta, Decision adjourning the commencement of trial, ICC-01/09-02/11, 31 October 2013

Prosecutor v Uhuru Muigai Kenyatta, Decision on Prosecution's application for a finding of non-compliance pursuant to Article 87(7) and for an adjournment of the provisional trial date, ICC-01/09-02/11, 31 March 2014

Prosecutor v Uhuru Muigai Kenyatta, Order vacating trial date of 7 October 2014, convening two status conferences, and addressing other procedural matters, ICC-01/09-02/11, 19 September 2014

Prosecutor v Uhuru Muigai Kenyatta, Decision on Prosecution's application for a further adjournment, ICC-01/09-02/11, 3 December 2014

Prosecutor v Uhuru Muigai Kenyatta, Public redacted version of 'decision on commencement date of trial', ICC-01/09-02/11, 20 June 2013

Prosecutor v William Samoei Ruto and Joshua Arap Sang, Decision on Mr Ruto's request for excusal from continuous presence at trial, ICC-01/09-01/11, 18 June 2013

Prosecutor v William Samoei Ruto and Joseph Arap Sang, Decision on the appeals of Mr William Samoei Ruto and Mr Joshua Arap Sang against the decision n of Pre-Trial Chamber II of 23 January 2012 entitled 'Decision on the Confirmation of Charges Pursuant to Article 61(7)(a) and (b) of the Rome Statute', ICC-01/09-01/11, 24 May 2012

Prosecutor v William Samoei Ruto, Henry Kiprono Kosgey and Joseph Arap Sang, Decision on the Confirmation of Charges Pursuant to Article 61(7)(a) and (b) of the Rome Statute, ICC-01/09-01/11, 23 January 2012

Republic of Kenya, Office of the President, 'Cabinet Decides on TJRC', 30 July 2009

Republic of Kenya, Office of the President, 'Special Tribunal to be set up', 17 December 2008

Republic of Kenya, Office of the President, 'Statement by His Excellency Hon Mwai Kibaki CGH MP, President and Commander-in-Chief of the Defence Forces of the Republic of Kenya following the decision by the International Criminal Court Pre-Trial Chamber', 23 January 2012

Republic of Kenya, Response to the Report of the Special Rapporteur on Extrajudicial. Arbitrary or Summary Executions, Professor Philip Alston, on his Mission to Kenya from 16-25 February, 2009

United Nations General Assembly Human Rights Council, Working Group of the Universal Periodic Review, *Report of the Working Group on the Universal Periodic Review, Kenya*, A/HRC/15/8, 17 June 2010

United Nations Human Rights Committee, Concluding observations adopted by the Human Rights Committee at its 105th session, 9-27 July 2012, CCPR/C/KEN/CO/3, 26 July 2012

Chapter 5
Prosecuting Perpetrators

The OTP's primary objective was to ensure that those responsible for the post-election violence were held accountable through prosecutions. Since prosecuting all suspects persons went well beyond the OTP's limited capacity, it sought to encourage the government to assume responsibility for these cases at the first instance, with the threat of prosecutions in The Hague should the government fail to comply. The Prosecutor emphasised that 'the primary responsibility of investigating and prosecuting crimes committed on Kenyan territory, including those for which the ICC is competent, lies with the Kenyan authorities'.[1] In response to the OTP's application of pressure, the government gave regular assurances that it was committed to ending impunity and ensuring that post-election violence suspects faced domestic trials. These commitments took various forms, with promises to establish a special tribunal; expedite police and judicial reforms so that suspects could be tried by the ordinary criminal courts; use the TJRC to handle suspects; try perpetrators through regional courts; and voluntarily referring the cases to the ICC. This chapter considers the extent to which those responsible for the post-election violence were held accountable through domestic or international trials and the contribution influence, if any, that the OTP's strategy of positive complementarity had on those prosecutions.

1 A Yardstick for Success

According to the OTP's own measure, a 'major success' for the strategy of positive complementarity would be 'the absence of trials before [the ICC] as a consequence of the regular functioning of national institutions'.[2] The question then becomes: what

---

[1] Gekara Emeka-Mayaka Gekara, 'Ocampo to step in if Kenya does shoddy job', *Daily Nation*, 19 June (2009).

[2] Luis Moreno-Ocampo, 'Statement Made at the Ceremony for the Solemn Undertaking of the Chief Prosecutor of the ICC', The Hague, 16 June 2003 ('Moreno-Ocampo June 2003 Statement').

would have satisfied the OTP that Kenyan legal system was 'regularly functioning' in its handling of the post-election violence cases?

First, the OTP expected prosecutions of both the organisers of the violence as well as the direct perpetrators. This much is clear from the OTP's three-pronged strategy for accountability and its regular insistence that domestic proceedings complement the ICC cases to avoid any impunity gap.[3] In other words, the OTP recognised the need for prosecution of both the direct perpetrators of the violence ('low-level perpetrators') as well as those responsible for organising, funding and inciting the violence ('high-level perpetrators'). Kenyans agreed, emphasising the necessity of prosecuting both the 'small fish' and the 'big fish'. In my focus group interviews in Nairobi, Nakuru, Naivasha and Eldoret, participants expressed their frustrations over the lack of accountability following the 1992 and 1997 electoral violence and insisted that there would be no end to impunity unless the organisers and financiers of the 2007/08 violence faced criminal prosecutions. Many also stressed, however, the importance of prosecuting low-level perpetrators, including their neighbours and the police, for the crimes that they committed. In December 2008, a KNDR poll of 4,000 households found that 81 % of Kenyans wanted the government to prosecute the leaders of the political leaders of the violence, while 75 % wanted non-political leaders prosecuted.[4] Even after the ICC confirmed the charges against four suspects in January 2012, 69 % of Kenyan households still wanted to see low-level perpetrators prosecuted.[5] Kenyans therefore agreed with the OTP in its assessment that ending impunity required the prosecution of both high-level and low-level perpetrators.

The OTP would not, however, require that perpetrators be tried for crimes against humanity and would have been satisfied with prosecutions for serious crimes under domestic criminal law.[6] At the local level it was only possible to prosecute persons for crimes against humanity committed after 1 January 2009. Any attempt to prosecute post-election violence suspects for crimes against humanity committed during the post-election violence would have been challenged in court due to the

---

[3] 'The Prosecutor will present in court a limited number of cases, two or three, against those persons considered the most responsible. Only some of the gravest incidents will be presented at trial'. Anthony Kariuki, 'Ocampo: ICC has strong case in Kenya chaos', Daily Nation, 7 November (2009).

'We cannot prosecute thousands of people at The Hague. Young men raped and killed, but who gave the order? Who paid the money?' Anthony Kariuki, 'Ocampo says no suspects in Kenya chaos', *Daily Nation*, 8 May 2010.

We still emphasise the need for a special tribunal and other national proceedings to ensure a holistic approach to criminal responsibility for these crimes'. 'Justice beckons as Ocampo visits Kenya', *Daily Nation*, 6 May 2010.

[4] South Consulting, Kenya National Dialogue and Reconciliation Monitoring Project, *National Baseline Survey*, January 2009 ('KNDR Baseline Survey').

[5] South Consulting, Kenya National Dialogue and Reconciliation Monitoring Project, *Progress in the Implementation of the Constitution and Preparedness for 2012, Review Report, January 2012* ('KNDR January 2012 Report'), 56.

[6] *Prosecutor v Saif Al-Islam Gaddafi and Abdullah Al-Senussi*, Prosecution response to application on behalf of the Government of Libya pursuant to article 19 of the ICC statute, ICC-01/11-01/11, 5 June 2012, [23].

constitutional protection against retroactive prosecutions. Nevertheless, it would have still been possible to prosecute suspects for committing ordinary domestic crimes. The Kenyan penal code criminalised murder, manslaughter, assault, rape, sexual assault and other offences against the person. Further, section 21 permitted two or more persons to be prosecuted where they had formed 'a common intention to prosecute an unlawful purpose', while section 22 criminalised the incitement of another to commit a crime, thereby making it possible to prosecute high-level perpetrators at the local level for conspiracy and inchoate offences.

Although it may not have been possible to prosecute *all* suspects, the OTP may have expected that a prosecutorial policy be developed which outlined a transparent set of criteria to explain the strategy for identifying the suspects to be investigated and prosecuted.[7] This strategy might have been expected to have taken into consideration the fact that perpetrators, victims and witnesses may have travelled during and after the violence and the respective investigatory challenges that this presented.[8] The OTP might also have expected that the security of witnesses be guaranteed by a well-resourced witness protection programme. Finally, the OTP would wish that suspects holding public office be suspended from duties pending the outcome of their trial.

To what extent were the low-level and high-level perpetrators prosecuted, either at the local or the international level, for either ordinary crimes or crimes against humanity? Did the OTP's strategy of positive complementarity contribute to any progress made? Did categories of persons evade accountability and, if so, was that the result of a justifiable prosecutorial strategy or was there another explanation? Finally, did the prosecutions that did take place, either at the local level or at The Hague, make a significant contribution to ending impunity, or did serious impunity gaps remain?

2 The Small Fish

A prosecutorial strategy of sorts appears to have been initiated by the Minister for Internal Security, George Saitoti, in mid-2008. Saitoti told newspapers that he had drawn up a list of cases that were to be handled with particular speed.[9] Included within this list of priority cases were 103 that were already before the courts and another 137 involving suspects on remand. No details, however, were provided on the categories of persons being prosecuted, the crimes with which they were charged or the criteria used to select these cases. In addition, no updates were ever provided on what progress, if any, was made in the prosecution of these suspects. It appears that any strategy which did exist was quickly abandoned, with the Director of Public

---

[7] Office of the United Nations High Commissioner for Human Rights, *Rule-of-Law Tools for Post-Conflict States: Prosecution Initiatives* (Office of the United Nations High Commissioner for Human Rights, 2006), 7.
[8] Human Rights Watch, *Turning Pebbles: Evading Accountability for Post-Election Violence in Kenya, 2011*, 75 ('HRW, Turning Pebbles').
[9] Fred Mukinda, 'Police won't free suspects', *Daily Nation*, 1 June 2008.

Prosecutions ('DPP') later admitting that he was not aware of the existence of such a priority list of suspects.[10]

Evaluating the extent of prosecutions for post-election violence crimes is a challenging exercise due to a lack of publicly available data. Kenya's investigatory and prosecutorial organs consistently demonstrated a reluctance to respond to requests for information on the status of cases. In 2011, Human Rights Watch wrote letters and made phone calls to the Commissioner of Police and the Criminal Investigations Division ('CID') to enquire into the progress of investigations but received no response.[11] My own approaches to these and other investigatory and prosecutorial agents equally failed to uncover data. Nevertheless, it is possible to provide a cursory overview of the progress of cases involving low-level perpetrators by reference to a variety of sources. Kenya's investigatory and prosecutorial organs released five reports on the status of the cases.[12] These are of limited assistance, however, as they themselves are lacking in data and the small amount produced appears to be inconsistent and unreliable. At least four reports were completed but not made public, although some of their content was reported in newspapers.[13] A Human Rights Watch report examined 76 court files and conducted interviews with police prosecutors, defence lawyers, magistrates, judicial officials, local administrative officials and local civil society in an attempt to assess the progress that had been made in prosecuting post-election violence cases as of December 2012.[14] Local newspapers also provide some limited assistance in the form of occasional reports on some high-profile cases and quotes from politicians and police spokespersons on the progress of the post-election violence cases.

---

[10] HRW, Turning Pebbles (see Footnote 8), 17.

[11] Ibid, 9.

[12] Office of the Attorney General, Report from Director of Public Prosecutions Keriako Tabiko to Attorney General Amos Wako on Meeting Between the Director of Public Prosecutions and the Criminal Investigation Department on Post Election Violence Cases, 19 June 2008 ('DPP 2008 Report'); Director of Public Prosecutions, A report to the Hon. Attorney General by the team on the review of post election violence related cases in Western, Nyanza, Central, Rift Valley, Eastern, Coast and Nairobi Provinces, February 2009 ('AG 2009 Report'); Office of the Attorney General, A Progress Report to the Hon. Attorney-General by the Team on Update of Post Election Violence Related Cases in Western, Nyanza, Central, Rift valley, Eastern, Coast and Nairobi Provinces, March 2011 ('AG March 2011 Report'); Office of the President, Criminal Investigation Department, Post Election Violence Investigations Progress Report, 5 May 2011 ('CID May 2011 Report'); Office of the President, Report from Director of Criminal Investigations Ndegwa Muhoro to Director of Public Prosecutions, 'Re: Update on investigation into Six ICC Suspects', 1 July 2011 ('CID July 2011 Report').

[13] Oliver Mathenge, 'New report says 5,000 election violence cases stalled due to lack of evidence', *Daily Nation*, 7 January 2012 ('DPP January 2012 Report'); Jeremiah Kilang' at, 'Lack of evidence derails local trials', *Daily Nation*, 17 August 2012 ('DPP August 2012 Report'); Marybeth Wambugu, '54 jailed over gender based post election violence crimes', *The Star*, 5 September 2013 ('DPP September 2013 Report'); Kenyans for Peace with Truth and Justice and Human Rights Watch, 'Kenya: Local Judicial Mechanism Should Complement ICC Cases', Press Release, 27 April 2012 ('Working Group 2012 Report').

[14] HRW, Turning Pebbles (see Footnote 8), 9.

2.1 Prosecutions by Numbers

The first source is a seven-page report compiled by the DPP for the Attorney General on 19 June 2008, the same month in which the Waki Commission was established. This reveals that a meeting was held on 16 June 2008 at which the Attorney General directed a joint team of CID officers to 'undertake a thorough review and re-evaluation of cases relating to post election violence' and to report to him within two weeks. The same report provides a working definition of post-election violence crimes and an agreed methodology for the CID team.[15]

It took eight months for this 398-page report to be completed by 'a team of State Counsels'. This was forwarded to the Attorney General in February 2009, the same month in which Parliament debated the establishment of the special tribunal. This was forwarded to the Prosecutor on 14 July 2009, five days after Annan had delivered the sealed envelope to the Prosecutor. It was made public on 26 November 2009 when the Prosecutor exercised his *proprio motu* powers.[16] The data from this report is summarised below (Table 5.1).

According to this data, as of February 2009 (approximately 12 months after the cessation of hostilities), there had been just 84 concluded post-election violence cases. The body of the report does not detail how many of these cases resulted in convictions but this data may be obtained from its appendices. This reveals convictions in just 45 cases throughout the country, involving a mere 80 persons. Included within these figures are those cases and persons in which the accused, although convicted, received a discharge and therefore escaped criminal sanction penalty. Although the report lists a further 157 cases as pending before the court, upon the Attorney General's instruction just 69 were to 'proceed to their logical conclusion', with the remainder to be withdrawn. This suggests that at this time there was little prospect of securing a considerable number of further convictions in the near future. In terms of raw figures, in the 12 months following the conclusion of the post-election violence there was an appallingly low number of prosecutions for crimes committed during the violence and pitifully few convictions during this time.

It would take more than two years for the same team to prepare another report for the Attorney General.[17] This 83-page report was completed in March 2011 and a copy was forwarded to the Pre-Trial Chamber in support of the government's Article 19 application.[18] This recorded an extra five convictions against nine persons in Western Province, two convictions against three persons in the Rift Valley, 25 convictions against approximately 46 persons in Nyanza Province and five convictions against approximately seven persons in Nairobi. According to the statistical summary on page

---

[15] DPP 2008 Report (see Footnote 12).

[16] International Criminal Court, Situation in the Republic of Kenya, Request for authorisation of an investigation pursuant to Article 15, ICC-01/09, 26 November 2009 ('OTP Request for Authorisation'), [16], Annex 29.

[17] AG March 2011 Report (n 403).

[18] *Prosecutor v William Samoei Ruto, Henry Kiprono Kosgey and Joshua Arap Sang*, ICC-01/11, Application on Behalf of the Government of the Republic of Kenya Pursuant to Article 19 of the ICC Statute, ICC-01/09–01/11–19, 31 March 2011 ('Article 19 Application').

Table 5.1 Record of domestic prosecutions for post-election violence crimes (February 2009)

Province	Cases pending before the court	AG directs trials to proceed to their logical conclusion	AG directs cases to be withdrawn due to lack of evidence	AG directs that the cases be withdrawn for further investigations	Concluded cases	Convictions	Inquests	Cases where there are no known suspects/Cases under investigation
Rift Valley	106 cases	42 cases	48 cases	16 cases	29 cases	19 cases	158 files	3,325 cases
	504 persons	123 persons	196 persons	185 persons	58 persons	27 persons		
Western Province	23 cases	16 cases	7 cases	0	19 cases	11 cases	18 files	0
	51 persons	29 persons	22 persons		58 persons	24 persons		
Nyanza Province	21 cases	11 cases	9 cases	1 case	23 cases	15 cases	51 files	0
	42 persons	18 persons	18 persons	1 person	113 persons	29 persons		
Central Province	1 case	0	1 case	0	0	0	1 file	0
	3 persons		3 persons					
Eastern Province	0	0	0	0	0	0	0	0
Nairobi Province	No data available							
Coast Province	6 cases	No data available	65 cases	17 cases	13 cases	No data available	19 files	0
	79 persons		239 persons	186 persons	51 persons			
Totals	157 cases	69 cases	65 cases	17 cases	84 cases	45 cases	228 files	3325 cases
	976 persons	170 persons	239 persons	186 persons	280 persons	80 persons		

70 of the report, as of March 2011 there had been a total of 94 convictions for crimes committed during the post-election violence: Rift Valley (50), Western Province (7), Nyanza Province (25), Coastal Province (5) and Nairobi (7). DPP Keriako Tobiko was a little more optimistic in his explanations to the media the following month, claiming that 'over 700' trials had been concluded, with a conviction rate of approximately 50 %.[19] This would suggest that, by March 2011, more than three years after the end of the post-election violence, there had been between 94 and 350 convictions.

As the ICC's Pre-Trial Chamber and Appeals Chamber considered whether it had jurisdiction on the basis that the Kenyan government was 'unwilling or unable' to conduct genuine prosecutions, the government produced two further reports.[20] These two 'reports' (more accurately described as letters) were limited to the issue of the government's attempts to investigate and prosecute the Ocampo Six since that was the matter being decided by judges at the ICC. As such, neither source provides any further detail on the progress being made by the government in its prosecution of low-level perpetrators.

The CID and DPP completed a further report on the status of the post-election violence cases in January 2012 which was leaked to the *Daily Nation* just days before the Pre-Trial Chamber's decision on whether to confirm the charges against the Ocampo Six.[21] This revealed that of the 6,081 post-election violence cases, approximately 500 had been prosecuted, resulting in 258 convictions. This figure suggests that Tobiko's claim nine months earlier that 'over 700' trials had been concluded, with a conviction rate of around 50 % was somewhat misleading. The report, which was prepared for the Attorney General, recommended that the government set up a multi-agency task force with officers from the Ministry of Internal Security, the DPP and the CID 'to urgently undertake a countrywide review of all the cases pending investigation and those cases pending trial'.

The DPP established such a multi-agency task force in February 2012. Chaired by Deputy DPP Dorcas Oduor, the agency comprised officers from the State Law Office, the Ministry of Justice, Kenya Police, the Witness Protection Agency and the DPP. The taskforce was made responsible for reviewing the progress of the post-election violence cases and to make recommendations on future prosecutions.[22] The task force completed its work in August 2012 and a summary of its conclusions were published in the *Daily Nation*[23]. This contained no further details on the number of prosecutions or convictions, but did reveal that most of the 8,869 reported post-election violence cases would not be prosecuted locally due to a lack of evidence. This report does not appear to have been made public.

In the meantime, the Attorney General established a working group of ten prominent Kenyan and international lawyers in March 2012 to advise the government on how to

---

[19] Bernard Naumnane, 'Kenya's fresh bid to stop Ocampo', *Daily Nation*, 22 April 2011.

[20] CID May 2011 Report (see Footnote 12); CID July 2011 Report (see Footnote 12).

[21] DPP January 2012 Report (see Footnote 13).

[22] 'Multi-agency task force on post-election violence begins sittings', *NAM News Network*, 11 February 2012.

[23] Working Group 2012 Report (see Footnote 13).

respond to the confirmation of charges against the Ocampo Four. This report was also not made public but, according to Human Rights Watch, journalists who had seen it said that the working group had concluded that there was no comprehensive government policy for dealing with crimes committed during the post-election violence.[24]

A further report appears to have been completed by the DPP sometime in September 2013 but again this does not seem to have been made public.[25] This does not provide any updates on overall figures, but instead focuses on crimes of gender-based violence. It also does not appear to provide any data on the number of convictions, merely stating that 'out of the 369 cases that were reported, 163 were taken to court and that 122 of them have been concluded'.

What conclusions may be drawn from this data on the extent of local prosecutions? Assuming the government's data is accurate, there were 8,869 reported post-election violence cases. By January 2012, four years had elapsed since the commencement of the violence and just 258 convictions had been secured. No further updates on the number of convictions were provided in the following two years but a significant increase in the rate of prosecutions or convictions would appear to be highly unlikely for three reasons. First, the time that had elapsed since the events in question would make it extremely difficult for prosecutors to gather sufficient evidence to support a conviction. Forensic and documentary evidence is likely to have been destroyed and there is the increasing likelihood that witnesses would recant their testimony or disappear.[26] Second, if such an increase were to have occurred, one might have expected the government to have reported this widely to bolster its claims to be ending impunity and justify its insistence that trials in The Hague be returned to Nairobi. The fact that there was no such wave of publicity suggests that little or no progress has been made. Finally, the government itself admitted on multiple occasions that it was having great difficulty securing convictions and that the vast majority of the post-election violence cases would not be prosecuted.[27] It is therefore reasonable to conclude that, of the 8,869 reported post-election violence cases, just 258 resulted in a conviction. This means a conviction rate of less than three percent. Included within this number are perpetrators who, although convicted, escaped any form of punishment by reason of having been discharged. It must also be recalled that a significant number of crimes went unreported, either because victims feared for their security or considered reporting crimes to the police to be futile. All of this provides compelling evidence to suggest that the overwhelming majority of persons responsible for crimes committed during the post-election violence entirely avoided accountability for their actions.

---

[24] Working Group 2012 Report (see Footnote 13).

[25] DPP September 2013 Report (see Footnote 13).

[26] Kenyans for Peace with Truth and Justice and Kenya Human Rights Commission, *Securing Justice: Establishing a Domestic Mechanism for the 2007/08 Post-Election Violence in Kenya* (Kenyans for Peace with Truth and Justice and Kenya Human Rights Commission, 2013), 11.

[27] Jeremiah Kilang'at, 'Lack of evidence derails local trials', *Daily Nation*, 17 August 2012; Oliver Mathenge, 'New report says 5,000 election violence cases stalled due to lack of evidence', *Daily Nation*, 7 January 2012; 'CID report says no charge can hold for PEV perpetrators', *Standard*, 16 February 2014.

2.2 Prosecutions by Crimes

The only reasonable justification for such a small number of convictions is if, owing to a lack of resources, the government adopted and pursued a prosecutorial strategy that focussed on the most serious crimes and the leaders of the violence. Once again, the data in this regard is far from comprehensive but the limited amount that does exist does support the existence of such a targeted prosecutorial strategy. Rather, it suggests that the vast majority of convictions were for less serious offences. The most detailed government report on the types of crimes prosecuted is in the report prepared for the Attorney General in February 2009 which recorded 84 prosecutions and 45 convictions by that time.[28] This report contained no details of any convictions for murder, rape, sexual assault or other serious offences against the person. Indeed, although more than 3,000 Rift Valley cases were listed as pending, not one related to an allegation of sexual violence. Instead, prosecutions tended to focus on minor offences such as obstruction of a police officer, conveying suspected stolen property, publishing false rumour and creating a disturbance.

According to the Waki Report 1,113 persons were killed during the violence.[29] Despite this, the DPP August 2012 Report revealed that just 152 murder files had been opened, of which only four had proceeded to trial, resulting in just two convictions. The first of these convictions occurred in July 2009 when the Kericho High Court found Robert Kemboi and Kirkland Langat guilty of murdering two police officers in Kisii District on 31 December 2007.[30] The two men were sentenced to death, but later had their sentence commuted to life imprisonment. The Court of Appeal, however, later overturned each of these convictions.[31] This therefore meant that the only post-election violence suspect to be convicted of murder was Paul Ruto, who was sentenced to life imprisonment by the Nakuru High Court in June 2012 for the murder of Kamau Kimani Thiongo on 1 January 2008.[32] While delivering her verdict, Justice Roselyan Wendoh questioned why the prosecution had not arrested two other suspects who during the course of the trial were identified as accomplices.[33] A third high-profile murder conviction, that of John Mwaniki, who was sentenced to 30 years in prison for his role in a mob attack in Molo, cannot be categorised as a successful post-election violence conviction since the incident took place on 27 November 2007, prior to the commencement of the post-election violence period.[34]

Other homicide trials did not lead to a conviction due to a lack of evidence. The most infamous example concerned the trial of four persons for their alleged role in the

---

[28] AG 2009 Report (see Footnote 12).

[29] *Final Report from Kenya's Commission of Inquiry into Post-Election Violence*, 15 October 2008, 305 ('Waki Report').

[30] Peter Mutai, 'Two to hang for killing policeman in poll upheaval', *Standard*, 31 July 2009.

[31] Wanjiru Macharia, 'Court frees two convicts in murder case', *Daily Nation*, 21 December 2012.

[32] Patrick Kibet, 'Man jailed for life over poll violence', *Standard*, 13 June 2012.

[33] Ibid.

[34] HRW, Turning Pebbles (see Footnote 8), 9.

Kiambaa church incident.[35] On 1 January 2008 mattresses and blankets were set ablaze with petrol and thrown into the church in which Kikuyu women and children had sought refuge. Seventeen persons were burned alive, while another 11 died on their way to hospital.[36] In delivering his judgment, Justice David Maraga expressed his 'outrage' at the behaviour of the police, describing their investigations as 'shoddy', before acquitting all four suspects.[37] Despite the fact that victims had recorded statements with police that identified many of the hundreds of persons responsible for the incident, no other suspects were arrested or brought to trial.[38]

Sexual and gender-based violence crimes also went largely unpunished. The Waki Report concluded that during the post-election violence there were more than 900 documented acts of rape and other forms of sexual violence, with many more cases unreported.[39] Despite this, the government's own data reveals that in the 12 months following the post-election violence not a single file had been opened for a crime of sexual violence. Even as late as August 2012, just 150 files had been opened for rape and other sexual assault crimes.[40] Details on how many of these cases resulted in convictions were not made public, but the AG March 2011 Report had earlier recorded that there had been 49 convictions for gender-based violence.[41] In September 2013, these figures were updated and it was reported that 54 persons had been imprisoned for gender-based violence.[42] There is good reason, however, to doubt the accuracy of the government's figures. According to Human Rights Watch, four of the claimed convictions actually resulted in acquittals, while two of the alleged 'convictions on gender-based post-election violence cases' involved men who were convicted of having 'carnal knowledge with a sheep'.[43] Other cases resulted in an acquittal on the sexual assault charges and a conviction for less serious offences, while for at least nine files the convictions appeared to be wholly unrelated to the post-election violence.[44] Human Rights Watch concluded that it was unclear whether there had been a single conviction for sexual and gender-based offences arising out of the post-election violence.[45]

It would also appear that there were very few prosecutions for property offences committed during the post-election violence. The Waki Report estimated that more than 80,000 houses, government buildings, businesses and vehicles were destroyed throughout the country.[46] The DPP August 2012 Report, however, revealed that just 3,446 property-related files had been opened, resulting in just 11 convictions.[47]

---

[35] *Republic v Stephen Kiprotich Leting & 3 others* [2009] eKLR, Criminal Case 34 of 2008.
[36] Waki Report (see Footnote 28), 46.
[37] *Republic v Leting* [2009] (see Footnote 34).
[38] HRW, Turning Pebbles (see Footnote 8), 30.
[39] Waki Report (see Footnote 28), 248.
[40] DPP August 2012 Report (see Footnote 13).
[41] AG March 2011 Report (see Footnote 12).
[42] DPP September 2013 Report (see Footnote 13).
[43] HRW, Turning Pebbles (see Footnote 8), 25.
[44] HRW, Turning Pebbles, (see Footnote 8), 25–26.
[45] Ibid, 26.
[46] Waki Report (see Footnote 28), 338–341.
[47] DPP August 2012 Report (see Footnote 13).

Finally, there also appears to have been only a small number of prosecutions for crimes against the person. The Waki Report documented 3,561 cases of persons being seriously injured during the post-election violence, often by guns, arrows and machetes.[48] Considering that there were only around 258 convictions for *all* crimes, it must be concluded that the overwhelming majority of persons responsible for crimes against the person also escaped criminal prosecution.

The above evidence suggests that the vast majority of low-level perpetrators responsible for the crimes committed during the post-election violence were never the subject of investigation. Of those cases that were investigated, very few ever made it to the trial stage. Of those cases that made it to court, most resulted either in acquittals or convictions on less serious charges. Apart from a small number of notable exceptions, low-level perpetrators who participated in the post-election violence completely avoided any form of accountability for their crimes.

2.3 The OTP's Influence

This then raises the question as to the extent to which the OTP's strategy of positive complementarity served as a catalyst for these small number of prosecutions. Once again, making this assessment is difficult due to the scarcity of publicly available data and the inaccuracies known to exist in that data. The first published data set is a report to the Attorney General from February 2009, which recorded 350 'concluded cases', of which 84 had resulted in convictions.[49] By this time, the OTP's actions were limited to the issuance of a 48-word statement in February 2008 and requests for further information that were made the following month.[50] This limited OTP involvement must be contrasted with the developments that were taking place at the local level during this period. By the time of the February 2009 report, the Waki Report had been published, the sealed envelope had come into existence and a special tribunal had been debated as an alternative to the ICC. Certainly the ICC's potential intervention may have had *some* influence on these prosecutions. Having said that, a mere 84 convictions (mostly for minor property offences) during a 12-month period can hardly be regarded as a major influence, particularly since effectively all of those responsible for murder, sexual violence and other offences against the person avoided criminal prosecution.

As suggested in the previous chapter, it was not until after the production of the February 2009 report that the OTP most actively pursued its strategy of positive complementarity. Between June 2009 and November 2009, the Prosecutor met with Kenyan officials on four occasions, took delivery of the sealed envelope, entered into a complementarity contract, outlined a division of labour, threatened international prosecutions and used his *proprio motu* powers. A March 2011 DPP report

---

[48] Ibid, 346.
[49] AG 2009 Report (see Footnote 12).
[50] International Criminal Court Office of the Prosecutor, 'OTP Statement in Relation to Events in Kenya', 5 February 2008 ('OTP February 2008 Statement'); OTP Request for Authorisation (see Footnote 16).

records that by that time there had been 94 convictions.[51] In other words, if this data is accurate, during the two years in which the OTP was imposing its greatest amount of pressure, there were a mere 10 convictions for post-election violence crimes at the local level. Once again, impunity continued to prevail for the perpetrators of the most serious crimes. It would therefore seem fair to conclude that the OTP's strategy of positive complementarity had little or no impact in serving as a catalyst for domestic prosecutions.

3 The Big Fish

The Waki Report concluded that politicians, businesspersons, religious leaders and tribal elders held meetings in town halls to organise the attacks, during which they promised cash payments to those who participated in the violence.[52] While the Waki Commission did not publicly name suspected perpetrators, the KNCHR report *On the Brink of a Precipice* named 219 persons believed to have organised, funded and incited the violence, including 20 MPs.[53] In addition, on 15 December 2010, the ICC Prosecutor named six persons whom he believed bore the greatest responsibility for the crimes against humanity committed during the violence, including three government ministers and two senior public servants.[54]

Despite this, no politician, businessperson, religious leader or tribal elder was ever held accountable at the local level for their role in organising the violence. The most infamous example of a senior figure evading prosecution was that of ODM politician Jackson Kibor. With the violence still ongoing, Kibor was interviewed by the BBC and used the opportunity to call for the removal of Kikuyu persons from Eldoret as part of a 'war'.[55] Kibor was arrested and charged with incitement to violence, but the Attorney General used his *nolle prosequi* powers to withdraw the case from prosecution. Another infamous example concerned former MP David Manyara and prominent businessman Zakayo Maina, who were arrested upon suspicion of funding some of the crimes committed by Mungiki members during the violence. The two men were later released without charge and, according to one lawyer, their case file then disappeared.[56]

---

[51] AG March 2011 Report (see Footnote 12).
[52] Waki Report (see Footnote 28), vii.
[53] Kenya National Commission on Human Rights, *On the brink of the precipice: a human rights account of Kenya's post-2007 election violence*, 15 August 2008 ('KNCHR Post-Election Violence Report').
[54] Situation in the Republic of Kenya, Prosecutor's Application Pursuant to Article 58 as to William Samoei Ruto, Henry Kiprono Kosgey and Joshua Arap Sang, Public Redacted Version of Document ICC-01/09-30-Conf-Exp, 15 December 2010 ('OTP Kenya One Application'); Situation in the Republic of Kenya, Prosecutor's Application Pursuant to Article 58 as to Francis Kirimi Muthaura, Uhuru Muigai Kenyatta and Mohammed Hussein Ali, Public Redacted Version of Document ICC-01/09-31-Conf-Exp, 15 December 2010 ('OTP Kenya Two Application').
[55] HRW, Turning Pebbles (see Footnote 8), 32.
[56] Ibid, 55.

Members of the police force also evaded accountability. The Waki Report found that Kenya's security forces were responsible for 405 deaths.[57] Despite this, just one case against a member of the security forces is known to have made it to trial, that of police officer Edward Kirui who was caught on film firing upon two unarmed protesters.[58] Although the film was admitted into evidence and 21 witnesses gave evidence against Kirui, Justice Fred Ochieng acquitted the accused on the basis that the prosecution had failed to prove that the bullets found in the victims' bodies matched the gun used by the officer.[59] The serial number of the murder weapon was identical to that issued to Kirui on the day of the shootings, but for the addition of the number '2' to the latter serial number. A representative from ICJ-Kenya described the trial as 'a classic case of police officers tampering with evidence in order to cover up for their colleague'.[60] The Waki Report also found that 'significant numbers of security forces' were responsible for crimes of sexual violence[61] but that, more than seven months after the post-election violence had ceased, 'no internal investigations into the conduct of police officers were being undertaken or contemplated'.[62] Similarly, Human Rights Watch noted that 'not a single police officer [had] been convicted for shootings or rapes directly related to the violence'.[63]

It can therefore be concluded that there was no serious attempt to try high-level perpetrators at the local level. Human Rights Watch's review of 76 post-election violence cases led that organisation to conclude that 'not one demonstrates any attempt to investigate those responsible for organising and directing the violence'.[64] Further, according to some journalists and civil society groups, the Working Group 2012 Report written by ten senior Kenyan and international lawyers was not made public because it concluded that Kenya lacked the political will to try the most senior perpetrators of the post-election violence.[65]

4 The Foreign Affairs Façade

Although the government made no serious attempt to prosecute either low-level or high-level perpetrators, it nevertheless continued to assure the OTP and the international community that it remained committed to trying the post-election violence cases at the local level. This 'foreign affairs façade' appears to have been created to protect Kenya's international reputation and to prevent the cases from being

---

[57] Waki Report (see Footnote 28), 331.
[58] 'It wasn't me, says officer accused of poll killings', *Daily Nation*, 30 April 2010.
[59] Humphrey Malalo, 'Kenya court acquits policeman of election killings', *Reuters*, 21 June 2010.
[60] HRW, Turning Pebbles (see Footnote 8), 34.
[61] Ibid, 349.
[62] Waki Report (see Footnote 28), 404.
[63] HRW, Turning Pebbles (see Footnote 8), 4.
[64] Ibid, 29.
[65] Working Group 2012 Report (see Footnote 13).

transferred to The Hague. In other words, despite the absence of investigations and prosecutions, the government sought to give the impression that progress was being made throughout this period. This foreign affairs façade began with the publication of the Waki Report, continued after the OTP commenced official investigations and remained in place even after the announcement of the Ocampo Six. It can be seen as having three phases. First, promises to establish a special tribunal; second, assurances that post-election violence suspects would be tried by local courts after the new Constitution was passed; and finally, the government's assertions that it was investigating the culpability of the Ocampo Six.

4.1 The Special Tribunal and Motion Without Movement

The first such example of this façade was the government's assurances in late 2008 and early 2009 that it would establish a special tribunal to try the post-election violence suspects. On 17 December 2008, Kibaki and Odinga signed an agreement to establish the tribunal, as required by the Waki Report.[66] The two principals promised 'accountability against persons bearing the greatest responsibility for crimes against humanity relating to the 2007 general elections'.[67] One month later, Kibaki issued a press release declaring that he was shortening Parliament's New Year recess to enable it 'to reconvene and deliberate and conclude important legislative matters that remained outstanding', with many understanding this to be an assurance of commitment to the special tribunal.[68] Despite these public commitments, the principals did very little to encourage their fellow parliamentarians to support the proposed legislation.[69] When the legislation debated by the National Assembly, MPs belied the lack of political leadership and pleaded with Kibaki and Odinga to express their support for the proposed special tribunal.[70] Mutula Kilonzo, who would later go on to become Justice Minister, criticised Kibaki and Odinga for being absent from the debate and said that they were 'failing in leadership'.[71] Indeed, the only evidence of the principals taking any proactive steps to secure the safe passage of the legislation occurred on 12 February 2009 when Kibaki wrote a letter to 80 MPs, directing them to attend Parliament to support the legislation.[72] The legislation was defeated later that same day, with Odinga not even present for the vote and no explanation provided for his absence.[73] Odinga was later to claim that he and Kibaki had

---

[66] Office of the President, 'Special Tribunal to be set up', 17 December 2008.
[67] Ibid.
[68] Office of the President, 'Parliament to reconvene on 20th January', 8 January 2009.
[69] International Centre for Policy and Conflict, *Post Election Violence: A Trail of Lies and Betrayal*, 2009 ('ICPC 2009 Report'), 7.
[70] Hansard, National Assembly, Official Report, 27 January 2009; Hansard, National Assembly, Official Report, 5 February 2009.
[71] Hansard, National Assembly, Official Report, 3 February 2009.
[72] Hansard, National Assembly, Official Report, 12 February 2009.
[73] Ibid.

'tried very hard to set up a local tribunal' and had 'spent eight hours in Parliament', although Hansard makes no record of this.[74] The Justice Minister, Martha Karua, who sponsored the legislation, later claimed that Kibaki and Odinga had provided 'little or no support' as it was being debated in Parliament.[75]

Nevertheless, just two days after Parliament's rejection of the special tribunal, Odinga issued a press release in which he said that its establishment was essential as it was the only mechanism suitable for trying the post-election violence suspects.[76] Later that week, Odinga assured Annan that the government remained committed to establishing the special tribunal as promised and persuaded him to grant an extension to the Waki deadline.[77] In the four months that followed, however, no discernible progress was made towards the establishment of the special tribunal. Kibaki and Odinga appear to have been disingenuous in their expressions of support for the special tribunal, with human rights activist Muthoni Wanyeki described this period as one of 'motion without movement'.[78]

A second attempt to establish the special tribunal was made in July 2009, the same month in which the Prosecutor took delivery of the sealed envelope. Although the special tribunal was again rejected, the government nevertheless insisted that it remained committed to holding post-election violence suspects accountable. A press release stated that its opposition to the special tribunal did not 'in any way reduce its desire to punish impunity' and that the TJRC would be employed to 'deal with post-election violence perpetrators'.[79] The TJRC, which was never intended to have a prosecutorial function, would have required a radical amendment to its founding statute in order to handle the thousands of post-election violence cases. No attempt was made to discuss these proposed changes with the TJRC's chairman, Bethuel Kiplagat and, ultimately, no such amendments were made.[80] The TJRC completed its work in May 2013 and never at any stage during its existence took steps to 'deal with' the post-election violence suspects.

Also in July 2009, the government promised accelerated reforms of the police and judiciary to allow the trial of suspects locally. More than two years later, however, Chief Justice Willy Mutunga described the judiciary as 'an institution so frail in its structures; so thin on resources; so low on its confidence; so deficient in integrity; so weak in its public support that to have expected it to deliver justice was to be wildly optimistic'.[81] This again suggests that the government was merely giving the appearance of being committed to prosecuting post-election violence suspects. It

---

[74] 'Kenyatta and Odinga in first Kenya presidential debate', *BBC News*, 11 February 2013; Sarah McGregor, 'Kenya must revive plan to create "credible" court, Odinga says', *Bloomberg*, 2 February 2011.
[75] Martin Mutua, 'Karua: Principals a stumbling block', *Standard*, 16 July 2009.
[76] 'How Kenya handled local tribunal process', *Daily Nation*, 17 September 2013.
[77] Abiya Ochola, 'Annan to delay envelope for two more months', *Standard*, 18 February 2009.
[78] Interview with Muthoni Wanyeki (Nairobi, 7 May 2010).
[79] Office of the President, 'Cabinet Decides on TJRC', 30 July 2009 ('Cabinet July 2009 Statement').
[80] Interview with Bethuel Kiplagat (Nairobi, 18 May 2010).
[81] Tom Maliti, 'Kenyan Chief Justice outlines progress in judicial transformation', *The International Criminal Court Kenya Monitor*, 25 October 2011.

would seem that the primary motivation for this lip service was the OTP's threat of international prosecutions. The government made these announcements two weeks after the delivery of the sealed envelope and three weeks after agreeing to the complementarity contract. The first resolution in the statement made explicit reference to the ICC. It also proclaimed that Kenya would 'not stand for impunity', just as a government delegation had said to the Prosecutor in The Hague earlier in the month.[82]

As evidence of this commitment to try suspects locally, the delegation delivered the 398-page AG 2009 Report to the Prosecutor detailing the progress that had been made up until February 2009.[83] This Report, however, in fact revealed that in 'a very high number of cases', a filed complaint was met with 'no subsequent follow-up' and that for many killings, inquest files were never opened.[84] In October 2009, Kibaki and Odinga assured Annan that it was 'accelerating the reform of the judiciary to be better placed to handle the bulk of the cases'.[85] This statement, however, was made during the midst of a two-month parliamentary recess.[86]

Despite committing to expedited reforms of the criminal justice system and the TJRC, these did not proceed in the second half of 2009. Instead, the government again threw its support behind a local mechanism. This may have been prompted by the Prosecutor's statement in August 2009 that he would be 'be closely monitoring the judicial mechanism that will be set up'.[87] The Justice Minister, Mutula Kilonzo, said that the TJRC proposal was unworkable and expressed his support for a third attempt to establish the special tribunal.[88] Kibaki and Odinga met with the Prosecutor in Nairobi on 5 November 2009 and again proclaimed that 'the government [remained] fully committed to [discharging] its primary responsibility in accordance with the Rome Statute to establish a local judicial mechanism to deal with the perpetrators of the post election violence'.[89] Less than one week later, a revised proposal for the special tribunal was introduced into Parliament but debates were boycotted by Kibaki, Odinga, Kilonzo and other senior government ministers.

4.2 *Justice Delayed but Justice Assured*

This foreign affairs façade continued even after the OTP commenced its investigations in Kenya. The government promised that local prosecutions would complement those in The Hague once a new Constitution had been passed. In March 2010,

---

[82] International Criminal Court Office of the Prosecutor, 'ICC Prosecutor Receives Materials on Post-Election Violence in Kenya', 16 July 2009 ('OTP First Statement on the Sealed Envelope').
[83] Ibid.
[84] Ibid.
[85] 'Kenya defends its reform record', *Capital News*, 5 October 2009.
[86] Dave Opiyo, 'Campaigners drum up support for Imanyara Bill', *Daily Nation*, 29 August 2009.
[87] 'Kenyan Cabinet in the eye of a storm', *Daily Nation*, 1 August 2009; Lucas Barasa, 'The Hague moving in for country's trials', *Daily Nation*, 27 August 2009.
[88] Ibid.
[89] Judie Kaberia, 'Kenya remains defiant over ICC trials' *Capital News* 5 November 2009.

Kilonzo promised that 'although I lost (on the special tribunal), I will come back to you (once the new Constitution is passed) and ask you to support us to try those people who committed crimes'.[90] The new Constitution was promulgated on 27 August 2010 and in the following month, Kilonzo reiterated that the reforms that would follow from this would make it possible for post-election violence cases to be heard by local courts.[91] Again, however, there is no evidence of any significant progress having been made in the investigation and prosecution of the post-election violence suspects during this period.

Approximately four months after Kenyans voted to adopt a new Constitution, the Prosecutor named the Ocampo Six. On the day of this announcement, Kibaki again affirmed that 'the government [was] fully committed to the establishment of a local tribunal to deal with those behind the post-election violence, in accordance with the stipulations of the new Constitution'.[92] On the following day, Odinga told Parliament that Cabinet was looking to 'establish a credible local process'.[93]

The government told the Pre-Trial Chamber in March 2011 that it was still six months from being able to fully conduct its own investigations. It argued that 'the adoption of the new Constitution and associated reforms [had] opened the way for Kenya to conduct its own prosecutions in Kenya' and promised that these reforms would be completed by the end of September 2011.[94] The Attorney General, who had not provided any report on the status of the post-election violence cases for over two years, assembled a team to provide an update on their progress and within three months of the announcement of the Ocampo Six a report was completed.[95] This report, however, was hastily compiled, contradicted the earlier report in places and included within its list of post-election violence convictions cases that actually resulted in acquittals and cases that were wholly unrelated to the post-election violence.[96] As the ICC judges considered the government's application, Wako released a letter addressed to the Police Commissioner in which he ordered that 'all cases pending investigations [be] concluded expeditiously and the investigation file submitted to [him] for appropriate directions'.[97] The government provided two further reports on the status of the cases in May 2011 and July 2011 but these were just four pages and six pages in length, respectively. Each report contained numerous typographical and spelling errors and contained very little new information, instead providing a narrative on the post-election violence and vague promises to continue investigations and prosecutions.[98] The government then

---

[90] Alphonce Shundu, 'Mutula Kilonzo vows new quest for Kenya's violence tribunal', *Daily Nation*, 23 March 2010.
[91] Lucas Barasa, 'Mutula to Ocampo: quit Kenyan probe', *Daily Nation*, 18 September 2010.
[92] Statement by His Excellency the President Hon Mwai Kibaki, Kenya State House, 15 December 2010.
[93] Hansard, National Assembly, Official Report, 16 December 2010.
[94] Ibid, [5].
[95] AG March 2011 Report (see Footnote 12).
[96] HRW, Turning Pebbles (see Footnote 8), 25–26.
[97] State Law Office, Letter from the Attorney General, Amos Wako, to the Commissioner of Police, Mathew Iteere, dated 14 April 2011 ('AG April 2011 Letter').
[98] CID May 2011 Report (see Footnote 12); CID July 2011 Report (see Footnote 12).

failed to meet its own deadline of 30 September 2011 for the commencement of local investigations and prosecutions. Despite the government's regular assurances, a special tribunal was never established, post-election violence suspects were never handled by the TJRC and the promised judicial and police reforms were not expedited.

4.3 Investigating the Ocampo Six

Perhaps the best example of this foreign affairs façade concerns the government's spurious attempts to prosecute the Ocampo Six. As early as August 2008, the KNCHR publicly named five members of the Ocampo Six as being persons suspected of having been involved in the post-election violence.[99] My interviews conducted in March 2010 and April 2010 revealed that victims of the post-election violence wanted to see the ICC prosecute three persons who would ultimately become members of the Ocampo Six—Ruto, Kenyatta and Ali. An Infotrak Research and Consulting poll conducted in the days following the announcement of the Ocampo Six revealed that nearly half of those surveyed were not surprised by the Prosecutor's choice of suspects.[100] As such, one might have expected the Kenyan authorities to have been conducting their own investigations into the Ocampo Six prior to the Prosecutor's announcement.

Despite this, there is no evidence that there had been any serious local investigations into the Ocampo Six's alleged role in organising, funding and inciting the violence. Indeed, in one document, the government admitted that there were no ongoing investigations against the Ocampo Six as of December 2010 when the Prosecutor made his announcement. A letter marked 'confidential' which was sent from the CID Director to the DPP on 5 May 2011 was made public as part of the government's Article 19 application to the ICC. The letter contains the following paragraph, which has been quoted *ver batim*:

> When the ICC Prosecutor finally disclosed the names of what came to be known as the ocampo six, the Police investigators were taken by surprise. This was because other than Hon William Ruto, non of the members of the ocampo six have been mentioned previously during the investigations. Nevertheless, the Commissioner of Police again tasked the team of investigators to carry out exhaustive investigations relating to the Ocampo six and other high ranking citizens.[101]

The government gave no reasons for why investigations failed to proceed against the Ocampo Six, leaving it up to senior English barristers to provide an explanation. They told the ICC's Pre-Trial Chamber that the lack of investigations against the Ocampo Six was because the government had made the decision to pursue a 'bottom-up' approach.

---

[99] The only member of the Ocampo Six not named in the KNCHR report was Francis Muthaura.

[100] Dave Opiyo, 'Kenyans not ready to re-elect Hague suspects: poll', *Daily Nation*, 18 December 2010.

[101] CID May 2011 Report (see Footnote 12).

According to their submissions, this strategy commenced with 'investigations against low-level perpetrators' which would serve as 'the foundation for extending investigations to senior leaders associated with the ODM and PNU for the most serious incidents'.[102] Given the observations made above regarding the lack of investigations and prosecutions associated with low-level perpetrators, this argument would also appear to be disingenuous.

With the ICC trials entering their pre-trial stages, the government increased its efforts to demonstrate that the post-election violence cases were being investigated and prosecuted locally. This included the government's Article 19 application challenging the admissibility of the Ocampo Six cases at the ICC on the ground that Kenyan authorities were conducting investigations.[103] The length of time taken by the government to commence investigations into the Ocampo Six is also indicative of the absence of a genuine commitment. The Waki Commission took less than four months to compile its list of high-level suspects who were named in the sealed envelope. The KNCHR took less than five months to name 219 high-level suspects. Nevertheless, the government's submission was that a delay of more than three years for the commencement of investigations against senior leaders could be justified.

Even if this justification is accepted, this does not explain why no attempt was made to prosecute these persons within Kenya *after* December 2010 when the Prosecutor publicly named them as suspects. The official government position was that investigations commenced immediately after the announcement of the Ocampo Six. One day after the Prosecutor's announcement, Odinga told Parliament that Cabinet's first preference was to 'establish a credible local process for the investigation and prosecution of the six persons'.[104] This was confirmed by the confidential letter of 5 May 2011, which again has been quoted *ver batim*:

> Following the disclosure by ICC prosecutor, Mr Louise Moren Ocampo of the involvement of prominent personalities (Ocampo six) in the post election violence, the Commissioner of Police has further directed the team to exhaustively investigate all the allegations.[105]

When the Pre-Trial Chamber was asked to consider this issue, however, it found that there was no 'documentary proof that there is or has been an investigation'.[106]

Two days after the Pre-Trial Chamber's decision, the Director of the CID wrote to the DPP, informing him that a team of ten senior police officers had been appointed and was 'on the ground conducting investigations as directed into all allegations made against the six ICC suspects'.[107] The letter advised that the team

---

[102] Article 19 Application (see Footnote 18), [34].

[103] Article 19 Application (see Footnote 18).

[104] Hansard, National Assembly, Official Report, 16 December 2010.

[105] CID May 2011 Report (see Footnote 12).

[106] Situation in the Republic of Kenya, Decision on the Request for Assistance Submitted on Behalf of the Government of the Republic of Kenya Pursuant to Article 93(10) of the Statute and Rule 194 of the Rules of Procedure and Evidence, Pre-Trial Chamber II, ICC-01/09, 29 June 2011 ('PTC Article 19 Decision'), [34].

[107] CID July 2011 Report (see Footnote 12).

had interviewed 'about 35 witnesses' but that 'to date no evidence [had] been received from any of these witnesses which could link any of the suspects to the crimes as alleged by the ICC Prosecutor, or any other crimes'.[108] In the following month, detectives questioned Ruto, Kosgey and Sang over their alleged role in the violence.[109] These interviews took place at the same time that the ICC's Appeals Chamber was reviewing the Pre-Trial Chamber's conclusion that there had been no local investigations of the Ocampo Six. The Appeals Chamber then unanimously dismissed the government's appeal and there appears to be no evidence of any further investigations taking place after this August 2011 decision.[110] Ultimately, the DPP never charged any member of the Ocampo Six with any crime arising out of the post-election violence.

In summary, one impact of the OTP's strategy of positive complementarity was to encourage the government to provide constant assurances that it was working to prosecute suspects, notwithstanding the fact that little or no progress was actually being made in this regard. In maintaining this foreign affairs façade, the government offered illusory undertakings that it would establish a special tribunal, try suspects through the TJRC, expedite criminal justice reforms (both before and after the passing of a new Constitution) and conduct investigations into the Ocampo Six. In other words, the OTP did not so much encourage the government to end impunity as much as it encouraged the government to give the appearance of ending impunity.

5   Kenyans in The Hague

5.1   *Local Support for ICC Intervention*

As no politician, businessperson, police officer or any other senior person was ever convicted at the local level for their involvement in the post-election violence, the prosecution of high-level perpetrators was limited to the two trials at the ICC. Although the Prosecutor had expressed a desire to have an impact in Kenya by the time of the 2013 elections, as Kenyans went to the polls neither of these trials had commenced. Nevertheless, it is possible that the progress of the cases through the pre-trial stage may have made a significant contribution to ending impunity.

Kenyans certainly believed that the ICC could have a major impact even if convictions were not secured prior to the start of the elections and welcomed the ICC's intervention on this basis. Local support for the trials remained high throughout the

---

[108] Ibid.

[109] 'Ruto quizzed in Kenya plan to stop Hague trials', *Daily Nation*, 8 August 2011.

[110] Situation in the Republic of Kenya, Decision on the admissibility of the 'Appeal of the Government of Kenya against the 'Decision on the Request for Assistance Submitted on Behalf of the Government of the Republic of Kenya Pursuant to Article 93(10) of the Statute and Rule 194 of the Rules of Procedure and Evidence', Appeals Chamber, ICC-01/09 OA, 10 August 2011 ('Appeals Chamber Article 19 Decision').

period of the OTP's intervention. A Synovate poll conducted in the days before the naming of the Ocampo Six revealed that 85 % of Kenyans were in favour of prosecuting high-level perpetrators at the ICC rather than before local courts.[111] An address by Ikolomoni MP Bonny Khalwale to the National Assembly in December 2010 provides an insight into Kenyans' enthusiasm for the ICC process at this time:

> Mr. Temporary Deputy Speaker, Sir, I have listened to Kenyans from all walks of life through Short text Messaging Service (SMS). Hundreds of them are saying that the solution is The Hague. I have read on my Face Book address, and Kenyans are saying 'The Hague!' I have listened to debate on FM radio stations and, again, it is a resounding case for The Hague. I have watched television stations' poll results on our handling of the post-election violence and, again, it is an overwhelmingly case for The Hague.
>
> As if that is not enough, if you go through the Mail Box in all the print media, you will see that the majority of Kenyans support The Hague option. I have attended funerals and church summons. I have been to wedding ceremonies as well as to bars, where people drink busaa or beer. When they were sober or drunk, the people have always insisted that we must take The Hague option.[112]

Support for ICC prosecutions remained high throughout the pre-trial stage of the two cases, with various opinion polls measuring support at between 56 and 70 %.[113] Such was the extent of the support that the ICC and its Prosecutor began to gain prominence in popular culture. Local *matatus*, the country's main form of public transport, displayed images of Moreno-Ocampo alongside fashionable hip-hop artists such as Snoop Dogg and Tupac Shakur.[114] A cheetah at a Nairobi national park was also named after the Prosecutor, some women named their children after him and one of the country's most popular newspapers, the *Daily Nation*, referred to him as the 'anti-impunity czar'.[115]

Much of this enthusiasm for the ICC was borne out of sense of frustration and hopelessness over the government's history of failed commitments to holding perpetrators accountable for their crimes. In April 2011, KNDR observed that Kenyans were supportive of prosecutions in The Hague because of 'widespread public disillusionment with the failure to complete investigations required to prosecute cases arising out of the post-election violence and the failure to establish a local special

---

[111] Jeff Otieno, 'Kenyans want suspects of poll chaos tried at Hague', *Daily Nation*, 14 December 2010.

[112] Hansard, National Assembly, Official Report, 22 December 2010.

[113] Judie Kaberia, 'Synovate survey contradicts rival pollster on ICC', *Capital News*, 6 February 2012; Lordrick Mayabi, 'Raila remains top contender—Synovate', *Capital News*, 19 January 2012; 'Support for ICC trials high', *Daily Nation*, 10 October 2012; South Consulting, Kenya National Dialogue and Reconciliation Monitoring Project, *Kenya's 2013 General Election: A Review of the Environment and Electoral Preparedness, October 2012* ('KNDR October 2012 Report').

[114] Scott Baldauf, 'Role over Snoop Dogg, Ocampo is new king of the matatu', *Christian Science Monitor*, 29 January 2010.

[115] Okech Kendo, 'See the fury of impunity fighting back', *Standard*, 8 December 2010; Mwauru Samora, 'Is this man Africa's only hope for justice?', *Daily Nation*, 7 December 2010; Radio Netherlands Worldwide, Interview with Luis Moreno-Ocampo, 6 February 2014.

tribunal to investigate and prosecute high-level perpetrators'.[116] Many Kenyans felt that the ICC's intervention was the country's only realistic prospect for ending impunity.

It is possible that this overwhelming support was the result of Kenyans' unrealistic expectations of the ICC's potential contribution. Residents of Haruma, for example, listed lack of water, lack of food and lack of housing as problems they expected the ICC to solve.[117] Consequently, part of the OTP's initial strategy was to manage Kenyans' expectations, which one OTP official described as being 'very scary'.[118] The Prosecutor told Kenyans that '[his] job [was] to prosecute, period'[119] and that the OTP would only seek to prosecute a small number of persons bearing the greatest responsibility for the violence.[120]

During interviews I conducted in Nairobi, Nakuru, Naivasha and Eldoret in March 2010, Kenyans revealed four broad desires with respect to the ICC process, each of which the OTP went some way to satisfying. First, there was a hope that those named would be senior public figures. Kenyans felt frustrated and disillusioned that at no time in the country's history had its leaders ever been held accountable for their actions, including for the post-election violence in 1992 and 1997. Many Kenyans remained supportive of the ICC process because it meant, for the first time, its leaders would tried for their crimes. The Ocampo Six included three ministers (including two presidential candidates), Kenya's most senior public servant and its former Commissioner of Police. Among those named as suspects included Uhuru Kenyatta, the Deputy Prime Minister and son of the country's first president; William Ruto, the leader of the Kalenjin in the Rift Valley; and Francis Muthaura, Kenya's former UN ambassador. For these reasons, 51 % of Kenyans said that they were satisfied with the Prosecutor's choice of suspects.[121]

Second, interviewees stressed the importance of the ICC being independent and impartial, since Kenyans were accustomed to local prosecutions being manipulated by elites. They were also aware that both ODM and PNU supporters bore responsibility for crimes committed during the violence. As a consequence, the only way that the ICC could demonstrate its independence and impartiality was for there to be an even number of prosecutions from both sides of the conflict. The Prosecutor initiated two cases, one against persons alleged to have been responsible for crimes committed against PNU supporters and the other against persons accused of organising violence against ODM supporters. Each case had three accused, including one person who was a presidential candidate. The composition of the Ocampo Six also reflected the geographical diversity that many Kenyans demanded, with three hailing from the Rift

---

[116] South Consulting, Kenya National Dialogue and Reconciliation Monitoring Project, *Draft Review Report*, April 2011 ('KNDR April 2011 Report').

[117] Christine Bjork and Juanita Goebertus, 'Complementarity in Action: The Role of Civil Society and the ICC in Rule of Law Strengthening in Kenya' (2011) 14 *Yale Human Rights & Development Law Journal* 205, 226.

[118] 'ICC team denies collecting evidence', *Standard*, 3 February 2010.

[119] Joe Mbuthia, 'ICC has 'no witness in Kenya'', *Daily Nation*, 24 March 2010.

[120] Kariuki (2009) (see Footnote 3).

[121] Dave Opiyo, 'Kenyans not ready to re-elect Hague suspects: poll', *Daily Nation*, 18 December 2010.

Valley, two from Nairobi and one from Eldoret. Even when the Ocampo Six was reduced to the Ocampo Four in January 2012, the balance remained, with one suspect from each side of the conflict having his charges dismissed.

Third, interviewees commonly expressed the view that, although the ideal was for convictions to be secured prior to the next elections, the ICC would nevertheless make a significant contribution to ending impunity if the suspects were merely to be named by this time. It took until September 2013 for the first of the cases to commence, by which time the country had already held its presidential election. Nevertheless, the Prosecutor's naming of the six accused on 15 December 2010, the suspects' initial appearances in April 2011 and their confirmation of charges hearings in September and October 2011 provided Kenyans with hope that even their leaders were not above the law, with this hope renewed in time for the holding of the elections.

Finally, Kenyans expressed a desire for the ICC process to reveal the full details of the country's post-election violence, including the crimes that were committed and how these were planned and organised. This first occurred in September 2011 when the Kenya One suspects appeared at The Hague for their confirmation of charges hearing. The Prosecutor told the Pre-Trial Chamber that Ruto was the leader of an ad hoc 'network of perpetrators' that also included Kosgey and Sang.[122] According to the Prosecutor, the three accused met on at least nine occasions between December 2007 and January 2008 to plan attacks on populations in the Rift Valley. The objective of this operation was to expel the Kikuyu, Kamba and Kisii from the region and to ensure that the Kalenjin voted as an ethnic bloc at the general elections. The Prosecutor alleged that Ruto and Kosgey assembled a network of politicians, businessmen, elders and police officers, then appointed commanders, arranged finances and purchased arms. This group promised monetary awards and immunity to subordinates and provided guns, fuel, telephones and transport to the perpetrators. Sang was alleged to have contributed to this plan by using his Kalenjin radio programme to recruit supporters and send messages. The Prosecutor alleged that from 30 December 2007 to 1 January 2008, five locations were attacked, during which the crimes against humanity of murder, torture, forcible transfer and persecution were committed.

In September and October 2011, the Prosecutor presented his the case against the three Kenya Two suspects. According to the Prosecutor, Kenyatta, Muthaura and Ali devised a plan to retaliate against perceived ODM supporters by organising attacks and ensuring that the police forces failed to take action to stop such attacks.[123] The Prosecutor alleged that Kenyatta used his existing connections with Mungiki members to solicit their support and to facilitate meetings that also included Muthaura, Ali, politicians and businessmen. During the course of at least eight

---

[122] *Prosecutor v William Samoei Ruto, Henry Kiprono Kosgey and Joshua Arap Sang*, Document Containing the Charges, ICC-01/09-01/11, 1 August 2011.

[123] *Prosecutor v Francis Kirimi Muthaura, Uhuru Muigai Kenyatta and Mohammed Hussein Ali*, Prosecution's Document Containing the Charges, List of Evidence and Comprehensive In-Depth Analysis Chart of Evidence Included in the List of Evidence Submitted Pursuant to Article 61(3) and Rule 121(3), ICC-01/09-02/11, 19 August 2011 ('Kenya Two Charges').

meetings in January 2008, including one at State House and another at the Nairobi Members Club, attacks against Luo, Luhya and Maasai were planned, organised and financed. According to the Prosecutor, at one of these meetings Muthaura instructed the Commissioner of Police, Ali, that the security forces were not to prevent these attacks from occurring. The Prosecutor told the Pre-Trial Chamber that from 24 January 2008 to 28 January 2008, Mungiki and PNU youths attacked the person and property of perceived ODM supporters in Nakuru and Naivasha. The Prosecutor alleged that during these attacks, the mobs killed over 150 persons and injured, raped, circumcised and forcibly displaced many others. Properties and businesses belonging to perceived ODM supporters were also looted and destroyed. The Prosecutor further alleged that throughout these attacks the police did not attempt to prevent or stop the crimes from being committed. On this basis, the Prosecutor accused Kenyatta, Muthaura and Ali of being criminally responsible for the crimes against humanity of murder, rape, forcible transfer, other inhumane acts and persecution.

5.2 A Blow to Impunity

For all of the above reasons, it must be recognised that the OTP's intervention in Kenya was a watershed moment in Kenya's long history of impunity. The symbolism of the announcement of the Ocampo Six should not be underestimated. On the day that the six suspects were announced, human activist Maina Kiai said 'finally we have our day. This is the first time we have high-ranking people facing the law where they have no control and they can't bribe their way out of it'.[124] Similarly, KHRC executive director, Muthoni Wanyeki, described the development as 'a strong step towards ending impunity in the country'.[125]

Between September 2011 and October 2011, the suspects spent a total of nineteen days in court as the judges determined whether there was a sufficient basis upon which to confirm the charges. According to an Ipsos Synovate poll, 77 % of Kenyans either watched the ICC proceedings live on television or followed other media coverage of the trials.[126] Human rights advocate Mwalimu Mati said 'We are not used to seeing our leaders have to account for anything in public … There may be a few people missing their Nigerian soaps but this is basically all that people are doing'.[127]

---

[124] Jeffrey Gettleman and Marlise Simons, 'International Court seeks indictments in Kenya vote violence', *New York Times*, 15 December 2010.
[125] International Federation for Human Rights, 'A big step towards ending impunity for 2008 post-election violence in Kenya: ICC Prosecutor announces list of 6 main suspects', 15 December 2010.
[126] Ipsos Synovate, Confirmation Hearings Boost Support for ICC Process, 4 November 2011.
[127] Daniel Howden, 'Kenyans gripped by latest TV soap: their leaders in the dock', *Independent*, 23 September 2011.

While these hearings were ongoing, I conducted interviews with victims of the violence residing in Nairobi's Kibera slum. The interviewees stated that they were following the proceedings closely and were encouraged by what they saw. Several interviewees excitedly explained one exchange they had witnessed between Ruto and presiding judge Ekaterina Trendafilova. The episode occurred during the initial appearance of the Kenya One suspects in The Hague on 7 April 2011. According to Article 60 of the Rome Statute and Rule 121 of the ICC's rules of procedure and evidence, the purpose of such hearings is simply to verify the identity of the accused persons and to ensure that they have been informed of the allegations against them. At one stage, however, Ruto attempted to make arguments in his defence, stating that the allegations against him 'can only be possible in a movie'.[128] Judge Trendafilova interrupted Ruto, told him to 'sit down', then reminded him of the purpose of the initial appearance hearing. Victims said this moment was 'significant' and 'symbolic' in Kenya's because it was the first time in Kenya's history that a senior politician had been shown 'who is boss'. They explained that such an exchange contributed to the ending of impunity in Kenya because it showed that 'even leaders can be brought to book'.

6 Impunity Gaps

Although the ICC's symbolic contribution to ending impunity should not be underestimated, it must also be recognised that, notwithstanding this intervention, serious impunity gaps remained. Six are identified here. The first concerned the absence of direct perpetrators before the ICC. Given that the OTP considered its mandate to be confined to holding leaders accountable, its decision not to try any 'small fish' did not come as a surprise. Nevertheless, since such persons almost entirely escaped accountability at the local level, the fact that they did not appear as suspects before the ICC meant that there was a significant impunity gap. Victims' representative Morris Anyah told the Pre-Trial Chamber:

> The victims ... are concerned about what you would call the foot soldiers, the actual direct perpetrators of the crimes. They still see some of these people from time to time. They recognise some of these people. Most of these persons have not been prosecuted, and it is a source of concern to the victims.[129]

Second, Kenyans expressed disappointment at the fact that many of the country's leaders were not held accountable for the role they were alleged to have played in the violence. In particular, some Kenyans felt disillusioned and frustrated that neither of the two principals, Kibaki or Odinga, were named as suspects. Suspicions over Kibaki's involvement in the post-election violence were based on the Waki

---

[128] *Prosecutor v William Samoei Ruto, Henry Kiprono Kosgey and Joshua Arap Sang*, ICC-01/11, Transcript 7 April 2011.

[129] *Prosecutor v Francis Kirimi Muthaura, Uhuru Muigai Kenyatta and Mohammed Hussein Ali*, ICC-01/09-02/11, Transcript 5 October 2011.

Report's finding that much of the planning of the crimes that were committed in Nakuru and Naivasha took place in State House.[130] As one lawyer noted, 'State House is not a hotel or kiosk where you just walk in and out at will. The retaliatory attacks must have been planned with the knowledge and blessings of State House'.[131] The case against Odinga gained momentum when his former chief of protocol, Tony Gachoka, announced that he had written to the Prosecutor indicting that he possessed evidence that implicated Odinga in the violence.[132] The omission of Kibaki and Odinga from the Ocampo Six therefore left some Kenyans unhappy. According to an Infotrak Harris poll of 1,500 persons in December 2010, 35 % of Kenyans were dissatisfied with the list of persons named, with common reasons provided including that 'the list is not exhaustive', 'it left out the two principals' and 'the hatchet men should also be brought to book'.[133] One IDP spokesperson said that 'Moreno-Ocampo's list [was] wanting', while another claimed that 'Ocampo [had] let Kenyans down'.[134] Kagundo MP Johnstone Muthama criticised the Prosecutor for leaving Kibaki and Odinga off the list.[135] On the day of the announcement of the Ocampo Six, a journalist asked the Prosecutor why the principals had not been included, with the Prosecutor responding that that OTP had 'followed the evidence strictly and [the list of suspects] was not based on political responsibility'.[136] He later disclosed that there was 'zero' evidence implicating either Kibaki or Odinga.[137] Although the two principals were not named, two of their closest political allies were. Muthaura, who served as Cabinet Secretary, was responsible for the hurried swearing in of Kibaki on 30 December 2007 and was regarded by some as being 'the power behind the throne'.[138] Meanwhile, Odinga was forced to deal with losing Kosgey, the chairman of his ODM party. Political analysts described the naming of Kosgey as being a 'big loss' for Odinga, since Kosgey was one of the few Rift Valley Kalenjins who had remained loyal to Odinga.[139] This led some Kenyans to speculate that the Prosecutor had named Muthaura and Kosgey as 'sacrificial lambs' or 'surrogates' for the principals.[140] The suspicion that the ICC process had become politicised led some Kenyans to question the extent to which the ICC had contributed to ending impunity.

---

[130] Waki Report (see Footnote 28), 121–122.

[131] Juma Kwayera, 'Why Ocampo spared the two principals', *Standard*, 17 December 2010.

[132] Tony Gachoka, 'Columnists were too quick to judge me', *Daily Nation*, 25 August 2012.

[133] Infotrak Research and Consulting, Infotrak Harris Poll, 'Kenyans take on the ICC and the Ocampo list of 6', December 2010.

[134] Vincent Mabatuk, Anthony Gitonga and Peter Mutai, 'IDPs praise list of suspects, as others claim it falls short of expectations', *Standard*, 16 December 2010.

[135] 'Kenya runs out of options as Ocampo strikes', *Standard*, 17 December 2010.

[136] Biketi Kikechi, 'Ocampo tells why he settled on the six, left out Principals', *Standard*, 15 December 2010.

[137] Radio Netherlands Worldwide, Interview with Luis Moreno-Ocampo, 6 February 2014.

[138] Emeka-Mayaka Gekara, 'Why Muthaura is an ICC suspect', *Daily Nation*, 18 December 2010.

[139] Peter Leftie, 'Raila faces tricky political situation after Ocampo fingers Kosgey and Ruto', *Daily Nation*, 18 December 2010.

[140] Juma Kwayera, 'Why Ocampo spared the two principals', *Standard*, 17 December 2010.

A third gap impunity gap concerned the absence of accountability in Kenya's security forces. The Waki Report found that police officers were responsible for 405 deaths as well as a significant number of crimes against the person, including sexual assaults and rapes, but it would appear that no police officer was convicted at the local level for their role in the violence. The ICC therefore presented the last hope for accountability. Kiai stressed that it was crucial that the limited number of ICC prosecutions include those who were most responsible for the actions of the security forces, including the Commissioner of Police, the National Security Committee and the Defence Minister.[141] The Prosecutor did name the Commissioner of Police as one of the six suspects, but did not charge him with being responsible for *ordering* the commission of such crimes. Rather, Ali was alleged to have been responsible for 'orchestrating a police failure to prevent the commission of crimes'.[142] According to the Prosecutor, Ali instructed the security forces 'not to obstruct the movement' of the persons committing the crimes and ensured that the police would not arrest or conduct investigations into the main perpetrators.[143] Those who were hopeful that the ICC would hold the security forces accountable were further disappointed when the Pre-Trial Chamber decided not to confirm the charges against Ali. The judges found that the inadequate police response to the crimes was because of 'ethnic bias' and the 'ineptitude' of senior police officers, rather than as part of a pre-conceived plan as alleged by the Prosecutor.[144] As a consequence of this decision, no member of the security forces or their superiors was held accountable for the hundreds of crimes committed by police officers during the post-election violence, either at the local level or at the international level.

A fourth gap impunity gap was that spontaneous acts of violence committed during Kenya's post-election violence period were excluded from the ICC's prosecutions. For example, according to the Waki Report, the violence started in Nairobi's slum area of Kibera immediately after the announcement of the presidential election results.[145] During this period, 125 persons were killed, 342 were seriously injured, a market housing over 3,000 traders was destroyed and a large number of persons were forcibly displaced.[146] For the ICC to have jurisdiction over these crimes, however, the Prosecutor had to satisfy the Pre-Trial Chamber that the crimes were committed as part of a 'state or organisational policy'.[147] The Prosecutor attempted to satisfy this legal requirement by alleging that Kenya's police officers 'indiscriminately shot at and killed more than a hundred ODM supporters in Kisumu and

---

[141] Interview with Maina Kiai (Naivasha, 30 April 2010).

[142] Kenya Two Charges (see Footnote 122), [18].

[143] Ibid [99].

[144] *Prosecutor v Francis Kirimi Muthaura, Uhuru Muigai Kenyatta and Mohammed Hussein Ali*, Judgment on the appeal of the Republic of Kenya against the decision of Pre-Trial Chamber II of 30 May 2011 entitled 'Decision on the Confirmation of Charges Pursuant to Article 61(7)(a) and (b) of the Rome Statute', ICC-01/09-02/11-274, 31 January 2012 ('PTC Confirmation of Charges, Kenya Two'), [226], [426].

[145] Waki Report (see Footnote 28), 196.

[146] Ibid, 198, 308, 333.

[147] Rome Statute, Article 7(2)(a).

Kibera'.[148] Although the Pre-Trial Chamber found that there were reasonable grounds for believing that there had been deaths, injuries and rapes in Kibera during the post-election violence period, it was not satisfied that these crimes were committed as part of a state or organisational policy and so dismissed these charges against the accused.[149] The Pre-Trial Chamber made the same finding in relation to crimes committed in Kisumu, where 81 persons were killed, 343 were seriously injured and there was widespread destruction of residential homes and government offices.[150] The two ICC cases therefore proceeded without any further evidence being adduced regarding any of the crimes committed in Kibera and Kisumu. Victims of these spontaneous acts of violence expressed their disappointment. A Kisumu resident said 'the first case of post-election violence was witnessed in Kisumu where nine police officers were killed and innocent Kenyans thrown into Lake Victoria but that one is not reflected anywhere in the ICC'.[151] Similarly, a victim of the violence in Kibera said 'if the ICC is going to abandon Kibera, it's a clear sign to Kibera residents that however much you kill one another the law will never catch up with you'.[152]

A fifth impunity gap was the lack of charges in relation to sexual and gender-based violence. As discussed above, there may not have been a single conviction at the local level for the more than 900 documented acts of rape and other forms of sexual violence, meaning victims placed much reliance on the ICC to ensure perpetrators were held accountable. The Prosecutor, however, again faced the challenge of demonstrating that these crimes were committed as part of a 'state or organisational policy'. In addition, the Prosecutor encountered difficulties in adducing sufficient evidence to sustain the charges because victims were reluctant to testify as a result of widespread harassment and intimidation.[153] Concerns over victims' security may have contributed to the Prosecutor's decision not to charge the suspects in the Kenya One case with rape as a crime against humanity. Judy Gitau from ICJ-Kenya suggested that 'the prosecutorial strategy was to expose victims as little as possible. He was keen not to expose them to too many risks and probably that is why he left out rape charges in Case One'.[154] Although the Prosecutor did elect to charge the three suspects in the Kenya Two case with rape as a crime against humanity in four locations, the Pre-Trial Chamber found that the Prosecutor had presented sufficient evidence to confirm only one the charges in Nakuru.[155] With the charges against Ali not confirmed and the Prosecutor electing not to pursue with the case against

---

[148] Kenya Two Charges (see Footnote 122) [6].

[149] *Prosecutor v Francis Kirimi Muthaura, Uhuru Muigai Kenyatta and Mohammed Hussein Ali*, Decision on the Prosecutor's Application for Summonses to Appear for Francis Kirimi Muthaura, Uhuru Muigai Kenyatta and Mohammed Hussein Ali, ICC-01/09-02/11, 8 March 2011 ('PTC Kenya Two Issuance of Summonses').

[150] Ibid; Waki Report (see Footnote 28), 308, 332, 337–338.

[151] Nandemu Barasa and Phanice Pkemei, 'PEV victims fault evidence in the ICC cases', *West FM*, 26 October 2012.

[152] Robbie Corey-Boulet, 'Frustration over limits of ICC charges', *IPS*, 29 April 2011.

[153] Judie Kaberia, 'Concerns over 'missing' rape charges at ICC', *Capital News*, 13 January 2012.

[154] Ibid.

[155] PTC Kenya Two Issuance of Summonses (see Footnote 148), [26].

Muthaura, it left Kenyatta as the only member of the Ocampo Six to stand accused of being criminally responsible for rape as a crime against humanity. Consequently, accountability for crimes of rape and other forms of sexual violence was limited to Kenyatta's alleged responsibility for crimes committed in Nakuru. Crimes committed in Naivasha, Kisumu, Kibera and elsewhere did not proceed before the ICC, prompting victims' groups such as the Women's Initiatives for Gender Justice to suggest that the ICC cases 'failed to reflect' the 'significant evidence' of such crimes having been committed.[156] The OTP later dropped its case against Kenyatta, meaning that the ICC trials contained no allegations at all concerning sexual and gender-based violence. Given that the prosecution of such crimes appears to have been entirely absent at the local level, this is a significant and disturbing impunity gap.

A final impunity gap which may be identified is the lack of accountability for property crimes. There were very few prosecutions at the local level for offences against property and the Prosecutor elected not to charge any members of the Ocampo Six with criminal responsibility for such crimes. Victims expressed their disappointment that neither of the two cases contained any allegations of looting or destruction of property, despite the extensive evidence of such crimes having been committed. On 15 August 2011, the victims' common legal representative for the Kenya One case, Sureta Chana, filed a document with the Pre-Trial Chamber seeking to include acts of destruction of property in the charges against the accused since almost all of the 327 represented victims had lost property during the violence and the Prosecutor had made reference to such acts in submissions to the Court.[157] Chana's counterpart in the Kenya Two case made similar submissions on behalf of 299 victims during the confirmation of charges hearing.[158] The Prosecutor nevertheless did not amend the charge sheet, nor did the Pre-Trial Chamber exercise its discretion under Article 61(7)(c)(ii) to include the charges. Consequently, no property offences were prosecuted before the ICC.

7 The Shadow Side of Complementarity

7.1 Increased Threats to Witnesses

The OTP's commencement of cases at The Hague as part of its strategy of positive complementarity also appears to have had at least two shadow sides. The first of these is that the ICC's presence in Kenya would seem to have led to an increase in the prevalence of witness intimidation. As discussed in Chap. 7, the Kenyan witness protection programme was not able to offer sufficient protection to witnesses and

---

[156] Women's Initiative for Gender Justice, *Gender 2011 Report Card on the International Criminal Court* (Women's Initiatives for Gender Justice, 2011), 169.

[157] *Prosecutor v William Samoei Ruto, Henry Kiprono Kosgey and Joshua Arap Sang*, Request by the Victims' Representative for authorisation by the Chamber to make written submissions on specific issues of law and/or fact, ICC-01/09-01/11, 15 August 2011.

[158] *Prosecutor v Francis Kirimi Muthaura, Uhuru Muigai Kenyatta and Mohammed Hussein Ali*, ICC-01/09-02/11, Transcript, 21 September 2011.

the ICC's protective measures extended only to the small number of witnesses giving evidence in The Hague. This therefore left other witnesses in a particularly vulnerable position. Persons believed to hold crucial information that might inculpate powerful persons were intimidated, harassed, threatened and, in some cases, killed. According to a report from the ICC's VPRS:

> The clearest message received during the Kenya mission was that there exist serious and well-founded fears for the security of those who contact the ICC, or who are even thought to have had contact with the ICC. There was overwhelming agreement that persons with knowledge or evidence about serious crimes have been and will continue to be harassed, intimidated, and even killed.[159]

The most high-profile example of ICC-related witness intimidation concerned retired Deputy Police Commissioner Bernard Kimeli, who was found murdered in his home in April 2011.[160] According to the Prosecutor, Kimeli was 'in possession of sensitive information in relation to the misuse of police resources by the government of Kenya and/or the PNU during the post-election violence'.[161] Civil society also reported the deaths of potential witnesses and claimed that intimidation had forced scores of others to go into hiding.[162] In May 2010, even the Justice Minister was forced to concede that 'some witnesses may have lost loved ones through intimidations, threats and killings'.[163]

Family members of suspected witnesses were also targeted, such as one woman who received an envelope containing 3,000 Kenyan shillings and a note reading 'this is our donation to help you purchase a coffin for your husband'.[164] The KNDR process monitored witness intimidation closely throughout this period and provided the following description of the pressures faced by witnesses and their families as a result of ICC investigations:

> Sometimes relatives of those perceived to be witnesses put pressure on the families by warning them against bringing the wrath of the community upon their households. They are perceived as 'traitors'. Individual members of households are under pressure from communities to demonstrate loyalty 'to the community' by not providing information lest they be construed as betraying their cause. In addition, there are simple, everyday measures to discredit those viewed as witnesses. They are painted as incorrigibly dishonest and out to extort money from the suspects. Such people and their families are threatened with 'a curse' for attempting to give 'false witness' about events that occurred during the violence. It is said that the curse will befall the witness in question as well as members of their household for generations.[165]

---

[159] International Criminal Court Pre Trial Chamber II, Situation in the Republic of Kenya, Public Redacted Version of Report Concerning Victims' Representations (ICC-01/09-6-Conf-Exp) and annexes 2–10, ICC-01/09, 29 March 2010 ('PTC Victims Report'), [25].

[160] Lucas Barasa, 'MP wants Govt to explain officer's killing', *Daily Nation*, 3 May 2011.

[161] Nzau Musau, 'Government explains Kimeli death to Ocampo', *The Star*, 20 May 2011.

[162] South Consulting, Kenya National Dialogue and Reconciliation Monitoring Project, *Status of Implementation of Agenda Items 1–4, Progress Report for January-March 2010*, April 2010 ('KNDR April 2010 Report'), 14.

[163] 'Interview with Mutula Kilonzo', UN Radio, *ReliefWeb*, 17 May 2010.

[164] Muchemi Wachira and Dennis Odunga, 'Speed up poll chaos trials, Hague court urged', *Daily Nation*, 7 January 2010.

[165] South Consulting, Kenya National Dialogue and Reconciliation Monitoring Project, *Review Report*, June 2011 ('KNDR June 2011 Report'), 9, 11.

Although witness intimidation occurred throughout this period, it increased markedly during times when there were debates or discussions over the ICC. According to one KNCHR member, 'the threats intensify during ICC Chief Prosecutor Luis Moreno-Ocampo's visits and when there is a debate around the Prosecutor's visit or next course of action'.[166] KNDR reported that 'the prospect of prosecution by the ICC triggered the disappearance and intimidation of potential witnesses'.[167] A representative of internally displaced persons said that 'when the ICC Prosecutor came temperatures on the ground went up'.[168] According to one witness, mobs 'kept shouting 'Hague! Hague!' as they threw stones on [her] house'.[169]

This is not to suggest that the OTP should abandon its attempts to seek accountability due to the potential for increased witness intimidation should cases be initiated. My focus groups interviews conducted with internally displaced persons who were victims of the post-election violence revealed that their desire to end impunity was so strong that many of these persons were willing to give evidence even if their personal safety could not be assured. This is verified by a KNDR survey conducted during the first quarter of 2010, in which 78 % of respondents said that they would like ICC prosecutions to proceed even if the protection of witnesses could not be guaranteed.[170] Nevertheless, with the Prosecutor on record as stating that protecting victims 'is the objective of [the OTP's] mission' and that 'addressing the interests of victims' is one of the OTP's four 'fundamental principles', this shadow side is one which demands consideration when deciding whether it would be appropriate to pursue a strategy of positive complementarity in a situation country.[171]

7.2 Politicisation of the ICC

A second shadow side of the OTP's commencement of investigations and prosecutions was that savvy politicians exploited the Court's threatened and actual presence to further their own political agendas. According to anti-corruption activist John Githongo, the OTP's strategy of positive complementarity introduced it to the 'most formidable, well-resourced and experienced political foe on the African continent'.[172] Politicisation of the ICC took three forms.

---

[166] Walter Menya, 'Rights body offers to protect chaos victims', *Daily Nation*, 11 May 2010.

[167] South Consulting, Kenya National Dialogue and Reconciliation Monitoring Project, *Review Report*, October 2010 ('KNDR October 2010 Report').

[168] Lucas Barasa, 'Kenya refugees fear renewed violence', *Daily Nation*, 23 June 2010.

[169] Dominic Wabala and Kamore Maina, 'Kenya: Families of Ocampo Witnesses Get Threats', *The Star*, 7 November 2011.

[170] KNDR April 2010 Report (see Footnote 161), 18.

[171] Moreno-Ocampo June 2003 Statement 3).(see Footnote 2); International Criminal Court, Office of the Prosecutor, *Paper on some policy issues before the Office of the Prosecutor*, September 2003' ('2003 OTP Policy Paper'), 3; International Criminal Court, Office of the Prosecutor, Prosecutorial Strategy 2009–2012, 1 February 2010 ('Prosecutorial Strategy 2009–2012'), [23].

[172] Interview with John Githongo (Nairobi, 21 April 2010).

First, leaders sought to pressure the OTP into prosecuting their political opponents. PNU members demanded that Odinga be indicted for his alleged role in the violence.[173] In response, Odinga and Ruto each called for prosecutions of those who had 'stolen the election'.[174] Other MPs mimicked the Waki Commission in producing their own sealed envelope containing names of persons they wished to see tried in The Hague.[175] Calls for particular persons to be prosecuted continued to be made even after the announcement of the Ocampo Six, suggesting that politicians' motivations were more political than legal. While speaking is his own defence during the confirmation of charges hearing, Kenyatta accused his main presidential rival, Odinga, of being 'politically responsible' for the killings that occurred during the post-election violence.[176] In the following month, Odinga said that Kibaki 'was personally and politically responsible for what police and other state agencies did during the post-election violence'.[177] Ruto, who had also announced his candidacy for the presidency, called upon the ICC to indict Kibaki, Odinga and Kilonzo.[178]

Second, those politicians who were named as suspects went to great lengths to discredit the ICC process by portraying the cases as politically motivated. Within minutes of the Prosecutor's naming of the Ocampo Six, PNU ministers called a press conference condemning his actions and motives.[179] In Parliament later that month, Isaac Ruto described the ICC as a 'colonial and imperialist court', while another MP, Robinson Githae, called the ICC a 'kangaroo court'.[180] Still others criticised the Prosecutor for failing to conduct independent and impartial investigations.[181] Some, such as MP Amina Abdalla, even went so far as to launch *ad hominem* attacks against the Prosecutor, saying 'Ocampo himself is a sex molester. He is on record to raping a woman journalist from South Africa. How can our women who have been raped get justice from somebody who is a rapist himself?'[182]

---

[173] 'Panic as ICC warns on alleged threats to witness families', *Standard*, 3 December 2010.

[174] Gakuu Mathenge, 'Kenya on tenterhooks as D-day draws nigh', *Standard*, 6 December 2010; Alex Ndegwa and Beauttah Omanga, 'Raila's parting shot to Ocampo', *Standard*, 2 December 2010; Mugumo Munene, 'Ocampo Six mount last assault on Hague trials', *Daily Nation*, 4 December 2010; Macharia Gaitho, 'You have no right to try anyone, says Ruto', *Daily Nation*, 19 July 2009.

[175] Njeri Rugene, 'MPs compile new port poll suspects list', *Daily Nation*, 25 July 2009.

[176] *Prosecutor v Francis Kirimi Muthaura, Uhuru Muigai Kenyatta and Mohammed Hussein Ali*, ICC-01/09-02/11, Transcript, 29 September 2011.

[177] 'Raila says Kibaki liable for 2008 post-poll chaos', *Capital FM*, 19 October 2011.

[178] Njenga Gicheha, 'Uhuru vows to prove his innocence at ICC', *The Star*, 13 February 2012.

[179] Gakuu Mathenge, 'Why Ocampo list has angered PNU members', *Standard*, 18 December (2010.)

[180] Alphonce Shiundu, 'Ruto's ICC motions falters in Parliament', *Daily Nation*, 16 December 2010.

[181] Hansard, National Assembly, Official Report, 22 December 2010.

[182] Ibid.

7 The Shadow Side of Complementarity

Finally, the suspects and their supporters claimed that they had become the victims of this politicised ICC process. The International Crisis Group observed that:

> Immediately after they were identified, the six suspects embarked upon an extensive and sophisticated campaign to cast themselves as victims of the court and of machinations by political opponents intent on preventing their participation in the 2012 elections.[183]

In particular, ICC suspects and presidential candidates Kenyatta and Ruto sought to mobilise their supporter bases by claiming that they were the victims of a conspiracy, involving the ICC and the international community, to sabotage their campaigns so that the leader of the Luo community, Odinga, could become president.[184] For example, in March 2012, Central Kenya leaders loyal to Kenyatta labelled the ICC trials as a plot by Odinga and western powers to remove Kenyatta from the ballot.[185] Some sought to prove the existence of this conspiracy by making reference to the distinctive first letter of the surnames shared by the Odinga, Ocampo and Obama, a feature of Luo surnames. For example, MO Gideon Mbuvi said:

> Hakuna vile tutakubali mtu wa jina linaanza na O asaidiwe na cousin yake huko America wa jina linaanza na O washikane na Ocampo kumaliza watu wetu … . tutapambana nao. (There is no way we can let someone with a name that starts with 'O' to be helped with his cousin in the US with a name that also starts with 'O' to work together with Ocampo to finish our people … we will deal with them.)[186]

In an attempt to mobilise political support for the ICC suspects, MP Lewis Nguyai even sought to draw parallels with political prisoners from the colonial period: 'we had the Kaneguria Six who were imprisoned by the colonial government and emerged to lead the country. Now we have the ICC Six, who will surely lead the country in the coming days'.[187] Another MP, Lucas Checpkitotony, compared the trials of Ruto and Kenyatta to the incarceration of Nelson Mandela.[188]

On 27 January 2012, Kenyatta and Ruto held a 'prayer rally' in Eldoret. The prayers lasted for just eleven minutes before Ruto spoke in Kalenjin and urged 'his people' to consider disrupting the presidential elections if the ICC process prevented him from campaigning.[189] At another rally, Assistant Minister Cecily Mbarire described the

---

[183] International Crisis Group, *Policy Briefing, 'Kenya: Impact of the ICC Proceedings'*, Africa Briefing No. 84, 9 January 2012 ('ICG January 2012 Briefing'), 11.

[184] Dave Opiyo, 'MPs allege plot to remove Uhuru, Ruto from 2012 race', *Daily Nation*, 4 December 2010; Jacob Ng'etich, 'Ruto; I'm prepared to face Ocampo', *Daily Nation*, 3 December 2010; Anthony Kariuki and Oliver Mathenge, 'Ocampo names Kenya chaos suspects', *Daily Nation*, 15 December 2010; Mathenge (2010) (see Footnote 178).

[185] Oliver Mathenge, 'Postpone Hague cases, Uhuru backers demand', *Daily Nation*, 23 March 2012.

[186] Samuel Omwenga, 'Kenya—Uhuru and Ruto Sowing Seeds of Discord', *Pambazuka News*, 16 February 2012.

[187] Vitalis Kimutai, 'Kenya MPs claim Ocampo move political', *Standard*, 20 December 2010.

[188] Omwenga (2012) (see Footnote 185).

[189] Omwenga (2012) (see Footnote 185).

ICC as a '*kichinjio*' (slaughterhouse).[190] These developments prompted the Law Society of Kenya to call for some politicians, including Ruto, to be prosecuted for inciting violence.[191] According to a national intelligence report, this emotive language in response to the ICC threatened national security:

> The recent trend where sections of the political elite have resorted to using ethnic groups for political mobilisation in order to advance personal and community interests to the exclusion of other sections of the Kenyan community is posing a threat to national cohesion and security ... The use of tribal groups to rally ethnic communities to denounce the ICC process may lead to deterioration of inter-ethnic tensions pitting those perceived to be for and against the process. The trend where most of the political parties attract bedrock support from specific ethnic groups is fuelling ethnic hostilities.[192]

In other words, the commencement of trials before the ICC not only led to the politicisation of these trials, but may also have fuelled ethnic tensions in Kenya in the lead-up to the 2013 presidential elections.

So effective was this victimisation campaign that it forced high-profile persons to publicly deny that the ICC cases were politically motivated. In March 2012, Odinga insisted that he 'was not involved in whichever way in naming the suspects'.[193] The Prosecutor also denied that political considerations had influenced the trials, even going so far as to say that he had 'nothing personal against' Ruto or Kenyatta.[194] They received support from Annan, who declared that the ICC had 'no interest in Kenyan politics' and that the country 'should not mix legal and political issues'.[195] Even the presiding judge of the ICC's Pre-Trial Chamber, Ekaterina Trendafilova, felt the need to assure Kenyans that all decisions would be reached 'independently and impartially'.[196]

With so many politicians seeking to use the ICC process for their own advantage, the trials became a major election issue that may have assisted the accused persons in obtaining positions of power. Two months prior to the holding of the elections, the International Crisis Group observed that 'the ICC process will potentially be the central plank of the election campaign, with battle lines drawn based on who supports or opposes it'.[197] Similarly, the KNDR monitoring process described the ICC issue as 'a political lightning rod' with debate focusing on the implications of the trials on individual political careers and the fortunes of the communities these persons represented.[198] One week before the elections, one human rights advocate from Eldoret claimed that if Kenyatta and Ruto were successful, 'they [would] owe it to the ICC'.[199]

---

[190] Mathenge (2012) (see Footnote 184).

[191] 'Charge Kiraitu and Ruto with incitement, says LSK', *Daily Nation*, 6 April 2012.

[192] Hansard, National Assembly, Official Report, 9 May 2012.

[193] Karanga (2012) (see Footnote 185).

[194] Mutwiri Mutuota, 'Ocampo: I am not playing politics', *Capital News*, 11 April 2011.

[195] Sarah Ambui, 'Annan disturbed by politics in Kenya ICC probe', *Capital News*, 4 December 2010.

[196] *Prosecutor v Francis Kirimi Muthaura, Uhuru Muigai Kenyatta and Mohammed Hussein Ali*, ICC-01/09-02/11, Transcript, 5 October 2011.

[197] International Crisis Group, *Kenya's 2013 Elections*, 17 January 2013, 10.

[198] KNDR October 2012 Report (see Footnote 112), 21, 27.

[199] International Crisis Group, *Policy Briefing, Kenya After the Elections*, 15 May 2013 ('ICG May 2013 Policy Briefing').

It would appear that the progress of the trials through the pre-trial stages did not reduce either Kenyatta's or Ruto's popularity. Ipsos Synovate polls revealed that initially 21 % of Kenyans supported Kenyatta in his presidential campaign. This figure increased to 24 % immediately following his confirmation of charges hearing in September and October 2011 and remained at 24 % after the charges against him were confirmed in January 2012. Ruto's popularity also remained steady throughout this period, recording a five percent approval rating prior to his hearing, five percent after it and four percent following the confirmation of charges.[200]

Kenyatta and Ruto were able to manipulate the ICC for their own electoral advantage, assisted by a leading British spin doctor.[201] Each were able to successfully deflect and rebut Odinga's claims that they would not be able to perform their presidential duties while standing trial in The Hague by portraying themselves as victims of a western conspiracy.[202] Annan urged Kenyans in October 2012 and again in December 2012 not to vote for the ICC suspects and, perhaps paradoxically, this may have bolstered support for Kenyatta and Ruto because it played into their victimhood narrative.[203] Leading Kenyan pollster Tom Wolfe revealed that 'people close to Kenyatta reckon that those declarations by diplomats helped them, for Kenyans are very proud and they remember that it is not long since they belonged to the colonial empire of another power'.[204] As Lynch explains, Kenyatta and Ruto succeeded in reframing the ICC story into 'a performance of injustice, neo-colonialism, and a threat to the country's sovereignty, peace, and stability'.[205] Political scientists Daniel Branch and Musambayi Katumanga also suggested that the ICC issue may have worked in Kenyatta's and Ruto's favour by ensuring that they remained in the public spotlight and providing an incentive behind which their respective ethnic communities could mobilise.[206]

Under the terms of the 2010 Constitution, a presidential candidate could only be elected at first instance if he or she: (a) secured more than 50 % of the total vote; and (b) received more than 25 % of the vote in at least 24 counties. According to the official results, Kenyatta secured victory with 6,173,433 votes (50.07 %). In other words, Kenyatta avoided the need for a run-off by a razor thin 8,400 votes.[207] Given the size of this margin, the prevalence of the ICC issue and the likelihood that it worked in favour of Kenyatta rather than against him, it is possible that the OTP's commencement of investigations and prosecutions in Kenya was a significant factor in one of the alleged masterminds of the post-election violence being elected to the country's highest office.

---

[200] Ipsos Synovate, Confirmation Hearings Boost Support for ICC Process, 4 November 2011.

[201] Andy Rowell, 'Former Tory PR advises Kenyans facing Hague trial', *Independent*, 14 Oct 2012.

[202] KNDR October 2012 Report (see Footnote 112), 21.

[203] Mwaniki Munuhe, 'Bensouda jets in as Uhuru, Ruto campaign intensifies', *Standard*, 21 October 2012; 'Kofi Annan urges Kenyans not to vote for indicted politicians', *BBC News*, 4 December 2012.

[204] 'Uhuru turned ICC indictment to his campaign advantage', *AFP*, 11 March 2013.

[205] Gabrielle Lynch, 'Electing the "alliance of the accused": the success of the Jubilee Alliance in Kenya's Rift Valley' (2013) 8(1) *Journal of Eastern African Studies* 93.

[206] Ibid.

[207] ICG May 2013 Policy Briefing (see Footnote 198).

8 Conclusion

The foregoing discussion suggests that the OTP's strategy of positive complementarity did not realise its desired objective of ensuring that post-election violence suspects were investigated and prosecuted at the local level. Nearly 9,000 post-election violence cases were reported to the authorities, but only approximately 258 resulted in successful convictions. These convictions were mostly of low-level perpetrators for less serious crimes, such as minor property offences and minor breaches of the peace. Serious crimes such as murder, assault and crimes of sexual gender-based violence went almost entirely unpunished. Senior figures also avoided sanctions, with no politician, public servant, businessperson, tribal elder or police officer ever convicted for their role in organising, funding, planning and executing the post-election violence crimes.

Nevertheless, throughout this period, the government consistently promised that it would try perpetrators locally. Initially, the government undertook to establish a special tribunal to perform this function, then claimed that a truth commission would handle the cases. Later, it gave assurances that suspects would be tried by local courts once the Constitution had been passed and implemented. These promises, however, proved to be little more than a foreign affairs façade, designed to protect Kenya's international reputation and prevent the ICC from causing further embarrassment through the commencement of proceedings.

This lack of accountability at the local level forced the OTP to commence its own investigations and prosecutions. The naming of the Ocampo Six, their initial appearances before the Court and the holding of the confirmation of charges hearings were all significant milestones in Kenya's long search for an end to impunity. The significance of these trials should not be underestimated, with millions of Kenyans watching on television or listening on radio as, for the first time in the country's history, senior politicians appeared in court to answer serious criminal charges. The proceedings provided Kenyans with hope that no person, no matter how powerful, was above the law.

This contribution from the ICC notwithstanding, significant impunity gaps nevertheless remained. At neither the local level nor the international level were members of the security forces held responsible for the crimes they committed during the post-election violence. Also absent were prosecutions for crimes committed during the spontaneous acts of violence in Kibera and Kisumu, sexual and gender-based crimes and crimes involving the destruction and looting of property.

Further, the OTP's initiation of prosecutions as part of its strategy of positive complementarity also appears to have had at least two shadow sides. First, the ICC's presence in Kenya is likely to have led to an increase in the prevalence of witness intimidation in a country ill-equipped to protect such persons. Second, opportunistic politicians used the ICC's intervention to their own advantage by calling for the prosecution of their opponents and constructing a victimhood narrative when they themselves were charged. This strategy proved effective in mobilising ethnic communities to support Kenyatta and Ruto and may have ultimately resulted in their being elected as president and vice president, respectively, despite being accused of committing crimes against humanity.

Given that the OTP had defined a 'major success' to be the absence of trials at The Hague as a result of investigations and prosecutions proceeding at the local level, the commencement of ICC proceedings must therefore be regarded as an unsuccessful implementation of the strategy of positive complementarity. But would it be correct to say that since local prosecutions did not take place the OTP had *no* influence over the government? Or is there evidence to suggest that at certain times the threat of international prosecutions influenced and perhaps even altered the government's decision-making calculus? The next chapter considers these questions and seeks to explain why it was that the OTP's encouragement of domestic investigations and prosecutions did not ultimately lead to the commencement of trials at the local level.

Bibliography

'Charge Kiraitu and Ruto with incitement, says LSK', *Daily Nation*, 6 April 2012
'CID report says no charge can hold for PEV perpetrators', *Standard*, 16 February 2014
'How Kenya handled local tribunal process', *Daily Nation*, 17 September 2013
'ICC team denies collecting evidence', *Standard*, 3 February 2010
'Interview with Luis Moreno-Ocampo', *Radio Netherlands*, 6 February 2014
'Interview with Mutula Kilonzo', UN Radio, *ReliefWeb*, 17 May 2010
'It wasn't me, says officer accused of poll killings', *Daily Nation*, 30 April 2010
'Justice beckons as Ocampo visits Kenya', *Daily Nation*, 6 May 2010
'Kenya defends its reform record', *Capital News*, 5 October 2009
'Kenya runs out of options as Ocampo strikes', *Standard*, 17 December 2010
'Kenyatta and Odinga in first Kenya presidential debate', *BBC News*, 11 February 2013
'Kofi Annan urges Kenyans not to vote for indicted politicians', *BBC News*, 4 December 2012
'Multi-agency task force on post-election violence begins sittings', *NAM News Network*, 11 February 2012
'Panic as ICC warns on alleged threats to witness families', *Standard*, 3 December 2010
'Raila says Kibaki liable for 2008 post-poll chaos', *Capital FM*, 19 October 2011
'Ruto quizzed in Kenya plan to stop Hague trials', *Daily Nation*, 8 August 2011
'Support for ICC trials high', *Daily Nation*, 10 October 2012
'Uhuru turned ICC indictment to his campaign advantage', *AFP*, 11 March 2013
Ambui, Sarah, 'Annan disturbed by politics in Kenya ICC probe', *Capital News*, 4 December2010
Baldauf, Scott, 'Role over Snoop Dogg, Ocampo is new king of the matatu', *Christian Science Monitor*, 29 January 2010
Barasa, Lucas, 'Kenya refugees fear renewed violence', *Daily Nation*, 23 June 2010
Barasa, Lucas, 'MP wants Govt to explain officer's killing', *Daily Nation*, 3 May 2011
Barasa, Lucas, 'Mutula to Ocampo: quit Kenyan probe', *Daily Nation*, 18 September 2010
Barasa, Lucas, 'The Hague moving in for country's trials', *Daily Nation*, 27 August 2009
Barasa, Nandemu and Pkemei, Phanice, 'PEV victims fault evidence in the ICC cases', *West FM*, 26 October 2012

Bjork, Christine and Goebertus, Juanita, 'Complementarity in Action: The Role of Civil Society and the ICC in Rule of Law Strengthening in Kenya' (2011) 14 *Yale Human Rights & Development Law Journal* 205

Corey-Boulet, Robbie, 'Frustration over limits of ICC charges', *IPS*, 29 April 2011

Director of Public Prosecutions, A report to the Hon. Attorney General by the team on the review of post election violence related cases in Western, Nyanza, Central, Rift Valley, Eastern, Coast and Nairobi Provinces, February 2009

Final Report from Kenya's Commission of Inquiry into Post-Election Violence, 15 October 2008

Gachoka, Tony, 'Columnists were too quick to judge me', *Daily Nation*, 25 August 2012

Gaitho, Macharia, 'You have no right to try anyone, says Ruto', *Daily Nation*, 19 July 2009

Gekara, Emeka-Mayaka, 'Ocampo to step in if Kenya does shoddy job', *Daily Nation*, 19 June 2009

Gekara, Emeka-Mayaka, 'Why Muthaura is an ICC suspect', *Daily Nation*, 18 December 2010

Gettleman, Jeffrey and Simons, Marlise 'International Court seeks indictments in Kenya vote violence', *New York Times*, 15 December 2010

Gicheha, Njenga, 'Uhuru vows to prove his innocence at ICC', *The Star*, 13 February 2012

Hansard, National Assembly, Official Report, 27 January 2009

Hansard, National Assembly, Official Report, 3 February 2009

Hansard, National Assembly, Official Report, 5 February 2009

Hansard, National Assembly, Official Report, 12 February 2009

Hansard, National Assembly, Official Report, 16 December 2010

Hansard, National Assembly, Official Report, 22 December 2010

Hansard, National Assembly, Official Report, 9 May 2012

Howden, Daniel, 'Kenyans gripped by latest TV soap: their leaders in the dock', *Independent*, 23 September 2011

Human Rights Watch, Turning Pebbles: Evading Accountability for Post-Election Violence in Kenya (Human Rights Watch, 2011)

Infotrak Research and Consulting, Infotrak Harris Poll, 'Kenyans take on the ICC and the Ocampo list of 6', December 2010

International Centre for Policy and Conflict, *Post Election Violence: A Trail of Lies and Betrayal* (International Centre for Policy and Conflict, 2009)

International Criminal Court Office of the Prosecutor, 'ICC Prosecutor Receives Materials on Post-Election Violence in Kenya', 16 July 2009

International Criminal Court, Office of the Prosecutor, 'OTP Statement in Relation to Events in Kenya', 5 February 2008

International Criminal Court, Office of the Prosecutor, *Prosecutorial Strategy 2009–2012*, 1 February 2010

International Criminal Court, Situation in the Republic of Kenya, Decision on the admissibility of the 'Appeal of the Government of Kenya against the 'Decision on the Request for Assistance Submitted on Behalf of the Government of the Republic of Kenya Pursuant to Article 93(10) of the Statute and Rule 194 of the Rules of Procedure and Evidence', Appeals Chamber, ICC-01/09 OA, 10 August 2011

International Criminal Court, Situation in the Republic of Kenya, Decision on the Request for Assistance Submitted on Behalf of the Government of the Republic of Kenya Pursuant to Article 93(10) of the Statute and Rule 194 of the Rules of Procedure and Evidence, Pre-Trial Chamber II, ICC-01/09, 29 June 2011

International Criminal Court, Situation in the Republic of Kenya, Prosecutor's Application Pursuant to Article 58 as to Francis Kirimi Muthaura, Uhuru Muigai Kenyatta and Mohammed Hussein Ali, Public Redacted Version of Document ICC-01/09-31-Conf-Exp, 15 December 2010

International Criminal Court, Situation in the Republic of Kenya, Prosecutor's Application Pursuant to Article 58 as to William Samoei Ruto, Henry Kiprono Kosgey and Joshua Arap Sang, Public Redacted Version of Document ICC-01/09-30-Conf-Exp, 15 December 2010

International Criminal Court, Situation in the Republic of Kenya, Decision on the Request for Assistance Submitted on Behalf of the Government of the Republic of Kenya Pursuant to Article 93(10) of the Statute and Rule 194 of the Rules of Procedure and Evidence, Pre-Trial Chamber II, ICC-01/09, 29 June 2011

Bibliography

International Criminal Court, Situation in the Republic of Kenya, Public Redacted Version of Report Concerning Victims' Representations (ICC-01/09-6-Conf-Exp) and annexes 2 to 10, ICC-01/09, 29 March 2010

International Criminal Court, Situation in the Republic of Kenya, Request for authorisation of an investigation pursuant to Article 15, ICC-01/09, 26 November 2009

International Crisis Group, *Kenya's 2013 Elections*, 17 January 2013

International Crisis Group, *Policy Briefing, 'Kenya: Impact of the ICC Proceedings'*, Africa Briefing No. 84, 9 January 2012

International Crisis Group, Policy Briefing, Kenya After the Elections, 15 May 2013

International Federation for Human Rights, 'A big step towards ending impunity for 2008 post-election violence in Kenya: ICC Prosecutor announces list of 6 main suspects', 15 December 2010

Interview with Bethuel Kiplagat (Nairobi, 18 May 2010)

Interview with John Githongo (Nairobi, 21 April 2010)

Interview with Maina Kiai (Naivasha, 30 April 2010)

Interview with Muthoni Wanyeki (Nairobi, 7 May 2010)

Ipsos Synovate, Confirmation Hearings Boost Support for ICC Process, 4 November 2011

Kaberia, Judie, 'Concerns over 'missing' rape charges at ICC', *Capital News*, 13 January 2012

Kaberia, Judie, 'Kenya remains defiant over ICC trials' *Capital News* 5 November 2009

Kaberia, Judie, 'Synovate survey contradicts rival pollster on ICC', *Capital News*, 6 February 2012

Karanga, Samuel, 'Raila denies role in ICC cases', *Daily Nation*, 19 March 2012

Kariuki, Anthony 'Ocampo: ICC has strong case in Kenya chaos', *Daily Nation,* 7 November 2009

Kariuki, Anthony, 'Ocampo says no suspects in Kenya chaos', *Daily Nation*, 8 May 2010

Kariuki, Anthony and Mathenge, Oliver, 'Ocampo names Kenya chaos suspects', *Daily Nation*, 15 December 2010

Kendo, Okech, 'See the fury of impunity fighting back', *Standard*, 8 December 2010

Kenya National Commission on Human Rights, On the brink of the precipice: a human rights account of Kenya's post-2007 election violence, 15 August 2008

Kenyans for Peace with Truth and Justice and Human Rights Watch, 'Kenya: Local Judicial Mechanism Should Complement ICC Cases', Press Release, 27 April 2012

Kenyans for Peace with Truth and Justice and Kenya Human Rights Commission, *Securing Justice: Establishing a Domestic Mechanism for the 2007/08 Post-Election Violence in Kenya* (Kenyans for Peace with Truth and Justice and Kenya Human Rights Commission, 2013)

Kibet, Patrick, 'Man jailed for life over poll violence', *Standard*, 13 June 2012

Kikechi, Biketi, 'Ocampo tells why he settled on the six, left out Principals', *Standard*, 15 December 2010

Kilang'at, Jeremiah, 'Lack of evidence derails local trials', *Daily Nation*, 17 August 2012

Kimutai, Vitalis, 'Kenya MPs claim Ocampo move political', *Standard*, 20 December 2010

Kwayera, Juma 'Why Ocampo spared the two principals', *Standard*, 17 December 2010

Leftie, Peter, 'Raila faces tricky political situation after Ocampo fingers Kosgey and Ruto', *Daily Nation*, 18 December 2010

Leftie, Peter, Wanyoro, Charles, Majefa, Mwakera and Mathenge, Oliver, 'Kenya Cabinet in the eye of a storm', *Daily Nation*, 2 August 2009

Lynch, Gabrielle, 'Electing the "alliance of the accused": the success of the Jubilee Alliance in Kenya's Rift Valley' (2013) 8(1) *Journal of Eastern African Studies* 93

Mabatuk, Vincent, Gitonga, Anthony and Mutai, Peter, 'IDPs praise list of suspects, as others claim it falls short of expectations', *Standard*, 16 December 2010

Macharia, Wanjiru, 'Court frees two convicts in murder case', *Daily Nation*, 21 December 2012

Malalo, Humphrey, 'Kenya court acquits policeman of election killings', *Reuters*, 21 June 2010

Maliti, Tom, 'Kenyan Chief Justice outlines progress in judicial transformation', *The International Criminal Court Kenya Monitor*, 25 October 2011

Mathenge, Gakuu, 'Kenya on tenterhooks as D-day draws nigh', *Standard*, 6 December 2010

Mathenge, Gakuu, 'Why Ocampo list has angered PNU members', *Standard*, 18 December 2010

Mathenge, Oliver, 'New report says 5,000 election violence cases stalled due to lack of evidence', *Daily Nation*, 7 January 2012

Mathenge, Oliver, 'Postpone Hague cases, Uhuru backers demand', *Daily Nation*, 23 March 2012

Mayabi, Lordrick, 'Raila remains top contender—Synovate', *Capital News*, 19 January 2012

Mbuthia, Joe, 'ICC has 'no witness in Kenya'', *Daily Nation*, 24 March 2010

McGregor, Sarah, 'Kenya must revive plan to create "credible" court, Odinga says', *Bloomberg*, 2 February 2011

Menya, Walter, 'Rights body offers to protect chaos victims', *Daily Nation*, 11 May 2010

Moreno-Ocampo, Luis, 'Statement Made at the Ceremony for the Solemn Undertaking of the Chief Prosecutor of the ICC', The Hague, 16 June 2003

Mutai, Peter, 'Two to hang for killing policeman in poll upheaval', *Standard*, 31 July 2009

Mutuota, Mutwiri, 'Ocampo: I am not playing politics', *Capital News*, 11 April 2011

Mukinda, Fred, 'Police won't free suspects', *Daily Nation*, 1 June 2008

Munene, Mugumo, 'Ocampo Six mount last assault on Hague trials', *Daily Nation*, 4 December 2010

Munuhe, Mwaniki, 'Bensouda jets in as Uhuru, Ruto campaign intensifies', *Standard*, 21 October 2012

Musau, Nzau, 'Government explains Kimeli death to Ocampo', *The Star*, 20 May 2011

Mutua, Martin, 'Karua: Principals a stumbling block', *Standard*, 16 July 2009

Naumnane, Bernard 'Kenya's fresh bid to stop Ocampo', *Daily Nation*, 22 April 2011

Ndegwa, Alex and Omanga, Beauttah, 'Raila's parting shot to Ocampo', *Standard*, 2 December 2010

Ng'etich, Jacob, 'Ruto; I'm prepared to face Ocampo', *Daily Nation*, 3 December 2010

Ochola, Abiya, 'Annan to delay envelope for two more months', *Standard*, 18 February 2009

Office of the Attorney General, A Progress Report to the Hon. Attorney-General by the Team on Update of Post Election Violence Related Cases in Western, Nyanza, Central, Rift valley, Eastern, Coast and Nairobi Provinces, March 2011

Office of the Attorney General, Report from Director of Public Prosecutions Keriako Tabiko to Attorney General Amos Wako on Meeting Between the Director of Public Prosecutions and the Criminal Investigation Department on Post Election Violence Cases, 19 June 2008

Office of the President, 'Cabinet Decides on TJRC', 30 July 2009

Office of the President, Criminal Investigation Department, Post Election Violence Investigations Progress Report, 5 May 2011

Office of the President, 'Parliament to reconvene on 20th January', 8 January 2009

Office of the President, Report from Director of Criminal Investigations Ndegwa Muhoro to Director of Public Prosecutions, 'Re: Update on investigation into Six ICC Suspects', 1 July 2011

Office of the President, 'Special Tribunal to be set up', 17 December 2008

Office of the President, 'Statement by His Excellency the President Hon Mwai Kibaki', Kenya State House, 15 December 2010

Office of the United Nations High Commissioner for Human Rights, *Rule-of-Law Tools for Post-Conflict States: Prosecution Initiatives* (Office of the United Nations High Commissioner for Human Rights, 2006)

Omwenga, Samuel, 'Kenya—Uhuru and Ruto Sowing Seeds of Discord', *Pambazuka News*, 16 February 2012

Opiyo, Dave, 'Campaigners drum up support for Imanyara Bill', *Daily Nation*, 29 August 2009

Opiyo, Dave, 'Kenyans not ready to re-elect Hague suspects: poll', *Daily Nation*, 18 December 2010

Opiyo, Dave, 'MPs allege plot to remove Uhuru, Ruto from 2012 race', *Daily Nation*, 4 December 2010

Otieno, Jeff, 'Kenyans want suspects of poll chaos tried at Hague', *Daily Nation*, 14 December 2010

Prosecutor v Francis Kirimi Muthaura, Uhuru Muigai Kenyatta and Mohammed Hussein Ali, Decision on the Prosecutor's Application for Summonses to Appear for Francis Kirimi Muthaura, Uhuru Muigai Kenyatta and Mohammed Hussein Ali, ICC-01/09-02/11, 8 March 2011

Prosecutor v Francis Kirimi Muthaura, Uhuru Muigai Kenyatta and Mohammed Hussein Ali, Prosecution's Document Containing the Charges, List of Evidence and Comprehensive In-Depth Analysis Chart of Evidence Included in the List of Evidence Submitted Pursuant to Article 61(3) and Rule 121(3), ICC-01/09-02/11, 19 August 2011

Prosecutor v Francis Kirimi Muthaura, Uhuru Muigai Kenyatta and Mohammed Hussein Ali, ICC-01/09-02/11, Transcript, 21 September 2011

Prosecutor v Francis Kirimi Muthaura, Uhuru Muigai Kenyatta and Mohammed Hussein Ali, ICC-01/09-02/11, Transcript, 29 September 2011

Prosecutor v Francis Kirimi Muthaura, Uhuru Muigai Kenyatta and Mohammed Hussein Ali, ICC-01/09-02/11, Transcript 5 October 2011

Prosecutor v Francis Kirimi Muthaura, Uhuru Muigai Kenyatta and Mohammed Hussein Ali, Judgment on the appeal of the Republic of Kenya against the decision of Pre-Trial Chamber II of 30 May 2011 entitled 'Decision on the Confirmation of Charges Pursuant to Article 61(7)(a) and (b) of the Rome Statute ', ICC-01/09-02/11-274, 31 January 2012

Prosecutor v Saif Al-Islam Gaddafi and Abdullah Al-Senussi, Prosecution response to application on behalf of the Government of Libya pursuant to article 19 of the ICC statute, ICC-01/11-01/11, 5 June 2012

Prosecutor v William Samoei Ruto, Henry Kiprono Kosgey and Joshua Arap Sang, ICC-01/11, Application on Behalf of the Government of the Republic of Kenya Pursuant to Article 19 of the ICC Statute, ICC-01/09-01/11-19, 31 March 2011

Prosecutor v William Samoei Ruto, Henry Kiprono Kosgey and Joshua Arap Sang, Document Containing the Charges, ICC-01/09-01/11, 1 August 2011

Prosecutor v William Samoei Ruto, Henry Kiprono Kosgey and Joshua Arap Sang, Request by the Victims' Representative for authorisation by the Chamber to make written submissions on specific issues of law and/or fact, ICC-01/09-01/11, 15 August 2011

Prosecutor v William Samoei Ruto, Henry Kiprono Kosgey and Joshua Arap Sang, ICC-01/11, Transcript 7 April 2011

Republic v Stephen Kiprotich Leting & 3 others [2009] eKLR, Criminal Case 34 of 2008

Rome Statute of the International Criminal Court, opened for signature 17 July 1998, 2187 UNTS 90 (entered into force 1 July 2002)

Rowell, Andy, 'Former Tory PR advises Kenyans facing Hague trial', *Independent*, 14 Oct 2012

Rugene, Njeri, 'MPs compile new port poll suspects list', *Daily Nation*, 25 July 2009

Samora, Mwauru, 'Is this man Africa's only hope for justice?', *Daily Nation*, 7 December 2010

Shundu, Alphonce, 'Mutula Kilonzo vows new quest for Kenya's violence tribunal', *Daily Nation*, 23 March 2010

Shiundu, Alphnce, 'Ruto's ICC motions falters in Parliament', *Daily Nation*, 16 December 2010

South Consulting, Kenya National Dialogue and Reconciliation Monitoring Project, *Draft Review Report*, April 2011

South Consulting, Kenya National Dialogue and Reconciliation Monitoring Project, Kenya's 2013 General Election: A Review of the Environment and Electoral Preparedness, October 2012

South Consulting, Kenya National Dialogue and Reconciliation Monitoring Project, *National Baseline Survey*, January 2009

South Consulting, Kenya National Dialogue and Reconciliation Monitoring Project, Progress in the Implementation of the Constitution and Preparedness for 2012, Review Report, January 2012

South Consulting, Kenya National Dialogue and Reconciliation Monitoring Project, *Review Report*, October 2010

South Consulting, Kenya National Dialogue and Reconciliation Monitoring Project, *Review Report*, June 2011

South Consulting, Kenya National Dialogue and Reconciliation Monitoring Project, *Status of Implementation of Agenda Items 1-4, Progress Report for January-March 2010*, April 2010

State Law Office, Letter from the Attorney General, Amos Wako, to the Commissioner of Police, Mathew Iteere, dated 14 April 2011

Wabala, Dominic and Maina, Kamore, 'Kenya: Families of Ocampo Witnesses Get Threats', *The Star*, 7 November 2011

Wachira, Muchemi and Odunga, Dennis, 'Speed up poll chaos trials, Hague court urged', *Daily Nation*, 7 January 2010

Wambugu, Marybeth, '54 jailed over gender based post election violence crimes', *The Star*, 5 September 2013

Women's Initiative for Gender Justice, *Gender 2011 Report Card on the International Criminal Court* (Women's Initiatives for Gender Justice, 2011)

Chapter 6
Don't Be Vague, Go to The Hague!

The OTP, through its strategy of positive complementarity, sought to persuade the government to conduct domestic prosecutions in the hope that international prosecutions would not be required. The Prosecutor held meetings with government delegations in Nairobi and The Hague at which he stressed that impunity would not be an option. The Prosecutor entered into a complementarity contract and outlined a division of labour. He promised that if domestic prosecutions did not occur, international prosecutions would swiftly follow. The literature on positive complementarity suggests that this pressure ought to have provided a positive incentive for the government to support domestic prosecutions. So why was the special tribunal rejected on three separate occasions? Why was it that so many members of government threw their support behind international prosecutions, united in the popular catch cry, 'Don't be vague, go to The Hague'?

Although the OTP was not successful in convincing the government to conduct its own investigations and prosecutions, it does not necessarily follow that the OTP's strategy of positive complementarity had no influence over the government. Legislation that would have established a special tribunal to try the perpetrators was drafted, then debated by Parliament in January and February 2009 and Cabinet in July 2009. Another attempt to establish the tribunal was made in November 2009. At other times, promises were made to handle the perpetrators through the TJRC, the regular Kenyan courts and regional justice mechanisms. No such measures were taken following the post-election violence in 1992 and 1997, suggesting that the OTP may have exerted some degree of influence over the government during this period. This chapter therefore considers the extent to which the OTP's strategy of positive complementarity served as a catalyst for these debates over local justice mechanisms. In doing so, it also attempts to provide answers to a number of other questions relating to the effectiveness of the strategy of positive complementarity. At what times was the OTP most influential? Why were local justice mechanisms ultimately not pursued? How did the government respond to this exertion of pressure? Did the strategy of positive complementarity have a shadow side?

What lessons may be learned when applying the strategy of positive complementarity in the future?

In seeking to answer these questions, reference is made to a variety of sources. First, interviews with politicians, senior public servants, civil society organisations and journalists. Second, speeches made by politicians in Parliament, as recorded in Hansard. Third, statements made by politicians to the media in the form of press releases and interviews. Finally, the published opinions of those who were closely monitoring the government's attempts to hold perpetrators accountable, including ambassadors, intergovernmental organisations, non-governmental organisations and consultancy firms.

This chapter argues that, although the OTP's threat of prosecutions influenced politicians during the period under consideration, the strategy was ultimately unsuccessful in persuading them to support a local mechanism because senior leaders with blood on their hands were simply not prepared to commit political suicide by supporting the prosecution of themselves or their allies. As a consequence, such persons expressed support for the mechanism they felt was most likely to result in themselves of their allies evading accountability. Some favoured a special tribunal they felt they could control, while others threw their support behind an ICC process they considered would take many years to conclude and perhaps even longer if steps were taken to frustrate the progress of the cases. At the same time, however, politicians were well aware of the need to publicly demonstrate that they were committed to ending impunity. The OTP's constant insistence of the need to end impunity therefore had the effect of encouraging politicians to engage in a foreign affairs façade whereby they gave assurances that they supported the ICC process but simultaneously took steps designed to frustrate the progress of the cases.

1   An Unsuitable Strategy

Chapter 2 demonstrated that the OTP, upon receiving a communication that crimes within the Court's jurisdiction may have been committed, undertakes a preliminary examination into the situation. Throughout this phase the OTP, as a matter of course, commences its strategy of positive complementarity. In other words, the OTP commits itself to this strategy without first undertaking any assessment as to whether it has a reasonable prospect of succeeding. This is despite the fact that some situations may not be suitable for the adoption of such a strategy.

First, the strategy may be unsuitable in a situation where the leaders who the OTP are seeking to persuade are either themselves criminally responsible for the crimes committed or are the allies of those perpetrators. It might be considered rather unlikely that the OTP would have success in convincing such leaders to ensure that they themselves are investigated and prosecuted. For the same reason, the strategy of positive complementarity is less likely to be effective where the state authorities responsible for investigating crimes are themselves implicated in the violence, such as where police officers or members of the armed services are involved in the commission of crimes against humanity.

Second, even where the leaders are willing to support local trials, the strategy of positive complementarity is likely to fail where the target state is lacking the present ability to conduct its own investigations and prosecutions. As shown in Chap. 2, the assistance that the OTP is prepared to offer in this regard is limited to the sharing of legal resources and information, with the OTP stating on a number of occasions that the development of domestic legal institutions is beyond its mandate. Given that any necessary rule of law reforms would require some time before they become effective, it would seem that the success of the strategy of positive complementarity is contingent upon the situation country possessing the ability to investigate and prosecute at the time the communication is first sent to the OTP. This would require, at a minimum, competent, impartial and well-resourced investigatory organs and judges, an effective witness protection programme and sufficient public confidence in these institutions to encourage victims and witnesses to report crimes and testify in court.

There is good evidence to suggest that, following the post-election violence and the swearing in of the power-sharing GNU, the Kenyan authorities were both unwilling to prosecute themselves or their allies and lacking in the present ability to undertake such a task, thereby rendering the strategy of positive complementarity unsuitable in the Kenyan situation.

1.1 Political Suicide

Kenya's post-election violence period concluded in February 2008 when the two warring parties agreed to form a power-sharing government. As a consequence, local investigations and prosecutions required bipartisan support. Given that politicians from both PNU and ODM were believed to be responsible for crimes committed during this period, the possibility of obtaining such a commitment appeared remote at best. As one MP told Parliament on 3 February 2009, 'those who perpetrated the violence are in the government'.[1] It was optimistic, perhaps even naïve, for the OTP to assume that it could convince Kenya's politicians to hold the perpetrators of the post-election violence accountable when to do so required the politicians prosecuting themselves or their allies. Human rights activist and former MP Koigi wa Wamwere said the OTP was essentially seeking to persuade Kenya's politicians to 'commit political suicide'.[2] This was also what Budalangi MP Ababu Namwamba hinted at during debates over the establishment of the special tribunal when he said 'one looks around this House and wonders whether there is sufficient political will for the passage of this Bill'.[3] Similarly, after Kenya's parliamentarians boycotted a debate over the establishment of the special tribunal in December 2009, former Justice Minister Martha Karua suggested that 'it could be that some of those who planned and funded the violence are in government and that is why they are

---

[1] Hansard, National Assembly, Official Report, 3 February 2009.
[2] Interview with Koigi wa Wamwere (Nairobi, 6 May 2010).
[3] Hansard, National Assembly, Official Report, 5 February 2009.

able to block this initiative'.⁴ It is on this basis that the US Ambassador to Kenya, Michael Ranneberger, described Kenya's politicians as persons with a 'great desire for self-preservation'.⁵

Even if the OTP were to secure the cooperation from these politicians, effective investigations would not necessarily follow, since they would have to be conducted by police officers who were themselves responsible for many of the crimes committed during the post-election violence. The Attorney General, Amos Wako, hinted at his limited influence over the investigating and prosecuting authorities when he said that he wished to have 'the power not only to control, but also to direct investigations'.⁶ His successor, Githu Muigai, adopted a similar position, telling Parliament in November 2011 that 'authority to prosecute lies with [the] DPP. Only what I can do now is share with him the anxiety of the government that cases should move and move expeditiously'.⁷ Meanwhile, the DPP blamed the police for the lack of prosecutions at the local level.⁸ Many police officers were reluctant to investigate post-election violence crimes, with some even going so far as to prevent investigations from proceeding. One woman told the Waki Commission that when she went to the Kilimani police station to report having been raped by a police officer in Nairobi, the police officers told her that she was to blame for the rape.⁹ A man from Kisumu who attempted to report a police shooting of two of his children was told by one police officer that 'if you continue to play around, you could be shot, too'.¹⁰ A significant number of politicians, police officers and prosecuting authorities either had blood on their hands or had an interest in shielding those who did. It would seem that no amount of encouragement or threats would convince such persons to lend support for local prosecutions.

1.2 Domestic Inability

Even if the OTP were to succeed in persuading both sides of government and the investigating authorities to try suspects locally, the strategy of positive complementarity might still have failed due to domestic inability to investigate and prosecute the thousands of cases arising from the post-election violence. There were at least four significant challenges facing Kenya's legal institutions in the prosecution of the post-election violence suspects.

---

⁴Caroline Wafula, 'Kenya MPs shun debate on tribunal bill', *Daily Nation*, 2 December 2009.
⁵'Can Kibaki be proactive?', *Standard*, 19 December 2010.
⁶Oliver Mathenge, 'Wako—No Mercy for Poll Violence Leaders', *Daily Nation*, 25 August 2008.
⁷Hansard, National Assembly, Official Report, 24 November 2011.
⁸Paul Juma, 'AG defends prosecution record', *Daily Nation*, 23 September 2009.
⁹*Final Report from Kenya's Commission of Inquiry into Post-Election Violence*, 15 October 2008 ('Waki Report'), 401.
¹⁰Ibid, 61–62.

1 An Unsuitable Strategy

First, the Kenyan authorities were faced with tremendous logistical challenges in conducting investigations, with many of the victims and witnesses displaced and difficult to locate. In November 2011, Muigai told Parliament that since victims had yet to return to their homes, criminal investigation officers were finding it difficult to trace them.[11] This challenge was reiterated by the DPP, Keriako Tobiko, in April 2012, when he said that 'police have had serious logistical constraints. Witnesses were not available; some have been displaced'.[12] Police were also overwhelmed by the sheer number of cases reported to them.[13]

Second, Kenya's investigatory and prosecutorial authorities also had to contend with budgetary and personnel constraints. The ratio of police officers to citizens was 1:850, far short of the UN recommended ratio of 1:450.[14] According to KNDR, resources within the police force were so scarce that police officers demanded that witnesses purchase fuel so that the officers could travel to the crime scene.[15] The DPP reported that the post-election violence cases required about 900 prosecutors, but the DPP's budget only allowed for the employment of 90 prosecutors.[16] Many of these prosecutors were not sufficiently qualified to handle complex cases, with some having completed no more than a primary-level education.[17] The DPP was also experiencing an acute shortage of equipment such as computers, printers and photocopiers.[18]

Consequently, there were serious flaws in the investigation of many cases, with forensic and documentary evidence often mishandled.[19] One glaring example of investigatory incompetence was revealed in the Kiambaa church case, where one witnesses giving evidence that on 9 April 2008 the police had entered her home to arrest her husband in connection with the incident, only to discover that he had died five years earlier.[20] At times, senior public servants and politicians who bore the ultimate responsibility for the effective functioning of the investigatory organs expressed their frustrations over this inability. In September 2009, Tobiko blamed

---

[11] Hansard, National Assembly, Official Report, 23 November 2011.

[12] Judie Kaberia, 'DPP not working to salvage Ocampo Four', *Capital News*, 12 April 2012.

[13] Director of Public Prosecutions, A report to the Hon. Attorney General by the team on the review of post election violence related cases in Western, Nyanza, Central, Rift Valley, Eastern, Coast and Nairobi Provinces, February 2009 ('AG 2009 Report'), 40.

[14] Patricia Kameri Mbote and Migai Akech, Kenya: Justice Sector and the Rule of Law (Open Society Foundation, March 2011) ('OSI Rule of Law Report'), 128.

[15] South Consulting, Kenya National Dialogue and Reconciliation Monitoring Project, *Review Report for October-December 2009*, January 2010) ('KNDR January 2010 Report'), 12.

[16] Ibid.

[17] Human Rights Watch, *Turning Pebbles: Evading Accountability for Post-Election Violence in Kenya, 2011*, 50 ('HRW, Turning Pebbles'); Oliver Mathenge, 'New report says 5,000 election violence cases stalled due to lack of evidence', *Daily Nation*, 7 January 2012.

[18] AG 2009 Report (see Footnote 13), 39.

[19] Eric White, *Putting Complementarity in Practice: Domestic Justice for International Crimes in DRC, Uganda, and Kenya* (Open Society Justice Initiative, 2011), 86–87; Philip Alston, *Mission to Kenya 16–25 February 2009* (United Nations Special Rapporteur on Extrajudicial Killings, Arbitrary or Summary Executions, 2009) ('Alston Report'), 27.

[20] *Republic v Stephen Kiprotich Leting & 3 others* [2009] eKLR, Criminal Case 34 of 2008.

the police, investigators and judges for the lack of prosecutions at the local level.[21] Similarly, when Justice Waki publicly asked Wako whether the police had the capacity to investigate crimes committed by the security forces, Wako responded by saying 'Your guess is as good as mine'.[22]

Third, the investigating authorities encountered great difficulties in convincing victims and witnesses to report crimes and give evidence in court. Victims and witnesses had little confidence in the criminal justice system and so were deterred from cooperating. In October 2011, KNDR reported that 58% of Kenyans believed that the government could not conduct local investigations and 64% believed that the government was not able to protect witnesses who gave evidence.[23] Many victims therefore instead either elected not to report crimes at all, or to report crimes to NGOs, local administrative officials or members of Parliament, thereby hampering the police force's ability to conduct investigations.[24] Of course, this lack of reporting contributed to an insufficient number of successful prosecutions, thereby leading to greater public cynicism in the criminal justice system and further withholding of cooperation.

Finally, it is possible that the judiciary, with a backlog of some 800,000 cases, may have struggled to handle the thousands of extra cases.[25] The DPP explained that the low number of convictions were because 'the judicial system [was] simply overwhelmed'.[26] In February 2010, ICJ-Kenya reported that there were 335 judges and magistrates working in Kenya but another 303 unfilled vacancies.[27] Even if all posts were filled, the ratio of judges to citizens would have been 1:61,000 which was well below the ratio of countries with comparable populations.[28] Indeed, in its Article 19 admissibility challenge, lodged in May 2011, the government stated that when promised judicial forms were completed, the 'national courts would *now* be capable of trying crimes from the [post-election violence]'.[29] In other words, the government was itself admitting that, as late as 2011, its courts did not have the capacity to try the post-election violence suspects.

---

[21] Paul Juma, 'AG defends prosecution record', *Daily Nation*, 23 September 2009.

[22] Oliver Mathenge, 'Wako: no mercy for poll violence leaders', *Daily Nation*, 25 August 2008.

[23] South Consulting, Kenya National Dialogue and Reconciliation Monitoring Project, *Progress in the Implementation of the Constitution and other reforms, Review Report*, October 2011 ('KNDR October 2011 Report'), viii, 57.

[24] HRW, Turning Pebbles (see Footnote 17), 61.

[25] Antonina Okuta, 'National Legislation for Prosecution of International Crimes in Kenya' (2009) 7(5) *Journal of International Criminal Justice* 1063.

[26] OSI Rule of Law Report (see Footnote 14), 124–125..

[27] International Bar Association and International Legal Assistance Consortium, *Restoring Integrity: An assessment of the needs of the justice system in the Republic of Kenya* (International Bar Association and International Legal Assistance Consortium, February 2010) ('IBA Report'), 75–76.

[28] Ibid.

[29] *Prosecutor v William Samoei Ruto, Henry Kiprono Kosgey and Joshua Arap Sang*, ICC-01/11, Application on Behalf of the Government of the Republic of Kenya Pursuant to Article 19 of the ICC Statute, ICC-01/09–01/11–19, 31 March 2011 ('Article 19 Application'), [2] (emphasis added).

In summary, the OTP's confidence in the government's ability to investigate and prosecute perpetrators may have been misplaced. For all of these reasons, the strategy of positive complementarity faced significant challenges in Kenya. Had an assessment been carried out during an early stage of the preliminary examinations phase, the OTP may have concluded that the strategy had little prospect of success and therefore considered its adoption to have been futile.

2 The OTP's Influence

2.1 Not the Initial Impetus

In assessing the extent to which the OTP served as a catalyst for domestic prosecutions in Kenya, it is first important to appreciate that the initial impetus for domestic accountability mechanisms does not appear to have come from the OTP. Although the OTP's threat to commence international prosecutions played a significant role in the debate over accountability mechanisms, it would be overly simplistic and misleading to suggest that such debates were the result of the OTP's strategy of positive complementarity. Rather, it is submitted that the initial impetus for holding perpetrators accountable was a sense of a national shame and an apprehension of future violence.

For decades, Kenya prided itself on being a stable country in an otherwise volatile region; a country that accepted refugees, not one that created them.[30] The scale and intensity of the post-election violence therefore shocked the country's conscience and became a source of national shame. MP Eugene Wamalwa told Parliament that during the violence 'we saw this nation at its lowest ebb'.[31] The Foreign Affairs Minister, Moses Wetangula was even more forthright, declaring that 'we defecated in our house and, therefore, must clean it'.[32] Expressing the concern of many MPs over the damage that the post-election violence had done to Kenya's international reputation, Abdul Bahari stressed that it was 'extremely important that we have an opportunity to repair our dented image'.[33] The Prosecutor himself recognised that Kenyans felt a sense a shame about their past, stating 'the reason I feel Kenya is good is because no one is proud of the violence. That's unique compared to other countries I have been to'.[34]

Coupled with this feeling of national shame was a widely held fear for Kenya's future. The Assistant Minister for Tourism, Cecily Mbarire, expressed concern that the post-election violence was 'the beginning of the end of Kenya' and predicted that

---

[30] Maina Kiai, 'The Crisis in Kenya' (2008) 19 *Journal of Democracy* 162; Jacqueline Klopp, 'Kenya's Unfinished Agendas' (2009) 62(2) *Journal of International Affairs* 162.
[31] Hansard, National Assembly, Official Report, 27 January 2009.
[32] Hansard, National Assembly, Official Report, 5 February 2009.
[33] Hansard, National Assembly, Official Report, 4 February 2009.
[34] Lucianne Limo, Beauttah Omanga and Vincent Bartoo, 'Ocampo asks Kenyans not to expect too much', *Standard*, 11 May (2010).

the country could witness even greater violence at the next general elections if the government did not respond appropriately.[35] Similarly, Rachael Shebesh told Parliament that Kenya risked 'turning into a failed state' before comparing the country to Rwanda, Uganda and Liberia.[36] Abdul Bahari and Mohammed Affey also expressed concerns that Kenya could suffer a similar fate to Rwanda in 1994, with the latter saying that 'what happened there could easily happen here'.[37] There was therefore a real sense that Kenya had reached a crossroads and that its future would be determined by the Tenth Parliament's response to the post-election violence. Kilonzo, for example, informed Parliament that the Chinese word for 'crisis' combined the words for 'danger' and 'opportunity' before going on to explain the importance of holding post-election violence suspects accountable.[38]

Perhaps the most pressing issue for Kenya's politicians was to 'end impunity', which Karua stressed was necessary to ensure Kenya's 'survival as a nation'.[39] For Karua, it was essential that Kenya rid itself of the 'ghost of election violence which started in the year 1992 … was repeated in 1997 and, finally came to haunt us in 2007'.[40] Similarly, the Minister for Lands, James Orengo, lamented Kenya's history of forming committees to investigate and report on previous instances of electoral violence, only for their recommendations to be ignored.[41] The Assistant Minister for Immigration, Francis Baya, told Parliament that 'those reports have been gathering dust instead of producing results' and that 'this time, as a country, we are more serious than before'.[42]

This process of ending impunity by holding post-election violence suspects accountable began long before the OTP began imposing serious pressure upon the government. On 24 January 2008, with the violence still ongoing, Annan initiated the KNDR process which ultimately resulted in agreement between the two conflicting parties on four agenda items that were designed to ensure long-lasting peace in Kenya. One of these items, Agenda Item IV, sought to address long-term issues and the root causes of the conflict by, *inter alia*, 'addressing impunity, transparency and accountability'.[43] This formed the basis for an agreement to establish the Waki Commission, which was mandated to provide a narration on the violence, examine its causes and make recommendations to prevent recurrence. The Waki Commission recommended the establishment of a special tribunal to try suspected perpetrators

---

[35] Hansard, National Assembly, Official Report, 5 February 2009.
[36] Hansard, National Assembly, Official Report, 22 December 2010.
[37] Ibid; Hansard, National Assembly, Official Report, 4 February 2009.
[38] Hansard, National Assembly, Official Report, 3 February 2009.
[39] Hansard, National Assembly, Official Report, 5 February 2009.
[40] Hansard, National Assembly, Official Report, 3 February 2009.
[41] Ibid.
[42] Hansard, National Assembly, Official Report, 27 January 2009.
[43] South Consulting, *The Kenya National Dialogue and Reconciliation (KNDR) Monitoring Project*, January 2009 ('KNDR January 2009 Report').

2   The OTP's Influence   141

and, on 16 December 2008, Kibaki and Odinga agreed to implement this recommendation. During the second reading speech in Parliament the following month, Karua said that:

> ... this Bill is as a result of the deliberations of the National Accord and the subsequent agreement by the parties which established the ... Waki Commission. Following those recommendations, it was agreed that a special tribunal be established to deal with these cases emanating from the post-election violence.[44]

By this time the OTP had done little to exert pressure upon the government to investigate and prosecute suspected perpetrators at the local level. The Prosecutor had yet to visit Kenya or receive a delegation in The Hague. Indeed, the OTP's actions appear to have been limited to the issuance of a 48-word statement in February 2008 announcing that it was 'carefully considering' whether crimes had been committed and its requests for further information that were made the following month.[45]

At this time, the major impetus for local investigations and prosecutions seems to have been national shame that followed from the violence, combined with a fear that future violence would occur should perpetrators not be held accountable. The OTP did little to encourage progress in this regard, instead leaving this for the Annan-led KNDR. Throughout 2008, Annan received regular updates on the government's progress and arranged meetings with both Kibaki and Odinga.[46]

Although it is suggested that the OTP and its strategy was not the catalyst for initiatives to ensure accountability, it is clear that it did exert a great deal of pressure over this period and influenced debates over local justice mechanisms. This is demonstrated below through an analysis of the references to the ICC and the Prosecutor in parliamentary debates and the media during this period. It is argued that the OTP's strategy of positive complementarity influenced leaders' decision-making calculus but that this influence was not constant throughout this period. It is also suggested that, although politicians were aware of the ICC and influenced by its threat of prosecutions, the majority ultimately responded to the OTP in accordance with their own vested interests, which most of the time did not include local prosecutions.

---

[44] Hansard, National Assembly, Official Report, 3 February 2009.

[45] International Criminal Court Office of the Prosecutor, 'OTP Statement in Relation to Events in Kenya', 5 February 2008 ('OTP February 2008 Statement'); International Criminal Court, Situation in the Republic of Kenya, Request for authorisation of an investigation pursuant to Article 15, ICC-01/09, 26 November 2009 ('OTP Request for Authorisation').

[46] African Union, Panel of Eminent African Personalities, Press Statement by Kofi Annan, 23 September 2008 ('Annan September 2008 Statement').

2.2 Influencing Leaders

There is strong evidence to suggest that during this period, the OTP's strategy of positive complementarity had some influence over Kenya's leaders. This section first demonstrates that politicians were aware of the OTP's threatened involvement, before providing three arguments to demonstrate that these politicians were influenced by the OTP's actions.

There can be little doubting that Kenya's politicians were conscious of the ICC and aware of the OTP's potential to conduct its own investigations and prosecutions. One month before the special tribunal legislation was debated in Parliament, the government passed the *International Crimes Act 2008*. The purpose of this legislation was 'to enable Kenya to co-operate with the ICC in the performance of its functions'.[47] During the Act's third reading, the Attorney General described it as 'an Act of Parliament to domestic the Rome Statute which establishes the International Criminal Court'.[48] The similarities between the *International Crimes Act 2008* and the *Special Tribunal for Kenya Bill 2009*, on the one hand, and the Rome Statute on the other, also suggests that Kenya's lawmakers were conscious of the ICC. The *International Crimes Act 2008* did not define the international crimes of genocide, crimes against humanity and war crimes, but instead referred to the Rome Statute for their definition.[49] In addition, the Act provided that certain provisions of the Rome Statute were directly applicable in Kenyan law, such as those relating to command responsibility, superior orders and the statute of limitations.[50] In the words of one of the drafters of the Act, 'the legislation very much copied the principles of the Rome Statute'.[51] Likewise, the *Special Tribunal for Kenya Bill 2009* was heavily influenced by the ICC. The Bill did not provide for the elements of each of the crimes within the proposed tribunal's jurisdiction, but instead made reference to the ICC.[52] Other indicators of ICC influence in the drafting of this legislation included the establishment of a defence office, the acceptance of victim involvement in the proceedings and recognition of victims' right to compensation.[53] It is clear, therefore, that legislators were aware of the ICC when deciding whether or not to establish a special tribunal.

The first piece of evidence to suggest that the OTP influenced Kenya's politicians relates to the statements made in Parliament during debates over the establishment of the special tribunal. The OTP's strategy of positive complementarity appears to have had the effect of altering the political calculus. Whereas politicians following the violence in 1992 and 1997 were faced with a choice between *domestic prosecutions* and *impunity*, the OTP's threatened involvement meant that on this occasion, many

---

[47] International Crimes Act 2008, Preamble.
[48] Hansard, National Assembly, Official Report, 11 December 2009.
[49] International Crimes Act 2008, section 6(4).
[50] Okuta (2009) (see Footnote 25).
[51] Interview with Fred Mwachi (Nairobi, 19 May 2010).
[52] Special Tribunal for Kenya Bill 2009, section 13.
[53] Ibid, sections 32, 50, 55.

regarded the choice as being between *domestic prosecutions* and *international prosecutions*. Statements from politicians suggest that their decision-making was influenced by a belief that if domestic prosecutions did not occur, international prosecutions would follow. Soon after the release of the Waki Report, Karua said 'we must ask ourselves: do we prefer this matter to be taken over by the ICC or do we set up a tribunal through an Act of Parliament?'.[54] Likewise, Wetengula warned that 'if we end up failing to rise to the occasion and give this country a tribunal, we are faced with The Hague option'.[55] Kilonzo told Parliament that 'if we say we cannot set up [the special tribunal] here, we are saying that a lot of [the post-election violence suspects] will, in fact, be arrested, investigated and taken to The Hague'.[56] On another occasion, Kilonzo stated that 'the best way to avoid the ICC is to establish as quickly as possible credible institutions as envisaged by the Rome Statute to handle the suspects'.[57] Minister for Lands James Orengo also supported the special tribunal because of a fear of ICC intervention: 'if we have local legislation that meets international standards, then there can be no intervention by any power, including the ICC, in any of the affairs in this country'.[58] In short, the government seemed to consider its decision to be binary in nature: either prosecutions in Kenya or prosecutions in The Hague.

The prospect of Kenyan citizens facing trial in The Hague appears to have motivated some politicians into supporting the special tribunal's establishment in order to preserve Kenya's state sovereignty. MP Joseph Lekuton, for example, argued that:

> Kenya should manage its own affairs and take charge of its sovereignty. We cannot surrender or cede it to any nation or agency. We must protect that treasured right … the moment we let people go to The Hague, we will cede our sovereignty and capability to think as a nation and as a society. We will forever be slaves to forces that are larger than us.[59]

Vice President Kalonzo Musyoka lobbied for his peers to support the special tribunal on the same basis: 'for goodness sake, let us not give away the sovereignty of this wonderful land'.[60] The Assistant Minister for Education, Asman Kamamba, told Parliament that 'sovereignty is like virginity. Once you lose it, it is gone forever'.[61] Perhaps the most impassioned plea came from Environment Minister, John Michuki, who said 'people have offered to be killed to defend their own sovereignty … In the same token, if [Kenyan citizens] are taken to The Hague, we shall cede our own sovereignty and shall cease to be sovereign'.[62]

---

[54] David Mugonyi and Bernard Namunane, 'MPs demand Waki's secret envelope', *Daily Nation*, 31 October 2008.
[55] Hansard, National Assembly, Official Report, 5 February 2009.
[56] Hansard, National Assembly, Official Report, 3 February 2009.
[57] Peter Leftie, 'Kilonzo: time running out for Ocampo Six', *Daily Nation*, 24 March 2011.
[58] Hansard, National Assembly, Official Report, 27 January 2009.
[59] Hansard, National Assembly, Official Report, 4 February 2009.
[60] Hansard, National Assembly, Official Report, 3 February 2009.
[61] Hansard, National Assembly, Official Report, 4 February 2009.
[62] Ibid.

In addition, the OTP's threatened intervention had the prospect of further bruising the national pride and this also had the effect of imposing pressure upon politicians to establish the special tribunal. The scale and intensity of the violence was already one cause for shame; revealing to the international community that the government did not have the capacity to adequately respond to the crisis risked becoming another. At a dinner honouring the appointment of Kenyan judge Joyce Aluoch to the ICC, Wako noted that 'the international community has honoured us … we would shame ourselves by letting the post-election matter go to The Hague'.[63] Njoroge Baiya also made reference to Kenya's international reputation in his address to Parliament: 'if this country wants to be seen, at the international level, as upholding the rule of law and democracy, at the very minimum we must demonstrate that we are in charge of our own affairs'.[64] Others, including Kilonzo, Musyoka and Assistant Minister for Nairobi Metropolitan Development, Elizabeth Ongoro, argued that the special tribunal should be established to demonstrate that Kenya was not a 'failed state'.[65]

A second example of the OTP's influence over politicians during this period concerned the frenzied speculation over the identity of persons in the sealed envelope. In November 2009, Odinga told Parliament that 'so many names may be in that list, even my name'.[66] Wealthy farmer and businessman Jackson Kibor admitted that his name was one of those contained in the sealed envelope.[67] Former Naivasha MP Jayne Kihara tearfully told the media that she was expecting to be indicted by the ICC.[68] In December 2010, just before the Ocampo Six was named, Eldoret South MP Peris Simam made the following statement in Parliament:

> Mr Speaker, there has been speculations about the Ocampo list and I have not been having enough sleep because I have been dreaming that I am on that list. My dreams normally come true but I hope that one doesn't become true because I am innocent.[69]

Even before the Prosecutor made his request for authorisation to conduct investigations in Kenya, two senior Cabinet ministers, a senior intelligence officer and a former senior security official had sought legal advice and commenced preparations for their defence.[70] In May 2010, MPs Edick Anyanga and John Pesa publicly announced that they were willing to meet with the Prosecutor in order to clear their names, while in October 2010 another unnamed Kenyan wrote to the OTP to promise that he would voluntarily surrender to the Court should he be named as a suspect.[71] Indeed, at one stage the speculation over who may be prosecuted became

---

[63] Bornice Biomndo, 'Pass tribunal law, Wako urges MPs', *Daily Nation*, 28 January 2009.

[64] Hansard, National Assembly, Official Report, 4 February 2009.

[65] Ibid; 'The Hague not an option, say Kalonzo', *Daily Nation*, 16 November 2008; Hansard, National Assembly, Official Report, 5 February 2009.

[66] Hansard, National Assembly, Official Report, 18 November 2009.

[67] 'Who is in the ICC list?', *Standard*, 5 March 2010.

[68] Ibid.

[69] Hansard, National Assembly, Official Report, 10 December 2010.

[70] Lucianne Limo, 'Ministers hire lawyers', *Standard*, 16 October 2009; Beauttah Omanga, 'Poll violence suspects seek legal help before Ocampo arrives', *Standard*, 2 May 2010.

[71] Samwel Kumba, 'December trial for Kenya violence suspects', *Daily Nation*, 11 May 2010; Eric Shimoli, 'Top Kenyan is ready to surrender at The Hague', *Daily Nation*, 13 October 2010.

so frenetic that Odinga publicly called on politicians not to panic over the ICC's involvement.[72]

The third and perhaps most compelling demonstration of the OTP's influence during this period, however, relates to senior politicians changing their position on accountability mechanisms at or around the same time that the OTP made progress with its investigations and prosecutions. The most obvious example is that of Ruto, who was long suspected of being one of the masterminds of the violence and was ultimately named in the Ocampo Six. Despite being one of the prime suspects for trial in The Hague, Ruto's initial position was to favour ICC prosecutions over the establishment of a special tribunal. In February 2009, he said 'Kofi Annan should hand over the envelope that contains the names of suspects to the International Criminal Court at The Hague so that proper investigations can start'.[73] Ruto's position appears to have been premised on a belief that his best hope for avoiding responsibility rested in the slow turning wheels of international criminal justice, because he famously told a Kalenjin rally that it would take 99 years for the ICC to begin its work.[74] Less than one week after Annan delivered the envelope to the OTP, Ruto changed his position, announcing that he supported the post-election violence cases being handled by the TJRC.[75] After Ruto was named as a suspect in December 2010, he and his Kalenjin allies from the Rift Valley again changed their position, this time calling for the suspects to be tried by the ordinary Kenyan courts.[76] They then commenced a campaign to discredit the ICC process, which they argued had become politicised. On the day that he was announced as a suspect, Ruto said 'all along I knew there was a deliberate scheme, hatched and executed by people who were not interested in justice'.[77] Odinga highlighted the contradictions and hypocrisy in Ruto opposing ICC trials, describing him as 'the conductor of the choir whose hit song was *"Don't be vague, go for The Hague"*'.[78]

Odinga himself, however, was not consistent in his position regarding the post-election violence cases. The Prime Minister was not present for the vote on the special tribunal legislation, made no speeches in favour of the tribunal and appears to have made no attempts to encourage his allies to support the legislation. Nevertheless, soon after the tribunal was rejected by Parliament, he appeared to support its establishment, saying 'the shooting down of the Bill is like a woman who has miscarried, which does not mean that is the end of her giving birth'.[79] He issued a press release in which he said that the special tribunal was the only mechanism

---

[72] Caroline Wafula, 'Don't Panic, Raila tells leaders', *Daily Nation*, 18 November 2009.

[73] 'Ruto: why I prefer The Hague route', *Daily Nation*, 21 February 2009.

[74] Oscar Obonyo, 'Beyond Ocampo 'Big Six' poll chaos suspects', *Standard*, 12 May 2010; Oscar Obonyo, 'Push and pull in search for justice for chaos victims', *Standard*, 11 December 2010.

[75] Daniel Otieno, Bernard Namunane and Lucas Barasa, 'Ruto beats a retreat, rejects Hague trials', *Daily Nation*, 15 July 2009.

[76] Peter Opiyo, 'MPs revive push for local tribunal, claim Hague partial', *Standard*, 13 December 2010; 'Ruto lawyer opposes ICC trials', *Daily Nation*, 1 May 2011.

[77] Anthony Kariuki and Oliver Mathenge, 'Ocampo names Kenya chaos suspects', *Daily Nation*, 15 December 2010.

[78] Eliud Owalo, Raila for President Secretariat, Press Release, 6 November 2012.

[79] 'Bid for local tribunal still on, says PM', *Daily Nation*, 15 February 2009.

suitable for trying the post-election violence suspects and later that same week persuaded Annan of the government's commitment to the local mechanism.[80] In July 2009, he again changed his position, supporting Cabinet's decision to have suspects dealt with by the TJRC. Just before the naming of the Ocampo Six, Odinga again changed his mind by throwing his support behind the ICC process: 'you know we tried to set up a local tribunal but MPs rejected it. This is how the envelope ended up with The Hague and we have no option but to co-operate with the ICC process'.[81] The day after the naming of the Ocampo Six, Odinga appeared to again change his stance as he told Parliament that Cabinet's first preference was to 'establish a credible local process for the investigation and prosecution of the six persons' so that the government could challenge the admissibility of the cases before the ICC.[82] In March 2011, Odinga again supported the establishment of a credible local mechanism,[83] but later in that month he said the Ocampo Six should go to The Hague to clear their names.[84] While campaigning for the presidency in Ruto's constituency of Eldoret, he changed his position once more, declaring that if he were to be elected, he would lobby for the four Kenyans facing charges at The Hague to be tried locally.[85]

While circumstantial, the fact that Ruto and Odinga (and their allies) so frequently changed positions on accountability mechanisms, often around the time of significant developments in the ICC process, suggests that the ICC was influencing the politicians' decision-making. As Kenyan-based international lawyer Godfrey Musila noted:

> Political elites, in particular those reported to be on the list of accused prepared by the Waki Commission, have vacillated between the various options, unsure which would safeguard their own agendas: trials in The Hague or local tribunals; trials before the special tribunal or nationals courts; and/or the TJRC.[86]

In summary, there is good evidence that the ICC's threatened presence influenced the government. It altered the decision-making calculus, prompted frenzied speculation over the names in the sealed envelope and is likely to have influenced leaders into flip-flopping between various positions. Having demonstrated that Kenya's politicians were aware of the ICC and were influenced by its actions, the next point to consider is whether this influence was constant throughout this period.

---

[80] 'How Kenya handled local tribunal process', *Daily Nation*, 17 September 2013; Abiya Ochola, 'Annan to delay envelope for two more months', *Standard*, 18 February 2009.

[81] 'Kenya committed to ICC and judicial reforms', *Kenya Broadcasting Commission*, 30 November 2010.

[82] Hansard, National Assembly, Official Report, 16 December 2010.

[83] Patrick Mayoyo and Bernard Namunane, 'ODM Pushes for ICC-Led Local Trials', *Daily Nation*, 23 March 2011.

[84] David Opiyo, 'Clear the Air on Trials, ODM Told', *Daily Nation*, 25 March 2011.

[85] 'Winning presidency won't assuage ICC—Raila', *Capital News*, 5 November 2012.

[86] Godfrey Musila, 'Options for Transitional Justice in Kenya: Autonomy and the Challenge of External Prescriptions' (2009) 3 *International Journal of Transitional Justice* 445, 450.

2.3 Imminent but not Inevitable

The OTP's influence over the government does not appear to have been constant throughout the period under investigation. Rather, it appears to have fluctuated depending on the government's perceptions of the likelihood and imminence of international prosecutions. When the OTP's threat of prosecutions was seen to be far-fetched or remote, the OTP had little influence over the government. When the threat was perceived to be real and imminent, however, the government responded with a flurry of activities to demonstrate that it was handling the post-election violence cases locally. Yet when the OTP moved beyond *threatening* prosecutions to *commencing* prosecutions, its influence over the government again diminished, possibly because the commencement of proceedings in The Hague removed a major incentive for domestic trials. It would therefore seem that the OTP's strategy of positive complementarity was most influential when the government perceived international prosecutions to be *imminent* but not *inevitable*.

The prospect of Kenyans being tried by the ICC first entered the public discourse in October 2008 when the Waki Commission published its report and delivered the sealed envelope to Annan. In order to avoid having this envelope forwarded to the OTP, the government was required to agree to the establishment of a special tribunal within 60 days and to pass legislation that would establish that tribunal within a further 45 days.[87] At this time, however, many regarded ICC prosecutions to be far-fetched, while others were of the opinion that even if they did commence, progress would be slow. There were good reasons for believing that any progress the OTP would make in the Kenyan situation would be measured not in days or weeks, but rather in years and possibly even decades. By October 2008 (when the Waki Report was published), the ICC had been in operation for over six years, but had indicted just twelve suspects and had yet to commence its first trial. Meanwhile, high-profile trials before other international courts were also proving to be laborious. The former president of the Republika Srpska, Radovan Karadžić had been arrested just three months earlier, having been a fugitive from the ICTY for almost 13 years. Similarly, more than five and a half years had passed since the Special Court for Sierra Leone indicted former Liberian president Charles Taylor, but the prosecution was only midway through the presentation of its case. As a consequence, Ruto was able to confidently assure his Kalenjin followers that the ICC would take 99 years for international prosecutions to commence.[88] With Hague trials considered to be a distant prospect, the government took no significant steps to ensure that post-election violence suspects would be held accountable either through a special tribunal or some other local mechanism.

As the Waki Report's two deadlines approached, however, the government regarded the ICC prosecutions to be more imminent and a great deal of activity fol-

---

[87] Waki Report (see Footnote 9) [473].
[88] Oscar Obonyo, 'Beyond Ocampo 'Big Six' poll chaos suspects', *Standard*, 12 May 2010; Oscar Obonyo, 'Push and pull in search for justice for chaos victims', *Standard*, 11 December 2010.

lowed. On 16 December 2008, one day before the expiration of the first deadline, Kibaki and Odinga signed a document agreeing to establish the special tribunal.[89] The following month, Kibaki recalled Parliament early to enable it 'to reconvene and deliberate and conclude important legislative matters that remained outstanding'.[90] At the top of the government's agenda was the passing of the necessary legislation to establish the special tribunal, which the Waki Report required to be completed by 29 January 2009. In order to meet this deadline, the legislation's sponsor, Martha Karua moved one motion to extend Parliament's sitting hours, and another motion to shorten the Bill's publication period from the customary fourteen days to one day.[91] The motion was defeated and debate took place in the week following the expiration of the deadline, with Annan retaining possession of the sealed envelope.

When Parliament voted against the establishment of the special tribunal, Annan responded by granting an extension until 31 August 2009.[92] This development caused many persons within the government to again doubt the imminence of ICC prosecutions and, consequently, the OTP's strategy of positive complementarity had little if any influence in encouraging the establishment of the special tribunal during this period. Indeed, in the five months from February 2009 to July 2009, there is no evidence of progress having been made in this regard. The government instead elected during this period to prioritise other issues, including the formation of a truth commission, electoral commission, boundary review commission and national cohesion commission.[93] According to the ICTJ's Njonjo Mue, the government saw Annan's granting of an extension as being an opportunity for them to 'push the envelope'.[94]

These politicians were again spurred into action following Annan's decision on 9 July 2009 to deliver the sealed envelope to the OTP. In the one week between Annan's delivery of the sealed envelope and its opening by the Prosecutor, the government made more progress in establishing the special tribunal than it had in the preceding five months. On the same day that Annan delivered the envelope, Kibaki hurriedly convened a crisis meeting of senior politicians to discuss the prospect of the OTP intervening and to receive an update on the progress that had been made in prosecuting the post-election violence suspects.[95] The government delegation held a press conference that evening during which they promised to comply with the Prosecutor's

---

[89] African Union, Panel of Eminent African Personalities, Statement of H E Kofi Annan on the Implementation of the Report of the Commission of Inquiry on Post-Election Violence (CIPEV) & Independent Review Commission (IREC), 19 December 2008.

[90] Office of the President, 'Parliament to reconvene on 20th January', 8 January 2009.

[91] Hansard, National Assembly, Official Report, 29 January 2009.

[92] African Union, Panel of Eminent African Personalities, Note on handover of CIPEV materials to the Prosecutor of the ICC, 29 July 2009 ('Annan Sealed Envelope Statement').

[93] Alphonce Shiundu, 'Reform tops agenda as Parliament opens', *Daily Nation*, 19 April 2009.

[94] Interview with Njonjo Mue (Nairobi, 10 May 2010).

[95] David Ohito, 'Government in crisis talks as Annan hands over secret envelope to the ICC', *Standard*, 10 July 2009.

demand for a special tribunal be established.[96] Also during this week, Wako sent the OTP two reports: one on the status of post-election violence cases and another on the operationalisation of Kenya's witness protection programme.[97] Kilonzo was also active during this week, presenting revised versions of the special tribunal legislation to Cabinet, which then spent four hours debating the proposal.[98]

Two days after Cabinet resolved not to establish a special tribunal, the Prosecutor announced that he had not yet decided whether to open an investigation in Kenya.[99] This appears to have once again caused the government to doubt the imminence of ICC prosecutions. Despite Cabinet's commitment to undertaking 'accelerated and far-reaching reforms',[100] no significant reforms occurred in the months that followed, with Parliament going on a two-month recess during this period.

As the government had made little or no progress in holding post-election perpetrators accountable, the Prosecutor decided to commence the OTP's investigatory progress, informing the government of his decision in writing on 27 October 2009 and in person during a visit to Nairobi on 5 November 2009.[101] One might have expected the imminence of ICC prosecutions to once again stimulate further activity at the local level, as it had done for the preceding twelve months, but, notably, this did not occur. This appears to have been because the government regarded the ICC process to have been not just *imminent* but also *inevitable*, thereby removing a major incentive for handling the post-election violence cases locally. When Imanyara introduced his proposal for a special tribunal, the local mechanism was no longer seen as an *alternative* to the ICC, but was instead regarded as *complementary* to it. Supporters of the legislation spoke about the need for the ICC process 'to continue' and for the special tribunal to 'collaborate with it'.[102] With the proposed special tribunal having no prospect of stopping an ICC process perceived to be inevitable, the vast majority of politicians did not even bother to attend the debate in Parliament and the Bill was scuppered for a lack of quorum.[103]

This perception that ICC trials were inevitable was reinforced through statements made by the Prosecutor during this period. The Prosecutor emphasised the strength of the OTP's case, assured Kenyans that no persons would be immune from

---

[96] David Ohito, 'Government in crisis talks as Annan hands over secret envelope to the ICC', *Standard*, 10 July 2009.

[97] International Criminal Court Office of the Prosecutor, 'ICC Prosecutor Receives Materials on Post-Election Violence in Kenya', 16 July 2009 ('OTP First Statement on the Sealed Envelope').

[98] Bernard Namunane and Lucas Barasa, 'Cabinet rejects draft laws on local tribunal', *Daily Nation*, 14 July 2009.

[99] 'Kenyan Cabinet in the eye of a storm', *Daily Nation*, 1 August 2009.

[100] Office of the President, 'Cabinet Decides on TJRC', 30 July 2009.

[101] OTP Request for Authorisation (see Footnote 45) [20]; Hansard, National Assembly, Official Report, 18 November 2009.

[102] Hansard, National Assembly, Official Report, 11 November 2009.

[103] Ibid.

prosecution and promised that all cases would be handled expeditiously.[104] Perhaps as a consequence of these statements, the OTP received little cooperation from the government in relation to its demands that a special tribunal or other local mechanism be established to complement the ICC. Despite the OTP's sustained insistence that ending impunity in Kenya required a local justice mechanism to complement the ICC trials, in the twelve months between December 2009 and December 2010, the government did not take any significant action to ensure that the post-election violence suspects were held accountable. At no stage did Cabinet or Parliament debate the formation of a local mechanism and, although a new Constitution was passed, the promised accelerated legal reforms never materialised.

In December 2010, the Prosecutor named the Ocampo Six but rather than confirming the inevitability of the ICC process, this development seems to have inspired many politicians to consider possible ways of deferring or subverting the progress of trials in The Hague. As discussed later in this chapter, sections of the government explored various options including withdrawal from the Rome Statute, Security Council deferral, arranging for suspects to be tried in regional courts and challenging the admissibility of the cases before the ICC. These attempts to defer and subvert demonstrate that at least some politicians no longer considered international prosecutions to be inevitable. As a consequence, there was again a stimulus of activity with respect to accountability for the post-election violence. On the day after the Prosecutor's announcement of the Ocampo Six, Odinga told Parliament that Cabinet was looking to

---

[104] 'I think I have a strong case because the Waki Commission is a very good report, it's full of information and there are other reports; the UN report; different other human rights groups reports. I believe I have a very strong case'. Anthony Kariuki, 'Ocampo: ICC has strong case in Kenya chaos', *Daily Nation*, 7 November 2009.

'There is no doubt that I will be able to present a very strong case against at least six key suspects before the ICC judges'. 'Why Ocampo needs two years on Kenya', *Standard*, 13 May 2010.

'We have great evidence. This includes details of meetings that planned the attacks'. Murithi Mutiga, 'Ocampo: I have solid evidence against six Kenyan suspects', *Daily Nation*, 21 September 2011; 'The important point is that no-one is immune from Prosecution before the ICC; politicians, businessmen or security officers may all potentially be brought to account in accordance with their criminal responsibility ... It happened with Slobodan Milosevic; it happened with Charles Taylor'. Emeka-Mayaka Gekara, 'Ocampo to step in if Kenya does shoddy job', *Daily Nation*, 19 June 2009.

'I saw in my country President Videla who had a lot of power when he took office and one day we prosecuted him in court ... I saw General Pinochet who was arrested when he was in London. I saw President Milosevic who was arrested in his own country. I saw Charles Taylor arrested and in The Hague. We are living in a new world in which power is not allowing you to commit massive crimes'. Michael Onyiego, 'ICC Prosecutor promises justice for Kenyans', Voice of America, 13 May 2010; 'We are investigating massive crimes against humanity faster than ever thought possible'. Emeka-Mayaka Gekara, 'Ocampo to step in if Kenya does shoddy job', *Daily Nation*, 19 June 2009.

'Everyone is worried about the next election in Kenya in 2012. That is why I understand the importance of speed'. 'ICC seeking speedy trials', *BBC News*, 7 November 2009.

'We are trying to be as fast as possible. Individuals should face justice in 2010'. Bernard Namunane, 'The Hague beckons for suspects', *Daily Nation*, 26 November 2009.

'It will be very fast. At the end of the year, we will present the cases that I want tried to the judges'. Bernard Namunane and Oliver Mathenge, 'I'll nail suspects in 6 months', *Daily Nation*, 8 May 2010.

'establish a credible local process for the investigation and prosecution of the six persons'.[105] As the ICC's Pre-Trial Chamber and Appeals Chamber considered the government's application to have the Ocampo Six tried locally, reports were prepared by the DPP and the Director of the CID on the status of the post-election violence cases; the Attorney General ordered that all cases be concluded expeditiously, a team of ten senior police officers was appointed to investigate the three members of the Ocampo Six were questioned by investigators for the first time.[106]

When both the ICC's Pre-Trial Chamber and Appeals Chamber dismissed the government's Article 19 application, this restored the perception that ICC trials were inevitable. Once again little, if any, action was taken to hold post-election violence perpetrators accountable. There were no further debates on the formation of a special tribunal, no further investigations of the Ocampo Six at the local level and the DPP announced that no further action would be taken in more than 8,000 post-election violence cases.[107]

The above discussion suggests that the OTP's influence over the government was not constant. Rather, it was most influential when Kenya's politicians perceived international prosecutions to be imminent, such as when the Waki Commission deadlines approached and when Annan handed the sealed envelope to the Prosecutor. When ICC prosecutions appeared inevitable, such as when the Prosecutor used his *proprio motu* powers and when the Appeals Chamber dismissed the government's Article 19 application, the ICC had little influence over Kenya's politicians. The OTP was therefore most influential when international prosecutions were perceived to be *imminent* but not *inevitable*. Having identified the periods during which the OTP was most influential, the next step is to examine the manner in which the OTP influenced the government during this period.

2.4 Vested Interests

Earlier in this chapter it was suggested that the OTP's strategy of positive complementarity might not be appropriate when members of the government are responsible for committing crimes within the ICC's jurisdiction because the OTP may find it difficult, if not impossible, to convince such persons to commit political suicide.

---

[105] Hansard, National Assembly, Official Report, 16 December 2010.

[106] Attorney-General by the Team on Update of Post Election Violence Related Cases in Western, Nyanza, Central, Rift valley, Eastern, Coast and Nairobi Provinces, March 2011 ('AG March 2011 Report'); Office of the President, Criminal Investigation Department, Post Election Violence Investigations Progress Report, 5 May 2011 ('CID May 2011 Report'); Office of the President, Report from Director of Criminal Investigations Ndegwa Muhoro to Director of Public Prosecutions, 'Re: Update on investigation into Six ICC Suspects', 1 July 2011 ('CID July 2011 Report'); Nzau Musau, 'Wako wants Ocampo 6 Prosecuted in Kenya', *The Star*, 13 April 2011; 'Ruto quizzed in Kenya plan to stop Hague trials', *Daily Nation*, 8 August 2011.

[107] Kenyans for Peace with Truth and Justice and Human Rights Watch, 'Kenya: Local Judicial Mechanism Should Complement ICC Cases', Press Release, 27 April 2012 ('Working Group 2012 Report') Bernard Naumnane, 'Kenya's fresh bid to stop Ocampo', *Daily Nation*, 22 April 2011.

It follows from this that, if the OTP nevertheless elects to pursue the strategy in such a situation, politicians are likely to respond according to their own vested interests. As Kleffner has observed, in such a situation 'the interest of that state's leaders to protect themselves and to stay in power would prevail over the benefits of retaining jurisdiction over the cases at hand and the reputation for compliance'.[108] This appears to have been what occurred in Kenya, with politicians from both PNU and ODM seeking to remain in power by protecting themselves from prosecution while at the same time trying to ensure that their political opponents faced trials. UN special rapporteur, Philip Alston, for example, observed that there were 'opportunistic efforts by politicians with a clear vested interest in promoting impunity to undermine the steps required to create the special tribunal'.[109] Similarly, KNDR reported to Annan that politicians mobilised for or against the special tribunal depending on how they thought it would 'impact their personal interests and ambitions'.[110] A leading Kenyan scholar described this process as one that was 'held hostage to the personal and political agendas of those with power', motivated 'not by the imperative to do justice for the victims but by the threat a particular approach could pose to political interests in the country'.[111]

This section considers the reasons for Parliament's rejection of the special tribunal in January and February 2009 and Cabinet's opposition to the tribunal in July 2009. During each of these debates, politicians tended to support positions that were the most likely to ensure that they and their allies would be shielded from prosecution. This strategy led to the exacerbation of both inter-party and intra-party divisions, as well as to the formation of some rather surprising alliances.

The first point to note is that politicians' responses to the ICC issue did not follow party lines. When MPs voted on the proposed special tribunal in February 2009, the issue split the house down the middle, with 101 voting in favour and 93 against.[112] This issue not only divided the National Assembly, but also each of the two major parties. Of those belonging to PNU, 50 voted in favour and 42 against, while from ODM 51 voted in favour and 49 against.[113] This data suggests that factors other than party loyalty influenced the manner in which MPs responded to the OTP's threatened prosecutions.

Although it is not possible to identify and analyse the motivations of all MPs at this time, it would appear that three distinct positions emerged. The first group, which consisted mainly of PNU members and others loyal to Kibaki, proposed and

---

[108] Jan Kleffner, *Complementarity in the Rome Statute and National Criminal Jurisdictions* (Oxford University Press, (2008), 34.

[109] Alston Report (see Footnote 19).

[110] South Consulting, Kenya National Dialogue and Reconciliation Monitoring Project, *Status of Implementation of Agenda Items 1–4, Progress Report for January-March 2010*, April 2010 ('KNDR April 2010 Report'), 63.

[111] Godfrey Musila, 'Options for Transitional Justice in Kenya: Autonomy and the Challenge of External Prescriptions' (2009) 3 *International Journal of Transitional Justice*, 459.

[112] Hansard, National Assembly, Official Report, 12 February 2009.

[113] South Consulting, Kenya National Dialogue and Reconciliation Monitoring Project, *Status of Implementation of Agenda Items 1-4, Draft Report*, May 2009, 35.

supported the special tribunal because they saw it as a mechanism for prosecuting opponents and shielding allies. As the legislation was being drafted, MP Jeremiah Kioni suggested that 'there are some MPs who do not want the issue going to The Hague. They find the formation of a local tribunal as one of the ways that they can manipulate the process'.[114] During the parliamentary debate over the legislation, the Minister for the Environment, John Michuki, may have inadvertently revealed the true intentions of many of those who supported the tribunal's establishment: 'it is being argued that in the proposed tribunal, we shall have some foreigners. Of course they will be there. They will be our employees and we shall control them! We cannot control The Hague'.[115] In other words, this first group sought to create a special tribunal that could be controlled by the executive to limit trials to political opponents. This group proposed a special tribunal that would be reliant upon the Justice Ministry for its funding, allowed the President to be immune from prosecution, permitted the Attorney General to discontinue any prosecution and allowed the President to grant mercy to any convicted persons.[116]

A second group, comprising mainly ODM supporters and those loyal to Ruto, opposed the establishment of this proposed special tribunal because they feared that it would target themselves and their allies. Instead, Ruto and his Kalenjin supporters from the Rift Valley called for a rejection of the proposed tribunal, arguing that the suspects should be tried by the ICC. According to the International Crisis Group, this group contained persons who were 'powerful individuals whose interest was to avoid accountability' by supporting a slow-moving international process that would allow the principal suspects to participate in the next general elections.[117] Ruto and his allies voted against the proposed legislation and called for Annan to deliver the sealed envelope to the OTP, believing that it would take the ICC 99 years to commence its work.[118]

Joining Ruto and his allies in opposing the special tribunal as proposed was a third group, comprising politicians from both sides of politics who had no involvement in the post-election violence and shared a genuine commitment to ending impunity. The champion of this group was Imanyara, a human rights lawyer who was imprisoned for two years during the 1980s for his activism against the oppressive Moi regime. Although this group supported the establishment of a special tri-

---

[114] Oliver Mathenge and Sadiki Sudhir, 'Lawyers fault proposed tribunal on Waki', *Daily Nation*, 3 December 2008.

[115] Hansard, National Assembly, Official Report, 4 February 2009.

[116] Funding provision—section 59; presidential immunity—section 6 of the Bill read with section 14 of the 1963 Constitution; AG *nolle prosequi*—section 30 of the Bill read with section 26 of the 1963 Constitution; presidential mercy—section 41 of the Bill read with section 60 of the 1963 Constitution.

[117] International Crisis Group, *Policy Briefing, 'Kenya: Impact of the ICC Proceedings'*, Africa Briefing No. 84, 9 January 2012 ('ICG January 2012 Briefing'), 6–7.

[118] Oscar Obonyo, 'Beyond Ocampo 'Big Six' poll chaos suspects', *Standard*, 12 May 2010; Oscar Obonyo, 'Push and pull in search for justice for chaos victims', *Standard*, 11 December 2010; Hansard, National Assembly, Official Report, 12 February 2009; 'Ruto: why I prefer The Hague route', *Daily Nation*, 21 February 2009.

bunal in principle, they opposed the proposal that was submitted to Parliament in January and February 2009 because they considered that the tribunal would be susceptible to political manipulation. Imanyara explained that 'we were never opposed to the local tribunal as such … We opposed the tribunal because the government had watered down the initial bill. It had too many loopholes'.[119] Imanyara's group supported the establishment of an independent and impartial tribunal as envisaged by the Waki Report and later proposed his own version of the special tribunal to Parliament in November 2009 and December 2009, only for other parliamentarians to boycott these debates.

The first attempt to establish a special tribunal was therefore defeated by an unholy alliance between those who thought that the tribunal would work and those who thought it would not. For Ruto and his supporters, the special tribunal posed a serious threat to the Kalenjin community in the Rift Valley so they rejected the tribunal in favour of an ICC process they hoped would never eventuate. For Imanyara and other like-minded MPs, however, the proposed mechanism had the potential to shield some perpetrators from prosecution, so they resolved that the only prospect for ending impunity was the ICC. A rather unlikely alliance was therefore formed, with each proclaiming that the ICC presented the only viable option for ending impunity. These two groups united behind the popular slogan, 'Don't be vague, go to The Hague'.[120]

When Cabinet met to debate the creation of the special tribunal in July 2009, its members again appear to have adopted positions that accorded with their own vested interests. The new proposal was presented by Kilonzo and sought to address many of the concerns that Imanyara and others had expressed in relation to the first proposal. Kilonzo proposed abolishing presidential immunity, presidential amnesty and the Attorney General's power of *nolle prosequi*.[121] Some Kenyans, however, questioned Kilonzo's motivations in proposing these amendments. They suggested that Kilonzo was seeking to prosecute both sides of politics only because it would result in both Ruto and Kenyatta facing criminal charges, which would in turn benefit Kilonzo's close political ally and potential presidential candidate, Vice President Kalonzo Musyoka.[122]

One group that opposed Kilonzo's proposal comprised those who were responsible for drafting the first proposed special tribunal—PNU ministers who sought to establish a proposal that could be controlled to only prosecute political opponents. Persons within this group included Kibaki, Wako, Wetangula and Saitoti.[123] It was reported

---

[119] Alphonce Shiundu, 'Imanyara: House will nail a big fish with proposed Bill', *Daily Nation*, 15 August 2009.

[120] Hansard, National Assembly, Official Report, 3 February 2009.

[121] Bernard Namunane and Lucas Barasa, 'Cabinet rejects draft laws on local tribunal', *Daily Nation*, 14 July 2009.

[122] Interview with Maina Kiai (Naivasha, 30 April 2010); Interview with Charles Kirudja (Nairobi, 4 May 2010); Interview with Njonjo Mue (Nairobi, 10 May 2010).

[123] Bernard Namunane and Lucas Barasa, 'Cabinet rejects draft laws on local tribunal', *Daily Nation*, 14 July 2009..

that these ministers told Kilonzo that their support was conditional upon the President's and the Attorney General's constitutional powers remaining unchanged.[124]

Opposed to each of these groups was a third coalition, comprising members from each of the major parties, who favoured the post-election violence cases being handled by the TJRC.[125] The most vocal advocate of this position was Ruto, who had suddenly abandoned his support for the ICC when Annan delivered the sealed envelope to the OTP.[126] Seemingly influencing this group's position was the complementarity contract that had been agreed just two weeks earlier, in which the government committed to either holding suspects accountable through a local mechanism or self-referring the situation to the ICC.[127] This group's strategy appeared to be to deny (or at least delay) ICC prosecutions by convincing the OTP that the cases were being handled domestically, while at the same time ensuring that perpetrators escaped accountability at the local level. This explains their decision to support the TJRC, a mechanism that was never designed for conducting individual prosecutions and which was never subsequently amended to allow for this possibility.

The difference of opinions between these three groups exacerbated a number of inter-party and intra-party divisions, while also encouraging the formation of some rather surprising alliances.[128] Perhaps the most surprising of these political alliances was that between Ruto and Kenyatta. During the post-election violence, Ruto was the undisputed leader of the Kalenjin, while Kenyatta assumed the leadership of the Kikuyu as they considered how to respond to the widespread evictions in the Rift Valley.[129] When the Prosecutor named the Ocampo Six, Ruto and Kenyatta were listed as the two key antagonists on opposite sides of the Rift Valley violence. The two leaders therefore each had good reason to oppose both the special tribunal and the ICC and so formed a political alliance that *The Economist* described as the 'coalition of the accused'.[130] They later joined with Kalonzo to form the 'KKK' in the lead-up to the 2013 elections, uniting the Kikuyu, the Kalenjin and the Kamba communities. This then became the 'Jubilee Alliance', in which four political parties supported the joint presidential ticket of Kenyatta and Ruto. The 'coalition of the accused' was ultimately successful in convincing Cabinet that the TJRC should handle the post-election violence cases. Cabinet's decision appeared to realise its

---

[124] Ibid.

[125] John Ngirachu, 'Draft laws on tribunal unchanged', *Daily Nation*, 29 July 2009.

[126] Daniel Otieno, Bernard Namunane and Lucas Barasa, 'Ruto beats a retreat, rejects Hague trials', *Daily Nation*, 15 July 2009.

[127] OTP First Statement on the Sealed Envelope (see Footnote 97); International Criminal Court Office of the Prosecutor, 'Agreed minutes of the meeting between Prosecutor Moreno-Ocampo and the delegation of the Kenyan Government', 3 July 2009 ('OTP Complementarity Contract Statement').

[128] 'ODM ministers walk out on Raila over tribunal', *Daily Nation*, 30 June 2009; Otieno Otieno, 'Waki envelope still causing ripples', *Daily Nation*, 20 February 2010.

[129] Macharia Gaitho, 'Annan has called the bluff on suspects against local trials', *Daily Nation*, 9 July 2009.

[130] 'Kenya and the international court: Will they go quietly?', *The Economist*, 29 December 2010.

objective of delaying ICC prosecutions, with the Prosecutor stating that he respected Kenyan authorities' efforts to end impunity and that no decision had been made on whether the ICC had to open an investigation'.[131]

3 Foreign Affairs Façade

From the time that the Prosecutor made his decision to intervene in Kenya, its government again engaged in a foreign affair façade. In the previous chapter, it was argued that, between December 2008 and August 2011, the government engaged in a foreign affairs façade whereby it continually provided assurances that it would try perpetrators locally while at the same time making little or no progress in this regard. This section argues that, from November 2009, the government engaged in another foreign affairs façade, this time by promising to cooperate with the ICC's investigations while simultaneously seeking to obstruct the Court's progress. Nine examples are provided to support this argument.

3.1 Reneging on Referral

The first instance of the government attempting to frustrate the OTP's investigations occurred in November 2009 when it reneged on the promise it had made in the complementarity contract to voluntary refer the situation should it fail to make sufficient progress in prosecuting the perpetrators locally. The government's official reason for this refusal was that it was not appropriate for Kenya to self-refer the situation since it had a 'functioning legal system' and there was no 'complete breakdown of law and order'.[132] The government had never previously expressed this opinion and certainly not when it was negotiating the complementarity contract just four months earlier when it made its promise to the Prosecutor. This suggests that when the government entered the complementarity contract, it was being disingenuous when it promised to self-refer the situation. Rather, this refusal to self-refer appears to have been an attempt to stall the ICC process.[133] By doing so, the government forced the Prosecutor to make a *proprio motu* application to the Pre-Trial Chamber for authorisation to conduct investigations, a process that took over four months.

As the OTP conducted its investigations and anticipation built over who the Prosecutor would ultimately name as suspects, the government regularly committed to cooperating with the OTP when the cases commenced. On 5 November 2009, the

---

[131] Peter Leftie, Charles Wanyoro, Mwakera Majefa and Oliver Mathenge, 'Kenya Cabinet in the eye of a storm', *Daily Nation*, 2 August 2009.

[132] Hansard, National Assembly, Official Report, 22 December 2010.

[133] Interview with Ndung'u Wainina (Nairobi, 14 April 2010); Interview with John Githongo (Nairobi, 21 April 2010); Interview with Harun N'Dubi (Nairobi, 27 April 2010).

day that the Prosecutor announced that he was opening a *proprio motu* investigation, Kibaki and Odinga issued a joint statement in which they said that the government remained committed to cooperating with the ICC.[134] In June 2010, the Attorney General promised that the government would abide by its obligations to the ICC.[135] In September 2010, the Minister for Foreign Affairs reiterated the government's firm support for the ICC, especially the investigations that were being undertaken at that time.[136] In October 2010, the Vice President guaranteed that the OTP would be granted all necessary support as it carried out its investigations.[137] In November 2010, Odinga said that the government had 'no options but to co-operate with the ICC process' and joined Kibaki in assuring that all suspects would be arrested if necessary.[138] On 1 December 2010, the Prosecutor met with Kibaki, Odinga and Annan in Nairobi and the principals reaffirmed their commitment to the ICC.[139] One week prior to the Prosecutor's announcement of the Ocampo Six, Orengo again insisted that cooperation would be forthcoming, declaring that it was 'too late to introduce sideshows in order to scuttle the process' and that the government would continue to cooperate with the ICC.[140]

3.2 Rescuing the Ocampo Six

Despite these pledges of cooperation, the government's immediate reaction to the naming of the Ocampo Six revealed that it was contemplating steps that would obstruct the ICC process. Ruto announced that he was 'determined to stop Ocampo and his dirty tricks on Kenya'.[141] He and the other suspects received an expression of support from the Vice President, who said that the suspects 'should not lose hope because of being named in the ICC list' as the government would 'do its best to assist [them]'.[142] Two days before the Prosecutor's announcement, Cabinet met to discuss options for how the government would respond. Odinga reported the outcome of these discussions to Parliament one day after the Ocampo Six were named.

---

[134] Judie Kaberia, 'Kenya remains defiant over ICC trials' *Capital News* 5 November 2009.

[135] Bernard Namunane, 'Kenya coalition rivalry plays out on the world stage', *Daily Nation*, 3 June 2010.

[136] International Criminal Court, Assembly of State Parties, 'President of Assembly meets Minister of Foreign Affairs in Kenya', 21 September 2010.

[137] Glena Nyamwayi, 'Kenya reiterates its commitment to ICC', Kenya Broadcasting Commission, 1 October 2010.

[138] Lucas Barasa, 'We'll arrest suspects, Big Two tell Ocampo', *Daily Nation*, 1 December 2010; 'Kenya committed to ICC and judicial reforms', *Kenya Broadcasting Commission*, 30 November 2010.

[139] Lucas Barasa, 'We'll arrest suspects, Big Two tell Ocampo', *Daily Nation*, 1 December 2010.

[140] Peter Leftie, 'It's late to scuttle ICC probe, says minister', *Daily Nation*, 8 December 2010.

[141] Gakuu Mathenge, 'Kenya on tenterhooks as D-day draws nigh', *Standard*, 6 December 2010.

[142] 'Raila rivals toy with single candidate plan', *Daily Nation*, 16 January 2011.

Hansard records that, at this session, two of the accused, Kenyatta and Kosgey, were applauded upon their entry into the National Assembly.[143] The House again applauded when Odinga informed his fellow lawmakers that Cabinet was considering withdrawing from the Rome Statute.[144] In a precursor of what was to come, the Prime Minister told Parliament that Cabinet had identified 'the following options in order of priority':

> Under Article 17 and 19(2) of the Rome Statute, to establish a credible local process for the investigation and prosecution of the six persons. This will entail genuine willingness and ability to carry out credible investigations and prosecutions before a special tribunal or a reformed Kenyan judiciary. The ICC will have to review and be convinced that the local process is credible before they cede jurisdiction.
>
> Option two is that under Article 16 of the Rome Statute, we can seek a Resolution of the UN Security Council under Chapter 6 of the Charter of the United Nations, deferring prosecutions of the six persons for a period of 12 months ...
>
> Option three is to withdraw from the Rome Statute
>
> (Applause)
>
> [...]
>
> Options four is that we let the current process take its course.[145]

The content and tone of Odinga's speech suggests that the impetus for Cabinet's consideration of these options was the announcement of the Ocampo Six and its desire to stall the progress of these cases. Revealingly, the Prime Minister's justification for these pursuing these options was not ending impunity, or providing justice for victims, or ensuring a peaceful and stable future for Kenya, but rather a desire to cause the ICC to 'cede jurisdiction'. Even if the local mechanisms were to be established, Odinga indicated that this would merely be 'for the investigation and prosecution of the six persons', suggesting that it would be designed not to exist complementary to the ICC, but rather to replace it. It was also notable that, according to Odinga's 'order of priority', the government favoured 'withdraw[ing] from the Rome Statute' over allowing the ICC process to 'take its course'. In other words, the Prime Minister appeared to be suggesting that the government would prefer the suspects to face no trials at all, rather than answer charges in The Hague.

3.3 Withdrawal from the Rome Statute

Within hours of the announcement of the Ocampo Six, the government pursued its next attempt to stall the progress of the cases when one of Ruto's closest allies, Chepalungu MP Isaac Ruto, filed a motion that sought to withdraw Kenya from the Rome Statute.[146] The timing of the resolution strongly suggests that this action was

---

[143] Hansard, National Assembly, Official Report, 16 December 2010; Laban Wanambisi, 'Plot to ditch the ICC hits a snag', *Capital News*, 17 December 2010.

[144] Hansard, National Assembly, Official Report, 16 December 2010.

[145] Hansard, National Assembly, Official Report, 16 December 2010.

[146] Anthony Kagiri, 'Ruto files motion to withdraw Kenya from ICC', *Capital News*, 15 December 2010.

motivated by a desire to protect the Ocampo Six by obstructing the ICC's investigations. Its wording would appear to confirm this suspicion:

> This House resolves that the government takes immediate action to have the International Crimes Act repealed so that Kenya is immediately released from any obligation to implement the Rome Statute and further that any criminal investigations or prosecutions arising out of the post-election violence 2007/2008 be undertaken under the framework of the new Constitution and that the government suspends any links, co-operation and assistance to the International Criminal Court forthwith.[147]

The motion was dismissed on constitutional grounds but an amended motion was introduced one week later, urging that 'the government takes appropriate action to withdraw from the Rome Statute'.[148] Only Karua spoke in opposition to the motion, which was eventually passed on 22 December 2010. Ultimately, the government took no action to remove itself from the Rome Statute because it realised that such a measure would not come into force for 12 months and, even then, would not halt the progress of the cases already underway.[149] Nevertheless, the President of the ICC's Assembly of States Parties, Christian Wenaweser, was sufficiently concerned with this development to schedule an impromptu official visit to Kenya in January 2011. At this meeting, the government reiterated its commitment to the Rome Statute and the principle of complementarity.[150]

3.4 Security Council Deferral and Shuttle Diplomacy

At the same time that the government was reassuring Wenaweser of its support for the ICC, it was embarking upon another attempt to obstruct the progress of the trials. This strategy relied upon Article 16 of the Rome Statute, which permits the deferral of investigations and prosecutions for a period of 12 months where the Security Council passes a resolution requesting the Court to do so. The government sought to persuade the Security Council that continuing to prosecute the Ocampo Six at the ICC would present a threat to peace and security. Kenya's Permanent Representative to the United Nations wrote a letter to Wenaweser containing the following passage:

> The pending ICC indictments pose a real and present danger to the exercise of government and the management of peace and security in the country ... the President believes that the ICC process in Kenya is being used by parties, both internal and external, to whip up emotions in ways in which the Rome Statute was never meant to be used.[151]

---

[147] Hansard, National Assembly, Official Report, 15 December 2010.

[148] Hansard, National Assembly, Official Report, 22 December 2010.

[149] Rome Statute, Article 127.

[150] International Criminal Court Assembly of States Parties, 'President of the Assembly of States Parties visits Kenya', 28 January 2011 ('ASP January 2011 Statement').

[151] Macharia Kamau, Kenya's Permanent Representative to the United Nations, Letter to Christian Wenaweser, President of the Assembly of State Parties to the Rome Statute 'Ref: Support for Kenya's reform movement', 28 February 2011 ('Kenya February 2011 Letter to ASP').

In January 2011, Kibaki arranged for senior government officials to visit various African destinations to lobby for support.[152] The African Union unanimously supported the government's initiative and so in March 2011 Kenyan officials then began lobbying members of the Security Council. The Office of the President released a press release confirming the government's objective:

> Kenya is set to begin the second phase of lobbying among members of the United Nations Security Council, for the deferment of the Hague process. In this regard, President Mwai Kibaki has nominated special envoys to lobby the member states to defer the Hague process for a period of one year.[153]

According to the Vice President, four members of the Security Council, including China and Russia, supported the government's initiative.[154] On 18 March 2011, the Security Council held a closed door 'interactive dialogue' with the Kenyan delegation, with no record made and no official statement issued. The Security Council was not persuaded by the delegation's arguments, prompting the government to send a letter, dated 23 March 2011, urging it to reconsider its decision. On 8 April 2011, the Security Council held an informal consultation to discuss the letter, after which the Council's President issued the following statement:

> Having received a request from the Kenyan Permanent Representative for a twelve-month deferral of the cases against six Kenyan nationals under Article 16 of the Rome Statute of the ICC, and taking into account the position expressed by the African Union, the Security Council held an informal dialogue on 18 March and informal consultations on 8 April 2011 in order to consider the issue. After full consideration, the members of the Security Council did not agree on the matter.[155]

A US state department official later admitted that the US did not support a resolution to defer the ICC investigation in Kenya.[156] It was also reported that the delegation had failed to win the support of both the United Kingdom and France.[157]

3.5 Article 19 Application

With this application for Security Council deferral unsuccessful, the government turned its attention to an alternative strategy for preventing the cases from proceeding. On 31 March 2011, the government submitted an application under Article 19 of the

---

[152] Bernard Namunane, 'Kenya seeks Africa support over Hague', *Daily Nation*, 12 January 2011; Dave Opiyo, 'President 'behind move on Hague'', *Daily Nation*, 16 January 2011.

[153] Office of the President, 'President appoints special envoys', 4 March 2011.

[154] Article 19 Application (see Footnote 29); Bernard Namunane, 'Kibaki, Raila plot way out for Ocampo 6', *Daily Nation*, 6 January 2011.

[155] ICG January 2012 Briefing (see Footnote 117), 9.

[156] Oliver Mathenge, Kevin Kelley, Bernard Namunane and Lucas Barasa, 'Govt fails to win US backing on poll trials', *Daily Nation*, 10 March 2011.

[157] Kevin Kelley, 'Why Kenya failed to defer ICC cases at Security Council', *Daily Nation*, 19 March 2011.

Rome Statute in which they challenged the admissibility of the cases before the ICC. In this application, the government promised swift implementation of the new Constitution so that perpetrators could be tried by a reformed Kenyan criminal justice system. There are at least five reasons, however, for believing that the arguments contained within this application were disingenuous and made with the primary objective of subverting the ICC process. First, despite the principals being aware of the Prosecutor's intention to initiate proceedings *proprio motu* from as early as October 2009, it took until March 2011 for the government to submit its admissibility challenge. This 18-month delay could hardly be considered as being the 'earliest opportunity' to submit the admissibility challenge, as required by Article 19 and appears to have been designed to stall the progress of the trials after other strategies had failed.[158] Second, in the weeks leading up to the submission of the application, Kibaki hurriedly appointed a new Chief Justice and Attorney General.[159] These appointments were made without legally required consultation, leading to scathing criticisms from the judicial service commission and ICJ-Kenya, before later being declared unconstitutional by the High Court.[160] The catalyst for these appointments appears to have been the Article 19 application and the necessity of convincing the ICC's judges that the promised reforms were progressing expeditiously. Just weeks before the appointments were made, Kilonzo linked this development to the government's desire to transfer the ICC cases from The Hague to Nairobi.[161] In other words, the government made illusory and unconstitutional appointments to give the impression of progress at the domestic level in the hope that this would convince the ICC to cede jurisdiction. Third, there does not appear to have been any attempt to investigate the Ocampo Six until the Pre-Trial Chamber rejected the government's application on the basis that there was no 'documentary proof that there is or has been an investigation' in the Ocampo Six that the government provided such evidence.[162] After this decision, investigators interviewed Ruto, Kosgey and Sang over their alleged role in the violence, with these interviews taking place while the Appeals Chamber considered the government's appeal.[163] After the Appeals Chamber dismissed the appeal no further investigations took place and none of the Ocampo Six were ever charged at the local level. This suggests that the government conducted such investigations as a façade in an attempt to fool the ICC's judges into discontinuing the trials. Fourth, the government promised further investigations and prosecutions

---

[158] Article 19 Application (see Footnote 29) [5].

[159] 'Kibaki appoints Justice Visram as CJ, Prof Muigai AG', *Standard*, 28 January 2011.

[160] Judy Ogutu, 'Court nullifies list of judicial nominees', *Standard*, 4 February 2011; International Commission of Jurists Kenya, 'ICJ Kenya's Position Paper on the appointment of the next Chief Justice as at Jan 2011', January 2011; Hansard, National Assembly, Official Report, 1 February 2011.

[161] Bernard Namunane and Oliver Mathenge, 'Nation seeks continental support over Hague', *Daily Nation*, 12 January 2011.

[162] PTC Article 19 Decision (n 496).

[163] 'Ruto quizzed in Kenya plan to stop Hague trials', *Daily Nation*, 8 August 2011.

after constitutional and criminal justice reforms had been completed. Although these reforms took place, little or no progress was made on cases at the local level. Finally, the arguments made before the ICC's judges contradicted the position that the government had adopted before the Security Council earlier in that same month. The government attempted to convince the Security Council that the trials of the Ocampo Six posed 'a real and present danger to the exercise of government and the management of peace and security in the country' and argued that the trials should be before for 12 months.[164] Just weeks later, however, the government indicated to the Pre-Trial Chamber, however, that 'all necessary steps have been and are being taken by Kenya to investigate and try all cases', with no suggestion of the need for a deferral in the interests of peace and security.[165] In summary, the government's Article 19 application was devoid of merit and pursued merely for the purpose of obstructing and delaying the progress of the ICC trials.

As the ICC's judges were deliberating on the government's application, the OTP began to express its first signs of frustration regarding the lack of cooperation. Senior OTP staff members visited Kenya in May 2011 'to understand the current position of the government in relation to the post-election violence'.[166] The OTP noted that there had been a change in the government's commitment to cooperating with the Court following the announcement of the Ocampo Six.[167] The Prosecutor suggested that 'the suspects or their allies [had been] able to influence the Kenyan government's position'.[168]

3.6 East African Court of Justice

Soon after the charges against the suspects were confirmed in January 2012, the government made another attempt to obstruct the ICC's progress. This involved seeking to have the trials of the Ocampo Six handled by the EACJ, a regional body set up to hear inter-state disputes and which did not have the jurisdiction to hear cases against individuals. On 28 April 2012, Kibaki used his influence as chair of the Extraordinary Summit of Heads of State of the East African Community to pass a resolution that extended the jurisdiction of the EACJ to include trials of individuals for crimes against humanity. Kibaki and the East African Legislative Assembly were clearly influenced by the impending ICC cases, with the Ocampo Four explicitly mentioned in the text of the resolution.[169] The motion was passed unanimously, with

---

[164] Kenya February 2011 Letter to ASP (n 748).

[165] Article 19 Application (see Footnote 29) [26].

[166] International Criminal Court Office of the Prosecutor, 'Statement of the Prosecutor on the Situation in Kenya', 29 May 2011 ('OTP May 2011 Statement').

[167] Ibid.

[168] Reed Stevenson, 'Hague court prosecutor to investigate Kenya violence', *Reuters*, 31 March 2010.

[169] East African Legislative Assembly, Hansard, 26 April 2012.

several speakers referring to the ICC as a 'neo-colonial court'.[170] The East African Law Society cautioned that the EACJ did not have the capacity, expertise or jurisdiction to entertain international criminal court matters.[171] ICC spokesperson Fadi Abdalla noted that it was 'technically impossible' for the cases to be transferred from the ICC to the EACJ and this appears to have stalled any momentum for these proposed amendments.[172] It took nearly six months for the relevant committee to discuss the implementation of the resolution, whereupon it deferred consideration until its next meeting.[173] At the time of writing, the EACJ still lacks jurisdiction to hear cases against individuals. Nevertheless, even as late as October 2012, the Attorney General still insisted that the EACJ could be used to try the ICC suspects.[174] ICJ-Kenya would therefore appear to be justified in describing measure as 'another blatant attempt to circumvent the ICC process'.[175]

3.7 African Court of Justice and Human Rights

In May 2012, the government commenced another initiative designed to prevent the suspects from being tried in The Hague. This attempt was perhaps the most audacious of all, given that it involved the suspects being tried by a regional court that had yet to come into existence. In 2004, the African Union passed a resolution agreeing to merge its two courts to form the African Court of Justice and Human Rights ('ACJHR'). A meeting of government legal advisors from all over Africa, including from Kenya, met in Addis Ababa in May 2012 to discuss how the ACJHR's statute could be amended to allow it to try individuals for crimes against humanity.[176] The ACJHR will only come into existence, however, when 15 states ratify the relevant protocol. To date, only five states have done so—Benin, Burkina Faso, Congo, Libya and Mali. The government provided no indication at this time that it was taking steps to ratify the relevant treaty and Kenya is still not a party. In other words, the government favoured the suspects being tried by a court that did not exist and that it did not support (ACJHR) over a court that did exist, that was already trying the suspects and that it did support (ICC). A coalition of African and international organisations expressed their doubts over the ACJHR's capacity to try the suspects, pointing out that the cost of a single trial was more than double the combined

---

[170] Ibid.

[171] Lillian Aluanga, 'Why EALA petition on ICC cases is futile', *Standard*, 29 April 2012.

[172] 'ICC says cases will not go to Arusha', *The Star*, 9 May 2012.

[173] East African Community, 'EAC Sectoral Council on Legal Affairs Okays Two Key Bills as 14th Meeting Ends', 24 October 2012.

[174] Felix Olick, 'AG hints at bid to postpone ICC cases', The *Standard*, 8 October 2012.

[175] International Commission of Jurists Kenya, 'Let the ICC Be', 10 May 2012.

[176] Action of Christian Activists for Human Rights in Shabunda et al., Letter to Justice Ministers and Attorneys General of African States Parties to the International Criminal Court, 3 May 2012.

budgets of the two African Union courts already in existence.[177] The ICTJ's James Gondi described this initiative as being 'part of a wider scheme to escape accountability and prepare the ground for non-cooperation with the ICC'.[178]

3.8 Motions Without Movement

In addition to the initiatives described above, the suspects also filed their own individual motions at the ICC. Muthaura's defence lawyer, Ken Ogeto, warned that the Prosecutor 'should brace himself for one of the most vicious legal battles of his career'.[179] Motions included a jurisdictional challenge on the basis that there was no organisational policy;[180] a jurisdictional challenge that the gravity threshold was not satisfied[181]; a request that the confirmation of charges hearings be postponed by six weeks[182] and three months[183]; a request that the Trial Chamber postpone its decision on the setting of the trial date[184] and a request that the trials be held in Kenya or Tanzania.[185] Some of these motions were frivolous, such as an application filed by Ruto, before he had been named as a suspect, alleging that the Prosecutor had failed to uphold his obligation to 'investigate incriminating and exonerating circumstances equally'.[186] In the 300-page application, Ruto argued that the Prosecutor had 'failed to investigate exonerating evidence in relation to [him] and also failed to afford him

---

[177] Ibid.

[178] James Gondi, 'How the search for accountability aborted', *Daily Nation*, 17 July 2012.

[179] Emeka Mayaka-Gekara, 'Lawyers accuse ICC of serving Kenyan political purpose', *Daily Nation*, 11 December 2010.

[180] *Prosecutor v William Samoei Ruto, Henry Kiprono Kosgey and Joseph Arap Sang*, Defence Challenge to Jurisdiction, ICC-01/09-01/11, 30 August 2011.

[181] *Prosecutor v Francis Kirimi Muthaura, Uhuru Muigai Kenyatta and Mohammed Hussein Ali*, Defence Challenge to Jurisdiction, Admissibility and Prosecutor's Failure to Meet the Requirements of Article 54, ICC-01/09-02/11-338, 19 September 2011 [56].

[182] *Prosecutor v William Samoei Ruto, Henry Kiprono Kosgey and Joseph Arap Sang*, Urgent Defence Application for Postponement of the Confirmation hearing and Extension of Time to Disclose and List Evidence, ICC-01/09-01/11-255, 11 August 2011.

[183] *Prosecutor v Francis Kirimi Muthaura, Uhuru Muigai Kenyatta and Mohammed Hussein Ali*, Defence Motion for an Adjournment of the Confirmation Hearing Scheduled for 21 September 2011, ICC-01/09-02/11-290, 5 September 2011; *Prosecutor v Francis Kirimi Muthaura, Uhuru Muigai Kenyatta and Mohammed Hussein Ali*, Application by the Defence for Uhuru Kenyatta under Article 61(3) and 67(1)(a) for an Adjournment of the Confirmation Hearing Schedule for 21 September 2011 and Request for Alteration to their Selected Viva Voce Witnesses, ICC-01/09-02/01/11-281, 2 September 2011.

[184] *Prosecutor v Francis Kirimi Muthaura, Uhuru Muigai Kenyatta and Mohammed Hussein Ali*, Request to Postpone Setting Trial Date Pending Appeals Chamber's Determination of Jurisdiction Appeal, ICC-01/09-02/11-417, 25 April 2012.

[185] *Prosecutor v Francis Kirimi Muthaura and Uhuru Muigai Kenyatta*, Defence application for a change of place where the court shall sit for trial, ICC-01/09-02/11-551, 3 December 2012; *Prosecutor v William Samoei Ruto and Joseph Arap Sang*, Joint Defence application for a change of place where the court shall sit for trial, ICC-01/09-01/11, 24 January 2013.

[186] Rome Statute, Article 54(1)(a).

an opportunity to present the exonerating evidence he has'.[187] This application was made despite the fact that just two weeks earlier, Ruto had voluntarily travelled to The Hague, where he spent more than 30 hours meeting with OTP officials.[188] Upon returning to Nairobi, Ruto said 'I used the opportunity to share my point of view and the information that I have on the issues the ICC is investigating in our country' and that the trip was 'worth every minute'.[189] Kenyatta's counsel adopted similar tactics. According to victims' representative Fergal Gaynor, the Kenyatta defence team filed 'application after application after application to seek to delay the start of this trial or to stop it taking place at all'.[190] These apparent attempts to frustrate and delay the progress of the trials seem to be contrary to the assurances that each of the suspects made that they would do everything necessary to cooperate with the Court in order to clear their names.[191]

3.9 Obstructing Investigations

The ninth and final means by which the government sought to frustrate the ICC process was by disrupting the OTP's attempts to conduct investigations. A senior ICC prosecutor described the government's strategy as one of 'pure obstructionism'.[192] This was achieved by four means.

First, Kenyan authorities withheld incriminating evidence. The OTP requested the government to provide it with post-mortem reports, police records, intelligence reports and minutes of national security meetings.[193] These documents, however, were not provided, prompting a senior OTP official to inform the Attorney General that 'the slow pace of processing these requests is a source of frustration for the OTP'.[194] In August 2010, the OTP requested the government to provide security-related documents relevant to the post-election violence but three and a half years later these had still not been pro-

---

[187] International Criminal Court, Situation in the Republic of Kenya, Transmission by the Registry of an Application Communicated by Katwa & Kemboy Advocates, Commissioners for Oaths on Behalf of Applicant William Ruto, ICC-01/09-32-AnxA, 1 December 2010.

[188] 'Ex-Kenyan minister defended himself at the ICC', *Associated Press*, 8 November 2010; Paul Juma, 'Ruto: My trip to The Hague', *Daily Nation*, 8 November 2010.

[189] 'Ruto returns, but no word from Ocampo', *Daily Nation*, 8 November 2010; Kikkirui K'Telwa, 'I got six names to present to ICC judges, says Ocampo', *Standard*, 16 November 2010.

[190] *Prosecutor v Uhuru Mauigai Kenyatta*, ICC-01/09-02/11, Transcript 5 February 2014 ('February 2014 Status Conference').

[191] Judie Kaberia, 'I knew it, Ruto says of ICC list', *Capital News*, 15 December 2010; Mutinda Mwanzia, 'I am innocent—Kass FM journalist tells Ocampo', *Standard*, 16 December 2010; Jacob Ng'etichp, 'Kosgey: I am ready to work with ICC', *Daily Nation*, 16 December 2010; 'Cases will ensure peaceful 2012 election, says Ocampo', *Daily Nation*, 15 December 2010; 'Kenya's suspects say will cooperate with ICC', *Reuters*, 15 December 2010; Bernard Momanyi, 'From army man, mail man, to suspect', *Capital News*, 15 December 2010.

[192] February 2014 Status Conference (see Footnote 190).

[193] Kamore Maina, 'How State gagged witnesses', *The Star*, 27 October 2012.

[194] Nzau Musau, 'ICC request for files has yet to reach me, says CJ', *The Star*, 25 October 2012.

vided.¹⁹⁵ Likewise, the OTP did not receive cooperation in its requests for copies of Kenyatta's financial records.¹⁹⁶ The OTP complained that its repeated requests for 19 months had been met with 'obfuscation and intransigence' and on this basis made a formal application to the Trial Chamber for a finding of non-compliance under Article 87(7) of the Rome Statute.¹⁹⁷ The OTP told the Trial Chamber that it had reason to believe that some documents that had been provided had been filtered. This included the redaction of pertinent information from key Kenyan intelligence committee reports without explanation.¹⁹⁸ In the words of victims' representative Fergal Gaynor, 'instead of immediately searching for, seizing and delivering key documents, the government has been dilatory and obstructive in providing documents and has deliberately filtered out those which appear to be most capable of revealing the truth'.¹⁹⁹

Second, the government introduced legal obstacles that made it more difficult for the OTP investigators to carry out their duties. Domestic regulations were passed that allowed a witness to refuse to answer any questions for certain reasons, such as if they were 'unable to answer ... for lack of sufficient particulars'.²⁰⁰ The difficulties that these rules posed for OTP investigators became apparent when they attempted to question senior security officers in 2010. The statement taking was initially delayed when the witnesses demanded to be provided with a list of questions in advance, further delayed when the witnesses insisted that they be guaranteed immunity from prosecution, then suspended indefinitely when an application was lodged claiming that one aspect of the procedure was in breach of the Constitution.²⁰¹ More than one year after the OTP's initial request for assistance, the statements had still not been taken, prompting the OTP to request access to the files related to the matter.²⁰² Aside from this, the OTP requested access to medical information and practitioners but it took the government more than a year to appoint relevant contact persons.²⁰³ In October 2012, Bensouda met with Kibaki and Odinga to express the OTP's 'concerns regarding delays in the government's response to a number of OTP

---

¹⁹⁵ *Prosecutor v Uhuru Muigai Kenyatta*, Prosecution opposition to the Defence request for the termination of the Kenyatta case, public redacted version of confidential Annex A, ICC-01/09-02/11, 31 January 2014 ('OTP opposition to Kenyatta termination').

¹⁹⁶ Ibid.

¹⁹⁷ *Prosecutor v Uhuru Muigai Kenyatta*, Prosecution application for a finding of non-compliance pursuant to Article 87(7) against the Government of Kenya, ICC-01/09-02/11, 29 November 2013.

¹⁹⁸ Ibid.

¹⁹⁹ February 2014 Status Conference (see Footnote 190).

²⁰⁰ *International Crimes (Procedures for Obtaining Evidence) Rules 2010*, Legal Notice No. 177, 22 October 2010, rule 10(5).

²⁰¹ Oliver Mathenge, 'Judge puts off quizzing security chiefs', *Daily Nation*, 7 December 2010; Cyrus Ombati, 'Kenya security chiefs scared of ICC grilling', *Standard*, 22 November 2010; Cyprus Ombati, 'ICC: Kenya's Security Chiefs testify on Dec 20', *Standard*, 7 December 2010; Walter Menya, 'ICC officers fail to jet in for statement taking', *Daily Nation*, 20 December 2010; Maureen Onyango, 'Court stops taking of ICC evidence', *Daily Nation*, 31 January 2011.

²⁰² Musau (2012) (see Footnote 194).

²⁰³ OTP opposition to Kenyatta termination (see Footnote 195).

requests related to its investigations'. The principals assured the Prosecutor of their willingness to ensure timely and effective execution of the pending requests.[204]

Third, the government inhibited the OTP's ability to conduct investigations by not requiring the suspects to resign from public office, contrary to its earlier promises. As early as December 2008, the government had promised that 'any person holding public office or any public servant charged with a criminal offence related to the 2008 post-election violence [would] be suspended from duty until the matter [was] fully adjudicated upon'.[205] When the Ocampo Six were named as suspects, there were widespread calls for those holding public office to either resign or be suspended. The issue was not just one of upholding the integrity of the respective offices, but also of ensuring that the OTP could conduct its investigations free from interference. For example, Muthaura was chair of the committee responsible for the police services, while Kenyatta was a member of the witness protection advisory board. As a consequence, the East African Law Society, the National Civil Society Congress, the Kenya National Commission on Human Rights, the Kenya Private Sector Alliance, the National Council of Churches, Muslims for Human Rights and others all expressed their concern over such persons continuing to occupy public office.[206] An Infotrak Harris opinion poll found that 82% of Kenyans supported the resignation or suspension of ICC suspects.[207] Despite these pressures, the government reversed its original position by supporting suspects' decisions to remain in office. On the day of the Ocampo Six announcement, State House issued a press release saying that calls for the suspects to resign were 'prejudicial, pre-emptive and against the rules of natural justice' and that the suspects should remain in office until the charges against them were confirmed.[208] The Prosecutor wrote to the government in March 2011 and July 2011 to express his concern over the suspects remaining in office, claiming that 'there is a public perception the individuals are very powerful and influential within government thus creating a climate of fear that is not conducive for impartial investigations and proceedings'.[209]

---

[204] International Criminal Court Office of the Prosecutor, 'Statement by the Prosecutor of the International Criminal Court Mrs. Fatou Bensouda at the press conference at the conclusion of Nairobi segment of ICC Prosecutor's visit to Kenya, Nairobi', 25 October 2012 ('OTP Second Statement on Bensouda's Visit to Kenya').

[205] Office of the President, 'Special Tribunal to be set up', 17 December 2008.

[206] Alex Kiprotich, 'Impunity: why not fire big four on Ocampos list?', *Standard*, 19 December 2010; Evelyne Njoroge and James Mburu, 'Atwoli throws weight behind Ocampo six', *Capital News*, 19 December 2010; Peter Leftie, 'Top four under pressure to step down from public jobs', *Daily Nation*, 16 December 2010; Linah Benyawa, 'Resign, the Ocampo six told', *Standard*, 16 December 2010; Athman Amran, 'Rights groups want Kibaki, Raila to back ICC', *Standard*, 9 December 2010; Beauttah Omanga, 'Githongo and Ghai rally Kenyans against impunity', *Standard*, 9 January 2011.

[207] Mugumo Munene, 'Last ditch effort to shield Ocampo six', *Daily Nation*, 18 December 2010.

[208] 'Statement by President Kibaki', *Standard*, 15 December 2010.

[209] Bernard Namunane, 'ICC wants Muthaura to leave key security team', *Daily Nation*, 14 March 2011; David Ochami and Peter Opiyo, 'ICC: Ocampo says Muthaura must leave by April 7', *Standard*, 15 March 2011; Cyrus Ombati, 'Ocampo demands to know why suspects are still holding office', *Standard*, 21 July 2011.

This 'climate of fear' to which the Prosecutor referred may have been a fourth way in which Kenya's politicians sought to hamper OTP investigations. In December 2010, the Prosecutor recognised that 'families of those believed to be ICC witnesses [had] been threatened' and hinted that suspects or their allies may have been responsible.[210] Later, the Prosecutor accused some politicians of pursuing 'political campaigns to stop the case', which was 'promoting a growing climate of fear that [was] intimidating potential witnesses and ultimately undermining national and international investigations'.[211] Bensouda made similar claims when she visited Kenya as Prosecutor in October 2012, suggesting that 'a climate of fear [was] being created for the witnesses not to come forward to give evidence'.[212] There was a great deal of speculation that senior politicians, including those suspected of being responsible for the post-election violence, were involved in the intimidation of witnesses. Mungiki leader Maina Njenga alleged that he had received death threats linked to a powerful politician within the Ocampo Six.[213] Further, the *Daily Nation* claimed to have seen minutes of a meeting in which allies of a Cabinet minister called for the elimination of some witnesses, while the *Standard* claimed that a Cabinet minister colluded with the National Security Intelligence Service to threaten witnesses.[214] Victims also claimed that senior politicians had urged them not to cooperate with the ICC's investigations.[215] The government did little to protect witnesses, with its witness protection programme chronically underfunded throughout this period.[216] Further, despite the government's assurances that those responsible for intimidating witnesses would be investigated and prosecuted, no person was ever convicted, or even charged.[217] The Trial Chamber acknowledged that the Kenyan situation had involved 'unprecedented levels of tampering and anti-witness activity'.[218] Almost certainly as a result of this climate of fear, one of the witnesses recanted part of his testimony, leaving the OTP with no alternative but to drop its case against one of the Ocampo Six.[219]

---

[210] International Criminal Court Office of the Prosecutor, 'ICC Prosecutor: threats will not stop ICC cases', 3 December 2010.

[211] OTP May 2011 Statement (see Footnote 166).

[212] 'ICC urges Kenya to cooperate on post-poll violence', *AFP*, 25 October 2012.

[213] Henry Kibira, 'Kenya: Former Mungiki Boss Seeks Kibaki Protection', *The Star*, 28 November 2011.

[214] Murithi Mutiga, 'Ocampo writes to judges over threats', *Daily Nation*, 30 January 2010; Kipchumba Some, 'Top NSIS official met minister, witnesses say', *Standard*, 30 April 2010.

[215] KNDR April 2010 Report (see Footnote 110), 14.

[216] Emmanuel Igunza, 'Witness protection fears in Kenya', *Institute for War and Peace Reporting*, 3 August 2012.

[217] OTP Second Statement on Bensouda's Visit to Kenya (see Footnote 204).

[218] *Prosecutor v Uhuru Muigai Kenyatta*, Public redacted version of the 'Additional Prosecution observations on Mr Kenyatta's Article 64 application, filed in accordance with order number ICC-01/09-02-11-699", ICC-01/09-02/11, 28 March 2013 [38].

[219] *Prosecutor v Francis Kirimi Muthaura and Uhuru Muigai Kenyatta*, Decision on the withdrawal of charges against Mr Muthaura, ICC-01/09-02/11, 18 March 2013 ('Decision to Withdraw Charges Against Muthaura').

The nine examples discussed above demonstrate that, from the time that the Prosecutor named the Ocampo Six, the government engaged in a foreign affairs façade whereby it promised to cooperate with the OTP, while at the same time making every effort to obstruct and delay the progress of the cases. In October 2012, the Prosecutor stated that of all of the cases she had handled, Kenya had been the 'most challenging'.[220] In May 2013, the OTP was even more scathing in its assessment of the government, stating that:

> [The OTP had] encountered serious difficulties in securing full and timely cooperation from the government of Kenya. The actions and inactions of the government have compromised the ability of the OTP to investigate the crimes in these cases, and limited the evidence available to assist the Chamber to adjudicate the crimes charged. Additionally, some public officials in Kenya have fostered an anti-ICC climate in the country, which has had a chilling effect on the willingness of potential witnesses and partners to cooperate with the OTP.
>
> [...]
>
> Since the beginning of the OTP's investigations in April 2010, the [government] has constructed an outward appearance of cooperation, while failing to execute fully the OTP's most important requests. Indeed, while the [government] has provided some cooperation and complied with a number of OTP requests, the most critical documents and records sought by the OTP remain outstanding, despite the OTP's exhaustive efforts to urge the [government] to furnish these items. The outstanding documents and records that the OTP has requested from the [government] have been pending for periods that range from one to three years. The individual and cumulative effect of the [government's] actions has been to undermine the investigation in these cases and limit the body of evidence available to the Chamber at trial.[221]

4 The Shadow Side of Complementarity

In the previous chapter, it was demonstrated that the OTP's decision to commence international prosecutions had at least two shadow sides—an increased threat to witnesses and the domestic politicisation of the trials. This section considers any shadow sides that may have been present as a result of the OTP's attempts to encourage domestic investigations and prosecutions. It is suggested that the OTP's implied and express threats of international trials produced two unexpected and undesirable shadow sides.

---

[220] Koome Kimonye and Alex Chamwada, 'Kenyan Gov't not cooperative, says ICC', *Citizen News*, 17 February 2013.

[221] *Prosecutor v William Samoei Ruto and Joshua Arap Sang*, Public redacted version of Prosecution response to the 'Government of Kenya's submissions on the status of cooperation with the International Criminal Court, or, in the alternative, Application for Leave to file observations pursuant to Rule 103(1) of the Rules of Procedure and Evidence', ICC-01/09-01/11, 10 May 2013 [1]–[4].

4.1 Discouragement of Local Prosecutions

The first of these shadow sides would perhaps be of greatest concern to OTP policy makers because it provides evidence that the strategy of positive complementarity may have had precisely the opposite effect from that intended. That is, somewhat paradoxically, the threat of international prosecutions may have *discouraged* some within the government from supporting initiatives that would allow suspects to be tried by a local mechanism. Three arguments are provided to support this position.

First, the OTP's threatened presence in Kenya meant that those MPs who genuinely wanted to see all post-election violence suspects held accountable voted against the proposed special tribunal because they regarded trials at the ICC to be a superior alternative. Imanyara, for example, said that supporting the proposed local mechanism with all of its flaws would 'have the effect of legalising impunity' and explained that it was on that basis that he 'stood for The Hague'.[222] For Imanyara and like-minded MPs, the ICC's impartiality provided an incentive for rejecting the proposed tribunal. As Alston observed in his report, the defeat of the proposed special tribunal could 'be attributed to the large number of people who believed that only an international tribunal could provide accountability'.[223] Had the prospect of international prosecutions not existed, it is possible that such persons would have worked harder to insist that the necessary amendments to the proposed local mechanism be made. The OTP's threatened intervention therefore provided persons with a genuine commitment to ending impunity with an incentive to oppose domestic investigations and prosecutions.

Second, the strategy of positive complementarity may have also discouraged politicians with blood on their hands from supporting a special tribunal. That is, the potential for ICC prosecutions provided those seeking to preserve impunity with a palatable excuse for voting against the establishment of a special tribunal. In other words, the presence of the ICC served as a 'pressure release valve'.[224] Lewis Nguyai, an MP who appeared as a defence witness for Kenyatta during the confirmation of charges hearing, said 'we want the key perpetrators of these particular atrocities to go to The Hague because we have developed a culture of impunity'.[225] Wilfred Machege, who went on to support Kenyatta's presidential campaign, called upon his fellow MPs to 'let the international community take charge of the full process'.[226] Lucas Chepkitony, an MP from the Keiyo North and ally of Ruto told Parliament:

> To me and, according to my constituents and the people I meet, they have no confidence in our systems, leave alone the tribunal that we are trying to establish. Let us try elsewhere this time. Let us allow The Hague to participate this time.[227]

---

[222] Gitobu Imanyara, 'The Hague is the better option', *Standard*, 8 February 2009; Alphonce Shiundu, 'Imanyara: House will nail a big fish with proposed Bill', *Daily Nation*, 15 August 2009.

[223] Alston Report (see Footnote 19), 27.

[224] Interview with Gichara Kibara (Nairobi, 17 May 2010).

[225] Hansard, National Assembly, Official Report, 4 February 2009.

[226] Ibid.

[227] Hansard, National Assembly, Official Report, 5 February 2009.

Cyrus Jirongo, who later assisted Ruto in launching the United Republican Party, told his fellow lawmakers that 'if we are genuine and we want those people to be punished, we should allow them to go [to The Hague]'.[228] Had the ICC not existed as an alternative forum for prosecutions, there may have been greater pressure at the local level for these politicians to support the special tribunal.

A third way in which the OTP's threatened presence may have acted as a disincentive for local investigations and prosecutions is that it took some pressure off Kenya's investigatory organs. In May 2011, the CID Director admitted that five members of the Ocampo Six were yet to be investigated and provided the following explanation for this omission, which has been quoted *ver batim*:

> The matter was tabled before Parliament and the Parliament overwhelmingly opted for I.C.C. rather than a local tribunal. This in turn also affected our investigations because members of the public viewed police as incompetent and instead waited for I.C.C. investigations.[229]

In other words, Kenya's most senior investigator claimed that the prospect of ICC prosecutions impeded his department's ability to conduct local investigations against those bearing the greatest responsibility for the crimes committed during the post-election violence. One of two conclusions may be drawn from this claim. On the one hand, the claim in the second sentence may be true, in which case it is evidence that the ICC process hampered domestic investigations. On the other hand, if the claim is false this would suggest that Kenya's investigatory organs used the ICC's presence as an excuse for not being able to conduct investigations at the local level. In other words, ICC intervention may have also served as a 'pressure release valve' for the Kenyan criminal justice system, just as it did for some of its politicians. Regardless of which of these is the correct conclusion, it provides further evidence to suggest that the OTP's strategy of positive complementarity in Kenya may have discouraged local investigations and prosecutions.

4.2 A Mechanism We Can Control

It was argued earlier in this chapter that the threat of ICC prosecutions encouraged some Kenyan politicians to support a special tribunal that could be manipulated so that it prosecuted rivals and shielded allies. In other words, it would seem that the OTP's strategy of positive complementarity encouraged the establishment of a local mechanism that was neither independent nor fair. The proposed special tribunal which was debated by Parliament in January and February 2009 suffered from several defects, including constitutional ambiguities, a lack of financial independence and an absence of lustration provisions.

---

[228] Hansard, National Assembly, Official Report, 3 February 2009.
[229] CID May 2011 Report (see Footnote 106).

Many of Kenya's most experienced and respected legal practitioners argued that the proposed special tribunal was not sufficiently shielded from constitutional challenge. PLO Lumumba, for example, predicted that:

> the accused will rush to courts and argue the offences are unconstitutional. And the courts will gladly agree. I have no doubt people will go to courts to sabotage justice. That is the gravest danger.[230]

As Parliament debated the proposal, the Law Society of Kenya identified several sections of the Constitution which would first need to be amended in order to protect the tribunal from constitutional challenge. To begin with, the proposed tribunal claimed to have jurisdiction over all persons, but did not explicitly repeal the constitutional guarantee of presidential immunity.[231] The special tribunal also assigned all responsibility for investigations and prosecutions to the tribunal's prosecutor, which may have contravened the Attorney General's constitutional powers to take over or discontinue criminal proceedings.[232] The proposed tribunal provided no possibility of pardon, despite the fact that the Constitution recognised the presidential prerogative of mercy.[233] The decisions of the special tribunal's appeals chamber were to be final, despite the fact that the Constitution granted the High Court unlimited jurisdiction in all criminal matters.[234] There was also the possibility that the proposed tribunal could not try persons for crimes against humanity without breaching the Constitution's protection against retrospectivity.[235] In summary, it was possible that, if established, the special tribunal would not have been able to try persons for crimes against humanity, its prosecutor would have been under the control of the presidentially appointed Attorney General, any decisions made by its panel of international judges could have been overturned by High Court beholden to the executive and any persons convicted could have been pardoned by the President.

Finally, the proposed special tribunal also lacked an independent funding source. Under the proposal, a special tribunal fund would be established, under the control of the tribunal's registrar, with money coming from Parliament, as well as grants and donations.[236] With no significant pledges having been made from international donors to support the tribunal, it was likely that its funding would have been reliant upon government support. This was particularly concerning for Imanyara, who argued that 'relying on the generosity of the Ministry of Justice when the incumbent will be busying campaigning for the presidency is not right'.[237]

---

[230] Stephen Mburu, 'Uncertain future for tribunal', *Daily Nation*, 7 February 2009.

[231] *Special Tribunal for Kenya Bill 2009*, section 6; Constitution of Kenya 1963, section 14.

[232] Ibid, section 30; Constitution of Kenya 1963, section 26.

[233] *Constitution of Kenya 1963*, section 27.

[234] *Special Tribunal for Kenya Bill 2009*, section 41; Constitution of Kenya 1963, section 60(1).

[235] *Constitution of Kenya 1963*, section 27.

[236] *Special Tribunal for Kenya Bill 2009*, section 58.

[237] Gitau Warigi, 'Local tribunal or The Hague?', *Daily Nation*, 31 July 2009.

Further, the proposed legislation contained no lustration provisions, despite the Waki Report recommending that these be included and the two principals undertaking to implement each of these recommendations. As a consequence, a person who was being investigated would have had the opportunity to remain in public office during the course of the investigations, raising the possibility of that person interfering with evidence or intimidating witnesses. With the Waki Report concluding that senior politicians planned and organised the violence and estimating that one third of all deaths were caused by police shootings, the absence of lustration provisions was a significant limitation of the proposed legislation.

The above evidence suggests that to the extent that the OTP's strategy of positive complementarity served as a catalyst for the establishment of the special tribunal, it was to encourage the creation of a local mechanism that would have been severely lacking in both independence and fairness. This finding raises a live debate within the field of international criminal justice—to what extent should the OTP have regard to the independence and fairness of the domestic proceedings when deciding whether or not to intervene? A case will be inadmissible at the ICC where it is being investigated or prosecuted at the local level, unless the state is unwilling or unable to carry out the investigation or prosecution. Certainly, where proceedings are commenced with the purpose of shielding certain persons from criminal responsibility, this is not sufficient to deny the admissibility of the case before the ICC.[238] As a consequence, it would appear to follow that if the special tribunal was set up to protect some politicians from prosecutions, this would not render the cases inadmissible.

A more contested issue, however, is whether the OTP could intervene if the special tribunal did not make it *more difficult* to convict suspects, but instead made it *easier*, such as by relaxing the rules of evidence. This debate in international criminal justice has become known as the 'due process thesis'.[239] Some scholars argue that the ICC's complementarity principle dictates that, in order to avoid cases being transferred to The Hague, domestic criminal justice systems are required to uphold certain fundamental due process rights that are recognised under international law, otherwise this will amount to 'inability' or 'unwillingness'.[240] This would appear to be the position favoured by the OTP, with a policy paper suggesting that the issue of admissibility 'should be based on *procedural* and *institutional* factors, not the substantive outcome'.[241] Others, including Heller, argue that the proper formulation that should be given to the complementarity regime is that, where a state's domestic legal proceedings make it easier to convict the accused person, the ICC must defer to that state's

---

[238] Article 20(3)(a).

[239] Kevin Jon Heller, 'The Shadow Side of Complementarity: The Effect of Article 17 of the Rome Statute on National Due Process' (2006) 17 *Criminal Law Forum* 255.

[240] Mark Ellis, 'The International Criminal Court and its Implications for Domestic Law and National Capacity Building' (2002–2003) 15 Florida Journal of International Law 215; Carsten Stahn, 'Complementarity, amnesties, and alternative forms of justice; some interpretive guidelines for the International Criminal Court' (2005) 3 *Journal of International Criminal Justice* 695.

[241] International Criminal Court Office of the Prosecutor, *Informal Expert Paper: The principle of complementarity in practice*, 2003 ('Informal Expert Paper') [46].

regime, no matter how unfair those proceedings may be.[242] The Pre-Trial Chamber appeared to lend some support to this position in May 2013 when it required the domestic state to adhere to its own substantive and procedural law, but not necessarily to the norms and principles recognised by international law.[243]

It is not necessary for the purposes of this study to express a position on this issue. However, given that the OTP has defined a 'major success' to be 'the absence of trials before [the ICC] as a consequence of the regular functioning of national institutions', the OTP might be expected to be particularly interested in the independence and fairness of the local mechanism. Consequently, where there is evidence that the strategy of positive complementarity encourages the establishment of a local mechanism that does not meet international standards of due process, such a shadow side might be expected to be of concern to the OTP.

5 Conclusion

This in-depth consideration of the OTP's impact in Kenya provides the opportunity to form some preliminary conclusions regarding the effectiveness of the strategy of positive complementarity. The first conclusion is one that seems to have received little attention in the literature to date—that the strategy of positive complementarity may not be appropriate in all situations. In particular, the strategy is unlikely to be successful where the persons responsible for ensuring the progress of investigations and prosecutions are themselves implicated in the violence. Local leaders with blood on their hands are unlikely to commit political suicide by supporting the establishment of a local mechanism. Likewise, where security forces are responsible for the commission of crimes, the prospect of these same persons or their colleagues conducting independent and effective investigations would appear to be bleak. The fact that senior politicians in the GNU were believed to have organised the violence, coupled with the police force's prominent role in committing crimes, suggests that it was optimistic to assume that the OTP could successfully encourage to progress of domestic investigations and prosecutions. Even in the unlikely event that local support were to be forthcoming, it is still quite possible that the strategy of positive complementarity may not have been successful in Kenya, owing to the apparent inability of the criminal justice system to handle such a large number of complicated cases. An insufficient number of adequately trained investigators and prosecutors, the logistical constraints in conducting investigations when so many persons had been displaced and the reluctance of witnesses to report crimes all suggest that, even with political will, successful domestic prosecutions would have been difficult to attain.

---

[242] Heller (2006) (see Footnote 239), 257.
[243] *Prosecutor v Saif Al-Islam Gaddafi and Abdullah Al-Senussi*, Decision on the admissibility of the case against Saif Al-Islam Gaddafi, ICC-01/11-01/11, 31 May 2013 [200].

Second, despite the Kenyan situation being perhaps ill-suited to the strategy of positive complementarity, there is evidence to suggest that the OTP's threat of prosecutions created positive incentives for the government to support domestic proceedings. Burke-White would appear to be correct, therefore, when he suggests that 'the threat of international prosecutions by the ICC may generate a positive set of incentives for national governments to pursue prosecutions themselves'.[244] The presence of the ICC altered the political calculus, with leaders considering their choice to no longer be between prosecutions and impunity, but instead between domestic prosecutions and international prosecutions. Likewise, there is support for Stahn's suggestion that the strategy of positive complementarity serves as a catalyst as states seek to avoid 'embarrassment resulting from ICC scrutiny'.[245] In Kenya, the strategy of positive complementarity created positive incentives for the establishment of a special tribunal by tapping into pre-existing domestic insecurities over state sovereignty and international embarrassment.

Third, the OTP's influence over the government appears not to have been constant, but instead fluctuated depending on the government's perceived imminence of the ICC prosecutions. The above evidence suggests that, when ICC prosecutions are considered to be far-fetched, the OTP's influence will be minimal. Where ICC intervention is perceived to be imminent, however, this influence increases, provided that such prosecutions are not regarded as being inevitable.

Fourth, the effect of this influence was not to encourage domestic investigations and prosecutions. This conclusion also challenges pre-conceived assumptions of the impact that the strategy would have upon domestic governments. Cryer, for example, has written that 'the system of complementarity creates a strong interest in states not to cheat by failing to prosecute'.[246] The OTP's experience in Kenya suggests that the strategy of positive complementarity in fact *creates* an incentive for States to 'cheat', at least where the persons responsible for the violence continue to serve in the government. For one matter, such persons are more likely to support a local mechanism designed to prosecute political opponents, or an ICC process they believe would never eventuate. For another, when ICC prosecutions commence, these persons are likely to protect their personal interests by attempting to obstruct their progress, while at the same time pledging support for the Court. By engaging in this foreign affairs façade, politicians may seek to protect themselves and their allies from prosecution yet remain publicly committed to ending impunity.

---

[244] William Burke-White, 'Reframing positive complementarity: reflections on the first decade and insights from the US federal criminal justice system' in Carsten Stahn and Mohamed M. El Zeidy (eds), *The International Criminal Court and Complementarity From Theory to Practice* (Cambridge University Press, (2011), 344.

[245] Carsten Stahn, 'Taking complementarity seriously: on the sense and sensibility of 'classical', 'positive' and 'negative' complementarity' in Carsten Stahn and Mohamed M. El Zeidy (eds), *The International Criminal Court and Complementarity From Theory to Practice* (Cambridge University Press, 2011), 250.

[246] Robert Cryer, *Prosecuting International Crimes: Selectivity and the International Criminal Law Regime* (Cambridge University Press, 2005), 164.

Finally, there is evidence that, in seeking to encourage national governments to pursue domestic prosecutions, the OTP's strategy of positive complementarity may have a shadow side where it is pursued while perpetrators remain in government. The OTP's threat of international prosecutions in Kenya may have, paradoxically, *discouraged* the establishment of local accountability mechanisms. Those seeking to preserve impunity were provided with a pressure-release valve, while those who genuinely remained committed to ending impunity were tempted into supporting ICC prosecutions which they considered to be a superior alternative. To the extent that the OTP was successful in serving as a catalyst for a local justice mechanism, it was to encourage the establishment of an institution that could be controlled by political elites and was lacking in independence and fairness.

The discussion to date has considered just one aspect of 'ending impunity'—the prosecution of persons responsible for the post-election violence. Although this appears to be what the OTP had in mind when it made its consistent promises to end impunity, Kenyans also hoped and expected that the OTP might make a significant contribution to this objective by serving as a catalyst for critical rule of law reforms. The next chapter considers the extent to which the OTP's strategy of positive complementarity influenced the government into pursuing such a reform agenda.

Bibliography

'Bid for local tribunal still on, says PM', *Daily Nation*, 15 February 2009
'Can Kibaki be proactive?', *Standard*, 19 December 2010
'Cases will ensure peaceful 2012 election, says Ocampo', *Daily Nation*, 15 December 2010
'Ex-Kenyan minister defended himself at the ICC', *Associated Press*, 8 November 2010
'How Kenya handled local tribunal process', *Daily Nation*, 17 September 2013
'ICC says cases will not go to Arusha', *The Star*, 9 May 2012
'ICC seeking speedy trials', *BBC News*, 7 November 2009
'ICC urges Kenya to cooperate on post-poll violence', *AFP*, 25 October 2012
'Kenya and the international court: Will they go quietly?', *The Economist*, 29 December 2010
'Kenya committed to ICC and judicial reforms', *Kenya Broadcasting Commission*, 30 November 2010
'Kenya's suspects say will cooperate with ICC', *Reuters*, 15 December 2010
'Kibaki appoints Justice Visram as CJ, Prof Muigai AG', *Standard*, 28 January 2011
'ODM ministers walk out on Raila over tribunal', *Daily Nation*, 30 June 2009
'Raila rivals toy with single candidate plan', *Daily Nation*, 16 January 2011
'Ruto lawyer opposes ICC trials', *Daily Nation*, 1 May 2011
'Ruto quizzed in Kenya plan to stop Hague trials', *Daily Nation*, 8 August 2011
'Ruto returns, but no word from Ocampo', *Daily Nation*, 8 November 2010
'Ruto: why I prefer The Hague route', *Daily Nation*, 21 February 2009
'Statement by President Kibaki', *Standard*, 15 December 2010
'The Hague not an option, say Kalonzo', *Daily Nation*, 16 November 2008
'Who is in the ICC list?', *Standard*, 5 March 2010
'Why Ocampo needs two years on Kenya', *Standard*, 13 May 2010

Bibliography

'Winning presidency won't assuage ICC—Raila', *Capital News*, 5 November 2012
Action of Christian Activists for Human Rights in Shabunda et al, Letter to Justice Ministers and Attorneys General of African States Parties to the International Criminal Court, 3 May 2012
Alston, Philip, *Mission to Kenya 16-25 February 2009* (United Nations Special Rapporteur on Extrajudicial Killings, Arbitrary or Summary Executions, 2009)
African Union, Panel of Eminent African Personalities, Note on handover of CIPEV materials to the Prosecutor of the ICC, 29 July 2009
African Union, Panel of Eminent African Personalities, Press Statement by Kofi Annan, 23 September 2008
African Union, Panel of Eminent African Personalities, Statement of H E Kofi Annan on the Implementation of the Report of the Commission of Inquiry on Post-Election Violence (CIPEV) & Independent Review Commission (IREC), 19 December 2008
Alston, Philip, *Mission to Kenya 16-25 February 2009* (United Nations Special Rapporteur on Extrajudicial Killings, Arbitrary or Summary Executions, 2009)
Aluanga, Lillian, 'Why EALA petition on ICC cases is futile', *Standard*, 29 April 2012
Amran, Athman, 'Rights groups want Kibaki, Raila to back ICC', *Standard*, 9 December 2010
Barasa, Lucas, 'We'll arrest suspects, Big Two tell Ocampo', *Daily Nation*, 1 December 2010
Benyawa, Linah, 'Resign, the Ocampo six told', *Standard*, 16 December 2010
Biomndo, Bornice, 'Pass tribunal law, Wako urges MPs', *Daily Nation*, 28 January 2009
Burke-White, William, 'Reframing positive complementarity: reflections on the first decade and insights from the US federal criminal justice system' in Carsten Stahn and Mohamed M. El Zeidy (eds), *The International Criminal Court and Complementarity From Theory to Practice* (Cambridge University Press, 2011)
Constitution of Kenya 1963
Cryer, Robert, Prosecuting International Crimes: Selectivity and the International Criminal Law Regime (Cambridge University Press, 2005)
Director of Public Prosecutions, A report to the Hon. Attorney General by the team on the review of post election violence related cases in Western, Nyanza, Central, Rift Valley, Eastern, Coast and Nairobi Provinces, February 2009
East African Community, 'EAC Sectoral Council on Legal Affairs Okays Two Key Bills as 14th Meeting Ends', 24 October 2012
East African Legislative Assembly, Hansard, 26 April 2012
Ellis, Mark, 'The International Criminal Court and its Implications for Domestic Law and National Capacity Building' (2002-2003) 15 *Florida Journal of International Law* 215
Final Report from Kenya's Commission of Inquiry into Post-Election Violence, 15 October 2008
Gaitho, Macharia, 'Annan has called the bluff on suspects against local trials', *Daily Nation*, 9 July 2009
Gekara, Emeka-Mayaka, 'Ocampo to step in if Kenya does shoddy job', *Daily Nation*, 19 June 2009
Gekara, Emeka-Mayaka, 'Lawyers accuse ICC of serving Kenyan political purpose', *Daily Nation*, 11 December 2010
Gondi, James, 'How the search for accountability aborted', *Daily Nation*, 17 July 2012
Hansard, National Assembly, Official Report, 27 January 2009
Hansard, National Assembly, Official Report, 3 February 2009
Hansard, National Assembly, Official Report, 4 February 2009
Hansard, National Assembly, Official Report, 5 February 2009
Hansard, National Assembly, Official Report, 12 February 2009
Hansard, National Assembly, Official Report, 11 November 2009
Hansard, National Assembly, Official Report, 18 November 2009
Hansard, National Assembly, Official Report, 11 December 2009
Hansard, National Assembly, Official Report, 10 December 2010
Hansard, National Assembly, Official Report, 16 December 2010
Hansard, National Assembly, Official Report, 22 December 2010
Hansard, National Assembly, Official Report, 1 February 2011
Hansard, National Assembly, Official Report, 23 November 2011

Hansard, National Assembly, Official Report, 24 November 2011

Heller, Kevin John, 'The Shadow Side of Complementarity: The Effect of Article 17 of the Rome Statute on National Due Process' (2006) 17 *Criminal Law Forum* 255

Human Rights Watch, Turning Pebbles: Evading Accountability for Post-Election Violence in Kenya (Human Rights Watch, 2011)

Igunza, Emmanuel, 'Witness protection fears in Kenya', *Institute for War and Peace Reporting*, 3 August 2012

Imanyara, Gitobu, 'The Hague is the better option', *Standard*, 8 February 2009

International Bar Association and International Legal Assistance Consortium, *Restoring Integrity: An assessment of the needs of the justice system in the Republic of Kenya* (International Bar Association and International Legal Assistance Consortium, February 2010)

International Commission of Jurists Kenya, 'ICJ Kenya's Position Paper on the appointment of the next Chief Justice as at Jan 2011', January 2011

International Commission of Jurists Kenya, 'Let the ICC Be', 10 May 2012

International Crimes Act 2008

International Crimes (Procedures for Obtaining Evidence) Rules 2010, Legal Notice No. 177, 22 October 2010, rule 10(5)

International Criminal Court, Assembly of State Parties, 'President of Assembly meets Minister of Foreign Affairs in Kenya', 21 September 2010

International Criminal Court Assembly of States Parties, 'President of the Assembly of States Parties visits Kenya', 28 January 2011

International Criminal Court, Office of the Prosecutor, 'Agreed minutes of the meeting between Prosecutor Moreno-Ocampo and the delegation of the Kenyan Government', 3 July 2009

International Criminal Court, Office of the Prosecutor, 'ICC Prosecutor Receives Materials on Post-Election Violence in Kenya', 16 July 2009

International Criminal Court, Office of the Prosecutor, 'ICC Prosecutor: threats will not stop ICC cases', 3 December 2010

International Criminal Court, Office of the Prosecutor, Informal Expert Paper: The principle of complementarity in practice, 2003

International Criminal Court, Office of the Prosecutor, 'OTP Statement in Relation to Events in Kenya', 5 February 2008

International Criminal Court, Office of the Prosecutor, 'Statement by the Prosecutor of the International Criminal Court Mrs. Fatou Bensouda at the press conference at the conclusion of Nairobi segment of ICC Prosecutor's visit to Kenya, Nairobi', 25 October 2012

International Criminal Court, Office of the Prosecutor, 'Statement of the Prosecutor on the Situation in Kenya', 29 May 2011

International Criminal Court, Situation in the Republic of Kenya, Decision on the Request for Assistance Submitted on Behalf of the Government of the Republic of Kenya Pursuant to Article 93(10) of the Statute and Rule 194 of the Rules of Procedure and Evidence, Pre-Trial Chamber II, ICC-01/09, 29 June 2011

International Criminal Court, Situation in the Republic of Kenya, Request for authorisation of an investigation pursuant to Article 15, ICC-01/09, 26 November 2009

International Criminal Court, Situation in the Republic of Kenya, Transmission by the Registry of an Application Communicated by Katwa & Kemboy Advocates, Commissioners for Oaths on Behalf of Applicant William Ruto, ICC-01/09-32-AnxA, 1 December 2010

International Crisis Group, *Policy Briefing, 'Kenya: Impact of the ICC Proceedings'*, Africa Briefing No. 84, 9 January 2012

Interview with Charles Kirudja (Nairobi, 4 May 2010)

Interview with Fred Mwachi (Nairobi, 19 May 2010)

Interview with John Githongo (Nairobi, 21 April 2010)

Interview with Gichara Kibara (Nairobi, 17 May 2010)

Interview with Harun N'Dubi (Nairobi, 27 April 2010)

Interview with Koigi wa Wamwere (Nairobi, 6 May 2010)

Interview with Maina Kiai (Naivasha, 30 April 2010)

Interview with Ndung'u Wainina (Nairobi, 14 April 2010)
Interview with Njonjo Mue (Nairobi, 10 May 2010)
Juma, Paul, 'AG defends prosecution record', *Daily Nation*, 23 September 2009
Juma, Paul, 'Ruto: My trip to The Hague', *Daily Nation*, 8 November 2010
Kaberia, Judie, 'DPP not working to salvage Ocampo Four', *Capital News*, 12 April 2012
Kaberia, Judie, 'I knew it, Ruto says of ICC list', *Capital News*, 15 December 2010
Kaberia, Judie, 'Kenya remains defiant over ICC trials' *Capital News* 5 November 2009
Kagiri, Anthony, 'Ruto files motion to withdraw Kenya from ICC', *Capital News*, 15 December 2010
Kamau, Macharia, Kenya's Permanent Representative to the United Nations, Letter to Christian Wenaweser, President of the Assembly of State Parties to the Rome Statute 'Ref: Support for Kenya's reform movement', 28 February 2011
Kariuki, Anthony, 'Ocampo: ICC has strong case in Kenya chaos', *Daily Nation*, 7 November 2009
Kariuki, Anthony and Mathenge, Oliver, 'Ocampo names Kenya chaos suspects', *Daily Nation*, 15 December 2010
Kelley, Kevin, 'Why Kenya failed to defer ICC cases at Security Council', *Daily Nation*, 19 March 2011
Kenyans for Peace with Truth and Justice and Human Rights Watch, 'Kenya: Local Judicial Mechanism Should Complement ICC Cases', Press Release, 27 April 2012
Kiai, Maina, 'The Crisis in Kenya' (2008) 19 *Journal of Democracy* 162
Kibira, Henry, 'Kenya: Former Mungiki Boss Seeks Kibaki Protection', *The Star*, 28 November 2011
Kimonye, Koome and Chamwada, Alex, 'Kenyan Gov't not cooperative, says ICC', *Citizen News*, 17 February 2013
Kiprotich, Alex, 'Impunity: why not fire big four on Ocampos list?', *Standard*, 19 December 2010
Kleffner, Jan, Complementarity in the Rome Statute and National Criminal Jurisdictions (Oxford University Press, 2008)
K'Telwa, Kikkirui, 'I got six names to present to ICC judges, says Ocampo', *Standard*, 16 November 2010
Kumba, Samwal, 'December trial for Kenya violence suspects', *Daily Nation*, 11 May 2010
Leftie, Peter, 'Kilonzo: time running out for Ocampo Six', *Daily Nation*, 24 March 2011
Leftie, Peter, 'It's late to scuttle ICC probe, says minister', *Daily Nation*, 8 December 2010
Leftie, Peter, 'Top four under pressure to step down from public jobs', *Daily Nation*, 16 December 2010
Leftie, Peter, Wanyoro, Charles, Majefa, Mwakera and Mathenge, Oliver, 'Kenya Cabinet in the eye of a storm', *Daily Nation*, 2 August 2009
Limo, Lucianne, 'Ministers hire lawyers', *Standard*, 16 October 2009
Limo, Lucianne, Omanga, Beauttah and Bartoo, Vincent, 'Ocampo asks Kenyans not to expect too much', *Standard*, 11 May 2010
Maina, Kamore, 'How State gagged witnesses', *The Star*, 27 October 2012
Mathenge, Gakuu, 'Kenya on tenterhooks as D-day draws nigh', *Standard*, 6 December 2010
Mathenge, Oliver, 'Judge puts off quizzing security chiefs', *Daily Nation*, 7 December 2010
Mathenge, Oliver, 'New report says 5,000 election violence cases stalled due to lack of evidence', *Daily Nation*, 7 January 2012
Mathenge, Oliver, 'Wako—No Mercy for Poll Violence Leaders', *Daily Nation*, 25 August 2008
Mathenge, Oliver, Kelley, Kevin, Namunane, Bernard and Barasa, Lucas, 'Govt fails to win US backing on poll trials', *Daily Nation*, 10 March 2011
Mathenge, Oliver and Sudhir, Sadiki, 'Lawyers fault proposed tribunal on Waki', *Daily Nation*, 3 December 2008
Mayoyo, Patrick and Namunane, Bernard, 'ODM Pushes for ICC-Led Local Trials', *Daily Nation*, 23 March 2011
Mbote, Patricia Kameria and Akech, Migai, *Kenya: Justice Sector and the Rule of Law* (Open Society Foundation, March 2011)
Mburu, Stephen, 'Uncertain future for tribunal', *Daily Nation*, 7 February 2009
Menya, Walter, 'ICC officers fail to jet in for statement taking', *Daily Nation*, 20 December 2010

Momanyi, Bernard, 'From army man, mail man, to suspect', *Capital News*, 15 December 2010
Mugonyi, David and Namunane, Bernard, 'MPs demand Waki's secret envelope', *Daily Nation*, 31 October 2008
Munene, Mugomo, 'Last ditch effort to shield Ocampo six', *Daily Nation*, 18 December 2010
Musau, Nzau, 'ICC request for files has yet to reach me, says CJ', *The Star*, 25 October 2012
Musau, Nzau, 'Wako wants Ocampo 6 Prosecuted in Kenya', *The Star*, 13 April 2011
Musila, Godfrey, 'Options for Transitional Justice in Kenya: Autonomy and the Challenge of External Prescriptions' (2009) 3 *International Journal of Transitional Justice* 445
Mutiga, Murithi, 'Ocampo: I have solid evidence against six Kenyan suspects', *Daily Nation*, 21 September 2011
Mutiga, Murithi, 'Ocampo writes to judges over threats', *Daily Nation*, 30 January 2010
Mwanzia, Mutinda, 'I am innocent—Kass FM journalist tells Ocampo', *Standard*, 16 December 2010
Namunane, Bernard, 'ICC wants Muthaura to leave key security team', *Daily Nation*, 14 March 2011
Namunane, Bernard, 'Kenya coalition rivalry plays out on the world stage', *Daily Nation*, 3 June 2010
Naumnane, Bernard, 'Kenya's fresh bid to stop Ocampo', *Daily Nation*, 22 April 2011
Namunane, Bernard, 'Kenya seeks Africa support over Hague', *Daily Nation*, 12 January 2011
Namunane, Bernard, 'Kibaki, Raila plot way out for Ocampo 6', *Daily Nation*, 6 January 2011
Namunane, Bernard, 'The Hague beckons for suspects', *Daily Nation*, 26 November 2009
Namunane, Bernard and Barasa, Lucas, 'Cabinet rejects draft laws on local tribunal', *Daily Nation*, 14 July 2009
Namunane, Bernard and Mathenge, Oliver, 'I'll nail suspects in 6 months', *Daily Nation*, 8 May 2010
Namunane, Bernard and Mathenge, Oliver, 'Nation seeks continental support over Hague', *Daily Nation*, 12 January 2011
Ng'etichp, Jacob, 'Kosgey: I am ready to work with ICC', *Daily Nation*, 16 December 2010
Ngirachu, John, 'Draft laws on tribunal unchanged', *Daily Nation*, 29 July 2009
Njoroge, Evelyne and Mburu, James, 'Atwoli throws weight behind Ocampo six', *Capital News*, 19 December 2010
Nyamwayi, Glena, 'Kenya reiterates its commitment to ICC', Kenya Broadcasting Commission, 1 October 2010
Obonyo, Oscar, 'Beyond Ocampo 'Big Six' poll chaos suspects', *Standard*, 12 May 2010
Obonyo, Oscar, 'Push and pull in search for justice for chaos victims', *Standard*, 11 December 2010
Ochami, David and Opiyo, Peter, 'ICC: Ocampo says Muthaura must leave by April 7', *Standard*, 15 March 2011
Ochola, Abiya, 'Annan to delay envelope for two more months', *Standard*, 18 February 2009
Office of the Attorney General, A Progress Report to the Hon. Attorney-General by the Team on Update of Post Election Violence Related Cases in Western, Nyanza, Central, Rift valley, Eastern, Coast and Nairobi Provinces, March 2011
Office of the President, 'Parliament to reconvene on 20th January', 8 January 2009
Office of the President, 'President appoints special envoys', 4 March 2011
Office of the President, 'Special Tribunal to be set up', 17 December 2008
Office of the President, Report from Director of Criminal Investigations Ndegwa Muhoro to Director of Public Prosecutions, 'Re: Update on investigation into Six ICC Suspects', 1 July 2011
Office of the President, Criminal Investigation Department, Post Election Violence Investigations Progress Report, 5 May 2011
Ogutu, Judy, 'Court nullifies list of judicial nominees', *Standard*, 4 February 2011
Ohito, David, 'Government in crisis talks as Annan hands over secret envelope to the ICC', *Standard*, 10 July 2009
Okuta, Antonina, 'National Legislation for Prosecution of International Crimes in Kenya' (2009) 7(5) *Journal of International Criminal Justice* 1063
Olick, Felix, 'AG hints at bid to postpone ICC cases', The *Standard*, 8 October 2012
Omanga, Beauttah, 'Githongo and Ghai rally Kenyans against impunity', *Standard*, 9 January 2011
Omanga, Beauttah, 'Poll violence suspects seek legal help before Ocampo arrives', *Standard*, 2 May 2010

Bibliography

Ombati, Cyrus, 'ICC: Kenya's Security Chiefs testify on Dec 20', *Standard*, 7 December 2010

Ombati, Cyrus, 'Kenya security chiefs scared of ICC grilling', *Standard*, 22 November 2010

Ombati, Cyrus, 'Ocampo demands to know why suspects are still holding office', *Standard*, 21 July 2011

Onyango, Maureen, 'Court stops taking of ICC evidence', *Daily Nation*, 31 January 2011

Onyiego, Michael, 'ICC Prosecutor promises justice for Kenyans', Voice of America, 13 May 2010

Opiyo, David, 'Clear the Air on Trials, ODM Told', *Daily Nation*, 25 March 2011

Opiyo, David, 'President 'behind move on Hague", *Daily Nation*, 16 January 2011

Opiyo, Peter, 'MPs revive push for local tribunal, claim Hague partial', *Standard*, 13 December 2010

Otieno, Otieno, 'Waki envelope still causing ripples', *Daily Nation*, 20 February 2010

Otieno, Daniel, Namunane, Bernard, and Barasa, Lucas, 'Ruto beats a retreat, rejects Hague trials', *Daily Nation*, 15 July 2009

Owalo, Eliud, Raila for President Secretariat, Press Release, 6 November 2012

Prosecutor v Francis Kirimi Muthaura, Uhuru Muigai Kenyatta and Mohammed Hussein Ali, Application by the Defence for Uhuru Kenyatta under Article 61(3) and 67(1)(a) for an Adjournment of the Confirmation Hearing Schedule for 21 September 2011 and Request for Alteration to their Selected Viva Voce Witnesses, ICC-01/09-02/01/11-281, 2 September 2011

Prosecutor v Francis Kirimi Muthaura and Uhuru Muigai Kenyatta, Decision on the withdrawal of charges against Mr Muthaura, ICC-01/09-02/11, 18 March 2013

Prosecutor v Francis Kirimi Muthaura and Uhuru Muigai Kenyatta, Defence application for a change of place where the court shall sit for trial, ICC-01/09-02/11-551, 3 December 2012

Prosecutor v Francis Kirimi Muthaura, Uhuru Muigai Kenyatta and Mohammed Hussein Ali, Defence Challenge to Jurisdiction, Admissibility and Prosecutor's Failure to Meet the Requirements of Article 54, ICC-01/09-02/11-338, 19 September 2011

Prosecutor v Francis Kirimi Muthaura, Uhuru Muigai Kenyatta and Mohammed Hussein Ali, Defence Motion for an Adjournment of the Confirmation Hearing Scheduled for 21 September 2011, ICC-01/09-02/11-290, 5 September 2011

Prosecutor v Francis Kirimi Muthaura, Uhuru Muigai Kenyatta and Mohammed Hussein Ali, Request to Postpone Setting Trial Date Pending Appeals Chamber's Determination of Jurisdiction Appeal, ICC-01/09-02/11-417, 25 April 2012

Prosecutor v Saif Al-Islam Gaddafi and Abdullah Al-Senussi, Decision on the admissibility of the case against Saif Al-Islam Gaddafi, ICC-01/11-01/11, 31 May 2013

Prosecutor v Uhuru Muigai Kenyatta, Prosecution application for a finding of non-compliance pursuant to Article 87(7) against the Government of Kenya, ICC-01/09-02/11, 29 November 2013

Prosecutor v Uhuru Muigai Kenyatta, Prosecution opposition to the Defence request for the termination of the Kenyatta case, public redacted version of confidential Annex A, ICC-01/09-02/11, 31 January 2014

Prosecutor v Uhuru Muigai Kenyatta, Public redacted version of the 'Additional Prosecution observations on Mr Kenyatta's Article 64 application, filed in accordance with order number ICC-01/09-02-11-699", ICC-01/09-02/11, 28 March 2013

Prosecutor v Uhuru Muigai Kenyatta, ICC-01/09-02/11, Transcript 5 February 2014

Prosecutor v William Samoei Ruto, Henry Kiprono Kosgey and Joshua Arap Sang, ICC-01/11, Application on Behalf of the Government of the Republic of Kenya Pursuant to Article 19 of the ICC Statute, ICC-01/09-01/11-19, 31 March 2011

Prosecutor v William Samoei Ruto, Henry Kiprono Kosgey and Joseph Arap Sang, Defence Challenge to Jurisdiction, ICC-01/09-01/11, 30 August 2011

Prosecutor v William Samoei Ruto and Joseph Arap Sang, Joint Defence application for a change of place where the court shall sit for trial, ICC-01/09-01/11, 24 January 2013

Prosecutor v William Samoei Ruto and Joshua Arap Sang, Public redacted version of Prosecution response to the 'Government of Kenya's submissions on the status of cooperation with the International Criminal Court, or, in the alternative, Application for Leave to file observations pursuant to Rule 103(1) of the Rules of Procedure and Evidence', ICC-01/09-01/11, 10 May 2013

Prosecutor v William Samoei Ruto, Henry Kiprono Kosgey and Joseph Arap Sang, Urgent Defence Application for Postponement of the Confirmation hearing and Extension of Time to Disclose and List Evidence, ICC-01/09-01/11-255, 11 August 2011

Republic v Stephen Kiprotich Leting & 3 others [2009] eKLR, Criminal Case 34 of 2008

Rome Statute of the International Criminal Court, opened for signature 17 July 1998, 2187 UNTS 90 (entered into force 1 July 2002)

Shimoli, Eric, 'Top Kenyan is ready to surrender at The Hague', *Daily Nation*, 13 October 2010

Shiundu, Alphonce, 'Imanyara: House will nail a big fish with proposed Bill', *Daily Nation*, 15 August 2009

Shiundu, Alphonce, 'Reform tops agenda as Parliament opens', *Daily Nation*, 19 April 2009

Some, Kipchumba, 'Top NSIS official met minister, witnesses say', *Standard*, 30 April 2010

South Consulting, Kenya National Dialogue and Reconciliation Monitoring Project, *Progress in the Implementation of the Constitution and other reforms, Review Report*, October 2011

South Consulting, Kenya National Dialogue and Reconciliation Monitoring Project, *Review Report for October-December 2009*, January 2010)

South Consulting, Kenya National Dialogue and Reconciliation Monitoring Project, *Status of Implementation of Agenda Items 1-4, Progress Report for January-March 2010*, April 2010

South Consulting, Kenya National Dialogue and Reconciliation Monitoring Project, *Status of Implementation of Agenda Items 1-4, Draft Report,* May 2009

South Consulting, The Kenya National Dialogue and Reconciliation (KNDR) Monitoring Project, January 2009

Special Tribunal for Kenya Bill 2009

Stahn, Carsten, 'Complementarity, amnesties, and alternative forms of justice; some interpretive guidelines for the International Criminal Court' (2005) 3 *Journal of International Criminal Justice* 695

Stahn, Carsten, 'Taking complementarity seriously: on the sense and sensibility of 'classical', 'positive' and 'negative' complementarity' in Carsten Stahn and Mohamed M. El Zeidy (eds), *The International Criminal Court and Complementarity From Theory to Practice* (Cambridge University Press, 2011)

Stevenson, Reed, 'Hague court prosecutor to investigate Kenya violence', *Reuters*, 31 March 2010

Wafula, 'Caroline, Don't Panic, Raila tells leaders', *Daily Nation*, 18 November 2009

Wafula, Caroline, 'Kenya MPs shun debate on tribunal bill', *Daily Nation*, 2 December 2009

Wanambisi, Laban, 'Plot to ditch the ICC hits a snag', *Capital News*, 17 December 2010

Warigi, Gitau, 'Local tribunal or The Hague?', *Daily Nation*, 31 July 2009

White, Eric, Putting Complementarity in Practice: Domestic Justice for International Crimes in DRC, Uganda, and Kenya (Open Society Justice Initiative, 2011)

Chapter 7
Rule of Law Reforms: Post Hoc Ergo Propter Hoc?

The ICC's intervention in Kenya coincided with the most sustained period of legal reforms in the country's history. A new constitution was passed and constitutional office holders replaced; a truth commission, a national cohesion commission and a new police commission were formed; judges were vetted; a new witness protection regime was established and new crimes were added to the statute book, including those within the ICC's jurisdiction. To what extent can the momentum for this widespread and fundamental rule of law reform be attributed to the OTP's strategy of positive complementarity and the commencement of trials in The Hague?

It would be easy to conclude, as Sriram and Brown do, that the OTP's intervention in Kenya served as a catalyst for these reforms. This chapter suggests, however, that this *post hoc ergo propter hoc* reasoning is misleading and does not accurately capture the most significant factors that were stimulating these reforms. Although the OTP's presence in Kenya may have had *some* impact on this reform agenda, it would appear that the reforms were part of an ongoing process that was accelerated by the scale of the post-election violence and the encouragement of the Annan-led KNDR. Indeed, there is even evidence to suggest that the OTPs intervention had a shadow side in that it may have at times been an *obstacle* to the reform agenda. First, the pressures emanating from the strategy of positive complementarity contributed to pre-existing tensions within the power-sharing government and this disunity threatened to derail the reform agenda. Second, the ICC's threatened intervention distracted from the ongoing reform agenda and the government's preoccupation with stalling trials in The Hague may have resulted in delays in implementing some reforms. Finally, the strategy of positive complementarity appears to have encouraged the government to pass illusory reforms in an attempt to frustrate the progress of the ICC's trials and in this way stalled the progress of effective reforms.

The focus of this chapter is not on the reforms themselves, but rather on the factors that stimulated and influenced them. In particular, this chapter considers the extent to which the OTP's strategy of positive complementarity served as a catalyst for these reforms. In conducting this analysis, a variety of sources were relied upon. First, speeches delivered in Parliament when legislation was being passed. This analysis involved the review of the Hansard records of 256 Parliamentary sessions, documenting the passing of 73 pieces of legislation between February 2008 and March 2013. Second, more than 2,000 statements made by politicians and other persons to media outlets, including television, radio and newspapers were also collated, coded and analysed. Third, particular regard was had to government reports that concerned one or more of the reforms under consideration and whether they identify any stimuli for reform. Fourth, I conducted a careful review of reports from international actors and local NGOs who were observing the reform process throughout this period. Finally, I have placed reliance upon my interviews with politicians, public servants and civil society.

1 The OTP and Rule of Law Reform

When assessing the OTP's impact on this reform process, it is first important to recognise that the OTP does not have an explicit mandate to actively participate in strengthening the rule of law.[1] Although the preamble to the Rome Statute recognises that 'it is the duty of every state to exercise its criminal jurisdiction over those responsible for international crimes', the Rome Statute does not provide any explicit reference to the OTP or any other organ of the Court as having an obligation to provide material support to states to assist them in upholding these duties. Rather, the Rome State envisages the ICC's organs acting only when a state has failed to uphold its obligation to investigate and prosecute international crimes.[2] Despite lacking an explicit mandate to assist with rule of law reforms, in its early years the OTP suggested that it saw its role as including the enhancement of domestic justice mechanisms[3].

In relation to the Kenyan situation, the OTP sought to emphasise that it would not actively assist the government in undertaking its rule of law reforms. While in Kenya conducting investigations in May 2010, Moreno-Ocampo said 'don't expect everything from me. I will only prosecute two to six cases and the rest is up to you'. The Prosecutor also stated that his job was 'to prosecute, period'; that the ICC's

---

[1] Robert Cryer, *Prosecuting International Crimes: Selectivity and the International Criminal Law Regime* (Cambridge University Press, 2005), 164.
[2] Rome Statute, Article 17.
[3] Luis Moreno-Ocampo, 'Address to the Assembly of States Parties', New York, 22 April 2003.

involvement was 'just the beginning of a journey to justice in Kenya'; and that 'Kenyans would be in the lead' in 'deciding on their own way forward'.[4]

Although the OTP did not consider domestic rule of law reform to be within its mandate, the linkage between the strategy of positive complementarity and rule of law reforms has been explored for four reasons. First, notwithstanding it's official position, the OTP did at times seek to encourage progress in certain reforms, particularly in respect of the truth commission and the country's witness protection regime. It is therefore important to consider what impact, if any, this may have had.

Second, it is entirely possible that the OTP's strategy of positive complementarity could fail to end impunity in the sense of ensuring accountability for post-election violence crimes, but nevertheless make a significant contribution to ending impunity according to some other understanding. Fairness to the OTP therefore requires consideration of all possible contributions to ending impunity that it may have had. Although such an impact would not have been intended by the OTP and was not part of its own assessment of success, if the strategy of positive complementarity did in fact have this impact in Kenya this should certainly be considered to have been a significant contribution to ending impunity.

Third, there has been very little academic consideration of the relationship between the strategy of positive complementarity and its impact on rule of law reforms in the target state. As Bjork and Goebertus note:

> The academic literature is rife with attacks on the ad hoc tribunals for failing to strengthen the rule of law in Rwanda and former Yugoslavia, but few have commented on the ICC's responsibilities in this area. Can the ICC—an international justice mechanism located far from the places in which it operates and staffed entirely by foreigners—encourage a restructuring of national legal systems?[5]

The assumption appears to be that the commencement of trials at the ICC may renew confidence in domestic criminal justice systems and inspire domestic rule of law reforms. Hampson has expressed hope that international tribunals such as the ICC may 'bring the element of impartiality necessary to restore faith in the judicial process and the rule of law'.[6] Likewise, Burke-White, Linjamuri, Mégret, Orentlicher, Robinson and Tillier suggest that international trials may serve a symbolic function that sets the rule of law through example and inspires societies to

---

[4] Joe Mbuthia, 'ICC has "no witness in Kenya"', *Daily Nation*, 24 March 2010; 'Cases will ensure peaceful 2012 election, says Ocampo', *Daily Nation*, 15 December 2010; Beauttah Omanga, 'Nowhere to hide as The Hague alerts states on chaos suspects', *Standard*, 27 April 2010; Luis Moreno-Ocampo, 'Kenya National Dialogue and Reconciliation, Two Year On, Where are We?', Statement, Nairobi, 2 December 2010.

[5] Christine Bjork and Juanita Goebertus, 'Complementarity in Action: The Role of Civil Society and the ICC in Rule of Law Strengthening in Kenya' (2011) 14 *Yale Human Rights & Development Law Journal* 205, 226.

[6] Fen Hampson, *Nurturing Peace: Why Peace Settlements Succeed or Fail* (United States Institute of Peace Press, 1996), 231.

affirm their respect for the rule of law.[7] Indeed, in the one academic study that has been completed on this issue, Sriram and Brown suggest that the OTP's strategy of positive complementarity *did* have such an influence on rule of law reforms in Kenya. They argue that 'the ICC's strategy of positive complementarity may have influenced the political calculus by influencing national debates on accountability mechanisms in response to the violence and provided extra momentum for broader rule of law reforms'.[8]

Finally, many in Kenya expected or hoped that the ICC would have such an impact. For many of the victims of the post-election violence, ending impunity in Kenya required not only prosecuting those responsible for the crimes, but also major structural reforms to the country's legal and political institutions which had allowed perpetrators of previous instances of electoral violence to evade accountability. Many local NGOs also had hope that the ICC's intervention would serve as a catalyst for reforms in Kenya.[9] Some, for example, explained that the ICC's prosecution of senior politicians would remove these 'lords of impunity' from the law-making process, thereby enabling crucial reforms to be passed without obstruction from these 'anti-reformers'. Others told me that the ICC's involvement demonstrated that the international community was monitoring the Kenyan situation closely and that this would have the effect of 'shaming' its politicians into supporting rule of law reforms.

2 The Tenth Parliament's Rule of Law Reforms

As demonstrated in Chap. 3, by the time Kenyans went to the polls in 2007, impunity had become institutionalised. Many electoral officials, police officers, prosecutors and judges lacked independence and were beholden to a president whose powers had been augmented by more than 30 constitutional amendments. Rule of law reforms were particularly necessary in Kenya, a country which the World Bank

---

[7] William Burke-White, 'Complementarity in Practice: The International Criminal Court as Part of a System of Multi-level Global Governance in the Democratic Republic of Congo' (2005) 18 *Leiden Journal of International Law* 569–572; Leslie Vinjamuri, 'Deterrence, Democracy and the Pursuit of International Justice' (2010) 24(2) *Ethics and International Affairs* 191, 197; Frédéric Mégret, 'Too much of a good thing? Implementation and the uses of complementarity' in Carsten Stahn and Mohamed M. El Zeidy (eds), *The International Criminal Court and Complementarity From Theory to Practice* (Cambridge University Press, 2011), 362; Diane Orentlicher, 'Settling Accounts: The Duty to Prosecute Human Rights Violations of a Prior Regime' (1991) 100 *Yale Law Journal* 2537, 2540; Darryl Robinson, 'The Rome Statute and its Impact on National Law' in Antonio Cassese, Paola Gaeta and John Jones (eds), *The Rome Statute of the International Criminal Court: a commentary* (Oxford University Press, 2002), 1849; Justine Tillier, 'The ICC Prosecutor and Positive Complementarity: Strengthening the Rule of Law?' (2013) 13(3) *International Criminal Law Review* 507.

[8] Chandra Sriram and Stephen Brown, 'Kenya in the Shadow of the ICC: Complementarity, Gravity and Impact' (2012) 12(2) International Criminal Law Review 219.

[9] Bjork and Goebertus (2011) (see Footnote 4), 226.

had consistently ranked in the bottom quintile on its rule of law index.[10] The Ministry of Justice had itself acknowledged that rule of law reform was essential in order to prevent future occurrences of violence and to end impunity in the country:

> Citizens have lost faith in the rule of law and often resort to extra-legal means to vindicate their rights or simply resign themselves to fate. Institutional failures and perceptions of selective and ineffective enforcement of the law have contributed to waning public confidence. This has, over time, led to a culture of impunity that partly explains the post-election violence witnessed in Kenya in 2007/2008.[11]

A major priority for the power-sharing government was the undertaking of fundamental and widespread rule of law reforms prior to the holding of the next presidential election. From 2008 until 2013, Kenya's Tenth Parliament was responsible for passing a new constitution, establishing a truth commission and implementing significant structural changes to the country's judiciary, security sector and witness protection programme. As Odinga told Parliament in December 2009:

> More than any other Parliament in our history, the Tenth Parliament has debated and enacted the highest number of reform-oriented legislation ... The honourable members of this house have also been relentless in their pursuit for accountability, transparency, good governance and an end to the culture of impunity.[12]

It is difficult to specify what should be considered to be a 'rule of law reform' for the purposes of this chapter because there is little consensus as to the essence of the rule of law or what it means for it to be strengthened. Tamanaha, for example, suggests that 'the rule of law is analogous to the notion of the 'good', in the sense that everyone is for it, but have contrasting convictions about what it is'.[13] The rule of law literature highlights the importance of avoiding reforms that are one-size-fits-all.[14] Consequently, for the purposes of this chapter a broad interpretation of 'rule of law reform' has been adopted to include all reforms that concern the administration of justice and the functioning of political institutions. In the case of Kenya, these reforms may be categorised as relating to: (1) the Constitution, (2) the criminal justice system, (3) the electoral process and (4) national reconciliation. Such reforms are often required in societies which have experienced periods of mass violence to ensure that public institutions within that society can have their legitimacy restored.[15] Police, courts and other institutions require legitimacy in order to secure voluntary

---

[10] World Bank Institute, *Country Data Report for Kenya, 1996–2011* (World Bank, 2011), 7.

[11] Ministry of Justice, National Cohesion and Constitutional Affairs, *GJLOS II Reform Programme 2011/12 to 2015/16*, 21 October 2011 ('GJLOS II Reform Programme'), 31.

[12] Hansard, National Assembly, Official Report, 2 December 2009.

[13] Brian Tamanaha, *On the Rule of Law: History, Politics, Theory* (Cambridge University Press, 2004).

[14] Thomas Carothers, *Promoting the Rule of Law Abroad: In Search of Knowledge* (Carnegie Endowment for International Peace, 2006); David Trubek and Alvaro Santos (eds), *The New Law and Economic Development: A Critical Appraisal* (Cambridge University Press, 2006).

[15] Colette Rausch (ed), *Combating Serious Crimes in Post-conflict Societies: a Handbook for Policymakers and Practitioners* (US Institute of Peace Press, 2006), 73–74.

cooperation, which in turn makes it easier for these institutions to maintain social order.[16] This chapter first outlines the Tenth Parliament's reforms, before going on to consider the catalysts for these reforms.

2.1 Constitution

Of all the reforms undertaken in Kenya between 2008 and 2013, none was more significant than the passing of the new Constitution. According to Teitel, when a society has experienced periods of repression or state-sponsored violence, the adoption of a new constitution is essential for re-establishing social order and respect for the rule of law.[17] This was particularly the case in Kenya because the new Constitution was a necessary pre-requisite for many other crucial reforms, including those relating to the judiciary, the security sector and the electoral process. The US Ambassador described this moment as the country's most important achievement since independence, while Odinga said that the new Constitution would be a 'powerful force' in 'ending 45 years of impunity'.[18]

The Constitution was approved by 67 % of Kenyan voters at a referendum held on 4 August 2010 and was promulgated later that same month. It reduced the concentration of power in the executive and provided for greater checks and balances between the three branches of government. For example, the Constitution required that Parliamentary approval be obtained for the appointment and dismissal of significant public office holders and prescribed the expectations and responsibilities of the persons occupying these positions. The Constitution also included a bill of rights and provided for a revamped and expanded human rights commission. Public satisfaction with the contents of the Constitution and its manner of implementation remained consistently high in the years following its promulgation. According to KNDR, the Constitution enjoyed 'huge public support and legitimacy' and its passing was a symbolic watershed that provided tremendous momentum for further reforms and hope for the future.[19]

---

[16] Tom Tyler, Anthony Braga, Jeffrey Fagan, Tracey Meares, Robert Sampson and Chris Winship, 'Legitimacy and Criminal Justice: International Perspectives' in Tom Tyler (ed), *Legitimacy and Criminal Justice: International Perspectives* (Russell Sage, 2007), 10–11.

[17] Ruti Teitel, *Transitional Justice* (Oxford University Press, 2002), 191–211.

[18] Remarks by the US Ambassador to Kenya at a forum on Civil Society and the Implementation of the New Constitution, Nairobi, 23 September 2010; Joy Wanja, 'Political detainees urge govt to resign', *Daily Nation*, 31 July 2009.

[19] South Consulting, Kenya National Dialogue and Reconciliation Monitoring Project, *Agenda Item IV Reforms, Long-standing Issues and Solutions, Progress Review Report*, March 2012 ('KNDR March 2012 Report'), i; South Consulting, Kenya National Dialogue and Reconciliation Monitoring Project, *Review Report*, October 2010 ('KNDR October 2010 Report'), v–vi.

2.2 Criminal Justice System

The new Constitution provided the foundations for other much-needed reforms of the criminal justice system, commencing with the judiciary. Upon assuming office in June 2011, Chief Justice Willy Mutunga said that he 'found an institution so frail in its structures; so thin on resources; so low on its confidence; so deficient in integrity; so weak in its public support that to have expected it to deliver justice was to be wildly optimistic'.[20] Chapter Ten of the Constitution sought to promote a more transparent, accountable and independent judiciary by providing for the establishment of a Supreme Court, the Judicial Services Commission ('JSC') and a judiciary fund. The Supreme Court was established to serve as check on executive power by resolving presidential election disputes, deciding on the validity of states of emergency and serving as the final court of appeal. The president retained the power to appoint judges to the Supreme Court, but appointments had to be supported by the independent JSC. The JSC's first high-profile task was to appoint a new Chief Justice. For eight days in May 2011, Kenyans were provided with an unprecedented transparent appointment process that included live television coverage of the candidates' interviews.[21] At the conclusion of the process, Mutunga's appointment was praised by academics and human rights activists, who paid tribute to his integrity and commitment to justice.[22]

The Constitution also provided for the establishment of the Judges and Magistrates Vetting Board ('JMVB'), which was charged with the responsibility of assessing the suitability of 58 judges and 352 magistrates to serve in the judiciary. The JMVB declared 13 judges to be unfit to serve, for reasons that included condoning the use of torture, accepting gifts from litigants and sanctioning the illegal transfer of public land.[23] Alongside these structural and personnel changes, the judiciary also sought to improve its management of cases by installing new information communication technology across the country.[24]

---

[20] Tom Maliti, 'Kenyan Chief Justice outlines progress in judicial transformation', *The International Criminal Court Kenya Monitor*, 25 October 2011.

[21] Tom Maliti, 'Outsiders nominated to be Kenya's next Chief Justice and Deputy Chief Justice', *The International Criminal Court Kenya Monitor*, 16 May 2011.

[22] Tom Maliti, 'Great expectations await new Kenyan Chief Justice', *The International Criminal Court Kenya Monitor*, 20 June 2011.

[23] Judges and Magistrates Vetting Board, 'Determination Concerning the Judges of the Court of Appeal', 25 April 2012 ('Vetting Board April 2012 Determination'); Pamela Chepkemei, 'Five judges sent home, 23 cleared as Rao turns to magistrates', *Daily Nation*, 22 December 2012.

[24] Patricia Kameri Mbote and Migai Akech, Kenya: Justice Sector and the Rule of Law (Open Society Foundation, March 2011) ('OSI Rule of Law Report'), 14; South Consulting, Kenya National Dialogue and Reconciliation Monitoring Project, *Status of Implementation of Agenda Items 1–4, Progress Report for January–March 2010*, April 2010 ('KNDR April 2010 Report'), 43.

The Constitution also facilitated significant reforms to Kenya's prosecutorial system. First, it required the sitting Attorney General, Amos Wako, to vacate office within twelve months. This was important, since Alston had accused Wako of being 'not just complicit in, but absolutely indispensable to, a system which has institutionalised impunity in Kenya'.[25] On 29 August 2011, Wako was replaced by Githu Muigai, a human rights lawyer who had previously served as a UN special rapporteur and had represented Mau Mau veterans attempting to sue the British government for torture committed during the 1950s.[26] The state's powers of prosecution were also taken out of the hands of the Attorney General and given to the independent DPP. The ancient and much-abused power to stop prosecutions (*nolle prosequi*) was amended so that it could not be exercised without the permission of the court.

The Constitution also provided the basis for necessary reforms in the security sector, including the establishment of a new police commission, which was to be responsible for overseeing the recruitment, promotion, transfer and disciplining of police officers. It also prescribed professional and ethical standards for the police force and required the president's appointee as head of the police to be approved by Parliament. Odinga said that 'when fully implemented, these reforms will transform the police institution from one associated with corruption, incompetence and brutality to one that exemplifies excellence, integrity and service to the people'.[27] Kenyatta declared that 'the police will salute you before any arrest and they will say "please may I arrest you?"'.[28] The promised reforms, however, were not fully implemented. In March 2012, KNDR described the security sector reform agenda to be 'a tale of motion without movement'.[29] The process of vetting senior officers commenced in May 2011, but was suspended when human rights organisations objected to the fact that the vetting was being carried out by other police officers.[30] According to Human Rights Watch, the restructuring of the police force and the vetting of officers were delayed for over a year because of resistance from senior officers.[31] Further, a lack of resources within the police force meant that officers had poor working conditions and were constrained in performing their duties through a lack of equipment.[32] Despite the Waki Report's damning findings regarding the police force's response to the post-election violence, the same policing structures that existed for the 2007 elections remained in place for the 2013 elections.

---

[25] Philip Alston, *Mission to Kenya 16–25 February 2009* (United Nations Special Rapporteur on Extrajudicial Killings, Arbitrary or Summary Executions, 2009) ('Alston Report'), 15–16.

[26] Jevans Nyabiage, 'Muigai sworn in as new Attorney General', *Standard*, 29 August 2011.

[27] Hansard, National Assembly, Official Report, 2 December 2009.

[28] 'Kenya's Constitution: a chance to improve how Kenya is run', *Economist*, 29 June 2010.

[29] KNDR March 2012 Report (see Footnote 18).

[30] Human Rights Watch, *Turning Pebbles: Evading Accountability for Post-Election Violence in Kenya, 2011*, 75 ('HRW, Turning Pebbles'), 72.

[31] Human Rights Watch, *World Report 2014* (Human Rights Watch, 2014).

[32] Amnesty International, *Police Reform in Kenya: 'A Drop in the Ocean'* (Amnesty International, 2013), 19.

While these reforms were ongoing, the Tenth Parliament also passed important pieces of criminal legislation. The first, the *International Crimes Act 2008* implemented Kenya's obligations under the Rome Statute by granting local courts jurisdiction to try persons for genocide, crimes against humanity and war crimes. Legislation was also enacted to prohibit female genital mutilation; permit courts to sentence persons convicted of terrorism or human trafficking to be imprisoned for up to 30 years; outlaw criminal gangs such as Mungiki; allow for the seizure of proceeds from money laundering and formalise the procedure for plea agreements.[33]

The Tenth Parliament was also responsible for much-needed amendments to the witness protection programme, aimed at making the responsible institutions more independent. The witness protection programme was granted financial autonomy, with its budgets approved by an independent advisory board, drawing funding from the country's consolidated fund. The powers of the Attorney General were conferred upon the newly established Witness Protection Agency ('WPA').[34] The WPA was officially launched on 12 August 2011 and by January 2013 had received over 100 applications for protection.[35]

2.3 Electoral Process

Another category of reforms upon which the Tenth Parliament focused was the electoral process. Reforming the electoral system was essential because the Electoral Commission of Kenya ('ECK') had lost all credibility over its handling of the 2007 elections. The ECK was disbanded and replaced with an Interim Independent Electoral Commission ('IIEC'). The IIEC organised and supervised the holding of the 2010 Constitutional referendum, which involved the registration of more than 12 million voters.[36] The Constitution then provided for the establishment of the Independent Electoral and Boundaries Commission ('IEBC') which was to be responsible for supervising elections and defining electoral boundaries. Although Constitutional ambiguity generated some controversy over when the next general election was required to be held, this was ultimately resolved peacefully through an open and transparent legal process, allowing IEBC chairman Issack Hassan to

---

[33] *Prevention of Terrorism Act 2012*; *Counter-Trafficking in Persons Act 2010*; *Prevention of Organised Crime Act 2010*; *Criminal Procedure Code (Amendment) Act 2008*; *Proceeds of Crime and Anti-Money Laundering Act 2009*; *Prohibition of Female Genital Mutilation Act 2011*.

[34] *Witness Protection (Amendment) Act 2010*.

[35] Lillian Aluanga-Delvaux, 'Lack of funds delays witness agency work', *Standard*, 6 January 2013.

[36] Anthony Kariuki, 'Kenya referendum date set', *Daily Nation*, 14 May 2010.

announce the election date as 4 March 2013. Legislation was also passed that regulated the registration and operation of political parties[37] and established penal offences for acts that interfered with the conduct of free and fair elections.[38]

2.4 National Reconciliation

Finally, the Tenth Parliament also focused on reforms that were intended to promote national reconciliation. The first of these occurred in October 2008 when legislation was passed to provide for the establishment of the TJRC. The TJRC's objective was to 'seek and promote justice, national unity, reconciliation and peace' by establishing a complete historical record of all human rights violations that had occurred in Kenya since independence.[39] The TJRC commenced its work in November 2009 and, although it was required to complete its work within two years, it took until May 2013 to publish its final report. Much of this delay can be attributed to the controversy concerning the appointment of the TJRC's chairperson, Bethuel Kiplagat, who had been the subject of two adverse findings by government commissions that related to matters within the TJRC's mandate.[40] As a result, one commissioner resigned in protest, the Justice Minister called for the TJRC to be disbanded and civil society dissociated itself from the process.[41] Kiplagat voluntarily stepped aside (on full salary) to allow the TJRC to continue its work and his appointment was subsequently cleared, but the TJRC itself was forced to admit that it 'lost a significant amount of time and credibility' as a result of this process.[42] Compounding the challenges faced by the TJRC was a 'lack of sufficient finances and resources'.[43] In the 2010/2011 financial year, the TJRC received less than 16 % of the funding that it requested for its operations, meaning that it was unable to pay staff salaries.[44] Funding from the donor community was not forthcoming because of the Kiplagat controversy and the government's failure to establish a special tribunal.[45]

---

[37] *Political Parties Act 2012.*

[38] *Elections Act 2011.*

[39] *Truth Justice and Reconciliation Act 2008.*

[40] International Centre for Transitional Justice, 'Kenya: Truth Commission Chair Should Step Down', 22 February 2010.

[41] Martin Mutua, 'Eyes on other TJRC officials as Murungi resigns', *Standard*, 19 April 2010; Michael Onyiego, 'Kenyan Justice Minister calls for disbanding of truth commission', *Voice of America*, 16 April 2010; Kenya Truth Justice and Reconciliation Commission, *Progress Report to the National Assembly Submitted Pursuant to Section 20(3) of the Truth, Justice and Reconciliation Act No. 6 of 2008*, 24 June 2011 ('TJRC Progress Report'), 38.

[42] TJRC Progress Report (see Footnote 40), iv.

[43] Ibid, 39–40.

[44] Ibid.

[45] Ibid.

Despite these setbacks, the TJRC was able to make some contribution to the process of national reconciliation. The TJRC received 43,000 statements and 1,600 memoranda from the public, the largest number of statements received by a truth commission anywhere in the world.[46] For the vast majority of victims and witnesses, the oral testimony they provided was their first opportunity to speak publicly about the crimes committed against themselves and their families.[47] On 3 May 2013, the TJRC published its report, comprising four volumes and 2,210 pages, documenting human rights violations committed by state agencies from 1893 until 2008. The report named persons believed to be responsible for these violations and recommended their prosecution, while also calling for the establishment of a reparation fund which would be responsible for compensating victims.[48]

Complementing the TJRC's reporting on historical injustices was the National Cohesion and Integration Commission ('NCIC'), which was established in October 2009 to 'facilitate and promote equality of opportunity, good relations, harmony and peaceful coexistence between persons of the different ethnic and racial communities'.[49] In seeking to realise this objective, the NCIC launched nationwide conflict management training programmes, nominated 'goodwill ambassadors' to 'promote tolerance, understanding and acceptance of diversity' and facilitated peace dialogues between communities.[50] The NCIC's most prominent activity, however, concerned the monitoring of hate speech. In particular, the NCIC investigated statements alleged to have been made by trade minister Chirau Ali Mwakwere, MPs Wilfred Machage and Fred Kapondi and four other unnamed MPs, although none resulted in prosecutions.[51] To support this work, the NCIC also produced guidelines for the media to assist it in guarding against the broadcasting of hate speech.[52] The cumulative effect of these reforms appears to have had some success, with KNDR reporting in April 2011 that 'over 80 % [of Kenyans had] no problems relating with members of other communities, and [that] they would readily work and invest in regions settled by people from other tribes'.[53]

---

[46] Patrick Beja, 'TJRC wants politicians charged over crimes', *Standard*, 6 February 2013.

[47] TJRC Progress Report (see Footnote 40), iii.

[48] Truth Justice and Reconciliation Commission, *Report of the Truth Justice and Reconciliation Commission*, 3 May 2013.

[49] *National Cohesion and Integration Act 2008*, section 25.

[50] Bernard Kwalia, 'NCIC Now Launches Workshops to Defuse Tension', *The Star*, 7 February 2012; National Cohesion and Integration Commission, 'Goodwill Ambassadors for Cohesion, Integration and Peaceful Coexistence', 4 February 2013; National Cohesion and Integration Commission, 'The National Cohesion Response to the Tana River Insecurity and the Riots in Mombasa', 5 September 2012.

[51] Walter Menya, 'AG, police faulted for derailing Mwakwere arrest', *Daily Nation*, 17 August 2010; Wahome Thuku, 'NCIC to withdraw hate speech charges against Machage, Kapondi', *Standard*, 4 August 2011; 'NCIC Probing Four MPS over Hate Speech During Rallies', *The Star*, 21 February 2012.

[52] National Cohesion and Integration Commission, Guidelines for Monitoring Hate Speech, August 2010.

[53] South Consulting, Kenya National Dialogue and Reconciliation Monitoring Project, *Draft Review Report*, April 2011 ('KNDR April 2011 Report').

It can therefore be seen that, from March 2008 until March 2013, the Tenth Parliament was responsible for a large number of rule of law reforms. What remains to be analysed is what factors served as catalyst for these reforms and, in particular, the extent to which the OTP's strategy of positive complementarity, which commenced in February 2008, had an influence.

3 Catalysts for Reform

Before discussing any impact that the OTP's strategy of positive complementarity may have had on Kenya's rule of law agenda, it is important to first consider any other factors that may have served as a catalyst for some or all of these reforms. It is argued that there are at least five alternative explanations for why it was that the Tenth Parliament was the most reformist in the country's history.

3.1 The Ongoing Reform Process

The Tenth Parliament's reforms should not be viewed in isolation, but should instead be considered to form part of an ongoing reform agenda that not only pre-dated the OTP's strategy of positive complementarity but even the establishment of the ICC itself. The momentum for reform may be traced back to Kenya's return to multi-partyism in 1992. This process of democratisation 'broadened political and social freedoms in Kenya significantly', thereby awakening political activism and providing the platform for a subsequent reform agenda.[54] In 1992, the government established 15 special task forces and commissions of inquiry to provide recommendations in relation to governance, justice and public order.[55] This led to the launch of a legal sector reform programme in 2000 and several proposals to reform laws relating to women, children, public order and the media.[56] These recommendations, however, resulted in little positive change until the election of the more reformist Kibaki government in 2002. The Kibaki administration oversaw the establishment of the KNCHR and the revamping of the Law Reform Commission.[57] In his first year in office, Kibaki also launched the Governance, Justice, Law and Order Sector reform programme ('GJLOS'), a multi-sectoral programme involving 32 government ministries with the objective of providing for the 'efficient, accountable and transparent

---

[54] David Throup and Charles Hornsby, *Multi-Party Politics in Kenya* (Ohio University Press, 1998), 592–594.
[55] GJLOS II Reform Programme (see Footnote 10).
[56] Ibid.
[57] OSI Rule of Law Report (see Footnote 23), 3.

administration of justice'.[58] Launched in November 2003 with the support of nine countries and eight international organisations, GJLOS built upon previous attempts to reform the legal sector by providing for an initial one-year plan, followed by a series of five-year plans.[59] Within six months of his re-election in December 2007, Kibaki launched Vision 2030, a 'long-term development blueprint for the country' that aimed to 'make Kenya a globally competitive and prosperous country with a high quality of life by 2030'.[60] According to the Justice Minister, Vision 2030 recognised that 'to achieve its social and economic development, Kenya needs to be a country that adheres to the rule of law'.[61] When assessing the impact that the OTP may have had on Kenya's rule of law reforms, it is therefore important to keep in mind that any transformations may have been part of a wider reform agenda that not only pre-dated the OTP's involvement, but also the ICC's existence.

For example, although it is true that the adoption of a new constitution in 2010 occurred at the same time that the OTP was pursuing its strategy of positive complementarity, its passing was in fact the culmination of a movement that had commenced even before to the ICC's establishment in 2002. Some, such as the Minister for Lands, James Orengo, civil society activist Njonjo Mue and international NGO Human Rights Watch considered the adoption of the new Constitution to be the culmination of more than 40 years of unrelenting efforts.[62] Others, including Kibaki, the Ministry of Justice, the KHRC and the Constitution's Committee of Experts suggested that the constitutional review process dated back to the end of one-party rule in 1992.[63] Certainly, a great deal of momentum for constitutional reform had been generated by 1997 when it had become the major election issue.[64] The Moi government created a review commission which oversaw the production of a draft

---

[58] Republic of Kenya, *Governance, Justice, Law and Order Sector Reform Programme, Short Term Priorities Programme, Fiscal Year 2003/04*, 11.

[59] Angela Reitmaier, *The African Peer Review Mechanism at Country Level: Views from Kenya, Occasional Paper No. 83, Governance and APRM Programme* (South African Institute of International Affairs, May 2011), 9; International Bar Association and International Legal Assistance Consortium, *Restoring Integrity: An assessment of the needs of the justice system in the Republic of Kenya* (International Bar Association and International Legal Assistance Consortium, February 2010) ('IBA Report'), 31.

[60] Office of the Prime Minister, Launch of Kenya Vision 2030 Speech by His Excellency Hon. Mwai Kibaki, 10 June 2008.

[61] GJLOS II Reform Programme (see Footnote 10), 31.

[62] Hansard, National Assembly, Official Report, 23 August 2011; Njonjo Mue, 'New Constitution major step towards justice in Kenya', *New Liberian*, 6 August 2010; Human Rights Watch, *World Report 2011* (Human Rights Watch, 2011), 133.

[63] Hansard, National Assembly, Official Report, 18 March 2008; GJLOS II Reform Programme (see Footnote 10); Kenya Human Rights Commission, *Surviving After Torture: A Case Digest on the Struggle for Justice by Torture Survivors in Kenya* (Kenya Human Rights Commission, 2009) ('KHRC, Surviving After Torture'); Committee of Experts on Constitutional Review, *Final Report of the Committee of Experts on Constitutional Review*, 11 October 2010 ('Committee of Experts Report'), 13.

[64] Mwangi wa Gĩthĩnji and Frank Holmquist, 'Reform and Political Impunity in Kenya: Transparency without Accountability' (2012) 55(1) *African Studies Review* 53, 65.

constitution, only for Moi to dissolve Parliament to ensure the process was derailed prior to the 2002 election.[65] Kibaki's 'Rainbow Coalition' won the election in a landslide, promising to enact a new constitution within 100 days and entering into a memorandum of understanding with Odinga that would see the latter become prime minister once the position was created.[66] Upon assuming office, however, Kibaki reneged on these promises and instead threw his support behind a heavily compromised draft constitution that did not significantly diminish the powers of the presidency.[67] Odinga refused to support the draft and was successful in ensuring that the proposal was defeated at a referendum held in 2005. With this history, it was perhaps not surprising that the issue of constitutional reform returned to the political agenda following the 2007 election.

The reforms to the judiciary provide a second example of an ongoing process that predated the ICC's formation. Judicial reforms may be traced back to at least 1998 when Justice Kwach was appointed to chair a committee to report on the administration of justice. The Kwach Committee found evidence of corruption, incompetence and neglect of duty and recommended that the Constitution be amended to allow for the removal of unsuitable judges.[68] Five years later, Judge Ringera was appointed to investigate corruption in the judiciary. The Ringera Committee found credible evidence implicating 32 % of magistrates, 50 % of High Court judges and 56 % of Court of Appeal judges.[69] During this vetting process, popularly known as the 'radical surgery' of the judiciary, the Chief Justice, 23 judges and 83 magistrates were suspended from office over corruption allegations.[70] In 2005 the Kibaki government adopted the *Judiciary Strategic Plan 2005–2008*, a strategy that was later replaced by the *Judiciary Strategic Plan 2009–2012*. These two policy documents provided a blueprint for judicial reform and led to the formation,

---

[65] Wauna Oluoch 'The Constitution Making Process in Kenya: A Crisis of Leadership and Illegalities?' in Philip Kichana (ed), *Judiciary Watch Report, Judicial Reform in Kenya* (International Commission of Jurists Kenya, 2005), 5–6; Grace Maingi, 'The Kenyan Constitutional Reform Process: A Case Study on the Work of FIDA Kenya in Securing Women's Rights' (2011) 15 *Feminist Africa* 63, 66; Alicia Bannon, 'Designing a Constitution-Drafting Process: Lessons from Kenya' (2007) 116 *Yale Law Journal* 1824, 1832.

[66] Axel Harneit-Sievers and Ralph-Michael Peters, 'Kenya's 2007 General Election and its Aftershocks' (2008) 43 *Africa Spectrum* 135; Edwin Odhiambo Abuya, 'Consequences of a Flawed Presidential Election' (2009) 29(1) *Legal Studies* 130.

[67] Matilda Lasseko, 'Role of Civil Society in Transitional Justice Process: the Evolving Kenyan Experience' in Godfrey Musila, 'The Accountability Process in Kenya: Context, Themes and Mechanisms' in Waruguru Kaguongo and Godfrey Musila (eds), *Judiciary Watch Report: Addressing Impunity and Options for Justice in Kenya—Mechanisms, Issues and Debates* (International Commission of Jurists, 2009) ('ICJ-K, Judiciary Watch Report'), 205.

[68] IBA Report (see Footnote 58), 30.

[69] *Report of the Integrity and Anti-Corruption Committee of the Judiciary in Kenya*, 30 September 2003 ('Ringera Report').

[70] Antony Laibuta, 'Constitutional and Institutional Reform: What role in Addressing Impunity' in ICJ-K, Judiciary Watch Report (see Footnote 66), 250.

in May 2009, of a taskforce on judicial reforms. The judicial taskforce provided its own recommendations, many of which were later adopted when the Constitution was passed in 2010.[71]

The reforms that took place in relation to the security sector may also be seen to have been part of a reform agenda that had been in existence for almost a decade. According to the Ministry of Justice, 'police reforms started in earnest in 2003 when the government set up the national taskforce on police reforms to make recommendations to transform the Kenya police into an effective, human rights-compliant, people-oriented and accountable institution'.[72] This led to the adoption of the *Police Strategic Plan 2004–2008* and other reforms as part of the GJLOS reform programme.[73] Following the post-election violence in 2007/2008, the government established a national taskforce on police reforms under the chairmanship of retired judge Philip Ransley.[74]

Proposals for a truth commission also existed well before the OTP's intervention in Kenya. Parliament had previously passed a motion to establish a truth commission to investigate ethnic violence during the 1992 and 1997 elections but Moi derailed this process by instead establishing a judicial commission and granting it much-reduced powers.[75] In 2000, MPs again rallied for the establishment of a truth commission and received support from a parliamentary report.[76] This was followed by a 2003 taskforce which found overwhelming support for a truth commission and recommended establishment by June 2004.[77] Momentum for the proposal was lost, however, following the government's decision in 2004 to form a government of national unity and therefore enter into a coalition with persons expected to be investigated by the truth commission.[78]

With this history, one should be careful in attributing too much credit to the OTP in respect of passing the new Constitution, reforms to the judiciary and the security sector or the establishment of the TJRC. This history does beg the question, however, after so many failed attempts at reform, why was so much progress made between 2008 and 2013?

---

[71] *Final Report of the Task Force on Judicial Reforms*, July 2010 ('Ouku Report').

[72] Republic of Kenya, Ministry of Justice, National Cohesion and Constitutional Affairs, *GJLOS Sector Policy Final Report*, 11 July 2011 ('GJLOS Sector Policy Final Report'), 25.

[73] OSI Rule of Law Report (see Footnote 23), 133–134.

[74] *Report of the National Task Force on Police Reforms*, October 2009 ('Ransley Report').

[75] Godfrey Musila, 'Options for Transitional Justice in Kenya: Autonomy and the Challenge of External Prescriptions' (2009) 3 *International Journal of Transitional Justice* 448.

[76] Ibid.

[77] Republic of Kenya, *Report of the Task Force on the Establishment of a Truth, Justice and Reconciliation Commission*, 2003.

[78] Kenya Human Rights Commission, International Centre for Policy and Conflict and International Commission of Jurists Kenya, *Transitional Justice in Kenya: A Toolkit for Training and Engagement* (International Commission of Jurists Kenya, 2010), 68.

3.2 The Post-Election Violence

If this ongoing reform agenda provided the blueprint for these reforms, then the scale and intensity of the post-election violence provided the stimulus. It is perhaps no coincidence that the most significant period of reforms in Kenya's history took place immediately after the nation's most tragic event. Although Kenyans were accustomed to violence accompanying elections, the scale and intensity of the hostilities in 2007/2008 appeared to surprise many and serve as a wake-up call. The two months of bloodshed seemed to bruise the national pride and spur its leaders into action. At the same time, many Kenyans began to fear for the future should its leaders fail to implement essential and overdue reforms. The crisis provided the nation with an opportunity to take the necessary measures to ensure that it would never again endure such a catastrophic period of carnage. As the Ministry of Justice observed, 'the 2007 post-election violence was a regrettable national tragedy which, however, served to draw attention to the need for deeper and far-reaching governance reforms in the country'.[79]

Kenyans had long regarded their nation to be one of stability in an otherwise volatile region. As Akech argues, 'many people wondered how a country that for many years was considered to be a rare island of peace in a sea of turmoil could descend into anarchy so rapidly'.[80] In his first address to Parliament following the violence, Kibaki told Parliament that the post-election violence had 'shook our sense of nationhood'.[81] Three MPs, including the Vice President and the Foreign Affairs Minister, described the post-election violence as 'embarrassing'.[82] According to the Vice President, the 'sad events deeply hurt our national pride and weakened our country's standing in the region and internationally'.[83]

Coupled with this was a fear that if urgent reforms were not undertaken, the violence that would accompany the next election could threaten the very survival of the nation. Upon arriving in the country to mediate the crisis, Annan compared the situation to Rwanda and the former Yugoslavia.[84] During Parliament's first sitting following the violence, Odinga told his fellow MPs that Kenya had 'moved to the precipice and we have realised that it is not very far away from where we were'.[85] In the following week, the Vice President also drew parallels with the Rwandan genocide before stressing the importance of 'saying 'no' to the culture of impunity'.[86] A few months later, Parliament passed the *Constitution of Kenya Review*

---

[79] GJLOS II Reform Programme (see Footnote 10), 21.

[80] Migai Akech, *Institutional Reform in the New Constitution of Kenya* (International Centre for Transitional Justice, October 2010), 17.

[81] Hansard, National Assembly, Official Report, 6 March 2008.

[82] Hansard, National Assembly, Official Report, 8 February 2011.

[83] Ibid.

[84] Martin Griffiths, 'The Prisoner of Peace: An interview with Kofi A. Annan', *Centre for Humanitarian Dialogue*, May 2008.

[85] Hansard, National Assembly, Official Report, 6 March 2008.

[86] Hansard, National Assembly, Official Report, 12 March 2008.

Bill, with government minister Mohammed Elmi stating that 'it is time we looked at our survival as a nation and really make sure that we have a constitution that takes care of all of us'.[87] When it came time for Parliament to debate amendments to the proposed draft constitution, MP Abdikadir Hussein Mohamed said that 'the lives of the people of Kenya and the nation are at stake'.[88] Forefront in the minds of these persons was the pressing need to complete reforms prior to the holding of the next elections. During his state of the nation address in March 2011, Kibaki made mention of the impending elections before proclaiming that 'it is in the interests of all of us to ensure that the elections are conducted within a framework that guarantees the free and fair exercise of people's choices'.[89] The mood of the Parliament was succinctly stated by MP Millie Odhiambo-Mabone who said 'We have seen what we have gone through as a country. God forbid that we go to the next election with the same law as we had in 2007!'[90]

The post-election violence therefore served as Kenya's line-in-the-sand moment. Wetangula spoke of the 'enormous opportunity' that the post-election violence had presented and told his fellow members of the Tenth Parliament that they would 'carry the burden of Kenyans'.[91] The Minister for Internal Security described the post-election violence as 'a moment of truth', the Vice President labelled it a 'constitutional moment', Ruto said it was 'an historic moment', while another MP said that Kenya had reached 'a crossroads'.[92] The Assistant Minister for Defence, Joseph Nkaissery, told Parliament that 'the issue of impunity must die with this new beginning'.[93] Throughout its existence, the Tenth Parliament therefore saw itself as being entrusted with a vital reformist agenda. As Odinga told Parliament in 2009, 'in our 40 years of independence, no government has been put in place with a specific agenda like that given to the grand coalition government. We were put in place specifically to pursue reforms'.[94]

Consequently, many of the reforms were passed with reference to the post-election violence. The Committee of Experts, charged with the responsibility of overseeing the constitutional review process, said that the post-election violence had 'offered Kenya a constitutional moment, an opportunity to reinvigorate the stalled constitutional process'.[95] The Vice President suggested to Kenya's politicians that the post-election violence had 'a direct bearing on the fact that we have failed as leaders to give Kenyans a new constitution'.[96] As Parliament passed the *Truth, Justice and*

---

[87] Hansard, National Assembly, Official Report, 6 August 2008.
[88] Hansard, National Assembly, Official Report, 23 March 2010.
[89] Hansard, National Assembly, Official Report, 22 March 2011.
[90] Hansard, National Assembly, Official Report, 16 December 2008.
[91] Hansard, National Assembly, Official Report, 6 March 2008.
[92] Hansard, National Assembly, Official Report, 18 March 2008; Hansard, National Assembly, Official Report, 6 March 2008; Hansard, National Assembly, Official Report, 5 May 2011.
[93] Hansard, National Assembly, Official Report, 6 March 2008.
[94] Hansard, National Assembly, Official Report, 2 December 2009.
[95] Committee of Experts (see Footnote 62), 22.
[96] Hansard, National Assembly, Official Report, 6 March 2008.

Reconciliation Act 2008, the Assistant Minister for Information, George Khaniri, said that the legislation was 'necessitated by the post-election violence'.[97] Similarly, at least five MPs made reference to the post-election violence when passing the electoral reforms.[98] When the Minister for Internal Security delivered his second reading speech for the *National Police Service Bill 2011*, he said 'the post-election violence that arose from the 2007 general election underscored the need to undertake comprehensive reforms in the police force in order to address structural, institutional and legislative weaknesses'.[99] It would therefore seem reasonable to conclude that the tragic events of December 2007–February 2008 served as a catalyst for the Tenth Parliament to pursue a reformist agenda.

3.3 Legacies and Campaigns

In the previous chapter, it was suggested that some politicians obstructed proposals for a special tribunal because it was not in their personal interest for it to be established. It logically follows that the undertaking of so many reforms suggests that some elites may have had some self-interest in ensuring that these proceeded without hindrance. For Kibaki, who was serving his second and final term as president, the passing of a new constitution and other associated reforms aimed at improving the quality of governance was necessary in order to protect his legacy.[100] Kibaki's career in public life would be remembered not for the international condemnation that followed the post-election violence, but rather for negotiating a fragile peace, holding together the power-sharing government and overseeing the rule of law reforms that would ensure that the country would never again witness such internal conflict.[101] Similarly, Wako, whose 21-year tenure as Attorney General came to an end in 2011, was able to rebut accusations that he was an 'anti-reformer' by pointing to the leading role he played in delivering the new Constitution.[102] For Odinga, the passing of the new Constitution and other associated reforms were essential in order

---

[97] Hansard, National Assembly, Official Report, 31 July 2008.

[98] Hansard, National Assembly, Official Report, 26 April 2011 (Martha Karua and Otieno Kajwang); Hansard, National Assembly, Official Report, 11 May 2011 (Christopher Obure); Hansard, National Assembly, Official Report, 31 May 2011 (Manson Nyamweya); Hansard, National Assembly, Official Report, 24 August 2011 (Mutula Kilonzo).

[99] Hansard, National Assembly, Official Report, 23 August 2011.

[100] Brian Kennedy and Lauren Bieniek, *Moving Forward with Constitutional Reform in Kenya* (Centre for Strategic International Studies, December 2010), 1.

[101] Pravin Bowry, 'Kibaki's legacy cemented by rule of law', *Standard*, 2 May 2012.

[102] Stephen Makabila, 'Focus on Wako's legacy as curtain falls on his tenure', *Standard*, 3 July 2011.

to bolster his credentials as a reformer ahead of the 2013 presidential election.[103] Other MPs also appear to have considered their political futures to be contingent upon successful implementation of reforms, such as MP Richard Onyonka, who said in relation to the proposed constitution:

> My feeling right now and from the mood out there, the feelings of Kenyans is that the Tenth Parliament is either going to commit political suicide by rejecting the document or enjoy political resuscitation by coming up with a document that Kenyans will be proud of.[104]

The passing of the reforms was not only in the interests of individual politicians, but also the government as a whole. The post-election violence and the global financial crisis had combined to threaten many of the fiscal and economic gains that had been made since 2003.[105] In his 2010 state of the nation address, Kibaki lamented that a growth rate of 7.1 % in 2007 had slowed to just 1.7 % following the post-election violence.[106] In addition, international donors threatened to withhold support unless reforms were forthcoming. With the violence still ongoing, US Secretary of State, Condoleezza Rice, said that the largest provider of aid to Kenya would not continue to conduct 'business as usual' unless the crisis was adequately resolved.[107] In March 2010, the EU threatened to withhold aid and to refuse to endorse Kenya to potential investors unless certain reforms were made.[108] Consequently, politicians often spoke of the economic importance of passing rule of law reforms. For example, the Assistant Minister for Tourism, Cecily Mbarire, said that such reforms were necessary in order for Kenya to be a 'destination that is sellable' and for 'tourism to grow'.[109] Likewise, Kibaki stated that 'an efficient and effective judiciary will be the cornerstone of a revived economy'.[110] As Parliament prepared to pass legislation that would implement the new Constitution, the speaker of the National Assembly, Kenneth Marende, referred to the positive impact that the Constitution had already had and cited the improved economy as an example.[111] It can therefore be seen that individual and collective interests conspired to provide a fertile ground for institutional reform.

---

[103] Karuti Kanyinga and James Long', The Political Economy of Reforms in Kenya: The Post-2007 Election Violence and a New Constitution' (2012) 55(1) *African Studies Review* 31, 35.

[104] Hansard, National Assembly, Official Report, 3 March 2010.

[105] GJLOS Sector Policy Final Report (see Footnote 71), 8; IBA Report (see Footnote 58), 14.

[106] Hansard, National Assembly, Official Report, 23 February 2010.

[107] Transcript of Statement of US Secretary of State Condoleezza Rice with Former UN Secretary General Kofi Annan, Serena Hotel, Nairobi, Kenya, 18 February 2008.

[108] 'EU threatens to cut aid over corruption', *Daily Nation*, 26 March 2010.

[109] Hansard, National Assembly, Official Report, 3 March 2010.

[110] Hansard, National Assembly, Official Report, 23 February 2010.

[111] Hansard, National Assembly, Official Report, 22 March 2011.

3.4 International Pressures

When considering the factors that may have influenced Kenya's rule of law reforms, regard must be had to the role played by the international community, particularly the Annan-led KNDR process. The KNDR mediations concluded in February 2008 when the two sides agreed to four agenda items that were designed to ensure that the country remained at peace. Agenda Item IV sought to identify the long-term causes of the violence and later served as the blueprint for the reform agenda that followed. The two parties committed to 'Constitutional, legal and institutional reforms, land reforms, tackling youth unemployment, tackling poverty, inequity and regional development imbalances, consolidating national unity and cohesion, and addressing impunity, transparency and accountability'.[112]

On 4 March 2008 the mediation team further clarified the coalition government's obligations by concluding agreements in relation to specific reforms. First, the team secured agreement to a five-stage process for constitutional reform which included a timetable, expert advisors and a referendum.[113] Second, the parties committed to the creation of a truth commission within four weeks and agreed that the principles would guide the formation, composition and procedures of the commission.[114] Finally, the mediation team secured commitments from the parties to establish a commission of inquiry into the post-election violence that would be mandated to investigate the facts and surrounding circumstances of the violence and make recommendations in relation to holding responsible persons accountable for their actions.[115]

With these agreements concluded, Annan announced that he would be leaving Nairobi but sought to maintain pressure upon the government by stating that he would 'never be far away' and 'would be looking in on the talks from time to time'.[116] At various stages during the term of the Tenth Parliament he made visits to Kenya or issued statements to encourage leaders to ensure that the reforms progressed expeditiously. As the government embarked upon this reform process, it regularly paid tribute to the role played by Annan and the KNDR.[117] The major reports on judicial, security sector and electoral reforms all explained that the respective reforms were being undertaken in response to the post-election violence

---

[112] South Consulting, *The Kenya National Dialogue and Reconciliation (KNDR) Monitoring Project*, January 2009 ('KNDR January 2009 Report').

[113] Kenya National Dialogue and Reconciliation, 'Longer–Term Issues and Solutions: Constitutional Review', 4 March 2008.

[114] Kenya National Dialogue and Reconciliation, 'Truth, Justice and Reconciliation Commission', 4 March 2008.

[115] Kenya National Dialogue and Reconciliation, 'Commission of Inquiry on Post-Election Violence', 4 March 2008.

[116] African Union Panel of Eminent African Personalities, Press Statement by Kofi Annan, 1 March 2008 ('Annan March 2008 Statement').

[117] See for example, the speeches of Kilonzo Musyoka, George Saitoti and Mutula Kilonzo: Hansard, National Assembly, Official Report, 18 March 2008.

and the commitments made in Agenda Item IV.[118] The TJRC's progress report also outlined the significant contribution that the KNDR process made to the truth commission's formation.[119] Speeches made in Parliament, reports of ad hoc law reform committees and my interviews with public servants, committee of experts and politicians involved in the reform process suggest that the government was being primarily guided by the KNDR process and, in particular, Agenda Item IV.

Pressures from other sources within the international community may also have convinced the government to pursue such an ambitious reform agenda. In addition to the threatened withholding of foreign aid discussed above, some states threatened travel bans against elites should the reform process stall.[120] Pressure was also placed upon the government by Alston's 2009 report on extrajudicial killings.[121] The Alston Report was scathing and received a great deal of publicity, prompting an official government response.[122] It called for fundamental reforms to the judiciary, witness protection programme and the criminal justice system. Within weeks of the Report's publication, the Attorney General's recruited a specialist from the United Nations Office of Drugs and Crimes to provide advice on how to amend its witness protection programme.[123]

The government was also scrutinised by other UN organs, such as the Human Rights Council, which conducted its periodic review of Kenya's human rights record in May 2010. The US delegation used this opportunity to express its concern over the allegations made in the Alston Report and to call upon the government to fully implement the recommendations.[124] Likewise, over three days in July 2012, the UN Human Rights Committee conducted its periodic review of Kenya, with the sessions broadcast live on Kenyan television.[125] It can therefore be concluded that the coalition government's progress in pursuing its reform agenda was being closely

---

[118] *Final Report of the Task Force on Judicial Reforms*, July 2010 ('Ouku Report'); *Report of the National Task Force on Police Reforms*, October 2009 ('Ransley Report'); *Independent Review Commission, Report of the Independent Review Commission on the General Elections Held in Kenya on 27 December 2007*, 17 September 2008 ('Kriegler Report').

[119] *TJRC Progress Report* (see Footnote 40).

[120] David Ohito, 'Travel ban: Obama jolts Cabinet ministers', *Standard*, 25 September 2009; Peter Leftie, 'Violence suspects may face UK travel ban', *Daily Nation*, 4 August 2009.

[121] Alston Report (see Footnote 24).

[122] Government of the Republic of Kenya, Response to the Report of the Special Rapporteur on Extrajudicial. Arbitrary or Summary Executions, Professor Philip Alston, on his Mission to Kenya from 16 to 25 February, 2009 ('Government Response to Alston Report').

[123] United Nations Office on Drugs and Crime, 'One step closer to witness protection in Kenya', *Reliefweb*, 14 January 2010.

[124] United Nations General Assembly Human Rights Council, Working Group of the Universal Periodic Review, *Report of the Working Group on the Universal Periodic Review, Kenya*, A/HRC/15/8, 17 June 2010 ('Human Rights Council Universal Periodic Review').

[125] United Nations Human Rights Committee, *Concluding observations adopted by the Human Rights Committee at its 105th session*, 9–27 July 2012, CCPR/C/KEN/CO/3, 26 July 2012 ('UN Human Rights Committee Concluding Observations').

observed by not just the OTP, but also by the international community at large. With pressure being applied from so many sources, it is extremely difficult to isolate the OTP's strategy of positive complementarity as being the catalyst for these reforms. Indeed, those responsible for the reforms credit the Annan-led KNDR as being the most influential international actor.

3.5 Domestic Pressures

The government was not only exposed to pressure from the international community, but also from domestic civil society. Kenyans longed for speedy and effective rule of law reform following two decades of broken promises and the tragedy of the post-election violence. In particular, my focus group interviews revealed that Kenyans demanded urgent reforms to the Constitution, judiciary and security sector.

A study conducted by Kanyinga and Long between 2008 and 2010 suggests that the Kenyan citizenry imposed strong pressure upon the coalition government for constitutional reform and that this pressure existed above and beyond partisan and ethnic divides.[126] The study included four rounds of household public opinion data and revealed that, throughout this period, between 80 % and 90 % of Kenyan households were in favour of constitutional reform.[127] Civil society organised a petition to lobby their leaders to support constitutional change. This appears to have had some influence, with Karua reading its contents aloud as Parliament debated the draft constitution:

> We are ... extremely fearful that if a new democratic constitution is not promulgated, there is a high likelihood of the post-election violence repeating itself with far reaching consequences than witnessed in 2007. Our prayer, therefore is that the Parliament of the Republic of Kenya secures the gains that we as citizens of Kenya have incrementally and cumulatively attained over the years in the context of the various proposed constitutions ... [128]

Other statements made by political leaders in Parliament also reveal the extent of civil society's influence over the reforms. In his state of the nation address in 2010, Kibaki said:

> Public concerns have also been constantly raised on the need to improve efficiency and integrity of our judicial system. The Government will, therefore, reintroduce the Judicial Service Bill, which will entrench the independence of the judiciary and make it more effective in the administration of justice.[129]

---

[126] Kanyinga and Long (2012) (see Footnote 102).
[127] Ibid, 42.
[128] Hansard, National Assembly, Official Report, 31 March 2010.
[129] Hansard, National Assembly, Official Report, 23 February 2010.

During the same speech, President Kibaki recognised the public's demands for reforms to the security sector and outlined that the government would pass legislation that would implement the new Constitution which was 'expected to improve accountability and enhance the public image of the police as servants of the people'.[130] Likewise, as Parliament debated proposed electoral reforms, Kilonzo made reference to domestic pressures:

> The entire country is watching us today to determine whether we are serious about setting up an electoral management system that would be able to take the country to the next level, away from the miasma of violence, corruption and the rest of it, of the past.[131]

Kenya's active non-governmental organisations supported and mobilised these demands for reforms, thereby placing even greater pressure upon the government. In particular, ICJ-Kenya, ICPC, KHRC and ICTJ regularly published reports and statements urging the government to fulfil its commitment to law reform. This then raises the issue of the extent to which the OTP's strategy of positive complementarity assisted Kenya's civil society organisations in their campaigns for rule of law reform. The ICC's Assembly of States Parties, for example, has recognised that 'the preliminary examination process provides an early and crucial opportunity to mobilise the efforts of ... civil society to support the national jurisdictions in their fight against impunity'.[132]

My interviews with these and other civil society organisations, however, suggest that, somewhat paradoxically, the OTP's strategy of positive complementarity may have in fact *discouraged* NGOs from advocating for rule of law reform. This is because of what Bjork and Goebertus describe as the 'perverse incentive' that positive complementarity created for NGOs in Kenya.[133] The OTP's threat of international prosecutions deterred several Kenyan NGOs from advocating for rule of law reforms because they feared that the government would respond by passing illusory reforms, primarily designed to demonstrate Kenya's ability to try suspects locally but which would ultimately have the effect of protecting elites from trials in The Hague.[134] The NGOs' lack of faith in the government's commitment to genuine rule of law reform meant that the OTP's strategy of positive complementarity instead encouraged these organisations to highlight deficiencies in the domestic criminal justice system so as to ensure that ICC trials proceeded and the main perpetrators did not evade prosecution.

That is not to say, however, that these organisations gained no leverage from the ICC's intervention in Kenya. First, with the ICC generally regarded by Kenyans to be a credible and impartial institution, the fact that the OTP's demands for prosecutions aligned with those of the NGOs served to increase the legitimacy of these

---

[130] Ibid.

[131] Hansard, National Assembly, Official Report, 26 April 2011.

[132] International Criminal Court Assembly of States Parties, *Report of the Court on Cooperation*, Tenth Session, New York, ICC-ASP/10/40, 18 November 2011 [8].

[133] Bjork and Goebertus (2011) (see Footnote 4).

[134] Ibid.

organisations within the local communities.[135] Second, NGOs used this increased legitimacy to advocate for the election of a new generation of political leaders who could in the future be entrusted to lead the rule of law reform agenda.[136] In other words, the OTP's strategy of positive complementarity may have assisted NGOs with their bottom-up approach to rule of law reform in the longer term.[137] The potential for this impact should not be underestimated, but measuring it is not possible in the short term and so it is beyond the scope of this study.

Having summarised the rule of law reforms that took place in Kenya during the life of the Tenth Parliament and five factors unrelated to the ICC that may have influenced this reform agenda, it is now possible to consider what impact, if any, the OTP's strategy of positive complementarity had on the reforms.

4 The OTP's Impact

4.1 The International Crimes Act 2008

It is perhaps not at all surprising that parliamentarians regularly referenced the ICC during the passing of domestic legislation that criminalised genocide, crimes against humanity and war crimes. Indeed, in the words of the Attorney General, the legislation was 'about domesticating the Rome Statute under which the ICC was constituted'.[138] There is no doubt that the ICC served as a catalyst for the drafting of this legislation, with the Attorney General admitting that the drafters were 'guided' by model legislation on domesticating the Rome Statute.[139]

Of greater interest for the purpose of this study, however, is the extent to which the OTP's strategy of positive complementarity had an impact on the passing of this legislation. There would appear to be circumstantial evidence to support the claim that positive complementarity influenced Kenya's domestication of the Rome Statute. According to the Attorney General, the Bill had 'been in existence since 2005'.[140] Despite this, it took until 14 April 2008 for the Bill to be published, with no explanation provided for this delay. It is perhaps noteworthy that this three-year delay ended approximately two months after the Prosecutor announced that the OTP was monitoring the situation in Kenya. It may therefore be possible to conclude that the OTP's commencement of its strategy of positive complementarity served as a catalyst for the publication of this legislation.

It is equally plausible, however, that Kenya's domestication of the Rome Statute was because of the factors identified above; namely, a damaged national pride, a fear

---

[135] Ibid.
[136] Ibid.
[137] Ibid.
[138] Hansard, National Assembly, Official Report, 7 May 2008.
[139] Ibid.
[140] Ibid.

for the future, an alignment of political interests and pressures from international and domestic sources. Indeed, at the time that the legislation was passed, OTP pressure consisted of a single brief statement and there had been no meetings between the OTP and the government. The Waki Commission had not been formed and the sealed envelope was yet to come into existence. If statements in Parliament are any indication, it would seem that ICC prosecutions in respect of the post-election violence were not even contemplated at this time. The Attorney General's second reading speech made no reference to the OTP's February 2008 statement, nor to the possibility of Kenyans being prosecuted for crimes committed during the post-election violence. Instead, the Attorney General insisted that the legislation was necessary to enable the government to assist the ICC in conducting prosecutions in *other* countries.[141] The Attorney General revealed that the government had already received a request for assistance from the ICC in relation to the Sudanese situation and that implementing the Rome Statute would allow Kenya to support the ICC's work in this regard. In a similar vein, MP Danson Mungatana suggested that the ICC would not prosecute Kenyans and instead argued that the legislation should be passed 'to help our country take the right position in international standing'.[142]

The threat of international prosecutions in the form of the sealed envelope may have provided an additional incentive for the passing of the legislation, which took place just two months after the publication of the Waki Report and the creation of the sealed envelope. During a speech to Parliament on 11 December 2008, MP David Ethuro noted that Kenya had signed and ratified many international protocols and statues but had yet to implement these through domestic legislation, before suggesting that the passing of the *International Crimes Act 2008* was a 'knee jerk' reaction to the publication of the Waki Report.[143] If this is the case, it would seem reasonable to conclude that the passing of the legislation owed more to Waki's ingenious self-implementing mechanism than any strategy of positive complementarity being pursued by the OTP.

Even if the OTP's strategy of positive complementarity went some way to persuading the government to domesticating the Rome Statute, this development had little, if any, *immediate* impact on ending impunity. On 5 June 2009, the government published a gazette notice declaring that the commencement date for the *International Crimes Act 2008* would be 1 January 2009.[144] As a result, it was not possible under the Act to prosecute persons for committing crimes against humanity during the post-election violence. Although setting an earlier commencement date would have violated the Constitutional protection against the enactment of retrospective legislation, no attempt was made to amend this Constitutional provision in order to allow for the prosecution of post-election violence suspects. This is of course not to underestimate the potential future impact of this legislation. Certainly, it is significant that any war crimes, crimes against humanity or acts of genocide committed in

---

[141] Ibid (emphasis added).
[142] Hansard, National Assembly, Official Report, 7 May 2008.
[143] Hansard, National Assembly, Official Report, 11 December 2008.
[144] International Centre for Policy and Conflict, *Post Election Violence: A Trail of Lies and Betrayal*, 2009 ('ICPC 2009 Report'), 7.

Kenya after 1 January 2009 may be prosecuted locally. Victims, however, expressed frustration that those most responsible for the post-election violence would not be prosecuted for international crimes and suggested that this process was itself a further example of impunity in Kenya.

4.2 Witness Protection

Perhaps the OTP's greatest involvement in Kenya's rule of law reforms was to encourage the strengthening of its witness protection programme. Although this involvement appears to have encouraged the government to prioritise the passing of necessary witness protection legislation, it seems that other factors served as the *catalyst* for the government's initial decision to amend the legislation. Indeed, this amendment process commenced months before the OTP began imposing overt pressure. As early as February 2009, personnel from the police, intelligence service and immigration department were seconded to the Attorney General's department to begin working on the reforms.[145] In the following month, the Attorney General requested that a witness protection expert be seconded to his office to advise on the amendments.[146] In other words, the reform process commenced at least three months before the OTP first raised the issue of Kenya's witness protection programme with the government delegation in The Hague.

This occurred in July 2009 when the Prosecutor secured a commitment that, by the end of September 2009, the government would provide a report on the status of its witness protection regime.[147] The government's immediate response was to provide the Prosecutor with a copy of the *Witness Protection Act 2006* and a letter outlining proposed amendments to the legislation.[148] As the 30 September 2009 deadline approached, the Attorney General gave public assurances that amendments were being discussed and would soon be finalised.[149] By November 2009 the drafting of the reforms had been completed.[150]

---

[145] Chris Mahony, *The Justice Sector Afterthought: Witness Protection in Africa* (Institute for Security Studies, 2010), 111.

[146] International Criminal Court, 'Focal points' compilation of examples of projects aimed at strengthening domestic jurisdictions to deal with Rome Statute Crimes', paper presented at the Review Conference of the Rome Statute (Kampala, 31 May 2010–11 June 2010).

[147] International Criminal Court Office of the Prosecutor, 'Agreed minutes of the meeting between Prosecutor Moreno-Ocampo and the delegation of the Kenyan Government', 3 July 2009 ('OTP Complementarity Contract Statement').

[148] Nzau Musau, 'Witnesses targeted over Waki envelope', *Nairobi Star*, 13 July 2009.

[149] 'Wako to publish witness protection Bill', *Daily Nation*, 15 September 2009; Lucas Barasa and Peter Leftie, 'ICC told to try poll chaos suspects', *Daily Nation*, 29 September 2009.

[150] Walter Menya, 'Law to shield chaos witnesses', *Daily Nation*, 12 November 2009.

Not satisfied with the pace of these reforms, the OTP continued to apply pressure upon the government to amend its witness protection programme. On 22 January 2010, the Prosecutor wrote a letter to the Justice Minister, urging the government to complete the necessary reforms to the witness protection programme:

> I wish to draw your attention to the fact that my office is aware of a growing number of reports suggesting that individuals who previously contributed to the enquiries by Kenya National Human Rights Commission and Waki Commission are perceived as the potential witnesses and had been threatened and intimidated. As we discussed before our meeting of 3rd July 2009 in The Hague, following which the Kenyan authority transmitted to my office a report on the operationalisation of the witness protection programme, the primary responsibility to protect persons at risk lies first and foremost with Kenyan authority.[151]

When cooperation was not forthcoming within a week, the Prosecutor wrote to the judges of the ICC's Pre-Trial Chamber to inform them of the threats that had been made against key prosecution witnesses.[152] At the same time, the OTP dispatched a team of investigators to Nairobi to discuss the status of the reforms and to emphasise that they should be passed 'as soon as possible'.[153]

This sustained pressure appears to have prompted a response from the government. Within three days of the government's meeting with OTP investigators, a meeting of a Cabinet sub-committee was arranged to discuss the proposed amendments to the witness protection regime.[154] In the same week, Kibaki announced that he was recalling Parliament from its recess to ensure that the government's reform agenda was not delayed.[155] Both the Attorney General and the Justice Minister then provided assurances that the amendments to the *Witness Protection Act 2006* would be passed as soon as Parliament had completed its review of the draft Constitution.[156] My interviews with persons involved in the drafting process revealed that the pressure imposed by the OTP led to witness protection amendments being prioritised over other reforms. Items on Parliament's agenda which were delayed so that the witness protection amendments could be debated included important bills relating to reform of the police, judiciary, electoral process, local government and company law.[157]

---

[151] Antony Gitonga and Peter Opiyo, 'Ocampo writes to Mutula over witness threats', *Standard*, 26 January 2010.

[152] Murithi Mutiga, 'Ocampo writes to judges over threats', *Daily Nation*, 30 January 2010.

[153] Beauttah Omanga, 'ICC sends team over threats to witnesses' lives', *Standard*, 31 January 2010.

[154] Ben Agina and Beauttah Omanga, 'ICC: State bows to pressure on safety of witnesses', *Standard*, 2 February 2010.

[155] Alex Ndegwa, 'House opens to a full diary', *Standard*, 5 February 2010.

[156] Barnard Namunane, 'Ocampo's team flying into Kenya', *Daily Nation*, 5 April 2010; Alphonce Shundu, 'Mutula Kilonzo vows new quest for Kenya's violence tribunal', *Daily Nation*, 23 March 2010.

[157] Pravin Bowry, 'Great prospects on law reform', *Standard*, 2 March 2010.

Although the prioritisation of witness protection reforms appears to have been made in response to the OTP's exertion of pressure, the government sought to deny the existence of any ICC influence. While moving the Bill, the Attorney General said 'I want to emphasise that what we are enacting, if it is enacted, it is not because of the ICC but because of our own criminal justice system here'.[158] Similarly, the Justice Minister said 'the law is not directly related to the ICC, that is a matter of little consequence'.[159] Some MPs criticised the government for failing to reform the witness protection programme for four years and suggested that the reforms were being made only in response to ICC pressure.[160] The Attorney General and the Justice Minister, however, emphasised that the reforms were made in response to difficulties encountered in investigating and prosecuting drug trafficking, pornography, money laundering, paedophilia and piracy offences.[161]

Notwithstanding the OTP's success in securing the passing of the amendments, it again appeared to have little immediate impact on ending impunity because the government declined to follow through on its commitment to protect witnesses. One month after the amendments to the *Witness Protection Act 2006* were made, the Prosecutor met with a government delegation to express his concern over the security of ICC witnesses.[162] The government responded by signing a commitment to protect all persons identified by the Prosecutor as being potential witnesses.[163] Despite this commitment, it took 16 months for the WPA to be launched.[164] When the WPA was finally established, it was massively underfunded, receiving just one-sixth of the funding it required in order to operate effectively.[165] Consequently, ad hoc measures were necessary in order to protect witnesses. Some were offered protection by the KHRC, the Institute for Peace and a consortium of other NGOs, while at least one other witness was forced to rely upon 24 hour police protection.[166] Even the Attorney General conceded that witnesses felt safer under the protection of NGOs than they did under the government's witness protection programme.[167]

---

[158] Hansard, National Assembly, Official Report, 6 April 2010.

[159] Caroline Wafula, 'Witness Bill gets House approval', *Daily Nation*, 7 April 2010.

[160] 'Parliament moves to protect Ocampo witnesses', *Standard*, 6 April 2010.

[161] Hansard, National Assembly, Official Report, 6 April 2010.

[162] Beauttah Omanga and David Ohito, 'Ocampo lists up to six suspects and trials start by October', *Standard*, 10 May 2010.

[163] KNDR October 2010 Report (see Footnote 19), 10–11.

[164] Steve Mkawale, 'Witness protection agency unveiled ahead of Hague hearing', *Standard*, 12 August 2011.

[165] Ibid; 'Sh1.2bn needed for witness protection', *The Star*, 27 May 2011.

[166] Walter Menya, 'Rights body offers to protect chaos victims', *Daily Nation*, 11 May 2010; Barnaba Bii, 'Chaos victims want security', *Daily Nation*, 12 April 2010; 'Kaunya's wife says her life under threat', *Daily Nation*, 25 April 2010; Mathews Ndanyi, 'High security at Nandi home of ICC witness', Nairobi Star, 29 September 2011.

[167] 'Forum asks Wako to act on chaos witnesses recanting evidence', *Daily Nation*, 3 December 2010.

According to an opinion poll conducted soon after the WPA had been launched, just 24 % of Kenyans believed that the government was able to protect witnesses giving evidence.[168]

The OTP accused 'high ranking members of the government' of 'promoting a growing climate of fear that [was] intimidating potential witnesses and ultimately undermining national and international investigations'.[169] In response, the ICC began protecting its own witnesses and by January 2013, more than 80 witnesses and their families had been placed under ICC protection.[170] The targeting of persons believed to be ICC witnesses, however, continued, with Moreno-Ocampo alleging that a 'person of interest' had had his email account hacked.[171] During her visit to Kenya in October 2012, Bensouda 'reiterated [her] concerns regarding witness intimidation and the increasing climate of fear affecting those perceived to be ICC witnesses, their family members, as well as those perceived to be associated with the ICC'.[172] Despite again securing a commitment to cooperate from the government, just five months later Bensouda revealed that ICC witnesses had been bribed and intimidated.[173] In February 2013, Bensouda informed the Pre-Trial Chamber that the OTP would no longer be relying upon a key insider witness because his credibility had been compromised by accepting a cash payment from persons holding themselves out to be associates of Kenyatta.[174] The OTP then successfully applied for a warrant to arrest journalist Warrant Barasa on suspicion of having bribed witnesses.[175]

In summary, the OTP's strategy of positive complementarity does not appear to have served as a catalyst for reforms to the witness protection programme, but did lead to their being prioritised over other reforms. Despite this prioritisation, however, the implementation of these reforms was tardy at best and the WPA was under-

---

[168] South Consulting, Kenya National Dialogue and Reconciliation Monitoring Project, *Progress in the Implementation of the Constitution and other reforms, Review Report*, October 2011 ('KNDR October 2011 Report'), viii, 58.

[169] International Criminal Court Office of the Prosecutor, 'Statement of the Prosecutor on the Situation in Kenya', 29 May 2011 ('OTP May 2011 Statement').

[170] '80 ICC witnesses in safe houses', *Standard*, 24 January 2013.

[171] Oliver Mathenge, 'Kenya AG orders probe on Ocampo witnesses' claim', *Daily Nation*, 15 March 2012.

[172] International Criminal Court Office of the Prosecutor, 'Statement by the Prosecutor of the International Criminal Court Mrs. Fatou Bensouda at the press conference at the conclusion of Nairobi segment of ICC Prosecutor's visit to Kenya, Nairobi', 25 October 2012 ('OTP Second Statement on Bensouda's Visit to Kenya').

[173] 'Kenyan Gov't Not Cooperative, Says ICC', *Citizen News*, 17 February 2013.

[174] *Prosecutor v Francis Kirimi Muthaura and Uhuru Muigai Kenyatta*, Public redacted version of the 25 February 2013 Consolidated Prosecution response to the Defence applications under Article 64 of the Statute to refer the confirmation decision back to the Pre-Trial Chamber, ICC-01/09-02/11, 25 February 2013 [17].

[175] *Prosecutor v Walter Osapiri Barasa*, Warrant of arrest of Osapiri Barasa, ICC-01/09-01/13, 2 August 2013.

funded, meaning that Kenya remained without a robust and effective witness protection programme throughout this period. It would appear that the OTP's sustained pressure did, however, influence the government into providing continued assurances that it would protect ICC witnesses. Despite these reforms and assurances, however, as Kenyans went to the polls in March 2013 the country was still without a well-resourced and credible witness protection programme.

4.3 Judicial and Security Sector Reforms

There is also a small amount of evidence that the OTP's strategy of positive complementarity encouraged the government to prioritise the passing of judicial and security sector reforms. The fifth schedule to the new Constitution provided deadlines for the passing of various pieces of legislation required to fully implement its principles and procedures. Legislation which was required to be prioritised and passed within one year included reforms related to the judiciary, parliamentary procedures, the electoral system, citizenship, ethics and anti-corruption, and human rights and equality.[176] The first pieces of legislation passed to implement the Constitution related to reforms of the judiciary.[177] It is possible that the OTP's strategy of positive complementarity encouraged the government to prioritise these two Bills over others that also shared a one-year Constitutional deadline for implementation. Each of the Bills was published on 27 January 2011 and introduced into Parliament one week later. These developments occurred in the month following the announcement of the Ocampo Six and Odinga's subsequent promise to 'establish a credible local process for the investigation and prosecution of the six persons' that would enable the government to challenge the admissibility of the cases before the ICC.[178] The Bills were published on the same day that the President of the Assembly of States Parties travelled to Nairobi to meet with members of the executive, whereupon he was assured that the government was moving expeditiously to implement judicial reforms that would enable suspects to be tried in Kenya.[179] While introducing the *Vetting of Judges and Magistrates Bill 2011* into Parliament, the Justice Minister made specific reference to the ICC:

> Allow me to remind this country, without fear, that this country is undergoing a terrible catharsis over the issue of the ICC and the Rome Statute where everybody is watching whether we are going to set up a judicial mechanism ... when we conclude the vetting of judges and magistrates, no judge, either in the ICC or the international court, will say that Kenya does not have quality judges who have been vetted.[180]

---

[176] *Constitution of Kenya 2010*, Schedule Five.
[177] *Vetting of Judges and Magistrates Act 2011* and *Judicial Services Act 2011*.
[178] Hansard, National Assembly, Official Report, 16 December 2010.
[179] International Criminal Court Assembly of States Parties, 'President of the Assembly of States Parties visits Kenya', 28 January 2011 ('ASP January 2011 Statement').
[180] Hansard, National Assembly, Official Report, 9 February 2011.

In the months that followed, Parliament also passed the *Supreme Court Act 2011* and the *National Police Service Act 2011*. For each piece of legislation, the Act's sponsor made reference to the ICC. When introducing the former, the Justice Minister said 'the presence of the International Criminal Court in Kenya was because of a huge constituency of this country refusing to go to court on the well-founded assertion that they did not have confidence in the judiciary'.[181] Similarly, the Minister for Internal Security spoke of the need for passing legislation that would reform the police service by making reference to the fact that Kenya's former Commissioner of Police was facing charges before the ICC.[182] This suggests that the commencement of the ICC trial process may have exposed serious deficiencies within the criminal justice system and this in turn appears to have provided a positive incentive for the government to prioritise some of the essential reforms that followed.

It must be recalled, however, that the legislation that was ultimately passed had its origins a reform agenda that pre-dated the establishment of the ICC and in large part involved the adoption of committee recommendations made prior to the commencement of the strategy of positive complementarity. Although brief mention was made of the ICC's intervention during debate over the legislation, this issue was given much less consideration by parliamentarians than others. MPs spoke in much greater detail about the KNDR process, the bruised national pride and their fear for the future. It would seem that the most that can be said of the OTP's impact is that it encouraged the prioritisation of certain reforms over others.

4.4 Simultaneous but Separate

The above legislation aside, there does not appear to be a great deal of evidence to support the claim that the OTP's strategy of positive complementarity served as a catalyst for rule of law reforms in Kenya. Rather, the passing of a new Constitution; the establishment of a truth commission and the transformation of the judiciary, security sector and electoral system seem appear to have proceeded simultaneously to, but separate from, the OTP's strategy of positive complementarity.

Given that the passing of the new Constitution had been on the political agenda since at least 1997, it perhaps should come as no surprise that this reform took place with very little reference to the ICC, despite the fact that the OTP was actively involved in Kenya throughout this period. As part of this reform process, the Committee of Experts produced a 159-page report which contained no reference to the ICC.[183] The draft Constitution was then debated by Parliament, with no MP mentioning the ICC, the OTP or the Prosecutor at any stage during this process. The ICC also received no attention as Parliament passed the legislation necessary for

---

[181] Hansard, National Assembly, Official Report, 2 June 2011.
[182] Hansard, National Assembly, Official Report, 23 August 2011.
[183] Committee of Experts (see Footnote 62).

implementing the new Constitution. My interviews with two members of the Committee of Experts about this reform process also contained no discussion of the ICC until I raised the matter, whereupon its influence was quickly and emphatically dismissed.

It was a similar story with respect to judicial reforms. The Ouko Committee produced a 253-page report on judicial reforms in July 2010. The Ouko Report was being drafted at the same time that the Prosecutor was making his high-profile visit to the country to commence the OTP's official investigations. Despite this, the Ouko Report contained no reference to the ICC.[184] The JMVB provided an overview of the judicial reform process as part of its first vetting determination but again contained no mention of the ongoing ICC process.[185] During my interviews with Justice Waki and Justice Ochieng, each provided various explanations for the judicial reforms which were taking place, with neither making any reference to the ICC. When asked about any influence that the ICC may have had, each strenuously denied such a possibility.[186] Although it is true that the Justice Minister made reference to the ICC when introducing the *Vetting of Judges and Magistrates Bill 2011* and the *Supreme Court Bill 2011* into Parliament, such references were only made in passing and no other MP mentioned the ICC at all during the debates. Further, no mention at all was made of the ICC as MPs debated the *Judicial Services Act 2011*. By contrast, when the proposed special tribunal was being debated, no less than 12 MPs made reference to the ICC, many on multiple occasions. It might therefore be concluded that any influence the ICC had over these reforms was minimal by comparison with the other factors identified above.

The reforms to the security sector provide a third example of the ICC's negligible influence. First, it must be recalled that by the time of the 2013 elections there had been only minimal reforms to the security sector. The existing policing structures remained in place, the police force's work continued to be compromised owing to a lack of resources and the promised vetting of officers did not eventuate. It is therefore difficult to see how the ICC or any other factor may be regarded as having provided the government with a positive incentive for ensuring that necessary security sector reforms took place. The Ransley Report was published in October 2009 which meant that it coincided with the period during which the OTP was most active in implementing its strategy of positive complementarity. As the Ransley Report was being written, the government entered into a complementarity contract with the OTP and later agreed to a division of labour, the latter occurring just one month before the Report's publication. Despite this, the 326-page report made no mention of the ICC.[187] Further, while the Internal Security Minister briefly

---

[184] Ouku Report (see Footnote 70).

[185] Judges and Magistrates Vetting Board, 'Determination Concerning the Judges of the Court of Appeal', 25 April 2012 ('Vetting Board April 2012 Determination').

[186] Interview with Philip Waki (Nairobi, 16 April 2010); Interview with Fred Ochieng (Nairobi, 19 April 2010).

[187] Ransley Report (see Footnote 73).

mentioned the ICC when sponsoring the introduction of the *National Police Service Bill 2011*, no other MP referred to the ICC and the Court's work was not discussed at all during debates over three other pieces of legislation relating to police reforms.[188]

The process of electoral reforms provides a fourth example of reforms proceeding with no apparent influence from the ICC. The electoral reform process commenced on 14 March 2008 when the government published the terms of reference for the Kriegler Commission. By this time, the OTP's involvement in Kenya was limited to a brief statement issued six weeks earlier announcing that it was considering whether crimes may have been committed during the post-election violence.[189] The 164-page Kriegler Report was published in September 2008 and likewise contained no discussion of the ICC's work.[190] Nor was the ICC mentioned during the debates over the three major pieces of electoral reform legislation or in any reports or press releases of the three electoral bodies to be established.[191]

The establishment of the TJRC provides a further example. Although it is true that the Prosecutor publicly supported a truth commission in Kenya, this announcement was first made in September 2009, nearly twelve months after Parliament had passed legislation to establish the TJRC. When debating this legislation, MPs made no reference to the ICC. Similarly, the TJRC made no mention of the ICC in its first progress report.[192] I also conducted interviews with two commissioners and two senior employees of the TJRC during which I asked what factors led to the TJRC's establishment. Several explanations were provided, none of which had any apparent relationship to the ICC.[193]

A sixth and final example of the ICC's minimal influence relates to criminal legislation enacted by the Tenth Parliament. Legislation was passed in relation to female genital mutilation, terrorism, organised crime and money laundering, but at no stage during these debates was the ICC's work discussed. One MP made mention of the Rome Statute during the passing of legislation that sought to prohibit human trafficking, but this was made only in passing and at the same time that the MP also referred to Kenya's international obligations under 15 other regional and international human rights instruments.[194]

---

[188] *National Police Service Commission Act 2011*; *National Police Service Act 2011*; *Independent Police Oversight Authority Act 2011*.

[189] International Criminal Court Office of the Prosecutor, 'OTP Statement in Relation to Events in Kenya', 5 February 2008 ('OTP February 2008 Statement').

[190] Kriegler Report (see Footnote 117).

[191] *Elections Act 2011; Independent Electoral Boundaries Commission Act 2011; Political Parties Act 2011*. The three electoral bodies that were established during this period were the Interim Independent Electoral Commission ('IIEC'), the Interim Independent Boundaries Review Commission ('IIBRC') and the Independent Electoral Boundaries Commission ('IEBC').

[192] TJRC Progress Report (see Footnote 40).

[193] Interview with Elijah Letangule (Nairobi, 5 August 2011); Interview with TJRC commissioner (Nairobi, 5 August 2011); Interview with TJRC commissioner (Nairobi, 5 August 2011).

[194] Hansard, National Assembly, Official Report, 22 June 2008.

The above discussion suggests that, although many of these reforms took place at the same time as the OTP's strategy of positive complementarity, there appears to be little evidential basis to conclude, *post hoc ergo proctor hoc*, that there was a correlation between the two. Instead, a more plausible explanation is that these reforms were part of a long-standing reform agenda and that the post-election violence served as the major catalyst for the Tenth Parliament's renewed commitment. Throughout this time, the international community, particularly Annan and the KNDR, continued to encourage efficient implementation of these reforms and MPs were eager to cooperate in order to preserve their legacy or support their upcoming electoral campaigns.

5 The Shadow Side of Complementarity

In assessing the impact that the OTP's strategy of positive complementarity had on rule of law reforms in Kenya, it is also important to consider whether there was a 'shadow side'. In other words, is there any evidence that the ICC's intervention in Kenya *discouraged* rule of law reforms or in some way jeopardised the successful implementation of these reforms? Three shadow sides are considered.

5.1 *The Government of National Disunity*

The first shadow side of the OTP's impact on Kenya's rule of law agenda is that it appears to have exacerbated existing divisions within the country's 'Government of National Unity'. This, in turn, had the potential to jeopardise the country's pursuit of its ambitious reform agenda and, in this way, served as a potential obstacle to ending impunity. When PNU and ODM entered into a power-sharing arrangement in February 2008 in order to bring an end to the post-election violence, this was just not an end in itself, it was also a means by which a process of institutional reform could commence which would address the long-term causes of the crisis.[195] As KNDR observed in January 2009, 'conflicts within the coalition and in the parties that make up the coalition have the potential of deflecting attention away from reforms to short-term interests'.[196] In its July 2009 report, KNDR suggested that such conflicts had in fact emerged in relation to the ICC issue:

> Where to try senior politicians and others who planned and financed the post-election violence is deepening divisions within government. Political conflicts over whether to try the perpetrators of the post-election violence locally or at the ICC have divided the government and created new factions within the main political parties.[197]

---

[195] KNDR January 2009 Report (see Footnote 111), 1.
[196] Ibid, 3.
[197] South Consulting, Kenya National Dialogue and Reconciliation Monitoring Project, *Status of Implementation of Agenda Items 1–4, Third Review Report*, July 2009, 4.

The pressure applied by the OTP as part of its strategy of positive complementarity contributed to *intra*-party divisions, particularly within ODM. As demonstrated in the previous chapter, the special tribunal issue split ODM down the middle, with 51 members voting in favour of the proposal and 49 voting against.[198] ODM members loyal to Ruto suggested that Odinga's support for the special tribunal was part of an objective to target the Kalenjin community in the Rift Valley.[199] A meeting arranged to resolve these differences ended abruptly when Kalenjin members walked out, telling Odinga that the tribunal would 'finish him and the party'.[200] When ODM members reneged on their promise to support the Imanyara Bill and instead formed part of the boycott to establish the special tribunal, Imanyara, pledged to 'never do business with the Prime Minister again because he showed himself as someone you cannot trust'.[201] Further tensions emerged when the government lobbied the Security Council to defer the ICC cases. ODM secretary general, Anyang' Nyong'o, wrote a letter to the Security Council stating that ODM did not support the deferral, only for Ruto and other ODM leaders to send their own letter claiming that Nyong'o did not speak for the party.[202] One week later, ODM's Parliamentary Secretary, Ababu Namwamba, joined other ODM leaders in committing the party to funding the defence costs of the three ODM members being tried by the ICC, only for Ruto to reject this assistance, comparing it to 'a hyena promising defence to the goats'.[203]

The ICC's involvement in Kenya also exacerbated *inter*-party tensions. Although many of Kenya's leaders altered their positions throughout this period, for the most part Odinga and his supporters within ODM supported trials at the ICC, while Kibaki and his allies in PNU opposed the ICC's intervention and sought to disrupt the progress of these trials. These tensions first became obvious in April 2010 when a Cabinet sub-committee formed to respond to ICC issues met to discuss whether to request the Prosecutor to postpone his investigations.[204] The PNU members of the sub-committee supported such action, but the ODM side opposed it, prompting the PNU members to schedule their own meeting.[205] At this meeting, the PNU members resolved to write a letter to the Prosecutor requesting that investigations be deferred until after the Constitutional referendum. In response, Orengo wrote to his PNU

---

[198] South Consulting, Kenya National Dialogue and Reconciliation Monitoring Project, *Status of Implementation of Agenda Items 1–4, Draft Report,* May 2009, 35.

[199] 'ODM ministers walk out on Raila over tribunal', *Daily Nation*, 30 June 2009.

[200] Ibid.

[201] 'Imanyara and Raila in dramatic fallout over Bill', *Daily Nation*, 14 November 2009.

[202] Peter Leftie, 'Reject Kenya Plea, Orange Asks UN', *Daily Nation*, 13 March 2011; 'Ruto allies write to UN Council on Hague Trials', *Daily Nation*, 16 March 2011.

[203] John Ngirachu and Njeri Rugene, 'ODM to Hire Lawyers for Ruto, Kosgey Over ICC Cases', *Daily Nation*, 24 March 2011; Benjamin Muindi, 'ICC: Uhuru, Ruto, Lash Out at PM', *Daily Nation*, 26 March 2011.

[204] 'Ministers push to keep Ocampo probe at bay', *Daily Nation*, 15 April 2010.

[205] Alex Ndegwa, 'How plot on Ocampo hit a dead end', *Standard*, 9 May 2010.

counterparts 'formally objecting to the decision made by a section of the government without the full participation or involvement of the ODM members of the committee'.[206] In the letter, Orengo argued that 'a section of the coalition cannot purport to make a decision of that magnitude without the full involvement and consent of both coalition partners'.[207]

These tensions played out on the international stage during the ICC's Kampala review conference held in June 2010. Wako officially informed the delegates that the government was undertaking institutional legal reforms to facilitate domestic investigations and prosecutions, but ODM members intervened by announcing that they had not been consulted in drafting the statement and that it reflected the position of only one side of the government.[208] Wako accused the ODM side of 'acting out of ignorance' and another member of the Kenyan delegation was shouted out of the meeting.[209]

A third episode of conflict occurred two days before the revelation of the Ocampo Six. Kibaki chaired a five-hour meeting at State House to discuss the government's response to the impending announcement. The PNU members argued that the government should create a local judicial process to prevent the ICC from having jurisdiction, but most of the ODM ministers rejected the proposal and demanded that the ICC be left to complete its work unencumbered. The ODM members left the meeting and held their own meeting in Odinga's office, only for Kibaki to issue a statement proclaiming that the government had resolved to establish a local mechanism to try post-election violence suspects.[210]

In the months that followed, the differences between the parties became even more obvious. During the first quarter of 2011, Kibaki arranged for senior government officials to lobby for Security Council support to defer the ICC cases.[211] Odinga, however, distanced himself from this process, claiming that Cabinet 'never talked about the issue of shuttle diplomacy'.[212] On 13 March 2011, Nyong'o wrote a letter on behalf of ODM, urging the Security Council not to agree to a deferral of the ICC cases.[213] When the government filed its Article 19 application, Odinga and

---

[206] Mugumo Munene and Peter Leftie, 'Why plot to stop Ocampo failed', *Daily Nation*, 8 May 2010.

[207] Ibid.

[208] Stephen Makabila, 'Annan, Ocampo comeback draws high anxiety', *Standard*, 27 November 2010.

[209] Bernard Namunane, 'Kenya coalition rivalry plays out on the world stage', *Daily Nation*, 3 June 2010.

[210] Biketi Kikechi, 'Fresh plan to block Ocampo', *Standard*, 14 December 2010; 'Cabinet Split Over Ocampo', *Nairobi Star*, 14 December 2010.

[211] Bernard Namunane, 'Kenya seeks Africa support over Hague', *Daily Nation*, 12 January 2011; Dave Opiyo, 'President "behind move on Hague"', *Daily Nation*, 16 January 2011; Office of the President, 'President appoints special envoys', 4 March 2011.

[212] Dave Opiyo, 'Kenya's PM disowns offensive against the Hague trials', *East African*, 26 January 2011.

[213] Peter Leftie, 'Reject Kenya Plea, Orange Asks UN', *Daily Nation*, 13 March 2011.

his supporters disowned this action.[214] Orengo said 'all the people who attended the meeting that arrived at that decision were from PNU. Not a single person from ODM was invited so this decision is self-serving; it is not a decision of the coalition government'.[215] Odinga himself said 'they are talking about a kangaroo court which they can manipulate to get these people acquitted and that is not acceptable to us'.[216]

These episodes led KNDR to conclude that there was no common government position over the ICC or other accountability mechanisms and that the Government of National Unity was in fact 'two government in one':

> Leaders continue to issue contradictory statements that stir controversy on whether to support the ICC or establish a local special tribunal—or have both—or even sometimes asking whether the ICC should stop handling [post-election violence] cases because there is a new Constitution.[217]

Kenyan lawyer Paul Muite made a similar observation: 'It is a very complicated situation; we have a section of the government supporting Ocampo and the other opposing his work. There is no collective government position on the matter'.[218]

It would be incorrect, however, to suggest that the ICC was the *cause* of divisions within the government, since there were points of conflict in 2008 even before debates over accountability mechanisms commenced. As Hansen has stated:

> … though it is fair to conclude that the ICC issue has been the dominating controversy between the coalition since Ocampo named the six suspects in December 2010, it is important to note that the coalition government has a track record of failing to agree on other major national issues. Even if the ICC controversy has intensified tensions between the two coalition partners, it should therefore not be viewed as something which has caused the breakdown an otherwise harmonious government.[219]

It would nevertheless seem reasonable to conclude that the OTP's encouragement of local investigations and prosecutions *exacerbated* these pre-existing tensions. In doing so, it may have inadvertently made it more difficult for the government to pursue the other impunity-ending measures to which it had committed. The ambitious Agenda Item IV reform agenda required support from both sides of politics. This was already going to be a massive challenged for a power-sharing government that had recently been on opposite sides of the bloodiest conflict in the country's history. Divisions within government and within parties over the ICC issue therefore had the potential to disrupt this vitally important reform agenda.

---

[214] John Ngirachu and Peter Leftie, 'ODM disowns efforts to challenge ICC cases', *Daily Nation*, 23 March 2011.

[215] Ibid.

[216] Anthony Kagiri, 'Raila: foreign judges must head local tribunal', *Capital News*, 26 March 2011.

[217] KNDR October 2010 Report (see Footnote 18), 10.

[218] James Macharia, 'Kenya names judge to help Hague investigators', *Reuters*, 6 October 2010.

[219] Thomas Obel Hansen, 'Transitional Justice in Kenya? An Assessment of the Accountability Process in Light of Domestic Politics and Security Concerns' (2011) 42(1) *California Western International Law Journal* 1, 17.

5.2 Delays and Distractions

Time was of the essence in the implementation of the Agenda Item IV reforms. There was a pressing need for these reforms to be passed as expeditiously as possible so as to ensure that the new laws, institutions and office holders were in place well before the holding of the next general elections. As such, any issue that distracted politicians from their primary responsibility of passing the reforms posed a threat to their successful implementation.

Several of the reforms took much longer to be passed than many had hoped and anticipated. In May 2009, KNDR reported that 'the progress towards implementing crucial actions under each of the agenda items has been slow'.[220] As of August 2011, Parliament had passed only 6 of the 24 Bills it was required to pass within the first year of the new Constitution.[221] Consequently, some Bills were hurriedly passed through Parliament with very little scrutiny, raising concerns over the quality of the reforms.[222] There are several explanations for these delays. Some MPs opposed and obstructed reforms on personal, parochial or ethnic grounds, while others neglected their law-making responsibilities as they focused on campaigning for their re-election.[223]

It would appear, however, that the OTP's commencement of investigations and prosecutions also contributed to delays in implementing the reform agenda. One prominent example was the government's reaction to the announcement of the Ocampo Six. On 22 December 2010, Parliament passed a motion calling upon the government to take 'appropriate action to withdraw from the Rome Statute'. The motion was passed under the threat that any failure to comply with its contents within 60 days would lead to the sabotage of future government business in Parliament, including the proposed reform agenda.[224] Despite the ever-increasing backlog of legislation necessary for implementing the new Constitution, scarce Parliamentary sitting hours were devoted to debating the government's options for obstructing the progress of the trials in The Hague. The legal affairs committee had tabled a report on electoral boundaries but this debate was delayed so that MPs could discuss the ICC motion.[225] In February 2011, Kenya's permanent representative to the United Nations wrote to the President of the ICC's Assembly of States Parties, stating that 'since the announcement of the names of the 'Ocampo Six' suspects, the pace of reforms has ground to a halt'.[226]

---

[220] KNDR May 2009 Report (see Footnote 197), vii.

[221] James Macharia, 'ICC trials main threat to Kenyan polls—electoral commission', *Reuters*, 17 April 2012.

[222] KNDR October 2011 Report (see Footnote 167), vii.

[223] Ibid, 34; KNDR May 2009 Report (see Footnote 197), 36.

[224] Hansen (2011) (see Footnote 218), 10–11.

[225] Peter Opiyo and David Ochami, 'MPs could miss Christmas break over ICC motion', *Standard*, 19 December 2010.

[226] Macharia Kamau, Kenya's Permanent Representative to the United Nations, Letter to Christian Wenaweser, President of the Assembly of State Parties to the Rome Statute 'Ref: Support for Kenya's reform movement', 28 February 2011 ('Kenya February 2011 Letter to ASP').

5 The Shadow Side of Complementarity

A second example relates to the government's lobbying at the Security Council to have the ICC cases deferred for a period of twelve months. Prior to approaching the Security Council, senior government ministers engaged in shuttle diplomacy to secure support for the proposal. This lobbying took place during the crucial first twelve months of the implementation of the Constitution and at a time that Parliament was struggling to meet the ambitious Constitutionally mandated deadlines for implementation. Delegations were sent to Botswana, Burundi, Djibouti, Ethiopia, Lesotho, Libya, Malawi, Nigeria, South Africa, Tanzania, Uganda and Zambia at a cost of $360,000.[227] The cost of this exercise was not insignificant, especially considering that the government was struggling to properly fund its TJRC, police force and witness protection programme.

The government's response to the suspects' confirmation of charges hearing provides a third example of the ICC process potentially serving as a distraction to the reform agenda. Despite the fact that not even the suspects themselves were required to attend, 41 Kenyan MPs travelled to The Hague for the hearings.[228] In response, a civil society group launched an online petition calling for attention to be diverted from the ICC process to more pressing national issues, such as the implementation of the new Constitution.[229] The Parliament Caucus for Reform also called for Constitutional implementation to be prioritised over the ICC issue.[230]

It would therefore appear that part of the explanation for the delay in implementing the reforms was the prominence that the ICC trials had on the political agenda. Arguably, progress in the rule of law reform agenda would have proceeded more expeditiously had the ICC trials not commenced. To the extent that the progress of the ICC cases distracted politicians from the reform agenda, it threatened to jeopardise the successful implementation of essential rule of law reforms. That is not to say, of course, that the OTP ought not to have proceeded with the trials. It does suggest, however, that if the OTP's objective is to end impunity, before committing itself to such prosecutions, it should consider the potential for the existence of this shadow side.

5.3 *Illusory Reforms*

A third shadow side is that the OTP's strategy of positive complementarity appears to have encouraged the government to pass illusory rule of law reforms in the hope that doing so would frustrate the progress of the ICC trials. This shadow side is not

---

[227] Hansard, National Assembly, Official Report, 8 February 2011.
[228] 'Embassy clears 41 MPs for trip to The Hague', *Daily Nation*, 4 April 2011.
[229] Daniel Wesangula, 'Plea to give Ocampo Six a blackout', *Daily Nation*, 12 April 2011.
[230] Anthony Kagiri, 'Mps urged to avoid sideshows in House', *Capital News*, 17 January 2011.

unlike the one identified in the previous chapter where it was suggested that one consequence of positive complementarity was to encourage the establishment of defective local justice mechanisms.

Following the announcement of the Ocampo Six in December 2010, senior government ministers began discussing options that would allow the cases to be transferred back to Kenya. One proposal which received some support was to quickly appoint a new Chief Justice, commit to rule of law reforms and convince the ICC that the suspects should be tried locally.[231] At this time, Kilonzo, said 'as soon as we have a new CJ and an AG, we can move ahead and have a three-judge bench to handle post-election cases'.[232] In the following month, Kilonzo said 'by August we will have a new CJ, AG, DPP, inspector general and Supreme Court. What would you need the ICC for?'[233]

On 28 January 2011, Kibaki appointed Justice Alnashir Visram, Professor Githu Muigai, Kioko Kilukumi and William Kirwa to the respective positions of Chief Justice, Attorney General, DPP and Controller of Budget.[234] In making these appointments, Kibaki ignored the Constitutional requirements that he act in accordance with the *National Accord and Reconciliation Act 2008* and that he first consult with Prime Minister Odinga.[235] Visram had not undergone a vetting process, Kirwa was allegedly being investigated by a Parliamentary committee and Kilukumi was acting as legal counsel for persons whom he would then be required to prosecute.[236] ICJ-Kenya described the appointments as the 'antithesis to international best practices that require the appointment process to be transparent, competitive and based on merit'.[237] The JSC also issued a statement in which it expressed its 'grave concern and misgivings about the nomination for the Chief Justice'.[238] In February 2011, the High Court ruled that these nominations were made in breach of the Constitution.[239]

These hurried appointments appear to have been made in response to the ICC's threat of prosecutions. The Ocampo Six were named on 15 December 2010 and on the following day the President and the Prime Minister met to discuss expediting judicial

---

[231] Mugumo Munene, 'Last ditch effort to shield Ocampo six', *Daily Nation*, 18 December 2010.

[232] Biketi Kikechi, 'Fresh plan to block Ocampo', *Standard*, 14 December 2010.

[233] Bernard Namunane, 'Kenya seeks Africa support over Hague', *Daily Nation*, 12 January 2011.

[234] Dave Opiyo and Bernard Namunane, 'Raila urges calm as PNU plots offensive', *Daily Nation*, 30 January 2011.

[235] Constitution of Kenya 2010, Schedule 6, Article 24(2); Lucas Barasa, 'Why I reject new Chief Justice', *Daily Nation*, 29 January 2011.

[236] Kenya Human Rights Commission, *Lest We Forget: The Faces of Impunity in Kenya* (Kenya Human Rights Commission, 2011) ('KHRC, Lest We Forget'), 12.

[237] International Commission of Jurists Kenya, 'ICJ Kenya's Position Paper on the appointment of the next Chief Justice as at Jan 2011', January 2011.

[238] Hansard, National Assembly, Official Report, 1 February 2011.

[239] Judy Ogutu, 'Court nullifies list of judicial nominees', *Standard*, 4 February 2011.

appointments so that the cases could be referred back to Kenya.[240] The government submitted this challenge on 31 March 2011, but before doing so, Kibaki hurriedly made the four appointments on 31 January 2011. Musyoka told Parliament that the appointments had to be finalised by this time because Kibaki was scheduled to attend an African Union heads of state meeting in Addis Ababa at which he would raise the issue of the ICC cases and seek the AU's support in having the cases deferred. According to Musyoka, the President wanted to strengthen his position by 'demonstrating before his colleagues that he was serious on this matter of appointments of the new judiciary officers'.[241]

In summary, the OTP's strategy of positive complementarity appears to have encouraged the government to hurriedly appoint persons to the country's most significant legal offices in a manner which was contrary to the Constitution and international best practice. In many ways, this marked a temporary return to the executive-controlled nepotism which had been a feature of Kenyan politics for decades. Although to some extent these problems were later rectified through a more thorough, transparent and meritorious appointment process (at least in the case of the Chief Justice), arguably this problem would not have arisen but for the ICC's intervention.

6 Conclusion

Between 2008 and 2013, Kenya's Tenth Parliament was responsible for the most sustained period of legal reforms in the country's history. The promulgation and implementation of a new Constitution, the establishment of a truth commission and substantial changes to the country's judiciary, security sector, electoral system, criminal justice system and witness protection programme meant that during this period Kenya made significant progress in ending impunity. After more than two decades of taskforces, commissions, inquiries, reports, recommendations and proposals, much-needed rule of law reforms were finally implemented.

Although these reforms occurred at the same time that the OTP was actively involved in Kenya, it must be recognised that the reforms were part of a wider reform agenda that not only pre-dated the commencement of the OTP's strategy of positive complementarity, but also the creation of the ICC itself. The new Constitution had its origins in failed attempts in 2002 and 2005 and, arguably, perhaps even earlier. The judicial reforms were part of a series of strategic plans for reforms that first commenced in 2005, and the security sector reforms were connected to strategic plans for the GJLOS programme dating back to 2004. Proposals for a truth commission dated back to at least 1997 and significant progress had been made in the establishment of the TJRC long before the OTP first turned its attention to the mechanism in September 2009.

---

[240] Hansard, National Assembly, Official Report, 1 February 2011.
[241] Ibid.

The major catalyst for these was the post-election violence, with MPs expressing dismay over this 'embarrassment' and admitting to anxiety over the future of the country should changes not be made. With many senior politicians eager to either preserve their legacy or boost their reform credentials in preparation for the next election, Kenya's leaders had powerful personal incentives to support the reform process. The Annan-led KNDR process seized this 'constitutional moment' to provide critical guidance for these reforms and imposed pressure to ensure that this valuable momentum was not lost. Likewise, the Human Rights Council, the Human Rights Committee, a UN special rapporteur and diplomatic embassies also kept a close eye on the government's progress.

The OTP, which explicitly stated on a number of occasions that assisting with rule of law reforms was beyond its mandate, made only a limited contribution to encouraging this reform process. This might explain why it was that judicial, security sector, electoral and criminal justice reforms proceeded with little or no reference to, or consideration of, the ongoing ICC process. These reforms appear to have been undertaken simultaneously to, but separate from, the OTP's investigations and prosecutions.

The OTP's greatest focus was on ensuring that Kenya had an effective witness protection programme. The OTP first raised this issue in July 2009, but by this time a UNODC adviser had been working with the State Law Office on these reforms for more than three months. The OTP's sustained pressure does, however, appear to have encouraged the government to prioritise the witness protection reforms over other reforms. Nevertheless, despite the government's continued assurances, these reforms appear to have been largely illusory, with the government delaying the operationalisation of the WPU and ensuring it remained chronically underfunded. This resulted in suspected witnesses being subjected to bribes and intimidation. Similarly, Kibaki's hurried appointment of the Chief Justice, Attorney General and DPP, made in contravention of the Constitution and contrary to international best practice, appears to have been a direct response to the OTP's threat of prosecutions.

It would therefore seem to be incorrect to assert that Kenya's rule of law reforms were made as a result of the ICC's intervention in Kenya. This conclusion challenges the work of Sriram and Brown, who argue that the ICC process in Kenya 'brought the public agenda extra momentum for broader reforms that would reinforce the rule of law'.[242] The greatest credit for these institutional reforms must be afforded to the Annan-led KNDR process, a conclusion that Moreno-Ocampo has himself acknowledged.[243]

Indeed, there is even evidence to suggest that the commencement of trials in The Hague may have *obstructed* the reforms. Following the announcement of the Ocampo Six, MPs focused on strategies aimed at circumventing the ICC process and this caused attention to be diverted away from the ongoing reform process.

---

[242] Sriram and Brown (2012) (see Footnote 7).

[243] Radio Netherlands Worldwide, Interview with Luis Moreno-Ocampo, 6 February 2014.

In addition, disagreements within the government over how it should respond placed further strains upon already-fractured relationships within the coalition government, which had the potential to derail the reform process altogether.

In reaching these conclusions, it must be recognised that this analysis has focused on the OTP's influence between 2008 and 2013. It might be, of course, that the OTP's greatest impact occurs in the longer term. Done properly, rule of law reform takes years and requires a significant amount of funding.[244] For one matter, the prosecution of those alleged to bear the greatest responsibility for the post-election violence might pave the way for further institutional reform once these 'lords of impunity' have been removed from the political landscape, as suggested by the US Ambassador.[245] For another matter, the ICC appears to have provided Kenya's NGOs with increased leverage and legitimacy, which these organisations are hoping will assist them in encouraging a new generation of leaders to enter politics. As such, it is possible that the ICC's greatest contribution to stimulating rule of law reform awaits to be seen.

Bibliography

'80 ICC witnesses in safe houses', *Standard*, 24 January 2013
'Cabinet Split Over Ocampo', *Nairobi Star*, 14 December 2010
'Cases will ensure peaceful 2012 election, says Ocampo', *Daily Nation*, 15 December 2010
'Embassy clears 41 MPs for trip to The Hague', *Daily Nation*, 4 April 2011
'EU threatens to cut aid over corruption', *Daily Nation*, 26 March 2010
'Forum asks Wako to act on chaos witnesses recanting evidence', *Daily Nation*, 3 December 2010
'Imanyara and Raila in dramatic fallout over Bill', *Daily Nation*, 14 November 2009
'Kaunya's wife says her life under threat', *Daily Nation*, 25 April 2010
'Kenyan Gov't Not Cooperative, Says ICC', *Citizen News*, 17 February 2013
'Kenya's Constitution: a chance to improve how Kenya is run', *Economist*, 29 June 2010
'Ministers push to keep Ocampo probe at bay', *Daily Nation*, 15 April 2010
'NCIC Probing Four MPS over Hate Speech During Rallies', *The Star*, 21 February 2012
'ODM ministers walk out on Raila over tribunal', *Daily Nation*, 30 June 2009
'Parliament moves to protect Ocampo witnesses', *Standard*, 6 April 2010
'Ruto allies write to UN Council on Hague Trials', *Daily Nation*, 16 March 2011
'Sh1.2bn needed for witness protection', *The Star*, 27 May 2011
'Wako to publish witness protection Bill', *Daily Nation*, 15 September 2009

---

[244] Naomi Roht-Arriaza, *Impunity and Human Rights in International Law and Practice* (Oxford University Press, 1995), 282; Office of the United Nations High Commissioner for Human Rights, *Rule-of-Law Tools for Post-Conflict States: Mapping the Justice Sector* (Office of the United Nations High Commissioner for Human Rights, 2006), 4.

[245] James Ratemo, 'Wikileaks: Kenya's old guard are masters of impunity', *Standard*, 9 December 2010.

African Union Panel of Eminent African Personalities, Press Statement by Kofi Annan, 1 March 2008
Agina, Ben and Omanga, Beauttah, 'ICC: State bows to pressure on safety of witnesses', *Standard*, 2 February 2010
Akech, Migai, *Institutional Reform in the New Constitution of Kenya* (International Centre for Transitional Justice, October 2010)
Alston, Philip, *Mission to Kenya 16-25 February 2009* (United Nations Special Rapporteur on Extrajudicial Killings, Arbitrary or Summary Executions, 2009)
Aluanga-Delvaux, Lillian, 'Lack of funds delays witness agency work', *Standard*, 6 January 2013
Amnesty International, *Police Reform in Kenya: 'A Drop in the Ocean'* (Amnesty International, 2013)
Bannon, Alicia, 'Designing a Constitution-Drafting Process: Lessons from Kenya' (2007 116 *Yale Law Journal* 1824
Barasa, Lucas, 'Why I reject new Chief Justice', *Daily Nation*, 29 January 2011
Barasa, Lucas and Leftie, Peter, 'ICC told to try poll chaos suspects', *Daily Nation*, 29 September 2009
Beja, Patrick, 'TJRC wants politicians charged over crimes', *Standard*, 6 February 2013
Bii, Bernaba, 'Chaos victims want security', *Daily Nation*, 12 April 2010
Bjork, Christine and Goebertus, Juanita, 'Complementarity in Action: The Role of Civil Society and the ICC in Rule of Law Strengthening in Kenya' (2011) 14 *Yale Human Rights & Development Law Journal* 205
Bowry, Pravin, 'Great prospects on law reform', *Standard*, 2 March 2010
Bowry, Pravin, 'Kibaki's legacy cemented by rule of law', *Standard*, 2 May 2012
Burke-White, William, 'Complementarity in Practice: The International Criminal Court as Part of a System of Multi-level Global Governance in the Democratic Republic of Congo' (2005) 18 *Leiden Journal of International Law* 557
Carothers, Thomas, *Promoting the Rule of Law Abroad: In Search of Knowledge* (Carnegie Endowment for International Peace, 2006); David Trubek and Alvaro Santos (eds), *The New Law and Economic Development: A Critical Appraisal* (Cambridge University Press, 2006)
Chepkemei, Pamela, 'Five judges sent home, 23 cleared as Rao turns to magistrates', *Daily Nation*, 22 December 2012
Committee of Experts on Constitutional Review, Final Report of the Committee of Experts on Constitutional Review, 11 October 2010
Constitution of Kenya 2010
Counter-Trafficking in Persons Act 2010
Criminal Procedure Code (Amendment) Act 2008
Elections Act 2011
Final Report of the Task Force on Judicial Reforms, July 2010
Gĩthĩnji, Mwangi wa and Holmquist, Frank, 'Reform and Political Impunity in Kenya: Transparency without Accountability' (2012) 55(1) *African Studies Review* 53
Gitonga, Antony and Opiyo, Peter, 'Ocampo writes to Mutula over witness threats', *Standard*, 26 January 2010
Government of the Republic of Kenya, Response to the Report of the Special Rapporteur on Extrajudicial. Arbitrary or Summary Executions, Professor Philip Alston, on his Mission to Kenya from 16-25 February, 2009
Griffiths, Martin, 'The Prisoner of Peace: An interview with Kofi A. Annan', *Centre for Humanitarian Dialogue*, May 2008
Hampson, Fen, *Nurturing Peace: Why Peace Settlements Succeed or Fail* (United States Institute of Peace Press, 1996)
Hansard, National Assembly, Official Report, 6 March 2008
Hansard, National Assembly, Official Report, 12 March 2008
Hansard, National Assembly, Official Report, 18 March 2008
Hansard, National Assembly, Official Report, 7 May 2008
Hansard, National Assembly, Official Report, 22 June 2008

Hansard, National Assembly, Official Report, 31 July 2008
Hansard, National Assembly, Official Report, 6 August 2008
Hansard, National Assembly, Official Report, 11 December 2008
Hansard, National Assembly, Official Report, 16 December 2008
Hansard, National Assembly, Official Report, 2 December 2009
Hansard, National Assembly, Official Report, 23 February 2010
Hansard, National Assembly, Official Report, 3 March 2010
Hansard, National Assembly, Official Report, 23 March 2010
Hansard, National Assembly, Official Report, 31 March 2010
Hansard, National Assembly, Official Report, 6 April 2010
Hansard, National Assembly, Official Report, 16 December 2010
Hansard, National Assembly, Official Report, 1 February 2011
Hansard, National Assembly, Official Report, 8 February 2011
Hansard, National Assembly, Official Report, 9 February 2011
Hansard, National Assembly, Official Report, 5 May 2011
Hansard, National Assembly, Official Report, 22 March 2011
Hansard, National Assembly, Official Report, 26 April 2011
Hansard, National Assembly, Official Report, 11 May 2011
Hansard, National Assembly, Official Report, 31 May 2011
Hansard, National Assembly, Official Report, 2 June 2011
Hansard, National Assembly, Official Report, 23 August 2011
Hansard, National Assembly, Official Report, 24 August 2011
Hansen, Thomas Obel, 'Transitional Justice in Kenya? An Assessment of the Accountability Process in Light of Domestic Politics and Security Concerns' (2011) 42(1) *California Western International Law Journal* 1
Harneit-Sievers, Axel and Peters, Ralph-Michael, 'Kenya's 2007 General Election and its Aftershocks' (2008) 43 *Africa Spectrum* 133
Human Rights Watch, Turning Pebbles: Evading Accountability for Post-Election Violence in Kenya (Human Rights Watch, 2011)
Human Rights Watch, *World Report 2011* (Human Rights Watch, 2011)
Human Rights Watch, *World Report 2014* (Human Rights Watch, 2014)
Independent Electoral Boundaries Commission Act 2011
Independent Police Oversight Authority Act 2011
Independent Review Commission, Report of the Independent Review Commission on the General Elections Held in Kenya on 27 December 2007, 17 September 2008
International Bar Association and International Legal Assistance Consortium, *Restoring Integrity: An assessment of the needs of the justice system in the Republic of Kenya* (International Bar Association and International Legal Assistance Consortium, February 2010)
International Centre for Policy and Conflict, *Post Election Violence: A Trail of Lies and Betrayal*, 2009
International Centre for Transitional Justice, 'Kenya: Truth Commission Chair Should Step Down', 22 February 2010
International Commission of Jurists Kenya, 'ICJ Kenya's Position Paper on the appointment of the next Chief Justice as at Jan 2011', January 2011
International Criminal Court, Assembly of States Parties, 'President of the Assembly of States Parties visits Kenya', 28 January 2011
International Criminal Court, Assembly of States Parties, *Report of the Court on Cooperation*, Tenth Session, New York, ICC-ASP/10/40, 18 November 2011
International Criminal Court, 'Focal points' compilation of examples of projects aimed at strengthening domestic jurisdictions to deal with Rome Statute Crimes', paper presented at the Review Conference of the Rome Statute (Kampala, 31 May 2010–11 June 2010)
International Criminal Court, Office of the Prosecutor, 'Agreed minutes of the meeting between Prosecutor Moreno-Ocampo and the delegation of the Kenyan Government', 3 July 2009
International Criminal Court, Office of the Prosecutor, 'OTP Statement in Relation to Events in Kenya', 5 February 2008

International Criminal Court, Office of the Prosecutor, 'Statement by the Prosecutor of the International Criminal Court Mrs. Fatou Bensouda at the press conference at the conclusion of Nairobi segment of ICC Prosecutor's visit to Kenya, Nairobi', 25 October 2012

International Criminal Court, Office of the Prosecutor, 'Statement of the Prosecutor on the Situation in Kenya', 29 May 2011

Interview with Elijah Letangule (Nairobi, 5 August 2011)

Interview with Fred Ochieng (Nairobi, 19 April 2010)

Interview with Philip Waki (Nairobi, 16 April 2010)

Interview with TJRC commissioner (Nairobi, 5 August 2011)

Judges and Magistrates Vetting Board, 'Determination Concerning the Judges of the Court of Appeal', 25 April 2012

Kagiri, Anthony, 'MPs urged to avoid sideshows in House', *Capital News*, 17 January 2011

Kagiri, Anthony, 'Raila: foreign judges must head local tribunal', *Capital News*, 26 March 2011

Kamau, Macharia, Kenya's Permanent Representative to the United Nations, Letter to Christian Wenaweser, President of the Assembly of State Parties to the Rome Statute 'Ref: Support for Kenya's reform movement', 28 February 2011

Kanyinga, Karuti and Long, James, ' The Political Economy of Reforms in Kenya: The Post-2007 Election Violence and a New Constitution' (2012) 55(1) *African Studies Review* 31

Kariuki, Anthony, 'Kenya referendum date set', *Daily Nation*, 14 May 2010

Kennedy, Brian and Bieniek, Lauren, *Moving Forward with Constitutional Reform in Kenya* (Centre for Strategic International Studies, December 2010)

Kenya Human Rights Commission, *Lest We Forget: The Faces of Impunity in Kenya* (Kenya Human Rights Commission, 2011)

Kenya Human Rights Commission, Surviving After Torture: A Case Digest on the Struggle for Justice by Torture Survivors in Kenya (Kenya Human Rights Commission, 2009)

Kenya Human Rights Commission, International Centre for Policy and Conflict and International Commission of Jurists Kenya, *Transitional Justice in Kenya: A Toolkit for Training and Engagement* (International Commission of Jurists Kenya, 2010)

Kenya National Dialogue and Reconciliation, 'Commission of Inquiry on Post-Election Violence', 4 March 2008

Kenya National Dialogue and Reconciliation, 'Longer-Term Issues and Solutions: Constitutional Review', 4 March 2008

Kenya National Dialogue and Reconciliation, 'Truth, Justice and Reconciliation Commission', 4 March 2008

Kenya Truth Justice and Reconciliation Commission, Progress Report to the National Assembly Submitted Pursuant to Section 20(3) of the Truth, Justice and Reconciliation Act No. 6 of 2008, 24 June 2011

Kikechi, Biketi, 'Fresh plan to block Ocampo', *Standard*, 14 December 2010

Kwalia, Bernard, 'NCIC Now Launches Workshops to Defuse Tension', *The Star*, 7 February 2012

Laibuta, Anthony, 'Constitutional and Institutional Reform: What role in Addressing Impunity' in Waruguru Kaguongo and Godfrey Musila (eds), *Judiciary Watch Report: Addressing Impunity and Options for Justice in Kenya—Mechanisms, Issues and Debates* (International Commission of Jurists, 2009)

Lasseko, Matilda, 'Role of Civil Society in Transitional Justice Process: the Evolving Kenyan Experience' in Waruguru Kaguongo and Godfrey Musila (eds), *Judiciary Watch Report: Addressing Impunity and Options for Justice in Kenya—Mechanisms, Issues and Debates* (International Commission of Jurists, 2009)

Leftie, Peter, 'Reject Kenya Plea, Orange Asks UN', *Daily Nation*, 13 March 2011

Leftie, Peter, 'Violence suspects may face UK travel ban', *Daily Nation*, 4 August 2009

Macharia, James, 'ICC trials main threat to Kenyan polls—electoral commission', *Reuters*, 17 April 2012

Macharia, James, 'Kenya names judge to help Hague investigators', *Reuters*, 6 October 2010

Mahony, Chris, The Justice Sector Afterthought: Witness Protection in Africa (Institute for Security Studies, 2010)

Maingi, Grace, 'The Kenyan Constitutional Reform Process: A Case Study on the Work of FIDA Kenya in Securing Women's Rights' (2011) 15 *Feminist Africa* 63
Makabila, Stephen, 'Annan, Ocampo comeback draws high anxiety', *Standard*, 27 November 2010
Makabila, Stephen, 'Focus on Wako's legacy as curtain falls on his tenure', *Standard*, 3 July 2011
Maliti, Tom, 'Great expectations await new Kenyan Chief Justice', *The International Criminal Court Kenya Monitor*, 20 June 2011
Maliti, Tom, 'Kenyan Chief Justice outlines progress in judicial transformation', *The International Criminal Court Kenya Monitor*, 25 October 2011
Maliti, Tom, 'Outsiders nominated to be Kenya's next Chief Justice and Deputy Chief Justice', *The International Criminal Court Kenya Monitor*, 16 May 2011
Mathenge, Oliver, 'Kenya AG orders probe on Ocampo witnesses' claim', *Daily Nation*, 15 March 2012
Mbote, Patricia Kameria and Akech, Migai, *Kenya: Justice Sector and the Rule of Law* (Open Society Foundation, March 2011)
Mbuthia, Joe, 'ICC has "no witness in Kenya"', *Daily Nation*, 24 March 2010
Mégret, Frédéric, 'Too much of a good thing? Implementation and the uses of complementarity' in Carsten Stahn and Mohamed M. El Zeidy (eds), *The International Criminal Court and Complementarity From Theory to Practice* (Cambridge University Press, 2011)
Menya, Walter, 'AG, police faulted for derailing Mwakwere arrest', *Daily Nation*, 17 August 2010
Menya, Walter, 'Law to shield chaos witnesses', *Daily Nation*, 12 November 2009
Menya, Walter, 'Rights body offers to protect chaos victims', *Daily Nation*, 11 May 2010
Ministry of Justice, National Cohesion and Constitutional Affairs, *GJLOS II Reform Programme 2011/12 to 2015/16*, 21 October 2011
Mkawale, Steve, 'Witness protection agency unveiled ahead of Hague hearing', *Standard*, 12 August 2011
Moreno-Ocampo, Luis, 'Address to the Assembly of States Parties', New York, 22 April 2003
Moreno-Ocampo, Luis, 'Kenya National Dialogue and Reconciliation, Two Year On, Where are We?', Statement, Nairobi, 2 December 2010
Mue, Njonjo, 'New Constitution major step towards justice in Kenya', *New Liberian*, 6 August 2010
Muindi, Benjamin, 'ICC: Uhuru, Ruto, Lash Out at PM', *Daily Nation*, 26 March 2011
Munene, Mugomo, 'Last ditch effort to shield Ocampo six', *Daily Nation*, 18 December 2010
Munene, Mugomo and Leftie, Peter, 'Why plot to stop Ocampo failed', *Daily Nation*, 8 May 2010
Musau, Nzau, 'Witnesses targeted over Waki envelope', *Nairobi Star*, 13 July 2009
Musila, Godfrey, 'Options for Transitional Justice in Kenya: Autonomy and the Challenge of External Prescriptions' (2009) 3 *International Journal of Transitional Justice* 445
Mutiga, Murithi 'Ocampo writes to judges over threats', *Daily Nation*, 30 January 2010
Mutua, Martin, 'Eyes on other TJRC officials as Murungi resigns', *Standard*, 19 April 2010
Namunane, Bernard, 'Kenya coalition rivalry plays out on the world stage', *Daily Nation*, 3 June 2010
Namunane, Bernard, 'Kenya seeks Africa support over Hague', *Daily Nation*, 12 January 2011
Namunane, Bernard, 'Ocampo's team flying into Kenya', *Daily Nation*, 5 April 2010
National Cohesion and Integration Act 2008
National Cohesion and Integration Commission, 'Goodwill Ambassadors for Cohesion, Integration and Peaceful Coexistence', 4 February 2013
National Cohesion and Integration Commission, Guidelines for Monitoring Hate Speech, August 2010
National Cohesion and Integration Commission, 'The National Cohesion Response to the Tana River Insecurity and the Riots in Mombasa', 5 September 2012
National Police Service Act 2011
National Police Service Commission Act 2011
Ndanyi, Mathews, 'High security at Nandi home of ICC witness', Nairobi Star, 29 September 2011
Ndegwa, Alex, 'House opens to a full diary', *Standard*, 5 February 2010

Ndegwa, Alex, 'How plot on Ocampo hit a dead end', *Standard*, 9 May 2010
Ngirachu, John and Leftie, Peter, 'ODM disowns efforts to challenge ICC cases', *Daily Nation*, 23 March 2011
Ngirachu, John and Rugene, Njeri, 'ODM to Hire Lawyers for Ruto, Kosgey Over ICC Cases', *Daily Nation*, 24 March 2011
Nyabiage, Jevans, 'Muigai sworn in as new Attorney General', *Standard*, 29 August 2011
Office of the President, 'President appoints special envoys', 4 March 2011
Office of the Prime Minister, Launch of Kenya Vision 2030 Speech by His Excellency Hon. Mwai Kibaki, 10 June 2008
Ogutu, Judy, 'Court nullifies list of judicial nominees', *Standard*, 4 February 2011
Ohito, David, 'Travel ban: Obama jolts Cabinet ministers', *Standard*, 25 September 2009
Oluoch, Wauna, 'The Constitution Making Process in Kenya: A Crisis of Leadership and Illegalities?' in Philip Kichana (ed), *Judiciary Watch Report, Judicial Reform in Kenya* (International Commission of Jurists Kenya, 2005)
Omanga, Beauttah, 'ICC sends team over threats to witnesses' lives', *Standard*, 31 January 2010
Omanga, 'Beauttah, 'Nowhere to hide as The Hague alerts states on chaos suspects', *Standard*, 27 April 2010
Omanga, Beauttah and Ohito, David, 'Ocampo lists up to six suspects and trials start by October', *Standard*, 10 May 2010
Onyiego, Michael 'Kenyan Justice Minister calls for disbanding of truth commission', *Voice of America*, 16 April 2010
Opiyo, Dave, 'Kenya's PM disowns offensive against the Hague trials', *East African*, 26 January 2011
Opiyo, Dave, 'President "behind move on Hague"', *Daily Nation*, 16 January 2011
Opiyo, Dave and Namunane, Bernard, 'Raila urges calm as PNU plots offensive', *Daily Nation*, 30 January 2011
Opiyo, Peter and Ochami, David, 'MPs could miss Christmas break over ICC motion', *Standard*, 19 December 2010
Orentlicher, Diane, 'Settling Accounts: The Duty to Prosecute Human Rights Violations of a Prior Regime' (1991) 100 *Yale Law Journal* 2537
Political Parties Act 2011
Political Parties Act 2012
Prevention of Organised Crime Act 2010
Prevention of Terrorism Act 2012
Proceeds of Crime and Anti-Money Laundering Act 2009
Prohibition of Female Genital Mutilation Act 2011
Prosecutor v Francis Kirimi Muthaura and Uhuru Muigai Kenyatta, Public redacted version of the 25 February 2013 Consolidated Prosecution response to the Defence applications under Article 64 of the Statute to refer the confirmation decision back to the Pre-Trial Chamber, ICC-01/09-02/11, 25 February 2013
Prosecutor v Walter Osapiri Barasa, Warrant of arrest of Osapiri Barasa, ICC-01/09-01/13, 2 August 2013
Rausch, Colette (ed), Combating Serious Crimes in Post-conflict Societies: a Handbook for Policymakers and Practitioners (US Institute of Peace Press, 2006)
Reitmaier, Angela, The African Peer Review Mechanism at Country Level: Views from Kenya, Occasional Paper No. 83, Governance and APRM Programme (South African Institute of International Affairs, May 2011)
Remarks by the US Ambassador to Kenya at a forum on Civil Society and the Implementation of the New Constitution, Nairobi, 23 September 2010
Report of the Integrity and Anti-Corruption Committee of the Judiciary in Kenya, 30 September 2003
Report of the National Task Force on Police Reforms, October 2009
Republic of Kenya, Governance, Justice, Law and Order Sector Reform Programme, Short Term Priorities Programme, Fiscal Year 2003/04
Republic of Kenya, Ministry of Justice, National Cohesion and Constitutional Affairs, *GJLOS Sector Policy Final Report*, 11 July 2011
Republic of Kenya, Report of the Task Force on the Establishment of a Truth, Justice and Reconciliation Commission, 2003

Robinson, Darryl, 'The Rome Statute and its Impact on National Law' in Antonio Cassese, Paola Gaeta and John Jones (eds), *The Rome Statute of the International Criminal Court: a commentary* (Oxford University Press, 2002)

Rome Statute of the International Criminal Court, opened for signature 17 July 1998, 2187 UNTS 90 (entered into force 1 July 2002)

Shundu, Alphonce, 'Mutula Kilonzo vows new quest for Kenya's violence tribunal', *Daily Nation*, 23 March 2010

South Consulting, Kenya National Dialogue and Reconciliation Monitoring Project, *Agenda Item IV Reforms, Long-standing Issues and Solutions, Progress Review Report*, March 2012

South Consulting, Kenya National Dialogue and Reconciliation Monitoring Project, *Draft Review Report*, April 2011

South Consulting, Kenya National Dialogue and Reconciliation Monitoring Project, *Progress in the Implementation of the Constitution and other reforms, Review Report*, October 2011

South Consulting, Kenya National Dialogue and Reconciliation Monitoring Project, *Review Report*, October 2010

South Consulting, Kenya National Dialogue and Reconciliation Monitoring Project, *Status of Implementation of Agenda Items 1-4, Progress Report for January-March 2010*, April 2010

South Consulting, Kenya National Dialogue and Reconciliation Monitoring Project, *Status of Implementation of Agenda Items 1-4, Draft Report*, May 2009

South Consulting, Kenya National Dialogue and Reconciliation Monitoring Project, *Status of Implementation of Agenda Items 1-4, Third Review Report*, July 2009

South Consulting, The Kenya National Dialogue and Reconciliation (KNDR) Monitoring Project, January 2009

Sriram, Chandra and Brown, Stephen, 'Kenya in the Shadow of the ICC: Complementarity, Gravity and Impact' (2012) 12(2) *International Criminal Law Review* 219

Tamanaha, Brian, *On the Rule of Law: History, Politics, Theory* (Cambridge University Press, 2004)

Teitel, Ruti, *Transitional Justice* (Oxford University Press, 2002)

Throup, David and Hornsby, Charles, *Multi-Party Politics in Kenya* (Ohio University Press, 1998)

Thuku, Wahome, 'NCIC to withdraw hate speech charges against Machage, Kapondi', *Standard*, 4 August 2011

Tillier, Justine, 'The ICC Prosecutor and Positive Complementarity: Strengthening the Rule of Law?' (2013) 13(3) *International Criminal Law Review* 507

Transcript of Statement of US Secretary of State Condoleezza Rice with Former UN Secretary General Kofi Annan, Serena Hotel, Nairobi, Kenya, 18 February 2008

Truth Justice and Reconciliation Act 2008

Truth Justice and Reconciliation Commission, *Report of the Truth Justice and Reconciliation Commission*, 3 May 2013

Tyler, Tom, Braga, Anthony, Fagan, Jeffrey Meares, Tracey, Sampson, Robert and Winship, Chris, 'Legitimacy and Criminal Justice: International Perspectives' in Tom Tyler (ed), *Legitimacy and Criminal Justice: International Perspectives* (Russell Sage, 2007)

United Nations General Assembly Human Rights Council, Working Group of the Universal Periodic Review, *Report of the Working Group on the Universal Periodic Review, Kenya*, A/HRC/15/8, 17 June 2010

United Nations Human Rights Committee, Concluding observations adopted by the Human Rights Committee at its 105th session, 9-27 July 2012, CCPR/C/KEN/CO/3, 26 July 2012

United Nations Office on Drugs and Crime, 'One step closer to witness protection in Kenya', *Reliefweb*, 14 January 2010

Vetting of Judges and Magistrates Act 2011

Vinjamuri, Leslie, 'Deterrence, Democracy and the Pursuit of International Justice' (2010) 24(2) *Ethics and International Affairs* 191

Wafula, Caroline, 'Witness Bill gets House approval', *Daily Nation*, 7 April 2010

Wanja, Joy, 'Political detainees urge govt to resign', *Daily Nation*, 31 July 2009

Wesangula, Daniel, 'Plea to give Ocampo Six a blackout', *Daily Nation*, 12 April 2011

Witness Protection (Amendment) Act 2010

World Bank Institute, *Country Data Report for Kenya, 1996-2011*(World Bank, 2011)

Chapter 8
Culture of Impunity

For a state to make progress in ending impunity, it must not only secure criminal convictions and a commitment to the rule of law, but also restore public confidence in the functioning of the criminal justice system. This is because effective investigations and prosecutions are contingent upon victims reporting crimes to the police and witnesses testifying in court. Such cooperation first requires that victims and witnesses have confidence in the criminal justice system. Witnesses must feel that reported crimes will be properly investigated, that cases will be fairly and impartially adjudicated and that their security (and that of their families) will be guaranteed at all times. Where witnesses do not feel confident in these matters, they will be less likely to report and testify, thereby making investigations and prosecutions even more challenging and contributing to a 'cycle of impunity'. The breaking of this cycle may only occur when steps are taken that have the effect of restoring public confidence in the criminal justice system. This chapter considers the extent to which the OTP's strategy of complementarity contributed to such a restoration of public confidence in Kenya and thereby helped in ending the country's 'culture of impunity'.

This analysis has been conducted by considering public perceptions of the police force and the judiciary between 2008 and 2013. Four data sets have been relied upon in measuring public confidence in these institutions. First, quantitative and qualitative data collected by KNDR, which took the form of quarterly national surveys of 2,500 respondents using multi-stage cluster sampling proportionate to the population size. The KNDR quantitative data was complemented by qualitative data obtained through interviews with government ministers, civil society organisations, the media and members of the public. The second data set has been produced by Transparency International, a non-governmental organisation that publishes annual reports on public perceptions of corruption within state institutions. This involves nationwide surveys of between 2,000 and 3,000 respondents who were asked whether they were confronted with demands for bribes in the preceding year, with follow-up questions in relation to the purpose, incidence, prevalence, severity, frequency and size of such bribes. These two sources are complemented by the third and fourth datasets—polls conducted by professional polling agencies Ipsos Synovate and Infotrak Harris. Each of these polls was carried out through face-to-face interviews of at least 1,500 respondents using stratified, random and systematic sampling techniques. All of this data has been compiled to identify any trends between February 2008 and March 2013 and whether any improvement in public confidence can be said to have taken place at significant moments during the OTP's intervention.

1 Ending the 'Culture of Impunity'

When there is little public confidence in the functioning of a criminal justice system, this will often lead to a 'culture of impunity' whereby people adjust their behaviours as a response to their distrust in state institutions. McSherry and Molina explain that this is the 'most poignant and tragic of all aspects of impunity' since 'if people believe there can be no justice, they resign themselves to political realities, adapt, and adjust in order to survive'.[1] Such a situation existed in Kenya at the time of the post-election violence. As the Waki Report notes, 'there was a perception by sections of the public that government institutions and officials, including the judiciary, were not independent of the presidency, were not impartial, and lacked integrity'.[2] Indeed, even the Justice Minister was forced to concede that there had been 'serious impunity' and that a great deal of confidence in state institutions had been lost.[3]

Where a culture of impunity exists, three consequences typically follow. First, disillusionment with respect to the state's ability to prevent or punish the commission of crimes may result in the forming of vigilante groups or militia in order to protect people from serious crimes, even though these groups may themselves be involved in the commission of such crimes.[4] In Kenya, this existed in the formation of gangs such as Mungiki, which became a 'gang for hire'.[5] Violence became commodified in a classic capitalist operation, with private security services being sold to the highest bidder, providing a major source of employment for Kenya's impecunious and uneducated youth. Second, the state will often respond to its lost monopoly on the legitimate use of force by attempting to reinstate its authority through increasing levels of oppression and brutality. Government officials, the police and the military them-

---

[1] Patrice McSherry and Mejia Molina, 'Confronting the Question of Justice in Guatemala' (1992) 19(3) *Social Justice* 1.

[2] *Final Report from Kenya's Commission of Inquiry into Post-Election Violence*, 15 October 2008 ('Waki Report'), 28. 28.

[3] Lucy Hannan and Maina Kiai, *Getting Justice: Kenya's Deadly Game of Wait and See* (Informaction, 2010).

[4] Colette Rausch 857).(ed), *Combating Serious Crimes in Post-conflict Societies: a Handbook for Policymakers and Practitioners* (US Institute of Peace Press, 2006), 73–74.

[5] Susanne Mueller, 'The Political Economy of Kenya's Crisis' (2008) 2(2) *Journal of Eastern African Studies* 185.

selves 'break the law without fear of punishment, for there is a shared understanding that each person will be silent about the other's abuses as long as the favour is returned'.[6] In Kenya, this occurred through state-sanctioned extrajudicial killings, torture and arbitrary detention. This further eroded the state's monopoly on legitimate force and public confidence in state institutions. A third consequence of a culture of impunity is a reluctance on the part of citizens to cooperate with state institutions, including the criminal justice system. The lawlessness of the state disempowers citizens, rendering them cynical, passive and fearful.[7] Within Kenya, crimes often went unreported because victims considered such action to be futile and held well-founded fears for their personal security should they cooperate with the criminal justice process. These three consequences then combine to further entrench the culture of impunity. A lack of confidence in state institutions leads to heavy-handed conduct from the state, which in turn encourages the establishment of vigilante groups and a reluctance to report crimes, making criminal prosecutions extremely difficult and thereby further diminishing public confidence in state institutions. In this way, a cycle of impunity is perpetuated.

Where such a cycle of impunity exists, what is often required is a circuit breaker to restore public confidence in state institutions. This might take the form of a change of government, major reforms to the institutions or removal of certain persons from public office. The OTP's strategy of positive complementarity, in seeking to hold leaders to account, has the potential to be such a circuit breaker in situation countries. Members of government, the public service, civil society and the public all expressed the view that the OTP's targeting of senior leaders would remove the 'lords of impunity', 'anti-reformers' and 'cronies' from public office and that this would make a significant contribution to restoring public confidence in state institutions.[8]

A culture of impunity may only be ended where respect for the rule of law is commanded not by force, but by public trust.[9] For Galligan, the object is for the criminal justice system to reach sound practical judgments about a matter in issue in

---

[6] David Crocker, 'Reckoning with Past Wrongs: A Normative Framework' (1999) 13 *Ethics International Affairs* 34.

[7] Naomi Roht-Arriaza, *Impunity and Human Rights in International Law and Practice* (Oxford University Press, 1995), 4.

[8] Paul Juma, 'New tribunal Bill on the way, says Kilonzo' *Daily Nation* 4 December 2009; Peter Clottey, 'Kenyan lawmakers says there's no rush to implement reforms', *Voice of America*, 8 December 2009; 'Interview with Mutula Kilonzo', UN Radio, *ReliefWeb*, 17 May 2010; Ng'ang'a Mbunga, 'Change of seismic proportion is on the way', *Daily Nation*, 26 December 2010; Interview with Alan Meso (Nairobi, 3 May 2010); Fred Oluoch, 'R Valley braces for new power balance', *Daily Nation*, 18 December 2010; Peter Kagwanga, 'ICC list merely stoking ethnic power politics', *Standard*, 21 December 2010; Interview with Lynne Muthoni Wanyeki (Nairobi, 7 May 2010); Christine Bjork and Juanita Goebertus, 'Complementarity in Action: The Role of Civil Society and the ICC in Rule of Law Strengthening in Kenya' (2011) 14 *Yale Human Rights & Development Law Journal* 205, 226; Interview with Charles Kirudja (Nairobi, 4 May 2010).

[9] Mike Hough and Julian Roberts, 'Confidence in Justice: An International Review' (2004) ICPR Research Paper No. 3, The Institute for Criminal Policy Research, School of Law, King's College, London, 6; Sir Gerard Brennan, 'The Third Branch and the Fourth Estate', Speech delivered at the Broadcasting Society and Law Lecture Series, University College, Dublin, 22 April 1997.

a manner that is regarded as rational and reasonable.[10] In other words, it is essential that 'justice should not only be done, but should manifestly and undoubtedly be seen to be done'.[11] For the judiciary, a branch of government that neither controls finances nor the use of force, the acceptance of its decisions rests not upon coercion, but upon public confidence.[12] Indeed, 'without public confidence, the judicial branch could not function'.[13] The same is true of the police service, which is dependent upon public confidence in order to secure the necessary cooperation for the investigation and prosecution of crimes. Only where the police service commands public confidence will citizens feel confident in reporting crimes.[14] The remainder of this chapter considers whether public confidence in the judiciary and the police service improved between 2008 and 2013 and, if so, the extent to which this might be attributed to the OTP's strategy of positive complementarity.

2 Judging the Judges

At the time of the 2007/2008 post-election violence, public confidence in the judiciary was extremely low. Decades of political patronage, an institutionalised history of corruption and massive delays in the delivery of judgments due to a lack of resources meant that Kenyans felt they could not rely upon the courts to deliver justice. As a consequence, ODM supporters who believed Kibaki's electoral victory to be illegitimate chose not to challenge this result through the courts and instead expressed their frustrations through spontaneous and organised violence. As of December 2008, less than one in three Kenyans expressed satisfaction with the performance of the courts.[15]

By September 2012, however, confidence in the judiciary had increased to 74 %, a figure that was maintained in subsequent surveys conducted in December 2012 and January 2013.[16] The last of these surveys was conducted two months before the March 2013 election and revealed that 75 % of respondents believed that the judi-

---

[10] Denis Galligan, *Due Process and Fair Procedures: A Study of Administrative Procedures* (Clarendon, 1996), 5.

[11] Ibid.

[12] Alexander Hamilton, 'The Federalist No. 78' in Clinton Rossiter (ed), *The Federalist Papers* (New American Library, 1961).

[13] *In re Raab*, 100 N.Y.2d 305, 315–316.

[14] David J Smith, 'The Foundations of Legitimacy' in Tom Tyler, Anthony Braga, Jeffrey Fagan, Tracey Meares, Robert Sampson and Chris Winship, 'Legitimacy and Criminal Justice: International Perspectives' in Tom Tyler (ed), *Legitimacy and Criminal Justice: International Perspectives* (Russell Sage, 2007), 10–11.

[15] South Consulting, *The Kenya National Dialogue and Reconciliation (KNDR) Monitoring Project*, January 2009 ('KNDR January 2009 Report').

[16] South Consulting, Kenya National Dialogue and Reconciliation Monitoring Project, *Kenya's 2013 General Election: A Review of Preparedness*, February 2013 ('KNDR February 2013 Report'), 15.

2 Judging the Judges 237

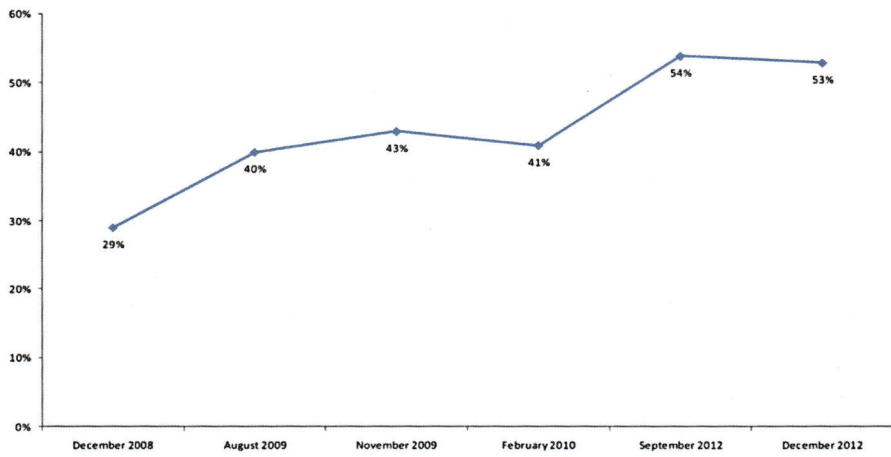

Fig. 8.1 How satisfied are you with the overall performance of the following institutions? The Police

ciary would settle any electoral disputes fairly.[17] This newly restored faith in the judiciary was put to the test when the IEBC declared that Kenyatta had won the presidential election with 50.07 % of the vote. Kenyatta had thus managed to avoid the need for a run-off ballot by a margin of fewer than 9,000 votes. Some anomalies in the conduct of the election had great potential to raise tensions: the IEBC's attempts to use biometric equipment to register voters suffered several setbacks and resulted in one-third of eligible voters not being registered; the registration equipment failed at many polling stations; and the IEBC was forced to abandon its electronic transmission system and instead tally votes manually.[18] Five days after the elections, the IEBC certified Kenyatta's victory. The runner-up, Odinga, urged his supporters not to resort to violence and filed a petition in the Supreme Court challenging the victory. Odinga's party argued that the IEBC had intentionally reverted to manual vote counting to facilitate manipulation and had fraudulently altered the voter registry.[19] On 25 March 2013, the Supreme Court ordered a recount in 22 polling stations and heard oral arguments over the next two days. The Supreme Court then dismissed the petition and declared that Kenyatta has been validly elected. Significantly, there was very little violence after the IEBC's announcement or after the Supreme Court's decision.[20] This would suggest that, on the whole, Kenyans were willing to accept the Supreme Court's decision, demonstrating a confidence in the judiciary that had not existed five years earlier. An opinion poll conducted soon

---

[17] KNDR February 2013 Report (see Footnote 16), 30.

[18] James Long, Karuti Kanyinga, Karen Ferree and Clark Gibson, 'Choosing Peace over Democracy' (2013) 24(3) *Journal of Democracy* 140.

[19] Long et al. (2013) (see Footnote 18), 149.

[20] International Crisis Group, *Policy Briefing, Kenya After the Elections*, 15 May 2013 ('ICG May 2013 Policy Briefing'), 6–7.

after the decision revealed that 69 % believed it to have been fair and impartial, while 78 % had either 'a lot' or 'some' trust in the Supreme Court.[21]

In assessing the factors that may have contributed to the public's dramatic increase in trust between elections, a useful starting point is to consider the time period during which support increased. Data from KNDR surveys throughout this period is helpful in this regard (Fig. 8.1). This suggests that public confidence in the judiciary remained at modest levels until sometime between February 2010 and November 2010, when there was a substantial increase, followed by another sudden improvement between November 2010 and September 2012.

The first point to note is that, as of August 2009, public confidence in the judiciary remained extremely low. By this time, the OTP had taken significant steps in implementing its strategy of positive complementarity. The OTP had issued two statements declaring that it was monitoring the situation in Kenya, the Prosecutor had threatened international prosecutions should a local mechanism fail to be established, two attempts had been made to form a special tribunal, a complementarity contract had been agreed and the government had given assurances that it would expedite reforms of the judiciary. Nevertheless, three out of four Kenyans said that the courts functioned 'about the same' or 'worse' than they did prior to the 2007 elections.[22] This would suggest that, at least until this stage, the strategy of positive complementarity did not make any significant contribution to restoring public confidence in the Kenyan judiciary.

Indeed, even as late as February 2010, there had still been no significant improvement. By this time, there had been three failed attempts to establish the special tribunal, the sealed envelope had been handed to the Prosecutor, the OTP had held several meetings with government leaders and had requested permission to initiate an investigation. In other words, the OTP's most active period of encouraging domestic investigations and prosecutions was drawing to a close, with little discernible impact on public confidence in the judiciary.

What action, if any, did the OTP take from February 2010 when there was a marked increase in public confidence? From this time, the OTP conducted its investigations, named its suspects and held its confirmation of charges hearings and during this period applied very little pressure upon the government to conduct its own proceedings. Nevertheless, it was during this period that local confidence in the judiciary increased significantly.

Although it is certainly possible that the OTP's commencement of investigations in March 2010 may have contributed to this renewed confidence, a more plausible explanation for this improvement was the passing of the new Constitution on 4 August 2010 and the implementation of associated judicial reforms. Chapter 10 of the new Constitution promised a more transparent, accountable and independent judiciary by providing for the establishment of a Supreme Court, the JSC and a judiciary fund. In the months that followed, major pieces of legislation were passed to implement these reforms. Then in May 2011, Kenyans were treated to the most

---

[21] Long et al. (2013) (see Footnote 18), 150.

[22] KNDR January 2009 Report (see Footnote 15).

open and transparent judicial appointment process in the country's history, which ultimately led to Mutunga's swearing in as Chief Justice. This process was complemented by the high profile work of the JMVB, which by December 2012 had declared 13 judges to be unfit to serve in public office. These reforms may also have contributed to significant reductions in levels of corruption in the judiciary over this period. The likelihood of Kenyans being solicited for bribes when interacting with the courts decreased from 92 % in 2008 to 35 % in 2012.[23]

By September 2012, the judicial reform process was close to completion and this coincided with unprecedented levels of public confidence in the institution. Respondents cited a number of factors as contributing to this increase, including 'transparency in the recruitment of judicial officers', 'efforts to demonstrate independence' and 'the ongoing vetting of judges and magistrates'.[24] Another survey conducted in the same month, funded by ICJ-Kenya and carried out by Infotrak Harris, revealed that the major reasons for this high level of public confidence in the judiciary were 'impartiality and fairness in recruiting' that 'judges had been vetted', that '[the judges were now] persons of high integrity' and '[the judges were now] the best qualified and experienced'.[25] Significantly for the purposes of this study, it appears that in neither of these surveys did the respondents suggest that their restored faith in the judiciary was in any way influenced either by the OTP's threat of prosecutions or the subsequent commencement of the trial process in The Hague.

It would therefore appear to be reasonable to conclude that, although the OTP's strategy of positive complementarity coincided with a period during which a tremendous amount of progress was made in restoring public confidence in the judiciary, this development was independent of the strategy. Instead, this improvement occurred because of the passing of the new Constitution, the implementation of judicial reforms and the much-publicised vetting and appointment process. As demonstrated in the previous chapter, these reforms were undertaken simultaneously to, but separately from, the OTP's investigations and prosecutions. In other words, it would seem to be incorrect to attribute the strengthening of public confidence in the judiciary to the OTP's strategy of positive complementarity.

3 Policing the Police

At the time of the post-election violence, the Kenyan police service was rated as one of the least trustworthy institutions in East Africa. Kenyans perceived the police to be an 'inefficient, brutal, anti-people institution that lacked transparency and

---

[23] Transparency International, *The East African Bribery Index 2012* (Transparency International, 2012) ('Transparency International, East African Bribery Index 2012').

[24] South Consulting, *Kenya National Dialogue and Reconciliation Monitoring Project, Kenya's 2013 General Election: A Review of the Environment and Electoral Preparedness, October 2012* (*'KNDR October* 2012 Report').

[25] International Commission of Jurists Kenya, *Judiciary, Perception Survey Presentation*, September 2012 ('ICJ-K Judiciary Perception Survey').

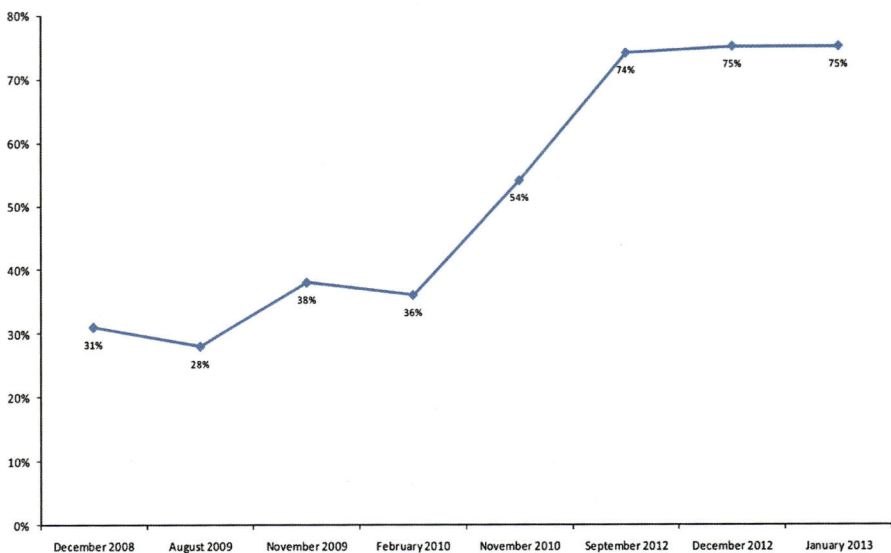

Fig. 8.2 How satisfied are you with the overall performance of the following institutions? Judiciary

accountability'.[26] Nearly half of all Kenyan households rated police performance as 'bad or very bad', ranking it as one of the worst in Africa.[27] This perception did not improve during the post-election violence, with police officers themselves believed to have been responsible for 405 deaths, while others 'simply refused to enforce the law' because of a 'reluctance to tread on the toes of powerful political personalities'.[28] Witnesses were reluctant to report crimes because when they did, the police officer would often treat them with 'callous indifference' or 'outright hostility'.[29] According to a US State Department human rights report, in 2008 an estimated 21,000 rapes were committed in Kenya, but just 627 were reported and it may be reasonably assumed that the lack of professionalism within the police force was partly to blame for this disparity.[30] In December 2008, only one in four Kenyans said that they were satisfied with the performance of the police. Disturbingly, a greater percentage said that they were more likely to either take the law into their

---

[26] Christine Alai and Njonjo Mue, Kenya: *Impact of the Rome Statute and the International Criminal Court* (International Centre for Transitional Justice, 2010).

[27] Economic Commission for Africa, African Governance Report 2005 (Economic Commission for Africa, 2005) ('African Governance Report 2005'), 177.

[28] Waki Report (see Footnote 2), 99, 102–104, 396.

[29] Ibid, 257.

[30] United States Department of State, *Human Rights Report 2010: Kenya*, 2010 ('US State Department Human Rights Report 2010').

own hands (15 %) or form neighbourhood watches (21 %) than they were to report crimes to the police (34 %).[31]

By December 2012, there had been a significant improvement in public confidence in the police service, with 53 % of Kenyans expressing satisfaction in the police, an increase of 24 percentage points over four years (Fig. 8.2). As with the judiciary, public confidence in the institution remained largely stable until February 2010, where there was a significant increase.

Public confidence in the police service, like with the judiciary, had shown some level of improvement by September 2012. By comparison with the judiciary, however, these improved perceptions in the police force took a little longer to eventuate. In September 2011, 60 % of Kenyans remained dissatisfied with the police and in December 2011, just 40 % reported having faith in the police service.[32] Even as late as May 2012, just 43 % of Kenyans said that they had confidence in the police.[33]

There are several possible explanations for these consistently poor levels of support. First, throughout much of this period, members of the police service continued to engage in acts of serious misconduct, including extrajudicial killings, with investigations often taking an unreasonably long time, if conducted at all.[34] Second, levels of corruption within the institution remained exceedingly high. In 2012, 60.4 % of clients were confronted with demands for bribes.[35] 94.5 % of those bribed said that they did not report the incident, mostly because they did not believe that any action would be taken if a report were to be made.[36] Finally, the slow pace of reforms to the police service, as compared with other reforms such as the judiciary and the electoral commission meant that the public had little cause for increased confidence. Put simply, the lack of significant reforms meant that citizens could not accept that there had been a clear break from the past and a commitment to change behaviours and practices.[37] In summary, as Ndungu observed in October 2011, 'public confidence in Kenya's police force has been eroded due to accusations of impunity,

---

[31] KNDR January 2009 Report (see Footnote 15).

[32] South Consulting, Kenya National Dialogue and Reconciliation Monitoring Project, Progress in the Implementation of the Constitution and other reforms, Review Report, October 2011 ('KNDR October 2011 Report'), viii, 57; South Consulting, Kenya National Dialogue and Reconciliation Monitoring Project, Progress in the Implementation of the Constitution and Preparedness for 2012, Review Report, January 2012 ('KNDR January Report'), 28.

[33] South Consulting, Kenya National Dialogue and Reconciliation Monitoring Project, *Reforms and Preparedness for Elections, Review Report*, May 2012 ('KNDR May 2012 Report').

[34] US State Department Human Rights Report 2010 (see Footnote 30).

[35] Transparency International, East African Bribery Index 2012 (see Footnote 23).

[36] Ibid.

[37] South Consulting, Kenya National Dialogue and Reconciliation Monitoring Project, *Agenda Item IV Reforms, Long-standing Issues and Solutions, Progress Review Report*, March 2012 16; KNDR October 2012 Report (see Footnote 24), viii, 12.

excessive use of force and brutality, disregard for human rights, abuse of due process and malignant corruption'.[38]

It was not until September 2012 that a majority of Kenyans (54 %) felt that they could trust the police. There appears to be little, if any, evidence that links this increase in confidence during the September quarter to the OTP's strategy of positive complementarity. No decisive actions were taken in the progress of the ICC cases in The Hague during this period and the Prosecutor did not arrange any meetings with members of the government. By contrast, one factor that appears to have contributed to this increase in support was Parliament's naming of six persons who would sit on the newly formed police commission.[39] These nominations seem to have renewed hope that the police force would be transformed into a more professional, responsible and impartial institution. The Chairman of the Law Society of Kenya, Erick Mutua, commended the nominees and expressed his belief that their appointment would allow the police service to be more functional and responsive to crime.[40]

These positive developments notwithstanding, the police service nevertheless continued to suffer from a poor public image. Nearly half of all Kenyans remained unsatisfied with the police service's performance and levels of corruption remained unacceptably high. As a consequence, large numbers of crimes committed within Kenya continued to go unreported. An Ipsos Synovate poll conducted in November 2012 revealed that, of the persons who had been the victim of a crime within the preceding three months, less than half (49 %) reported that crime to the police.[41] Similarly, the US State Department estimated that as many as 95 % of sexual offences were not reported to the police.[42]

In summary, public confidence in the police service remained unsatisfactorily low more than five years after the commencement of the OTP's strategy of positive complementarity, resulting in a substantial underreporting of crimes. A culture of impunity therefore continued to exist in relation to the police service. While perceptions of the police force improved throughout this period, much of this progress took place well after the most intense phase of positive complementarity and with seemingly no discernible link to the activities of the strategy of positive complementarity. Rather, public confidence increased mainly because of progress in the reform agenda and the potential that this provided for a break from the past.

---

[38] Irene Ndungu, 'Police Reforms Crucial to Restore Public Confidence', *Institute for Security Studies*, 20 October 2011.

[39] 'House urged to speed up vetting of nominees', *Daily Nation*, 9 September 2009.

[40] Patrick Otieno, 'Police commission nominees raise hope for peaceful elections in Kenya', *Soomaali*, 19 September 2012.

[41] Ipsos Synovate, SPEC Barometer Survey, 20 November 2012.

[42] US State Department Human Rights Report 2010 (see Footnote 30).

4 The Shadow Side of Complementarity

The above discussion suggests that the OTP's strategy of positive complementarity does not appear to have made any significant contribution to ending Kenya's culture of impunity. Indeed, the strategy may have, paradoxically, *undermined* attempts to restore faith in domestic institutions. Four consequences of the ICC's intervention in Kenya might be seen to have *reduced* public confidence in Kenya's legal institutions.

First, the prospect of ICC intervention created positive incentives for a number of groups to comment disparagingly about the Kenyan criminal justice system. As discussed in the previous chapter, the OTP's threat to conduct investigations encouraged civil society to highlight the inadequacies of the local justice process so as to ensure that the progress of the ICC cases was not stalled by arguments over admissibility. As such, many NGOs regularly suggested that Kenya's justice institutions were not capable of investigating or prosecuting the post-election violence cases.[43]

The Prosecutor joined civil society in criticising Kenya's criminal justice system. In his *proprio motu* application, the Prosecutor told the Pre-Trial Chamber that 'there are no domestic prosecution (*sic*) for the crimes against humanity allegedly committed in Kenya, nor is there any prospect that there will be'.[44] Later in the application, the Prosecutor made reference to the statement from the judge in the Kiambaa church case that there had been 'shoddy police investigations'.[45] In January 2010, the Prosecutor wrote an open letter to the Justice Minister highlighting reports that witnesses had been threatened and intimidated.[46] In the same week, the Prosecutor wrote to the judges of the ICC's Pre-Trial Chamber to inform them that threats had been made against key prosecution witnesses.[47] In March 2011, the Prosecutor again raised concerns over witness protection, since two of the suspects, Muthaura and Kenyatta, continued to hold public office in positions that could interfere with the witness protection programme.[48] In May 2011, the Prosecutor again highlighted deficiencies in Kenya's witness protection programme, referring to 'a

---

[43] International Centre for Policy and Conflict, 'Independent investigation for widespread and astonishingly high rights of impunity for enforced disappearance and extrajudicial killings by police', 29 April 2011; Lucas Barasa, 'Mutula to Ocampo—Quit Probe', *Daily Nation*, 18 September 2010; Caroline Wafula, 'Lobby calls for forum on Kenya reforms', *Daily Nation*, 13 April 2009; Lucas Barasa, 'Police reforms report out soon', *Daily Nation*, 7 October 2009.

[44] International Criminal Court, Situation in the Republic of Kenya, Request for authorisation of an investigation pursuant to Article 15, ICC-01/09, 26 November 2009 ('OTP Request for Authorisation') [53].

[45] Ibid [54].

[46] Anthony Gitonga and Peter Opiyo, 'Ocampo writes to Mutula over witness threats', *Standard*, 26 January 2010.

[47] Murithi Mutiga, 'Ocampo writes to judges over threats', *Daily Nation*, 30 January 2010.

[48] Bernard Namunane, 'Ocampo—Muthaura may interfere with witnesses', *Daily Nation*, 14 March 2011.

growing climate of fear that [was] intimidating potential witnesses and ultimately undermining national and international investigations'.[49] When Bensouda became Prosecutor, she too 'reiterated [her] concerns regarding witness intimidation and the increasing climate of fear affecting those perceived to be ICC witnesses'.[50] Just five months later, Bensouda was forced to admit that an ICC witnesses had been intimidated.[51] In short, throughout the period of the OTP's involvement, its citizens regularly heard civil society and the ICC, two groups generally regarded by Kenyans to be credible and trustworthy, commenting negatively about the country's police, judiciary and witness protection programme. Such statements may well have had the effect of undermining public confidence in these institutions.

A second consequence of the strategy of positive complementarity is that the OTP's commencement of investigations demonstrated that the government was unwilling or unable to handle the cases itself. An editorial in the *Daily Nation* labelled the ICC's involvement as 'one of the lowest points in [Kenya's] institutional history of governance' and said that the police force, the judiciary and the Attorney General's office bore the greatest responsibility for this development.[52] Another piece published seven months later stated that 'Moreno-Ocampo's very presence in Kenya … is a demonstration that our institutions have failed'.[53] Social commentators, the Africa Centre for Open Governance and the Centre for Multi Party Democracy each made similar claims.[54] Indeed, in May 2011, even the country's most senior criminal investigator, the CID Director, admitted that the ICC's presence in Kenya caused the public to view the police as being 'incompetent'.[55] A consistently reinforced message, therefore, was that the ICC's intervention was evidence of a failure of Kenya's justice system, a message that is likely to have undermined public confidence in these institutions.

Third, the existence of the ICC as a forum for prosecutions appears to have increased reliance upon the Court, to the detriment of the local justice system. As was suggested in Chap. 6, the ICC's presence may have served as a disincentive to the establishment of a special tribunal because the ICC was perceived to be a superior alternative to any local mechanism. A large percentage of the population

---

[49] International Criminal Court Office of the Prosecutor, 'Statement of the Prosecutor on the Situation in Kenya', 29 May 2011 ('OTP May 2011 Statement').

[50] International Criminal Court Office of the Prosecutor, 'Statement by the Prosecutor of the International Criminal Court Mrs. Fatou Bensouda at the press conference at the conclusion of Nairobi segment of ICC Prosecutor's visit to Kenya, Nairobi', 25 October 2012 ('OTP Second Statement on Bensouda's Visit to Kenya').

[51] 'Kenyan Gov't not cooperative, says ICC', *Citizen News*, 17 February 2013.

[52] 'ICC move an indictment of our justice system', *Daily Nation*, 3 October 2009.

[53] 'ICC role painful but necessary', *Daily Nation*, 8 May 2010.

[54] Okech Kendo, 'Kibaki should keep his cool as MPs lose theirs', *Standard*, 30 December 2010; Judie Kaberia, 'Civil society backs ICC ruling in Kenya cases', *Capital News*, 23 January 2012; Dave Opiyo, 'Lobbies petition UN Council to reject ICC deferral', *The East African*, 15 March 2011.

[55] Office of the President, Criminal Investigation Department, Post Election Violence Investigations Progress Report, 5 May 2011 ('CID May 2011 Report').

also appear to have regarded ICC trials to have been superior to domestic trials. According to a poll conducted in September 2012, 58 % of respondents said that they did not want post-election violence suspects tried by local courts. When asked for their reasons for their lack of support for this option, the most common response was that 'only the ICC [could] deliver justice'.[56] This faith in the ICC led for calls for the Court to investigate and prosecute crimes other than those committed during the post-election violence because the justice at the international level was regarded as being a significant improvement upon what could be delivered domestically. Increasingly, Kenyans became reliant upon the ICC to provide justice. The Chief Justice, for example, described the ICC as having become a part of the Kenyan judicial system.[57] Orengo also stated that the ICC was now a part of Kenyan law.[58] According to an ICJ-Kenya study conducted by Infotrak, Kenyans regard the ICC as one of the organisations that most promoted and enhanced access to justice in Kenya. Given that the ICC did not train prosecutors or judges, provide any support for local trials or lead to the establishment of a local mechanism, this expression of confidence seems likely to have been the result of the ICC's trials in The Hague.[59] In April 2009, the national civil society congress called upon the ICC to investigate extrajudicial killings in Kenya and one human rights lawyer wrote to the OTP to request that indictments be issued.[60] Similarly, in a 2011 report, Human Rights Watch urged the ICC to investigate crimes that were alleged to have been committed in Mount Elgon.[61] This increased reliance upon the ICC to provide justice may have reinforced the belief that the Kenyan criminal justice system was incapable of delivering this outcome, thereby reducing public confidence in these institutions.

Finally, a more direct consequence of the strategy of positive complementarity is that it provided the government with an incentive to make hurried appointments to public office, without proper vetting or appointment procedures being followed, thereby giving the impression that the appointees were lacking in merit or impartiality. As demonstrated in the previous chapter, the government's immediate response to the naming of the Ocampo Six was to hurriedly appoint a new Chief Justice and DPP in anticipation of its forthcoming admissibility challenge. These appointments were made in breach of the Constitution and without proper consultation, drawing damning criticism from ICJ-Kenya, the JSC and the High Court. In a country long accustomed to presidential appointments lacking in transparency, merit and accountability, such a development must surely have fostered further public cynicism of the

---

[56] ICJ-K Judiciary Perception Survey (see Footnote 25).

[57] Ramadhan Rajab, 'ICC part of judicial system, says CJ', *The Star*, 27 April 2012.

[58] Peter Leftie, 'It's too late to scuttle ICC Kenya probe, says Orengo', *Daily Nation*, 8 December 2010.

[59] Ipsos Synovate, SPEC Barometer Survey, 20 November 2012.

[60] Joyce Mulama, 'Kenya cannot fail to prosecute extrajudicial killings', *Inter Press Service*, 27 April 2009.

[61] Human Rights Watch, *'Hold Your Heart': Waiting for Justice in Kenya's Mt Elgon Region* (Human Rights Watch, 2011).

investigative and judicial institutions and made the restoration of public confidence in the criminal justice system even more challenging.

5 Conclusion

During the first five years of the OTP's strategy of positive complementarity in Kenya, some progress was made in ending the culture of impunity in the country, particularly with respect to the restoration of public confidence in the judiciary. There does not, however, appear to be any discernible link between this increased public confidence in the criminal justice system and the strategy of positive complementarity. Rather, this enhanced faith in local institutions seems likely to be the result of progress having been made in the reform of these institutions and, in particular, the much-publicised appointments of new persons to public office through a transparent and meritocratic process. Indeed, it might even be the case that the ICC's involvement in Kenya in some ways undermined public confidence in the local justice institutions, thereby exhibiting a further shadow side. ICC intervention created incentives for both the OTP and civil society to publicly critique the Kenyan justice system, provided *prima facie* evidence that Kenyan institutions had failed, increased domestic reliance upon the ICC and encouraged the hurried and illegitimate appointments to key offices in a manner that was lacking in transparency. These shadow sides of complementarity, either individually or cumulatively, may in fact have made the challenge of restoring public confidence in these institutions more difficult and in this way been counterproductive to the objective of ending impunity.

Bibliography

'House urged to speed up vetting of nominees', *Daily Nation*, 9 September 2009
'ICC move an indictment of our justice system', *Daily Nation*, 3 October 2009
'ICC role painful but necessary', *Daily Nation*, 8 May 2010
'Interview with Mutula Kilonzo', UN Radio, *ReliefWeb*, 17 May 2010
'Kenyan Gov't not cooperative, says ICC', *Citizen News*, 17 February 2013
Alai, Christine, and Mue, Njonjo, *Kenya: Impact of the Rome Statute and the International Criminal Court* (International Centre for Transitional Justice, 2010)
Barasa, Lucas, 'Mutula to Ocampo—Quit Probe', *Daily Nation*, 18 September 2010
Barasa, Lucas, 'Police reforms report out soon', *Daily Nation*, 7 October 2009
Bjork, Christine and Goebertus, Juanita, 'Complementarity in Action: The Role of Civil Society and the ICC in Rule of Law Strengthening in Kenya' (2011) 14 *Yale Human Rights & Development Law Journal* 205

Clottey, Peter, 'Kenyan lawmakers says there's no rush to implement reforms', *Voice of America*, 8 December 2009
Crocker, David, 'Reckoning with Past Wrongs: A Normative Framework' (1999) 13 *Ethics International Affairs* 34
Economic Commission for Africa, *African Governance Report 2005* (Economic Commission for Africa, 2005)
Final Report from Kenya's Commission of Inquiry into Post-Election Violence, 15 October 2008
Galligan, Dennis, Due Process and Fair Procedures: A Study of Administrative Procedures (Clarendon, 1996), 5
Gitonga, Anthony and Opiyo, Peter, 'Ocampo writes to Mutula over witness threats', *Standard*, 26 January 2010
Hamilton, Alexander, 'The Federalist No. 78' in Clinton Rossiter (ed), *The Federalist Papers* (New American Library, 1961)
Hannan, Lucy and Kiai, Maina, Getting Justice: Kenya's Deadly Game of Wait and See (Informaction, 2010)
Hough, Mike and Roberts, Julian, 'Confidence in Justice: An International Review' (2004) ICPR Research Paper No. 3, The Institute for Criminal Policy Research, School of Law, King's College, London, 6; Sir Gerard Brennan, 'The Third Branch and the Fourth Estate', Speech delivered at the Broadcasting Society and Law Lecture Series, University College, Dublin, 22 April 1997
Human Rights Watch, *'Hold Your Heart': Waiting for Justice in Kenya's Mt Elgon Region* (Human Rights Watch, 2011)
In re Raab, 100 N.Y.2d 305
International Centre for Policy and Conflict, 'Independent investigation for widespread and astonishingly high rights of impunity for enforced disappearance and extrajudicial killings by police', 29 April 2011
International Commission of Jurists Kenya, *Judiciary, Perception Survey Presentation*, September 2012
International Criminal Court, Office of the Prosecutor, 'Statement of the Prosecutor on the Situation in Kenya', 29 May 2011
International Criminal Court, Situation in the Republic of Kenya, Request for authorisation of an investigation pursuant to Article 15, ICC-01/09, 26 November 2009
International Criminal Court, Office of the Prosecutor, 'Statement by the Prosecutor of the International Criminal Court Mrs. Fatou Bensouda at the press conference at the conclusion of Nairobi segment of ICC Prosecutor's visit to Kenya, Nairobi', 25 October 2012
International Crisis Group, Policy Briefing, Kenya After the Elections, 15 May 2013
Interview with Alan Meso (Nairobi, 3 May 2010)
Interview with Charles Kirudja (Nairobi, 4 May 2010)
Interview with Lynne Muthoni Wanyeki (Nairobi, 7 May 2010)
Ipsos Synovate, SPEC Barometer Survey, 20 November 2012
Juma, Paul, 'New tribunal Bill on the way, says Kilonzo' *Daily Nation* 4 December 2009
Kaberia, Judie, 'Civil society backs ICC ruling in Kenya cases', *Capital News*, 23 January 2012
Kagwanga, Peter, 'ICC list merely stoking ethnic power politics', *Standard*, 21 December 2010
Kendo, Okech, 'Kibaki should keep his cool as MPs lose theirs', *Standard*, 30 December 2010
Leftie, Peter, 'It's too late to scuttle ICC Kenya probe, says Orengo', *Daily Nation*, 8 December 2010
Long, James, Kanyinga, Karuti, Ferree, Karen and Gibson, Clark, 'Choosing Peace over Democracy', (2013) 24(3) *Journal of Democracy* 140
Mbunga, Ng'ang'a, 'Change of seismic proportion is on the way', *Daily Nation*, 26 December 2010
McSherry, Patrice and Molina, Mejia, 'Confronting the Question of Justice in Guatemala' (1992) 19(3) *Social Justice* 1
Mueller, Susanne, 'The Political Economy of Kenya's Crisis' (2008) 2(2) *Journal of Eastern African Studies* 185
Mulama, Joyce, 'Kenya cannot fail to prosecute extrajudicial killings', *Inter Press Service*, 27 April 2009

Mutiga, Murithi, 'Ocampo writes to judges over threats', *Daily Nation*, 30 January 2010

Namunane, Bernard, 'Ocampo—Muthaura may interfere with witnesses', *Daily Nation*, 14 March 2011

Ndungu, Irene, 'Police Reforms Crucial to Restore Public Confidence', *Institute for Security Studies*, 20 October 2011

Office of the President, Criminal Investigation Department, Post Election Violence Investigations Progress Report, 5 May 2011

Oluoch, Fred, 'R Valley braces for new power balance', *Daily Nation*, 18 December 2010

Opiyo, Dave, 'Lobbies petition UN Council to reject ICC deferral', *The East African*, 15 March 2011

Otieno, Patrick, 'Police commission nominees raise hope for peaceful elections in Kenya', *Soomaali*, 19 September 2012

Rajab, Ramadhan, 'ICC part of judicial system, says CJ', *The Star*, 27 April 2012

Rausch, Colette (ed), Combating Serious Crimes in Post-conflict Societies: a Handbook for Policymakers and Practitioners (US Institute of Peace Press, 2006)

Roht-Arriaza, Naomi, Impunity and Human Rights in International Law and Practice (Oxford University Press, 1995)

Smith, David J 'The Foundations of Legitimacy' in Tyler, Tom, Braga, Anthony, Fagan, Jeffrey Meares, Tracey, Sampson, Robert and Winship, Chris, 'Legitimacy and Criminal Justice: International Perspectives' in Tom Tyler (ed), *Legitimacy and Criminal Justice: International Perspectives* (Russell Sage, 2007)

South Consulting, Kenya National Dialogue and Reconciliation Monitoring Project, *Agenda Item IV Reforms, Long-standing Issues and Solutions, Progress Review Report*, March 2012

South Consulting, Kenya National Dialogue and Reconciliation Monitoring Project, *Kenya's 2013 General Election: A Review of the Environment and Electoral Preparedness*, October 2012

South Consulting, Kenya National Dialogue and Reconciliation Monitoring Project, *Kenya's 2013 General Election: A Review of Preparedness*, February 2013

South Consulting, The Kenya National Dialogue and Reconciliation (KNDR) Monitoring Project, January 2009

South Consulting, Kenya National Dialogue and Reconciliation Monitoring Project, *Progress in the Implementation of the Constitution and other reforms, Review Report*, October 2011

South Consulting, Kenya National Dialogue and Reconciliation Monitoring Project, *Progress in the Implementation of the Constitution and Preparedness for 2012*, Review Report, January 2012

South Consulting, Kenya National Dialogue and Reconciliation Monitoring Project, *Reforms and Preparedness for Elections, Review Report*, May 2012

Transparency International, *The East African Bribery Index 2012* (Transparency International, 2012) ('Transparency International, East African Bribery Index 2012')

United States Department of State, *Human Rights Report 2010: Kenya*, 2010

Wafula, Caroline, 'Lobby calls for forum on Kenya reforms', *Daily Nation*, 13 April 2009

Chapter 9
Conclusion

Between 2008 and 2013, there is little evidence that the OTP's strategy of positive complementarity made any significant contribution to its stated objective of ending impunity. The OTP's own interpretation of a 'major success' ('the absence of trials before [the ICC] as a consequence of the regular functioning of national institutions') was clearly not realised.[1] Although the government's figures are incomplete and in some cases unreliable, it would seem that less than 3 % of reported post-election violence crimes resulted in conviction. These convictions were mainly for property and public order offences, with trials for serious crimes such as murders, sexual violence and offences against the person going almost entirely unpunished. Further, convictions were almost exclusively limited to lower-level perpetrators, with politicians, police officers, business persons and tribal elders escaping accountability for their role in organising, funding and inciting the post-election violence. The passage of time since the post-election violence means that the prospect of further convictions remains bleak. In February 2014 the Director of Public Prosecutions was forced to concede that there was insufficient evidence to sustain a prosecution at the domestic level for any of the 5,000 pending post-election violence cases.[2]

It therefore seems that the trials in The Hague are Kenya's last remaining hope for accountability. Certainly the symbolism of seeing the Ocampo Six sitting in court for their initial appearances and confirmation of charges hearings should not be underestimated. For the first time in the country's long history of impunity, its leaders appeared in a court of law to answer serious charges, with proceedings broadcast live on Kenyan television. Civil society proclaimed this as being a 'strong step towards ending impunity in this country'.[3]

---

[1] Luis Moreno-Ocampo, 'Statement Made at the Ceremony for the Solemn Undertaking of the Chief Prosecutor of the ICC', The Hague, 16 June 2003 ('Moreno-Ocampo June 2003 Statement').

[2] Macharia Mwangi, 'JSC, Tobiko in row over special court', *Daily Nation*, 6 February 2014.

[3] International Federation for Human Rights, 'A big step towards ending impunity for 2008 post-election violence in Kenya: ICC Prosecutor announces list of 6 main suspects', 15 December 2010.

Subsequent developments, however, tempered this enthusiasm. The two most senior members of the Ocampo Six, Uhuru Kenyatta and William Ruto, were elected President and Vice President, respectively. Upon their return to Kenya following the confirmation of charges hearing, each were greeted as heroes by thousands of supporters at a prayer rally in Nairobi's Uhuru Park.[4] According to KNDR, citizens had returned to the belief that those involved in the post-election violence and were allied to politicians 'tended to be untouchable'.[5] Such sentiments could only have been strengthened following the Prosecutor's decision in December 2014 to withdraw the charges against Kenyatta. In September 2013, Annan stated that he continued to closely follow the Kenyan situation and that he was of the opinion that 'impunity [remained] one of the greatest sources of underlying tensions'.[6]

Meanwhile the trials themselves, particularly Kenyatta's, continued to encounter obstacles and delays. In the words of the victims' legal representative Fergal Gaynor, 'after thousands of hours of work by prosecution investigators and lawyers and the expenditure of untold millions of Euros, the ICC's most high profile case has suffered such a devastating series of setbacks'.[7] After five postponements in the Kenyatta trial, the OTP ultimately decided to withdraw the charges against the Kenyan President. The OTP's hopes now rest on securing convictions against Vice President Ruto and radio broadcaster Sang.

A major cause of these delays is that the government continues to engage in a foreign affairs façade whereby it promises cooperation with the Court while simultaneously frustrating the progress of the trials.[8] According to Human Rights Watch, Kenyatta and Ruto have used their electoral victory to 'deploy all the resources of the state toward stopping their prosecution by the International Criminal Court'.[9] First, in May 2013, the government requested the UN Security Council to exercise its powers to 'terminate' the proceedings 'as soon as possible'.[10] Once again, however, the Security Council rejected the government's proposal.[11] Then, in September 2013, just five days before the commencement of Ruto's trial, the National Assembly passed a motion calling upon the executive to withdraw from the Rome Statute, not unlike the motion passed in December 2010.[12] Next, in November 2013,

---

[4] Tom Odula, 'Hero's welcome for Kenya's int'l court suspects', *Associated Press*, 11 April 2011.

[5] KNDR May 2009 Report (South Consulting, Kenya National Dialogue and Reconciliation Monitoring Project, *Status of Implementation of Agenda Items 1–4, Draft Report,* May 2009).

[6] Kofi Annan, 'Justice for Kenya', *New York Times*, 9 September 2013.

[7] *Prosecutor v Uhuru Mauigai Kenyatta,* ICC-01/09-02/11, Transcript 5 February 2014 ('February 2014 Status Conference').

[8] Francis Mreithi and Nzau Musau, 'We will not block International Criminal Court cases', *The Star*, 10 October 2012.

[9] Human Rights Watch, *World Report 2014* (Human Rights Watch, 2014), 10.

[10] 'Kenya makes new plea to UN Council over ICC charges', *The Star*, 24 May 2013.

[11] Michelle Nichols, 'Africa fails to get Kenya ICC trials deferred at United Nations', *Reuters*, 15 Nov 2013.

[12] Mike Pflanz, 'Kenya votes to withdraw from ICC ahead of trials', *The Telegraph*, 5 September 2013.

the government proposed an amendment to the Rome Statute which would permit heads of state such as Kenyatta to be exempt from prosecution during their term of office.[13] Meanwhile, the accused's defence teams continued to submit legal motions, including a request for a one-week adjournment so that Ruto could return to Kenya following the Westgate terrorist attacks[14]; a request that Kenyatta be permitted to participate in his trial via video link[15] and a request for Kenyatta be granted permission to be absent from a large proportion of his trial.[16] Further, throughout this period, the government continued to withhold documents from the OTP and did little if anything to address the climate of fear that discouraged witnesses from testifying before the Court. This prompted the Prosecutor to make a formal application to the Trial Chamber for a finding of non-cooperation under Article 87(7) of the Rome Statute.[17] On 19 December 2013, the Prosecutor requested a three-month adjournment of the Kenyatta trial following the withdrawal of two witnesses.[18] Kenyatta's defence team responded by inviting the Court to terminate the proceedings.[19]

Even if Ruto and Sang are convicted of all charges, significant impunity gaps will nevertheless remain. No member of the security forces will be tried in The Hague, spontaneous acts of violence in Kibera and Kisumu have been omitted from the indictments, property crimes have not been charged and accountability for sexual and gender-based violence is totally absent from proceedings in The Hague.

When one looks beyond merely criminal prosecutions and adopts a broader understanding of ending impunity, again there is little cause for celebration for the OTP. Although the OTP's strategy of positive complementarity coincided with the most sustained period of legal reforms in the country's history, there is little or no evidence linking the two. Indeed, if anything, the ICC's intervention in Kenya appears to have served as a distraction from, and obstacle to, the country's much-needed rule of law reforms. Similarly, with respect to the culture of impunity in

---

[13] Charles Jalloh, "Reflections on the Indictment of Sitting Heads of State and Government and its consequences for peace and stability and reconciliation in Africa", *Legal Studies Research Paper Series*, Working Paper No. 2014-02, January 2014.

[14] *Prosecutor v William Samoei Ruto and Joshua Arap Sang*, Defence request for adjournment, ICC-01/09-01/11, 22 September 2013.

[15] *Prosecutor v Uhuru Muigai Kenyatta*, Order on submissions regarding the accused's presence at trial via video link, ICC-01/09-02/11, 26 March 2013.

[16] *Prosecutor v Uhuru Muigai Kenyatta*, Decision on defence request for conditional excusal from continuous presence at trial, ICC-01/09-02/11, 18 October 2013.

[17] *Prosecutor v Uhuru Muigai Kenyatta*, Prosecution application for a finding of non-compliance pursuant to Article 87(7) against the Government of Kenya, ICC-01/09-02/11, 29 November 2013.

[18] *Prosecutor v Uhuru Muigai Kenyatta*, Notification and removal of a witness from the Prosecution's witness list and application for an adjournment of the provisional trial date, ICC-01/09-02/11, 19 December 2013.

[19] *Prosecutor v Uhuru Muigai Kenyatta*, Public redacted version of the 13 January 2014 'Defence response to the Prosecution's "Notification of the removal of a witness from the Prosecution's witness list and application for an adjournment of the provisional trial date"', ICC-01/09-02/11-878-Conf, 24 January 2014.

Kenya, the ICC's involvement seems to have had little impact on restoring faith in the criminal justice system and has perhaps even contributed to the undermining of public confidence in state institutions.

It might be of course that the OTP's strategy of positive complementarity contributed to the ending of impunity in a manner that is beyond the scope of this project, such as by deterring persons from committing crimes during the holding of the 2013 elections. Moreno-Ocampo, for example, has suggested that the ICC contributed to the holding of a peaceful election.[20] Given Kenya's history of violence during the holding of presidential elections, if the ICC's intervention contributed to peaceful polls this impact ought not to be discounted. For the reasons explained in the first chapter, methodological challenges associated with studying deterrence make it extremely difficult to demonstrate any significant impact that the OTP may have had in this regard. It would, however, seem to be premature and perhaps a little simplistic to conclude that it was the ICC's presence which ensured no repeat of the 2007/2008 post-election violence. Although it is true that relatively peaceful elections were held at a time when Kenyatta and Ruto were about to commence their trials, other explanations for a reduction in violence also exist. Long, Karnyinga, Ferree and Gibson, for example, point to factors such as Kenyans' desire for peace, the visible presence of a well-prepared security force and the creation of a Supreme Court with new-found legitimacy as all contributing to the absence of violence.[21] Indeed, Cheeseman, Lynch and Willis suggest that to the extent that the ICC contributed to peace, it was by accidentally bringing together two former rivals in Kenyatta and Ruto, which reduced the prospect of violence between their respective Kikuyu and Kalenjin communities.[22]

Aside from the holding of peaceful elections in 2013, there appears to be little evidence of the ICC serving as a deterrent. It is true that in 2008 the Attorney General admitted that the Rome Statute was a deterrent to himself and anyone else in a leadership position.[23] Likewise, one month after the Pre-Trial Chamber warned suspects that it would issue arrest warrants should they engage in dangerous speeches, Ruto told youths at a prayer rally to shun politicians who were attempting to incite violence.[24] Such limited evidence, however, does little to assist one in concluding with any degree of confidence that the ICC had a deterrent effect and in this way contributed to the ending of impunity.

In addition, a further shadow side may be emerging in the form of increased African Union hostility towards the Court. Even before the OTP's commencement of investigations in Kenya, the African Union had been critical of the ICC's focus on Africa. Its chairperson had accused the West of using Africa as its 'laboratory to

---

[20] Radio Netherlands Worldwide, Interview with Luis Moreno-Ocampo, 6 February 2014.

[21] James Long, Karuti Kanyinga, Karen Ferree and Clark Gibson, 'Choosing Peace over Democracy' (2013) 24(3) *Journal of Democracy* 140.

[22] Nic Cheeseman, Gabrielle Lynch and Justin Willis, 'Democracy and its discontents: understanding Kenya's 2013 elections' (2014) *Journal of Eastern African Studies* 2.

[23] Hansard, National Assembly, Official Report, 7 May 2008.

[24] Peter Leftie, 'Uhuru and Ruto Vow to Preach Peace', *Daily Nation*, 11 April 2011.

test the new international law', while Rwandan President Paul Kagame had described the ICC as a 'fraudulent institution' reminiscent of 'colonialism' and 'imperialism' which was seeking to undermine and control Africa.[25] The ICC's prosecution of the Kenyan President and Vice President provided a further justification for the African Union's resistance to the ICC. The African Union has since requested the ICC to suspend the trials, held an extraordinary summit to discuss withdrawing support for the Court, threatened to withhold cooperation with the Court unless reforms are undertaken and accused the Court of being engaged in 'some kind of race hunting'.[26] It is therefore possible that by choosing to prosecute two of Africa's most high-profile politicians, the OTP may have made it more difficult to prosecute other suspects from the continent in future. Again, this is not to suggest that this should deter the OTP from prosecuting such persons. Rather, it is suggested this may be a potential shadow to which the OTP ought to give due consideration when deciding whether to implement its strategy of positive complementarity.

Despite the apparent lack of success at ending impunity in Kenya, Bensouda's OTP remains committed to the strategy of positive complementarity. Bensouda has described the strategy as 'a proactive policy of cooperation and consultation, aimed at promoting national proceedings and at positioning itself as a sword of Damocles, ready to intervene in the event of unwillingness or inability by national authorities'.[27] In its first policy paper published after Bensouda's appointment as Prosecutor, the OTP affirmed its commitment to the strategy.[28] Given this commitment, it is important that lessons be learned in applying the situation in future situations. It is too easy, and almost certainly incorrect, for Moreno-Ocampo to suggest that the OTP did all that it could in Kenya and that any failure in the implementation of its strategy was because of a lack of local leadership.[29]

So, what lessons can the OTP learn from its Kenyan experience? This study suggests that the most important lesson is that the strategy of positive complementarity may not be appropriate for all situations. The strategy is more likely to succeed where the target state has the present ability to investigate and prosecute suspects, the domestic criminal justice system commands public confidence, suspected perpetrators do not occupy positions of power and the target state considers international prosecutions to be imminent but not inevitable. Where some or all of these precursors for positive complementarity are lacking, the strategy of positive

---

[25] 'Vow to pursue Sudan over "crimes"', *BBC News*, 27 September 2008; Kezio Musoke, 'Kagama tells why he is against ICC charging Bashir', *Daily Nation*, 3 August 2008.

[26] African Union, Letter to ICC President Sang-Hyun Songdated 10 September 2013; African Union, Letter to ICC President Sang-Hyun Songdated 29 January 2014; 'African Union accuses ICC of "hunting" Africans', *BBC News*, 27 May 2013; 'African Union summit on ICC pullout over Ruto trial', *BBC News*, 20 September 2013.

[27] Fatou Bensouda, 'Reflections from the International Criminal Court Prosecutor' (2012) 45 *Case Western Reserve Journal of International Law* 503, 507.

[28] International Criminal Court Office of the Prosecutor, *Strategic Plan June 2012–2015*, 11 October 2013 ('OTP Strategic Plan 2012–2015').

[29] Radio Netherlands Worldwide, Interview with Luis Moreno-Ocampo, 6 February 2014.

complementarity is less likely to succeed and it is possible that the target state may engage in a foreign affairs façade.

Instead of automatically implementing the strategy of positive complementarity when a situation is referred, the OTP should first consider whether the strategy is likely to be successful. Further, before adopting the strategy, the OTP should take into account whether intervention is likely to have shadow sides. Such considerations would require the OTP consulting persons who are intimately familiar with domestic politics, the history of the conflict, the applicable national law and any relevant cultural norms.[30] One option might be to diversify the OTP's staff composition so that it includes not only legal experts, but also country experts and anthropologists, to assist in this decision-making process.[31]

The OTP's laudable objective of ending impunity should remain its primary focus and the strategy of positive complementarity would still appear to be its best hope for realising this goal. It is essential, however, that the OTP critically evaluates its impact in situations to date so that mistakes are not repeated and it can enhance its ability to persuade future domestic governments. Further in-depth empirical studies are therefore necessary in the other situation countries in which the OTP has conducted preliminary examinations. By doing so, it is possible to improve the effectiveness of the strategy of positive complementarity and increase the likelihood of the OTP making a significant contribution to ending impunity.

Bibliography

'African Union accuses ICC of "hunting" Africans', *BBC News*, 27 May 2013
'African Union summit on ICC pullout over Ruto trial', *BBC News*, 20 September 2013
'Interview with Luis Moreno-Ocampo', *Radio Netherlands Worldwide*, 6 February 2014
'Kenya makes new plea to UN Council over ICC charges', *The Star*, 24 May 2013
'Vow to pursue Sudan over "crimes"', *BBC News*, 27 September 2008
African Union, Letter to ICC President Sang-Hyun Song dated 10 September 2013
African Union, Letter to ICC President Sang-Hyun Song dated 29 January 2014
Annan, Kofi, 'Justice for Kenya', *New York Times*, 9 September 2013
Bensouda, Fatou, 'Reflections from the International Criminal Court Prosecutor' (2012) 45 *Case Western Reserve Journal of International Law* 503
Cheeseman, Nic, Lynch, Gabrielle and Willis, Justin, 'Democracy and its discontents: understanding Kenya's 2013 elections' (2014) *Journal of Eastern African Studies* 2
Hansard, National Assembly, Official Report, 7 May 2008
Human Rights Watch, *Courting History: the Landmark International Criminal Court's First Years* (Human Rights Watch, 2008)

---

[30] Human Rights Watch, *Courting History: the Landmark International Criminal Court's First Years* (Human Rights Watch, 2008).

[31] Jane Stromseth, 'Justice on the Ground: Can International Criminal Courts Strengthen Domestic Rule of Law in Post-Conflict Societies?' (2009) 1 *Hague Journal on Rule of Law* 87, 91–92.

Human Rights Watch, *World Report 2014* (Human Rights Watch, 2014)
International Criminal Court, Office of the Prosecutor, *Strategic Plan June 2012-2015*, 11 October 2013
International Federation for Human Rights, 'A big step towards ending impunity for 2008 post-election violence in Kenya: ICC Prosecutor announces list of 6 main suspects', 15 December 2010
Jalloh, Charles, 'Reflections on the Indictment of Sitting Heads of State and Government and its consequences for peace and stability and reconciliation in Africa', *Legal Studies Research Paper Series*, Working Paper No. 2014-02, January 2014
Leftie, Peter, 'Uhuru and Ruto Vow to Preach Peace', *Daily Nation*, 11 April 2011
Long, James, Kanyinga, Karuti, Ferree, Karen and Gibson, Clark, 'Choosing Peace over Democracy', (2013) 24(3) *Journal of Democracy* 140
Moreno-Ocampo, Luis, 'Statement Made at the Ceremony for the Solemn Undertaking of the Chief Prosecutor of the ICC', The Hague, 16 June 2003
Mreithi, Francis and Musau, Nzau, 'We will not block International Criminal Court cases', *The Star*, 10 October 2012
Musoke, Kezio, 'Kagama tells why he is against ICC charging Bashir', *Daily Nation*, 3 August 2008
Mwangi, Macharia, 'JSC, Tobiko in row over special court', *Daily Nation*, 6 February 2014
Nichols, Michelle, 'Africa fails to get Kenya ICC trials deferred at United Nations', *Reuters*, 15 Nov 2013
Odula, Tom, 'Hero's welcome for Kenya's int'l court suspects', *Associated Press*, 11 April 2011
Pflanz, Mike, 'Kenya votes to withdraw from ICC ahead of trials', *The Telegraph*, 5 September 2013
Prosecutor v Francis Kirimi Muthaura and Uhuru Muigai Kenyatta, Decision on the schedule leading up to trial, ICC-01/09-02/11, 9 July 2012
Prosecutor v Francis Kirimi Muthaura and Uhuru Muigai Kenyatta, Order concerning the state date of trial, ICC-01/09-02/11, 7 March 2013
Prosecutor v Uhuru Muigai Kenyatta, Decision adjourning the commencement of trial, ICC-01/09-02/11, 31 October 2013
Prosecutor v Uhuru Muigai Kenyatta, Decision on defence request for conditional excusal from continuous presence at trial, ICC-01/09-02/11, 18 October 2013
Prosecutor v Uhuru Muigai Kenyatta, Decision on Prosecution's application for a finding of non-compliance pursuant to Article 87(7) and for an adjournment of the provisional trial date, ICC-01/09-02/11, 31 March 2014
Prosecutor v Uhuru Muigai Kenyatta, Notification and removal of a witness from the Prosecution's witness list and application for an adjournment of the provisional trial date, ICC-01/09-02/11, 19 December 2013
Prosecutor v Uhuru Muigai Kenyatta, Order on submissions regarding the accused's presence at trial via video link, ICC-01/09-02/11, 26 March 2013
Prosecutor v Uhuru Muigai Kenyatta, Prosecution application for a finding of non-compliance pursuant to Article 87(7) against the Government of Kenya, ICC-01/09-02/11, 29 November 2013
Prosecutor v Uhuru Muigai Kenyatta, Public redacted version of 'decision on commencement date of trial', ICC-01/09-02/11, 20 June 2013
Prosecutor v Uhuru Muigai Kenyatta, Public redacted version of the 13 January 2014 'Defence response to the Prosecution's "Notification of the removal of a witness from the Prosecution's witness list and application for an adjournment of the provisional trial date"', ICC-01/09-02/11-878-Conf, 24 January 2014
Prosecutor v Uhuru Muigai Kenyatta, ICC-01/09-02/11, Transcript 5 February 2014
Prosecutor v William Samoei Ruto and Joshua Arap Sang, Defence request for adjournment, ICC-01/09-01/11, 22 September 2013
Stromseth, Jane, 'Justice on the Ground: Can International Criminal Courts Strengthen Domestic Rule of Law in Post-Conflict Societies?' (2009) 1 *Hague Journal on Rule of Law* 87
South Consulting, Kenya National Dialogue and Reconciliation Monitoring Project, *Status of Implementation of Agenda Items 1-4, Draft Report*, May 2009

Appendix
Timeline

27 Dec 2007	Presidential and parliamentary elections held in Kenya
30 Dec 2007	The Electoral Commission of Kenya declares Kibaki to be the victor of the presidential election and he is sworn in as president. ODM supporters protest the result through spontaneous acts of violence
Jan 2008	ODM and PNU supporters organise violence against opponents, including the Kiamba church incident and Naivasha arson incident
Mid-Jan 2008	ODM sends a communication to the OTP, advising that serious crimes had been committed in Kenya
24 Jan 2008	Annan and the Panel of Eminent African Personalities commence mediation process
5 Feb 2008	The OTP commences its strategy of positive complementarity by issuing a statement declaring that it was 'carefully considering all information' on crimes that may have been committed in Kenya
28 Feb 2008	Kibaki and Odinga sign a power-sharing agreement, signalling the end of the post-election violence period
4 Mar 2008	The KNDR mediation team secures agreement from the two parties to: (1) a five-stage process for Constitutional reform; (2) the creation of a TJRC; and (3) the establishment of a commission of inquiry into the post-election violence
1 Jun 2008	The Minister for Internal Security, George Saitoti, announces that he has drawn up a list of post-election violence cases that were to be handled with particular speed
10 Jun 2008	Kibaki launches Vision 2030, designed to 'make Kenya a globally competitive and prosperous country with a high quality of life by 2030'
19 Jun 2008	The DPP publishes its first report on the status of investigation and prosecution of post-election violence suspects
15 Aug 2008	The KNCHR publishes its report on the post-election violence, naming 219 alleged perpetrators, including Kenyatta and Ruto
17 Sep 2008	The Kriegler Report on the integrity of the electoral process is published
15 Oct 2008	The Waki Report is published, recommending the establishment of a special tribunal to try post-election violence suspects. Names of suspected perpetrators placed into a sealed envelope and handed to Kofi Annan.

(continued)

23 Oct 2008	The Truth, Justice and Reconciliation Act 2008 is passed
19 Nov 2008	The EU insists on full implementation of the Waki Report and the Kriegler Report
27 Nov 2008	The National Cohesion and Integration Act 2008 is passed
11 Dec 2008	The International Crimes Act 2008 is passed
16 Dec 2008	One day before the expiration of the Waki Report's first deadline, Kibaki and Odinga sign a document agreeing to implement the Report's recommendations, including the establishment of a special tribunal
Jan 2009	The first of the quarterly KNDR review reports is published
29 Jan 2009	The Waki Report's second deadline passes without the establishment of the special tribunal
11 Feb 2009	The OTP issues a statement, affirming that it 'continues to follow-up whether national proceedings into the post-election violence in Kenya in early 2008 are being conducted'
12 Feb 2009	Parliament votes against the establishment of the special tribunal (101 in support and 93 against)
18 Feb 2009	Odinga meets with Annan and states that the government remains committed to establishing the special tribunal
23 Feb 2009	Annan grants an extension for the establishment of the special tribunal, imposing a new deadline of 31 August 2009
Feb 2009	The AG publishes a report that concludes that 350 cases relating to the post-election violence have been concluded
30 Mar 2009	The Prosecutor's special advisor, Beatrice le Fraper Du Hellen, tells Cabinet ministers that the OTP would act 'relentlessly and immediately' should a special tribunal not be established
26 May 2009	Alston Report published, recommending comprehensive and urgent reforms, commencing with the immediate dismissal of the Police Commissioner and the Attorney General
19 Jun 2009	The Prosecutor is interviewed by the *Daily Nation* and states that if the government does not investigate and prosecute then the OTP would intervene
3 Jul 2009	A government delegation meets with the Prosecutor in The Hague. The two parties declare that impunity is not an option and agree to a 'complementarity contract' whereby the government agreed that if a specific judicial mechanism for the post-election violence cases was not established by June 2010, it would voluntarily refer the situation to the ICC. The government also agreed that, by 30 Sep 2009, it would provide the OTP with reports on the status of (1) domestic prosecutions; (2) the witness protection programme and (3) the establishment of the special tribunal
9 Jul 2009	Annan delivers the sealed envelope and six boxes of supporting material to the OTP to assist the OTP in assessing the extent to which the government was in a position to initiate local investigations and prosecutions
14 Jul 2009	The Justice Minister presents revised legislation of the establishment of the special tribunal to Cabinet. At the conclusion of the 4-h meeting no consensus is reached
16 Jul 2009	The Prosecutor opens the sealed envelope, reads the names contained within it and then reseals the envelope. The Prosecutor affirms that he had received from government on the status of prosecutions and the witness protection programme

(continued)

27 Jul 2009	The EU calls for the establishment of a special tribunal and urges the government to move at a greater speed in relation to reforms of the constitution, electoral system, police and judiciary
30 Jul 2009	Cabinet declares that the government will not establish the special tribunal but would instead accelerate reforms of the police and judiciary to enable them to investigate and prosecute suspects. Cabinet states that, in the interim, cases will be handled by the TJRC
1 Aug 2009	The Prosecutor states that he respected the government's efforts to end impunity and confirmed that he had not yet decided whether to open an investigation
3 Aug 2009	The TJRC is inaugurated
4 Aug 2009	London declares that over 20 Kenyans had been the subject of travel bans preventing them from entering the UK
7 Aug 2009	The EU announces that it is considering withholding funds for the TJRC if it will be used to try post-election violence suspects
10 Aug 2009	The Prosecutor states that he will be 'closely monitoring the judicial mechanisms that will be utilised to conduct national investigations and prosecutions of those most responsible for the post-election violence'
16 Aug 2009	The US warns that it will not conduct 'business as usual with those who do not support the reform agenda or who support violence'
10 Sep 2009	Kibaki appoints commissioners to the NCIC
17 Sep 2009	The Prosecutor tells the Minister for Lands that he favoured a three-tiered approach to ending impunity, in which the OTP would prosecute individuals bearing the greatest responsibility, the special tribunal would prosecute low-level perpetrators and the TJRC would address historical injustice and underlying causes of the violence
25 Sep 2009	The US threatens 15 prominent Kenyans with travel bans should they continue to obstruct the reform agenda
29 Sep 2009	One day before the expiration of the government's 30 Sept 2009 deadline for providing the OTP with a report on the status of the special tribunal, the Foreign Affairs Minister states that he had spoken to the Prosecutor in New York and had received no indications that the OTP was preparing to initiate its own investigations
30 Sep 2009	The Prosecutor outlines a 'division of labour' in which the OTP would prosecute individuals bearing the greatest responsibility, the special tribunal would prosecute low-level perpetrators and the TJRC would address historical injustice and underlying causes of the violence
27 Oct 2009	The Prosecutor writes to Kibaki and Odinga, informing them that the OTP would commence investigations in Kenya and requesting that the government uphold its promise to voluntarily self-refer the situation
Oct 2009	The Report of the National Task Force on Police Reforms ('Ransley Report') is published
5 Nov 2009	The Prosecutor meets with Kibaki, Odinga and other Cabinet ministers in Nairobi but is informed that the government will not be voluntarily self-referring the situation. The Prosecutor informs the delegation that he will commence an investigation *proprio motu* and writes to the President of the ICC to inform him of these developments. The principals issue a statement promising to cooperate with the OTP in its investigations and to establish a local judicial mechanism to prosecute the perpetrators of the post-election violence

(continued)

7 Nov 2009	The Prosecutor declares that he will end impunity in Kenya
12 Nov 2009	MPs boycott a parliamentary debate of Imanyara's proposal for the establishment of a special tribunal
19 Nov 2009	MPs again boycott a parliamentary debate of Imanyara's proposal for the establishment of a special tribunal
26 Nov 2009	The Prosecutor requests the Pre-Trial Chamber for authorisation to conduct investigations in Kenya
Dec 2009	The Victims Participation and Reparations Section visits Kenya to meet with victims and receive their representations
22 Jan 2010	The Prosecutor writes to the Justice Minister, urging the government to complete the necessary reforms to the witness protection programme
30 Jan 2010	The Prosecutor writes to the PTC to inform the judges of threat made against key prosecution witnesses. A team of investigators travels to Nairobi to emphasise that reforms must be passed 'as soon as possible'
2 Feb 2010	A meeting of a Cabinet sub-committee is arranged to discuss proposed amendments to the witness protection programme
18 Feb 2010	The Pre-Trial Chamber requests the OTP to provide it with further information on the individuals to be investigated and their alleged links to the crimes committed
3 Mar 2010	The OTP provides the Pre-Trial Chamber with a confidential list of 20 persons believed to have been involved in the organisation, incitement or financing of widespread or systematic attacks against civilians
23 Mar 2010	The Justice Minister, Mutula Kilonzo, promises that suspects will be tried locally after the new constitution is passed
31 Mar 2010	A majority of the Pre-Trial Chamber (Justice Kaul dissenting) finds that there is a reasonable basis for believing that crimes against humanity have been committed in Kenya during the post-election violence and therefore authorises the OTP to commence investigations
7 Apr 2010	The Witness Protection (Amendment) Act 2010 is passed
6 May 2010	The UN Human Rights Council conducts a universal periodic review of Kenya
8 May 2010–12 May 2010	The Prosecutor visits Kenya, meeting with victims, civil society and Cabinet ministers
Jul 2010	The Report of the Taskforce on Judicial Reforms ('Ouku Report') is published
Aug 2010	The NCIC publishes its guidelines for monitoring hate speech
4 Aug 2010	A constitutional referendum is held with 67 % of voters supporting the proposed new Constitution
4 Sep 2010	The Outreach Unit distributes 200,000 copies of a publication entitled *Understanding the ICC*
18 Sep 2010	The Justice Minister, Mutula Kilonzo, promises that suspects will be tried locally after the new constitution is implemented
21 Sep 2010	The President of the ASP, Christian Wenaweser, meets with the Minister of Foreign Affairs, Moses Wetangula, to encourage the government to cooperate with the Court
11 Oct 2010	The Committee of Experts on Constitutional Review publishes its final report
6 Nov 2010	The OTP meets with Ruto in The Hague to discuss Ruto's role in the post-election violence

(continued)

Appendix: Timeline

1 Dec 2010	The Prosecutor meets with Kibaki, Odinga and Annan in Nairobi to provide an update on the progress of the investigations
2 Dec 2010	The Prosecutor announces that investigations had been completed and that in the next 2 weeks he would reveal the identity of six suspects
3 Dec 2010	The Outreach Unit launches a programme entitled *Understanding the International Criminal Court*, which is broadcast through 13 vernacular and community radio stations
	On the same day, the Prosecutor issues a press release claiming that 'families of those believed to be ICC witnesses have been threatened'
13 Dec 2010	Cabinet meets to discuss possible responses to the impending OTP announcement. It resolves that its first preference is to 'establish a credible local process for the investigation and prosecution of the six persons' that would enable the government to challenge the admissibility of the cases before the ICC. Its second preference was to seek a Security Council deferral. Its third preference was to withdraw from the Rome Statute. Its fourth and least-preferred response was to allow the ICC process to 'take its own course'
15 Dec 2010	The Prosecutor announces to 'Ocampo Six'. Kenya One—William Ruto, Henry Kosgey and Joshua Sang. Kenya Two—Uhuru Kenyatta, Francis Muthaura and Mohammed Ali. Kibaki affirms that 'the government is fully committed to the establishment of a local tribunal to deal with those behind the post-election violence, in accordance with the stipulations of the new Constitution'
22 Dec 2010	Parliament passes a motion calling upon the government to take immediate action to withdraw from the Rome Statute and suspend any links, cooperation and assistance with the ICC
Jan 2011	Kibaki dispatches envoys to African capitals to lobby for support for the government's application to the Security Council for a deferral of the cases
28 Jan 2011	The President of the ASP, Christian Wenaweser, visits Nairobi to meet with the government and receives an expression of commitment to the ICC
	On the same day, Kibaki appoints a new Chief Justice, Attorney General, DPP and Controller of Budget
4 Feb 2011	The High Court rules that Kibaki's appointments of a new Chief Justice, Attorney General, DPP and Controller of Budget were unconstitutional
16 Feb 2011	The Vetting of Judges and Magistrate Act 2011 is passed
23 Feb 2011	The Judicial Services Act 2011 is passed
4 Mar 2011	Kibaki issues a press release confirming that envoys will lobby Security Council members for support to defer the ICC cases for 1 year
8 Mar 2011	The Pre-Trial Chamber issues summonses for the Ocampo Six to appear before the ICC
	On the same day, the AG orders the creation of a unit to provide an update on the progress of the post-election violence cases
14 Mar 2011	The Prosecutor writes to the government to express his concern over the suspects remaining in office
18 Mar 2011	The Security Council holds a closed door 'interactive dialogue' with the Kenyan delegation
7 Apr 2011	Suspects in the Kenya One case make their initial appearance
8 Apr 2011	Suspects in the Kenya Two case make their initial appearance
	On the same day, the Security Council issues a statement announcing that its members do not support the government's request to defer the cases

(continued)

14 Apr 2011	The AG writes to the Commissioner of Police, directing him to 'ensure that all the cases, pending investigations are concluded expeditiously' and to investigate all other potential suspects, including the Ocampo Six
22 Apr 2011	The DPP delivers a report to the AG, concluding that over 700 post-election violence cases had been concluded and more than 1,000 cases had been investigated and were awaiting prosecution
31 Mar 2011	The government submits its Article 19 application to the Pre-Trial Chamber, arguing that the cases are inadmissible before the ICC since investigations and prosecutions were ongoing in Kenya.
5 May 2011	The Director of Criminal Investigations writes to the DPP and the Commissioner of Police, informing that 'the team is currently on the ground conducting investigations as directed', including investigations into the role of the Ocampo Six
May 2011	Candidates undergo an 8-day interview process for the position of Chief Justice, with proceedings broadcast live on television
29 May 2011	The OTP releases a statement accusing some politicians of pursuing 'political campaigns to stop the case' which is 'promoting a growing climate of fear that is intimidating potential witnesses and ultimately undermining national and international investigations'
20 Jun 2011	Willy Mutunga becomes Chief Justice
29 Jun 2011	The Pre-Trial Chamber finds that there is no 'documentary proof that there is or has been an investigation' in Kenya and dismisses the government's Article 19 application
1 Jul 2011	The Director of Criminal Investigations writes to the DPP and the Commissioner of Police, informing that witnesses had been interviewed in relation to the role of the Ocampo Six but that 'no evidence has been received from any of these witnesses which could link any of the suspects to the crimes as alleged by the ICC Prosecutor, or any other crimes'
11 Jul 2011	The Ministry of Justice publishes its final report on GJLOS sector policy
21 Jul 2011	The Prosecutor writes to the government to express his concern over the suspects remaining in office
8 Aug 2011	Kenyan investigators question Ruto, Kosgey and Sang over their alleged role in the violence
10 Aug 2011	The Appeals Chamber dismisses the government's appeal against the Pre-Trial Chamber's decision that the cases are admissible before the ICC
12 Aug 2011	The Witness Protection Agency is launched
25 Aug 2011	The National Police Service Act 2011 is passed
29 Aug 2011	Githu Muigai succeeds Amos Wako as AG
1 Sep 2011–8 Sep 2011	Confirmation of charges hearings for the Kenya One suspects
21 Sep 2011–5 Oct 2011	Confirmation of charges hearings for the Kenya Two suspects
18 Oct 2011	The Independent Policing Authority Act 2011 is passed
21 Oct 2011	The Ministry of Justice publishes its report on the GJLOS II Reform Programme for 2011/12–2015/16
7 Jan 2012	A report from the DPP to the AG that is not made public concludes that there had been 258 convictions for cases relating to the post-election violence

(continued)

23 Jan 2012	A majority of the Pre-Trial Chamber (Justice Kaul dissenting) confirms the charges against Ruto, Sang, Kenyatta and Muthaura. Charges against Kosgey and Ali are dismissed
24 Jan 2012	The Prosecutor calls upon the government to address the concerns of the country's displaced persons and states that it is 'in the hands of Kenyans themselves to solve the problems in Kenya'
25 Apr 2012	The JMVB issues its first determination
28 Apr 2012	Kibaki chairs the Extraordinary Summit of Heads of State of the East African Community, which passes a resolution agreeing to extend the jurisdiction of the EACJ to include trials of individuals for crimes against humanity
7 May 2012–15 May 2012	A government delegation attends the meeting of Government Experts and Ministers of Justice and Attorneys General on Legal Matters in Addis Ababa to discuss how the ACJHR statute could be amended to allow it to try individuals for crimes against humanity
24 May 2012	The Appeals Chamber upholds the Pre-Trial Chamber's decision to confirm the charges against Ruto, Sang, Kenyatta and Muthaura
15 Jun 2012	Fatou Bensouda succeeds Luis Moreno-Ocampo as Prosecutor
9 Jul 2012	The Pre-Trial Chamber orders that that Kenya One case will commence on 10 April 2013 and the Kenya Two case will commence on 11 April 2013
17 Jul 2012	The UN Human Rights Committee conducts its periodic review of Kenya's compliance with human rights, with sessions broadcast live on television
27 Jul 2012	The head of the OTP's JCCD division, Phakiso Mochochoko, travels to Nairobi and announces that the trials will continue, irrespective of the outcome of the presidential election
17 Aug 2012	The DPP completes a report that is not made public, concluding that there were 8,869 post-election violence cases
1 Sep 2012	The DPP announces that it will not prosecute more than 8,000 post-election violence cases due to a lack of evidence
21 Oct 2012–25 Oct 2012	The Prosecutor visits Kenya and meets with Kibaki, Odinga, Chief Justice Willy Mutunga, members of civil society and victims. The Prosecutor revealed that the OTP was 'facing challenges' such as interference with witnesses and the government's withholding of evidence
25 Oct 2012	An OTP official informs the AG that 'the slow pace of processing [requests for information] is a source of frustration for the OTP'
4 Mar 2013	Presidential election held in Kenya. Kenyatta is declared the victor with 50.07 of the votes
18 Mar 2013	The OTP withdraws the charges against Muthaura after a key insider witness recanted his testimony
25 Mar 2013	The Supreme Court upholds Kenyatta's presidential election victory
4 Apr 2013	Kenyatta is sworn in as the country's fourth president
3 May 2013	The TJRC publishes its final report
10 May 2013	The OTP states that it 'has encountered serious difficulties in securing full and timely cooperation from the government' and that the effect of the government's actions has been to undermine the investigation in [the ICC] cases and limit the body of evidence available to the Chamber at trial'
24 May 2013	The government lobbies the Security Council to 'terminate' the proceedings 'as soon as possible'
5 Sep 2013	Parliament passes a motion calling upon the government to withdraw from the Rome Statute

(continued)

10 Sep 2013	The trial of Kenya One suspects (William Ruto and Joshua Sang) commences in The Hague
	The African Union writes to the President of the ICC, Judge Sang-Hyun Song, saying that it is seriously concerned that the trials are beginning to adversely affect the ability of Kenyatta and Ruto to discharge their constitutional responsibilities
23 Sep 2013	The Trial Chamber grants Ruto 1-week leave from the trial to return to Kenya and respond to the Westgate terrorist attacks
11–12 Oct 2013	The African Union holds an extraordinary summit to discuss its relationship with the ICC and calls for the Kenyatta and Ruto trials to be suspended until the defendants complete their terms of office
18 Oct 2013	The Trial Chamber grants Kenyatta permission to be absent from a large proportion of his trial
15 Nov 2013	The Security Council rejects the African Union's request for the two trials to be deferred
28 Nov 2013	The Assembly of States Parties rejects Kenya's proposed amendment to the Rome Statute to exempt heads of state from prosecution during their term of office but accepts an amendment permitting accused persons to participate in their trial via video link
29 Nov 2013	The Prosecutor makes a formal application to the Trial Chamber for a finding of non-compliance under Article 87(7) of the Rome Statute
19 Dec 2013	The Prosecutor requests a 3-month adjournment of the Kenyatta trial following the withdrawal of two witnesses
13 Jan 2014	Kenyatta's defence team files an application inviting the Trial Chamber to terminate his trial
29 Jan 2014	The African Union writes to the President of the ICC, Judge Sang-Hyun Song, threatening to withhold cooperation with the ICC unless reforms are undertaken
5 Feb 2014	The Trial Chamber holds a status conference for the Kenyatta case. A senior prosecutor admits that the OTP will have difficulty proving its case against Kenyatta beyond a reasonable doubt
31 Mar 2014	The Trial Chamber orders the government to comply with the Prosecutor's requests for assistance, including copies of Kenyatta's financial records
5 Oct 2014	The Prosecutor announces the withdrawal of charges against Uhuru Kenyatta
7 Oct 2014	The trial of Uhuru Kenyatta is scheduled to commence

Index

A
African Court of Justice and Human Rights (ACJHR), 83, 163–164, 263
African Union, 71–73, 148, 160, 163, 164, 223, 253, 264
Alston, Philip, 58, 74, 152
Annan, Kofi, 1, 47, 51, 71, 72, 125, 145, 148, 198, 201, 250, 257
Appeals chamber, 97, 110, 151, 161, 172, 262, 263
Article 19 application, 15, 95, 108, 109, 138, 151, 160–162, 218, 262
Assembly of States Parties, 3, 34, 36, 37, 39, 159, 205, 212, 220, 264
Attorney General, 60, 63, 73, 74, 77, 94, 95, 97, 99, 101, 102, 107, 136, 142, 151, 153–155, 157, 161, 163, 165, 172, 190, 191, 200, 203, 206, 208–210, 222, 224, 244, 252, 258, 261

B
Bensouda, Fatou, 3, 84, 85, 253, 263
Bribery, 61, 239, 241

C
CID. *See* Criminal Investigations Division (CID)
Colombia, 34–36, 38, 40, 41
Constitution, 14, 22, 51, 56, 59, 61, 62, 73, 81, 93, 104, 106, 107, 110, 125, 126, 138, 150, 153, 159, 161, 166, 172, 183, 186–191, 195–201, 204, 209, 212–214, 219–223, 238, 239, 245, 259–261
Criminal Investigations Division (CID), 94, 95, 97, 98, 107–109, 151, 171, 244
Culture of impunity, 18, 21, 61–63, 72, 170, 187, 198, 233–245

D
Democratic Republic of the Congo (DRC), 6–8, 20, 35, 38–40, 139
Deterrence, 16, 17, 186, 252
Director of Public Prosecutions (DPP), 94, 95, 97–101, 108–110, 136–138, 151, 190, 222, 224, 245, 249, 257, 261–263
DPP. *See* Director of Public Prosecutions (DPP)
Due process thesis, 173

E
East African Court of Justice (EACJ), 83, 162–163, 263
Electoral Commission of Kenya (ECK), 49, 191, 257

F
Foreign Affairs Façade, 18, 22, 23, 43, 103–110, 126, 134, 156–169, 175, 250, 254
Foreign Affairs Minister, 57, 76, 139, 198, 259

G

Governance, Justice, Law and Order Sector reform programme (GJLOS), 187, 194, 195, 197, 198, 201, 223, 262

Government of National Unity (GNU), 47, 51, 58, 69, 71, 135, 174, 197, 216, 219

H

Human Rights Watch, 31, 43, 48, 56, 93, 94, 98, 100, 103, 190, 195, 245, 250, 254

I

ICG. *See* International Crisis Group (ICG)

ICTR. *See* International Criminal Tribunal for Rwanda (ICTR)

ICTY. *See* International Criminal Tribunal for the former Yugoslavia (ICTY)

Imanyara, Gitobu, 78, 170

Impunity, 1, 29, 47, 69, 91, 133, 185, 233, 249

Impunity gaps, 3, 4, 13, 14, 21, 31, 33, 87, 92, 93, 115–119, 126, 251

Institutionalised impunity, 47, 53–64, 190

International Centre for Policy and Conflict (ICPC), 70, 75, 104, 197, 205, 243

International Commission of Jurists-Kenya (ICJ-Kenya), 61, 103, 118, 138, 161, 163, 205, 222, 239, 245

International Criminal Court (ICC), 1, 29, 64, 70, 91, 134, 183, 235, 249

International Criminal Tribunal for Rwanda (ICTR), 5, 30, 31, 43

International Criminal Tribunal for the former Yugoslavia (ICTY), 5, 30, 31, 43, 147

International Crisis Group (ICG), 48–50, 123–125, 153, 160, 237

J

Judges and Magistrates Vetting Board (JMVB), 189, 214, 239, 263

Judicial reforms, 146, 157, 196, 197, 203, 212, 214, 223, 238, 239, 260

Judicial Services Commission (JSC), 189, 222, 238, 245, 249

Judicial vetting, 212, 214, 239

Justice Minister, 35, 42, 58, 74, 104, 106, 120, 135, 163, 192, 195, 209, 210, 212–214, 234, 243, 258, 260

K

Kenya Human Rights Commission (KHRC), 54–57, 64, 70, 98, 114, 195, 197, 205, 210, 222

Kenya National Commission on Human Rights (KNCHR), 48–50, 58, 60, 71, 102, 108, 109, 121, 167, 194, 257

Kenya National Dialogue and Reconciliation (KNDR), 13–15, 22, 23, 51, 71, 72, 86, 92, 111, 120, 121, 124, 137, 138, 140, 141, 152, 168, 183, 184, 189, 190, 193, 202, 203, 210, 213, 216, 217, 219, 220, 224, 236–241, 250, 257, 258

Kenyatta, Uhuru, 1, 69, 70, 82, 112, 126, 164, 179, 250, 261, 264

KHRC. *See* Kenya Human Rights Commission (KHRC)

Kibaki, Mwai, 47, 75, 84, 107, 160, 194

Kilonzo, Mutula, 58, 74, 104, 106, 120, 200, 202, 209, 235, 260

KNCHR. *See* Kenya National Commission on Human Rights (KNCHR)

KNDR. *See* Kenya National Dialogue and Reconciliation (KNDR)

L

Law Society of Kenya (LSK), 70, 124, 172, 242

M

Moreno-Ocampo, Luis, 1, 3, 4, 13, 36, 39, 111, 116, 121, 184, 224, 252, 253, 263

Muigai, Githu, 136, 190, 222, 262

O

Ocampo Six, 1, 3, 69, 82–86, 97, 104, 107–110, 112, 114, 116, 119, 122, 126, 143, 144, 146, 150, 155, 157–159, 161, 162, 167, 168, 171, 212, 218, 220–222, 224, 245, 249, 250, 261

Odinga, Raila, 47, 75

ODM. *See* Orange Democratic Movement (ODM)

Office of the High Commissioner for Human Rights (OHCHR), 48

Office of the Prosecutor (OTP), 1, 30, 70, 91, 134, 184, 234, 249

Index 267

OHCHR. *See* Office of the High Commissioner for Human Rights (OHCHR)
Orange Democratic Movement (ODM), 47, 49–52, 63, 70, 82, 102, 109, 112–114, 116, 117, 135, 146, 152, 153, 155, 216–219, 236, 257

P

Party of National Unity (PNU), 15, 47, 51, 52, 70, 82, 109, 112, 114, 120, 122, 135, 152, 154, 216–219, 222, 257
Police reforms, 108, 197, 202, 215, 242, 243, 259
Political suicide, 134–139, 151, 174, 201
Politicisation of the ICC, 22, 121–125
Positive complementarity, 1, 29–44, 69, 91, 134, 183, 235, 249
Post-election violence, 1, 44, 47–64, 69, 92, 133, 183, 234, 249
Precursors of positive complementarity, 23
Pre-trial chamber, 14, 36, 39, 40, 50, 78, 79, 82–84, 95, 97, 107–109, 113, 115, 117–119, 124, 151, 156, 161, 162, 174, 209, 211, 243, 252, 260–263
Proactive complementarity, 6, 36
Proprio Motu, 3, 36, 38, 69, 77, 87, 95, 101, 151, 156, 161, 243, 259
Public confidence, 18, 20, 23, 64, 135, 187, 233–246, 252

R

Ruto, William, 1, 69, 71, 82, 108, 112, 165, 250, 261, 264

S

Sealed envelope, 1, 3, 9, 69, 71–75, 77, 87, 95, 101, 105, 109, 122, 144, 146–148, 151, 153, 155, 207, 238, 257, 258
Security Council, 8, 31, 34, 82, 150, 158–162, 217, 218, 221, 250, 261, 263, 264

Shadow side of complementarity, 8, 20, 23, 30, 42–44, 119–127, 169–174, 216–223, 243–246
Special tribunal for Kenya, 73, 142, 172

T

TJRC. *See* Truth, Justice and Reconciliation Commission (TJRC)
Tobiko, Keriako, 94, 97, 137
Trial chamber, 16, 164, 166, 168, 251, 264
Truth, Justice and Reconciliation Commission (TJRC), 75, 76, 91, 105–108, 110, 133, 146, 149, 155, 192, 193, 197, 202, 203, 215, 221, 223, 257, 259, 263

U

Uganda, 2, 7, 8, 38–40, 43, 137, 140, 221

V

Vice President, 1, 22, 58, 69, 85, 127, 143, 154, 157, 160, 198, 199, 250, 253
Victims Participation and Reparations Section (VPRS), 79, 120, 260

W

Waki Report, 1, 47–53, 57, 59, 60, 63, 71–72, 99–104, 116–118, 136, 143, 147, 154, 173, 190, 207, 234, 239, 257, 258
Wako, Amos, 73, 74, 94, 107, 136, 190, 262
Witness intimidation, 119–121, 126, 211, 244
Witness protection agency (WPA), 97, 191, 210–212, 262
Witness protection programme, 15–17, 19, 22, 71, 93, 119, 135, 149, 168, 187, 191, 203, 208–211, 221, 223, 224, 243, 258, 260
WPA. *See* Witness protection agency (WPA)

Printed by Printforce, the Netherlands